William Cunningham

S. Austin and His Place in the History of Christian Thought

William Cunningham

S. Austin and His Place in the History of Christian Thought

ISBN/EAN: 9783337167479

Printed in Europe, USA, Canada, Australia, Japan

Cover: Foto ©Lupo / pixelio.de

More available books at **www.hansebooks.com**

THE HULSEAN LECTURES, 1885.

S. AUSTIN

AND HIS PLACE IN THE

HISTORY OF CHRISTIAN THOUGHT.

BY

W. CUNNINGHAM, B.D.,

CHAPLAIN AND BIRKBECK LECTURER, TRINITY COLLEGE, CAMBRIDGE.

LONDON: C. J. CLAY & SONS,
CAMBRIDGE UNIVERSITY PRESS WAREHOUSE
1886

[All Rights reserved.]

PREFACE.

The Hulsean Lectures of 1885 are now published in the form in which they were delivered: some verbal changes have been made, but there are no substantial alterations. My object in writing them was to give such an account of S. Austin's philosophical and theological doctrines as might form a suitable introduction to the study of his works. I have tried while preparing them for the press, to render them better adapted to serve this purpose, and have added in an appendix brief discussions of several important points which could not be conveniently treated within the limits of the lectures. I have also printed at length in the footnotes passages which may enable the reader to judge for himself how far the statements in the text can be substantiated. S. Austin has suffered so much from the way in which isolated expressions have been quoted to give the weight of his authority to opinions he would have repudiated, that I have been careful to avoid the very appearance of such unfairness, by making my citations both frequent and full; while I trust that I have done something to show that there is less ground than is commonly supposed for the alleged inconsistencies in his writings and changes in his doctrine.

I have ventured to depart so far from the prevailing fashion as to speak to an English congregation of the great African doctor by the English name which was in common use for centuries, and was adopted by English men of letters from Langland onwards. Were it merely a matter of literary taste I might be satisfied to plead the examples of Sir W. Hamilton and Dr Munro: but in the case of one who exercised such a striking influence upon English theologians, the fact that his name became a household word is not without significance. There is besides a difference in the theological associations of the two forms of the name which Chillingworth seems to have recognised when he appealed from S. Augustine as quoted by his Roman adversary to the calmer judgment of S. Austin; while there is reason to believe that the longer form came into common use in connexion with the Genevan interpretation of his doctrine.

I have reason to thank the Rev. E. G. de S. Wood, Vicar of S. Clement's, the Rev. R. S. J. Parry, Assistant Tutor of Trinity College, and other friends for reading the proof sheets and giving me many valuable suggestions. To Mr Parry I am specially indebted for the care he has taken in verifying and correcting the quotations from S. Austin's writings. These are printed from Migne's Edition, though the somewhat peculiar punctuation there used has not invariably been retained.

The discussion of S. Austin's teaching in regard to the Eucharist by George Smith has been transcribed from the copy of his *Epistolary Dissertation* in the library of the British Museum.

W. CUNNINGHAM.

TRINITY COLLEGE,
28 *August*, 1886.

CONTENTS.

INTRODUCTION.

	PAGE
PRELIMINARY CONSIDERATIONS	3

1. Christian Life in the Fourth Century. S. Ambrose and Pastoral Work, S. Jerome and Christian Scholarship, S. Austin and Christian Thought.   3
2. Christian Thought
   - (a) Neglected in our day.   4
   - (b) Its work in formulating doctrine.   5
   - (c) And in harmonizing our knowledge—Christian Philosophy.   6
3. No finality in Christian Philosophy.   7

S. AUSTIN AS THE EXAMPLE OF A CHRISTIAN PHILOSOPHER . .   8

1. Personal Characteristics.   10
   - (a) Love of truth and especial carefulness in regard to external facts.   10
   - (b) His convictions the fruit of personal experience.   11
2. Circumstances of his age.   12
3. The Range of his Studies, and consequent difficulty of any survey of his teaching.   12
4. The extraordinary influence he has exercised.   15
   - (a) Mediæval Church, monastic life, scholastic theology, mysticism.   15
   - (b) Post-Reformation Controversies—Lutherans, Calvinists, Jansenists.   16
   - (c) Consequent misinterpretation of his teaching and prejudice against him.   16
     - (α) Was his influence baneful?   17
     - (β) How far was any evil that ensued due to him personally?   18

I.

TRUTH AND THE POSSIBILITY OF ATTAINING IT.

	PAGE
S. Austin's Philosophical Doctrines	19
1. "What is Truth?" Academic Scepticism.	21
2. *Si enim fallor, sum.*	22
3. Intellectual elements in our knowledge, and intellectual principles which are common to all intelligents, while sensations are special to each.	25
4. Numbers and Harmony.	27
5. The Light of Truth, self manifesting, and manifesting intellectual principles.	29
6. The fruitfulness of this analogy. Mysticism and Scholasticism.	32
(a) The unique position of S. Austin.	32
(b) Belief and knowledge.	35
(c) Argument for Christian verities rests on the nature, not on the limitations of human knowledge.	35
Contrast with other Thinkers, Ancient and Modern	36
1. Plato and thought of God. Plato's theology is difficult to interpret, while S. Austin's is definitely Theistic.	36
2. Neoplatonists and doctrine of Man's nature.	37
3. Schoolmen. Application of Aristotelian categories to knowledge of God.	38
4. Descartes. *Cogito ergo sum.* Contrast in the argument for the trustworthiness of the senses.	39
5. High place which may be assigned S. Austin, though he has not said the last word on any philosophical problem, and despite the defects in his mode of treatment. Philosophy was not his main pursuit.	41

II.

THE ORIGIN OF EVIL AND THE PUNISHMENT OF SIN.

The Manichæans and the Nature of Evil	45
1. The teaching of Mani.	45
(a) Public Disputations.	46
(b) The attractiveness of Mani's teaching.	47
(c) Its relation to other faiths, Buddha, Zoroaster; the religion of the Jains. Esoteric Buddhism.	48

	PAGE
2. Goodness and Happiness.	49
(a) Influence of Greek Thought.	49
(b) External Goods.	50
(c) The Unreality of Evil and harmony of the Universe.	51

II. THE ORIGIN OF EVIL. 54

1. How is Evil Possible? 54
   (a) Beings that are good but changeable. . . 54
   (b) Defect of Will. 55
2. How did Evil actually arise? 55
   (a) The Scriptural story of the Fall, as symbolical or the account of an actual event. . . . 56
      (α) S. Austin superadds the literal interpretation. . 56
      (β) Partly from antagonism to the Manichæans, partly from the bent of his mind. . . 57
   (b) Pre-Adamite Death. 58
3. The Sting of Death. 59

III. THE PUNISHMENT OF SIN 61

1. The nature of punishment, as assertory not merely remedial or exemplary. 61
2. The physical effects of sin. 62
3. Its punishment—Ignorance and Incapacity. . . 63
4. S. Austin's horror of sin—
   (a) Incontinence. 64
   (b) Was his opinion still partly Manichæan or not? . 65
5. The proportion of the Divine Punishments. . . 68
6. Are future punishments material as well as spiritual? . 69
7. The question of final salvation is not a question of time, but of the possibility of restoration. . . . 70
8. Is there any limit to the power of God's grace? . . 71
9. A harmonious whole, or the restoration of each creature to the fullest life of which it is capable. . . . 72

III.

HUMAN FREEDOM AND THE DIVINE WILL.

THE PELAGIAN CONTROVERSY. 77

1. Its origin and character. 77
2. Its value and bearing on modern discussions. . . 78
3. A necessary question, though little considered in the East. 79

		PAGE
4.	Personal importance for S. Austin.	80
	(a) His own experience.	80
	(b) A psychological question as to the nature of evil, and thus connected with the metaphysical question he had discussed with the Manichæans.	81

COMMONLY RECOGNISED FACTS OF HUMAN NATURE. . . . 81

1. Heredity, and evil dispositions. 81
    - (a) Perfectionism out of date. 81
    - (b) S. Austin's doctrine of original sin. 82
    - (c) Contrast with Calvin and the doctrine of total depravity. 83
2. My responsibility for what I do. 84
    - (a) Strongly held by S. Austin. 84
    - (b) Contrast with Calvin. 85
3. Pessimism. 86
    - (a) Is a not uncommon and a consistent (though incomplete) view of life. 87
    - (b) A difficulty is created by the Christian revelation. 87
    - (c) The rejection of Christianity may remove this difficulty, but does not give us a gospel. 88

DIVINE FOREKNOWLEDGE. 88

1. Knowledge and Control. This distinction rejected by Calvin as a superstition. 88
2. The creation of a mutable will, liable to defect. 91
    - (a) The true freedom of the will. 91
    - (b) Distinct from the Pelagian liberty of indifference. 93
    - (c) Man's will, when free, comes to be at harmony with other men, and with God. 94
    - (d) Freedom for caprice, and freedom from sin. 95
    - (e) The fallacy of discussing the Will of God apart from the Character of God, and the Will of Man apart from the Nature of Man—Abstract reasonings about concrete realities. 96
3. The effects of the defect of the mutable will. 97
    - (a) S. Austin's view. 97
        - (i) Permitting not causing evil. 97
        - (ii) The will is a noble power still. 98
        - (iii) The unknown good in evil. 99

		PAGE
(b)	These considerations are not a proof of the goodness of God, but they serve to confirm our belief in His goodness as made known by Christ.	99
(c)	This belief as a key to knowledge of what is otherwise unintelligible—it renders knowledge possible.	100
(d)	The argument from the limits of our experience is of weight to warn us against trusting our power of criticising God's purpose.	101

DIVINE OMNIPOTENCE. 102
1. Is the use of means derogatory, or the use of the particular means He has ordained? . . . 102
2. The true nature of Omnipotence, which can never be arbitrary. Contrast with Calvin's teaching. . . . 102
3. S. Austin's doctrine of the Will. . . . 104
    (a) Pelagius and Calvin. . . . 105
    (b) Similarity to that of Kant. . . . 105
    (c) The distinctive testimony from the English Church. . . . 106

IV.

THE KINGDOM OF GOD AND THE MEANS OF GRACE.

THE CITY OF GOD 111
1. The Goths and Rome. Fugitives in Africa. . . . 111
2. Christ as a protector against temporal evil. . . . 112
3. Christians and the discipline of temporal evils. . . . 113
4. Was this misery due to the vengeance of the old gods, or how is it to be explained? By a faith in the Holy Catholic Church. . . . 113
5. S. Austin's Philosophy of History; its originality and value. . . . 115
6. The Church, not merely as ideal, but as actual. . . . 116
7. The failure to realise the ideal in S. Austin's day. . . . 116
    (a) Schismatics. . . . 117
    (b) Unworthy Members. . . . 119

THE DONATIST CONTROVERSY 120
1. Its character and the point at issue. . . . 120
    (a) Breach of continuity. . . . 121
    (b) Self-opinionated schismatics. . . . 121
2. The validity of baptism by heretics. . . . 122
    (a) F. D. Maurice and re-baptism. . . . 122
    (b) Is the worthiness of the minister a *sine qua non* . . . 123

		PAGE
FOURTH CENTURY DOCTRINE OF THE MEANS OF GRACE		123
1. Regeneration and Conversion.		124
2. Baptismal Regeneration.		125
3. The limits to the operation of God's grace.		126

    (a) The area of administration, and its bearing on the doctrine of predestination. No excuse is furnished for Antinomianism when the doctrine is stated thus. 126

    (b) The hardness of human hearts. Pelagian liberty of indifference. 128

    (c) Article XVII. 128

4. Contrast with more modern schools of thought. 129

    (a) The Sacraments are only means of grace. 129

    (b) The divinely ordained Sacraments are not the only means of grace. Repentance. The truth, and the implicit danger of Evangelicalism. 130

        (i) Fixing attention on divine power in unexpected and exceptional phenomena. 131

        (ii) Undervaluing the divinely appointed means of grace. 132

        (iii) Pelagianism in regard to Preaching. 132

    (c) The sacraments are real means of grace. Formalism and self-deception. 133

5. Importance of his doctrine on this point and its place in his theological system. 134

APPENDIX.

Excursus A. S. AUSTIN AND THE OBSERVATION OF NATURE . 137

Excursus B. S. AUSTIN'S INFLUENCE IN THE MIDDLE AGES . 142
1. Mode of Testing it. 142
2. The System of Study. 143
3. Erigena on Reason and Authority. 143
4. Erigena on Prescience and Predestination. 145
5. Erigena on Eternal Punishment. 146
6. S. Anselm. 150
7. The Decline of S. Austin's influence. 152

Excursus C. S. AUSTIN'S KNOWLEDGE OF GREEK. 154

Excursus D. THE AUTHORITY AND INTERPRETATION OF SCRIPTURE . . 157
1. Eternal Truth. 157
2. The Bible and the Church. 159

	PAGE
3. How is a conflict between "Reason" and "Authority" possible?	160
4. False pretensions to Authority and the limits of Empirical Opinion.	162
5. The Interpretation of Authority.	165
6. The conditions for apprehending Bible Truth.	166

Excursus E. CONTINENCE IN MARRIED LIFE . . . 168

Excursus F. THE FREEDOM OF THE WILL 171
1. Freedom as a faculty and differences of moral condition. 171
2. S. Austin's originality. 174
3. The asserted modification of his views. 175

Excursus G. THE INFLUENCE OF S. AUSTIN ON THE ENGLISH CHURCH . 177
1. The negative and positive proofs of his influence. 177
2. Its duration. 178
3. The Prayer Book, and Articles. 180
4. The Brownists—Gyffard. 184
5. The Penal Laws against Dissenters. 189
6. Passive Obedience. 192
7. His popular influence in the Seventeenth Century. 195
8. The Eighteenth Century. 196
9. His Eucharistic Doctrine. 197

An Epistolary Dissertation addressed to the Clergy of Middlesex wherein the Doctrine of S. Austin concerning the Christian Sacrifice is set in a true light: by a Divine of the University of Cambridge. London, 1739 199

Excursus H. The Chronology of S. Austin's Life . . . 277

LECTURE I.

And Pilate saith unto Him, What is Truth?

S. John xviii. 38.

INTRODUCTION.

I. Preliminary Considerations.

The end of the fourth century of our era was marked by the work of three men who have left an impress on all subsequent ages. Amidst the ruin that was overtaking civilisation and culture around them these three preserved that which was to show itself in a new and worthier growth, for each contributed something to the progress of Christian life. At Milan, S. Ambrose devoted himself to teaching his flock, to enriching the services of his church, and to the pastoral care of his people. In his cell at Bethlehem, S. Jerome was busy in studying the text of the Scriptures and in sending forth those volumes which were among the firstfruits of Christian scholarship. At Hippo, S. Austin was defending the Christian verities against the open attacks of the enemies of the cross or the more insidious errors of mistaken brethren. Pastoral work, Christian scholarship and Christian thought had each found a worthy representative.

In the revived Christian life of the present century there are everywhere traces of earnest pastoral work such as once distinguished the see of Milan. More frequent and more hearty services abound, and at no time in the history of the English Church have greater efforts been made to render the parochial ministry available for the spiritual needs of all the dwellers in our parishes. The revised translation of the Bible, issued this year, is a monumental work which shows that the Church in our day has fully maintained the progress made by the Christian scholarship of other ages. There is no need to dwell now on the example of fourth century saints to quicken our energies in these directions.

But with the work of S. Austin it is different: he still towers, as a master of Christian thought, above all who have followed him in Western Christendom; there has been no crisis of religious history in later days, when men have not turned to him for direction. And not only has he thus proved himself worthy our study, but the department of Christian life in which he was pre-eminent is one in which our age is singularly weak, and singularly blind to its own weakness; for it is much easier to depreciate what we do not understand, than to try and understand what we do not appreciate. In the outcry which greeted the teaching of Frederick Maurice, or the publication of the *Essays and Reviews*, we have recent examples of the jealousy with which freshness of thought on theological subjects is apt to be regarded in religious circles; while in the literary world there are not a few who speak as if thought about the Christian Faith were wholly thrown away. Religious sentiment in any land, the spirit of our age can respect and admire: religious benevolence it will even applaud and hail as the only worthy expression of the devout spirit: but of the results of thought about God, and man's relation to Him it takes no heed. And to those who thus disparage the results of such thinking it seems to be a not wholly harmless waste of time, since they feel that dogmatic discussions have caused and do cause so much bitterness among those who engage in them, and that they thus interfere with the united and harmonious prosecution of works of Christian philanthropy.

Yet after all, however highly we prize the personal earnestness of a devout man or woman, it may be an ensample, but it cannot be a possession for ever: however devoted Christian work may be, it is limited both in time and place. The life of S. Ambrose is an example for all time, but his work has to be begun anew in each new age; his course is over, his task completed. And Christian scholarship too takes us away into the long past. As it sets forth the written revelation of God in its greatest fulness, and accumulates proofs of the authenticity of each part of the message, it leads us back to the beginnings of our Faith, to the first manifestation of the Truth. Very different is the work of Christian thought: it has to set before us the meaning for all time of the events to which Christian scholarship testifies, and of the Divine words it has treasured and preserved. Be it so that there was One mysteriously born, living strangely, inspiring strong enthusiasm and wild hatred, suffering death and rising from the grave to a new life among men, what is the import of that story for all time? what is the full force of the message He had to give, the real measure of the authority with which He spake? And the answer to these questions—of desperate interest as they are to us here and now—comes to us in those dogmas as to the person of Christ which were formulated by the earnest thought of the Fathers of the Church. The unifying power of their thought gathered into one the scattered sayings, and the records of Divine doings, and set their meaning forth in a form in which it may be treasured for all time, as a precious possession for every age.

But there is other work for Christian thought to do: it is not only through Christ that we know of God; there is evidence of Him in the heart of man and in the world around us. It is not only through His death that we may see that sin has entered the world, though we may learn its heinousness at the foot of the cross—as nowhere else. It is not only by conscious reliance on His Spirit that we may begin to overcome evil and attain to a true freedom; it is not merely in the history of God's ancient people, or of the planting of the Church, that we learn His dealings with men, though we see them most fully there. Philosophy had discussed the being of God, and the nature of good and evil, of human freedom, and of human society, before the Christian revelation came. It was tempting, but not wholly safe, to accept "the rational residuum of centuries of Greek mental activity[1]" and express the Christian verities in terms which should harmonise with it; and it was no light or easy task to re-cast the current philosophic thoughts of God and Man and the World in the light of the new revelation regarding each, which was given in the person and work of Christ.

The earlier Fathers, in defining Christian dogmas, had thought out the meaning of the Christian revelation for all time: they did not aspire to be Christian philosophers, or to combine the knowledge which we have from all sources, in one consistent scheme of thought. This was the work on which Origen[2] entered for Greek-speaking Christians and the East, and which S. Austin began for Latin Christianity, to which time after time he returned as the exigencies of new controversy led him once more to the fray: and if for the present we try to concentrate attention on the work of the Bishop of Hippo, it is from no special desire to draw a comparison in his favour with other workers in

[1] Mark Pattison, *Sermons*, 165.
[2] The suspicion which his contemporaries felt of Origen's orthodoxy was due to the fact that rightly or wrongly they believed he was accommodating Christian truth to non-Christian philosophy, not building a Christian philosophy on the enlarged basis given by the Christian revelation of divine truth. It was on precisely similar grounds that the teaching of Erigena was subsequently repudiated by the orthodox in the middle ages.

the same field, but because his writings are more akin to our Western modes of thought.

And since these great problems about the being of God and the nature of Man press on us too, the solutions at which the earliest of Christian philosophers arrived may have a real and living interest for us to-day: they can never be out of date. Even though the solutions offered were necessarily partial, they have a worth for all time. For here we must distinguish: so far as the great events of Christ's life and work are concerned, the duty of thinking out their import for all time was done once, and need not be done again: it is embodied for us in the three Creeds. But there is no such finality in Christian philosophy: apart from the continual self-revelation of God in His Church, there is a continual change in the material which is submitted to us to think about, and a change from age to age in human habits of thinking about it. Great advances have been made in both respects in our own century, and the difficulty of co-ordinating older and newer truths is forced upon us day by day in many lines of study. The discoveries and inventions which abound in our day have opened up fields of knowledge that were undreamed of by S. Austin. The post-Kantian account of the development of Thought has affected every department of human study, for it has affected the habits of study themselves. No philosophy, Christian or other, can make itself heard which does not take this new material into account, or recognise these new habits of thinking. As the ages pass we get, time after time, new light on the way in which God rules the world; there can be no finality in philosophy, though the partial solutions of other ages, the phases of Truth they apprehended, must be kept in full view, if our own knowledge is to be more complete[1].

[1] G. W. F. Hegel, *Geschichte der Philosophie*, I. 42.

II. S. Austin as the Example of a Christian Philosopher.

Since the old questions about God, and Man and the World are before us still, if any of us feel that we cannot ignore them, that we must strive to face them and to consider how far the old solutions harmonise with new experience, we can surely prepare ourselves for this task in no better way than by sitting at the feet of the greatest of Christian thinkers. We shall turn to S. Austin, not as a dogmatic teacher[1], but as the greatest example of a Christian Philosopher. It is to follow in his steps that we may look to him now,—not to accept his teaching as a ready

[1] Compare his own language in regard to the respect due to his opinion: Sane cum in omnibus litteris meis non solum pium lectorem, sed etiam liberum correctorem desiderem, multo maxime in his, ubi ipsa magnitudo quæstionis utinam tam multos inventores habere posset, quam multos contradictores habet. Verumtamen sicut lectorem meum nolo mihi esse deditum, ita correctorem nolo sibi. Ille me non amet amplius quam catholicam fidem, iste se non amet amplius quam catholicam veritatem. Sicut illi dico, Noli meis litteris quasi Scripturis canonicis inservire; sed in illis et quod non credebas, cum inveneris, incunctanter crede, in istis autem quod certum non habebas, nisi certum intellexeris, noli firmiter retinere: ita illi dico, Noli meas litteras ex tua opinione vel contentione, sed ex divina lectione vel inconcussa ratione corrigere. Si quid in eis veri comprehenderis, existendo non est meum, at intelligendo et amando et tuum sit et meum: si quid autem falsi convinceris, errando fuerit meum, sed jam cavendo nec tuum sit nec meum. *De Trin.* III. 2.
 Libera me, Deus, a multiloquio quod patior intus in anima mea, misera in conspectu tuo, et confugiente ad misericordiam tuam. Non enim cogitationibus taceo, etiam tacens vocibus. Et si quidem non cogitarem nisi quod placeret tibi, non utique rogarem ut me ab hoc multiloquio liberares. Sed multæ sunt cogitationes meæ, tales quales nosti, cogitationes hominum, quoniam vanæ sunt. Dona mihi non eis consentire, et si quando me delectant, eas nihilominus improbare, nec in eis velut dormitando immorari. Nec in tantum valeant apud me, ut aliquid in opera mea procedat ex illis; sed ab eis mea saltem sit tuta sententia, tuta conscientia te tuente. *De Trin.* xv. 51.

made solution of the difficulties that press on us to-day. Old controversies return, but in new forms; yet the way which he pursued in his search for truth is open to us too; it is still the path of faith that leads to knowledge[1]. And

[1] Aderit enim Deus, et nos intelligere quod credidimus, faciet. Præscriptum enim per prophetam gradum, qui ait, *Nisi credideritis, non intelligetis* (Isai. vii. 9, *sec.* LXX), tenere nos, bene nobis conscii sumus. *De Lib. Arb.* I. 4.

Credibilium tria sunt genera. Alia sunt quæ semper creduntur, et nunquam intelliguntur: sicut est omnis historia, temporalia et humana gesta percurrens. Alia quæ mox ut creduntur, intelliguntur: sicut sunt omnes rationes humanæ, vel de numeris, vel de quibuslibet disciplinis. Tertium, quæ primo creduntur, et postea intelliguntur: qualia sunt ea quæ de divinis rebus non possunt intelligi, nisi ab his qui mundo sunt corde; quod fit præceptis servatis, quæ de bene vivendo accipiuntur. *De Div. Quæst. LXXXIII.* qu. xlviii.

Quo cognito, satis apparebit, quantum homo assequi potest, quam necessariis et invictis et justis legibus Deo et Domino suo cuncta subjecta sint: ex quo illa omnia, quæ primo credidimus, nihil nisi auctoritatem secuti, partim sic intelliguntur, ut videamus esse certissima; partim sic, ut videamus fieri posse, atque ita fieri oportuisse, doleamusque illos hæc non credentes, qui nos antea credentes irridere, quam nobiscum credere maluerunt. *De Vera Religione*, 14.

Fides quaerit, intellectus invenit. *De Trin.* xv. 2.

As a personal trust in its parents and its reliance on them is the first step which a child takes in knowledge of social relationships and ethical duty, so our trust in the Eternal God, in so far as He has revealed Himself, is the first step towards a right understanding of the relations of man to the Eternal and Unseen Realities. There is even an analogy in the progress of empirical science from hypothesis tentatively accepted (or believed) till by being verified it becomes knowledge. On the whole subject compare Gangauf, *Metaph. Psych.* I. 31, also Excursus D. p. 157.

Credulity, according to S. Austin, is the state of mind of those who think they know what they know not, and who therefore rest satisfied with mere belief and never try to advance to knowledge. *De Util. Cred.* 22. 23. He has no sympathy with the standpoint of Tertullian or any of those whose motto is *Credo quia absurdum*. S. Anselm reiterates his view excellently when he says, Negligentia mihi videtur, si postquam confirmati sumus in fide, non studemus, quod credimus intelligere. *Cur Deus Homo*, I. ii.

It is often said that there is much in common between Christian philosophy and such theosophies as are contained in Buddhist or Hermetic writings. But these, generally speaking, regard γνῶσις as a thing

we in our day, distracted with anxiety and doubt, may well turn to him,—to him perhaps rather than any of the Fathers of the Church. He above all others may be our guide, philosopher and friend, both because of his personal qualities and of the times in which he wrote, because of the range of his studies and the effect they have produced in Christendom throughout all subsequent ages.

1. Perhaps the most striking trait in the personal character of S. Austin as it stands out before us in his own writings is his devotion to truth wherever it is found. Not only truth as set before us in revelation, or reached by patient argument and intellectual discussion, but also in the form in which it is specially prized by our generation—empirical truth as detected through the senses in scientific investigation[1]. He pours his contempt on the physical philosophers of his own day who ignored such inquiries. "For pray because they dispute most truly and persuade "us by most certain proofs that all things in time depend "upon eternal principles, are they therefore able to discover "*a priori* or to deduce from their principles the different "kinds of animals there are, the original seeds of each, the "rule of their growth, the limits that run through their con- "ception, births, ages, decease, their natural attractions and "repulsions? Are they not forced to leave that unchange- "able wisdom, and to look for all these things to the actual "particulars of place and time, and to the experience and

to which few can attain, and thus separate the *electi* from the *auditores*. Christianity imposes no such hard-and-fast line, but offers its doctrines in a form in which they can be apprehended and believed by the most uncultivated, and which may afford those who believe a guide to action. From this platform the more thoughtful and devout may advance to greater and greater degrees of knowledge of divine things.

[1] See Excursus A. on *S. Austin and the Observation of Nature*, p. 138; also Excursus B. § 3, on *Erigena on Reason and Authority*, p. 143; also Excursus D. § 3, on *The Possibility of a Conflict between Reason and Authority*, p. 160.

"records of others[1]?" Nor does he spare those who would prejudge such enquiries on the supposed authority of Scripture. "It is a very disgraceful and pernicious thing, and "one greatly to be watched against, that any infidel should "hear a Christian talking wild nonsense about the earth "and the heaven, about the motions and magnitude and "intervals of the stars, the courses of years and times, the "natures of animals, stones and other matters of the same "kind, pretending that he has the authority of the Scriptures "on his side. The other who understands these things from "reason or experience, seeing that the Christian is utterly "ignorant of the subject, that he is wide of the mark by a "whole heaven, cannot refrain from laughter[2]." Again and again we see what an attraction physical science and the experimental investigation of facts had for his own mind, and how his reasonings are affected by the influence it exercised over him.

While his writings thus show that his mind remained ever open to the reception of new evidence, the story of his life brings clearly before us the passionateness of his search for an intellectual truth which should render the world and his own being less incomprehensible. It almost seems when we read his *Confessions* as if Christianity won him, not so much through the promise of deliverance from sin, as by affording him a solution of the mysteries of this unintelligible world. The personality of the writer in all its intellectual earnestness has left an indelible mark on his treatment of the most abstruse problems. Each of the positions of his philosophy owes its strength, not to a mere series of rigid logical demonstrations, but to the convictions which had been formed in his own experience by his eager wrestling for Truth. He found a certainty through

[1] *De Trin.* IV. 21.
[2] *De Genes. ad Lit.* I. 39. Quoted by F. D. Maurice, *The Old Testament*, 14.

struggling with every form of doubt. He knew the nature of evil, since he had sounded its depths himself. He understood human freedom, since he was himself attaining it: and he could realise something of God's working in the world, since he had traced it in his own life.

2. While the cast of S. Austin's mind was so similar to that of many men to-day, the circumstances of his age were very different to ours. Deep metaphysical problems which some of us are tempted to ignore as insoluble or unintelligible were pressed upon his attention : he was forced to deal with them, and his age was one in which no debater could hold his own who did not wield the weapons of speculative thought most warily. The wonders of the physical universe excite the enthusiasm of our contemporaries; attention and thought are so generally directed to these matters that the cultured public of to-day has little interest and less appreciation for philosophy. But in days when the points of the Arian controversy were frequently debated in the streets, when public disputations between Christians and Manichaeans were matters of eager interest to a whole population, there was a wide field for speculative energy. He who won the honours then, may fairly claim the attention of all who think on such subjects now.

3. S. Austin may also move our admiration and attract us by the extraordinary range of his studies[1]. Some of his earlier writings from a heathen standpoint[2], as well as his treatises on particular branches of science, are lost to us[3].

[1] A. Dorner, *Augustinus*, 324.

[2] Et ista consideratio scaturivit in animo meo ex intimo corde meo ; et scripsi libros de Pulchro et Apto; puto, duos aut tres. Tu scis, Deus: nam excidit mihi. Non enim habemus eos, sed aberraverunt a nobis, nescio quomodo. *Conf.* IV. 20.

[3] Per idem tempus quo Mediolani fui, Baptismum percepturus, etiam Disciplinarum libros conatus sum scribere, interrogans eos qui mecum erant, atque ab hujusmodi studiis non abhorrebant ; per corporalia

But more than enough remains to impress us with the marvellous fertility of his pen, and the versatility of his talents. There is hardly a topic in the whole range of theology and philosophy on which he has not something to say. However diverse our interests may be, whichever of the many problems of life weighs on us most heavily, we may learn that it is not peculiarly our own, but that the great African Father wrestled with something similar in his time. Indeed we dare not neglect him, for though he lived so long ago his work is by no means antiquated; he deals with many of the questions that vex us now, and raise restless longings for a certainty that seems unattainable, or give place to the bitter hopelessness that weighs on our hearts and hampers our efforts to struggle after good and for good.

Thus to set S. Austin before you, as a man whose work is of living interest to-day, is no light undertaking, both because of the difficulty of the subject and the shortness of the term allotted to a lecturer. To do so at all one must touch lightly on many deep matters, must state questions rather than discuss them, and pass rapidly from one broad issue to another. But even the most hasty and inadequate sketch is not wholly useless, if it can help any of us to realise that we are blameworthy indeed, in so far as we ignore S. Austin now, or let ourselves fancy that the points he discussed have lost their importance, or that his treatment of them is wholly out of date.

cupiens ad incorporalia quibusdam quasi passibus certis vel pervenire vel ducere. Sed earum solum de Grammatica librum absolvere potui, quem postea de armario nostro perdidi: et de Musica sex volumina; quantum attinet ad eam partem quæ Rythmus vocatur. Sed eosdem sex libros jam baptizatus, jamque ex Italia regressus in Africam scripsi; inchoaveram quippe tantummodo istam apud Mediolanum disciplinam. De aliis vero quinque disciplinis illic similiter inchoatis, de Dialectica, de Rhetorica, de Geometria, de Arithmetica, de Philosophia, sola principia remanserunt, quæ tamen etiam ipsa perdidimus: sed haberi ab aliquibus existimo. *Retract.* I. vi.

There is a peculiar difficulty in attempting a rapid survey of S. Austin's work, for he has not given us a systematic exposition of his views in a single treatise: and besides this, the views expressed in the books he wrote as a catechumen before his baptism appear to have undergone some modification in his later years: the works published during his episcopate are not obviously in complete harmony with his first essays, and he was at the trouble to revise and correct his earlier writings only with respect to the statements they contained on one particular question[1]. The difficulty is farther increased by the fact that there are frequent and hasty expressions of his opinions in private letters, or thrown out in the heat of controversy, and one cannot hope to be always successful in choosing statements which fairly embody his view on the whole.

The want of system in his teaching gives rise to another difficulty—in what order are we to delineate the many doctrines discussed here and there throughout his numerous treatises? By expounding his teaching in a regular system, as Dorner has done, we may get the means of summarising the value of his conclusions, but we cannot hope to preserve the living personal interest which attaches to his doctrines in the less rigid sequence in which he has expressed them. The very form of his writings— the dialogues which make no pretence to art but which purport to represent actual conversations[2]—the correspon-

---

[1] At the same time it may be said that there is far less alteration in his standpoint during the period of his authorship than has been the case with many philosophers, notably, the Platonic dialogues, Berkeley or Schelling. Compare Excursus A. p. 139 note, for the alleged alteration in his view of secular studies; also Excursus F. p. 175, for the asserted modification in his doctrine of the Will. On the changes in his attitude towards the Platonic philosophy see p. 29 note 4, and p. 36 note 1 below.

[2] Idibus novembris mihi natalis dies erat: post tam tenue prandium, ut ab eo nihil ingeniorum impediretur, omnes qui simul non modo illo die, sed quotidie convivabamur, in balneas ad consedendum vocavi; nam

dence which was called forth by special opportunities of conveying letters[1]—the *Confessions* and *Soliloquies* which tell of his own personal experience—the treatises and public debating which were required for the special instruction of his flock in connexion with blatant or novel errors, all have an occasional interest, besides their permanent value, either in their matter or their form. With the view of retaining something of this personal interest, it may be wisest for us to review the more important subjects on which he wrote, as they successively attracted his own attention. The order in which the various controversies arose will serve at any rate to indicate the order in which we may begin the discussion of them now.

4. The practical cast of his mind, together with the wide range of the subjects of which he treats, goes far to account for the extraordinary influence he has exercised on Christendom. The whole life of the mediæval Church was framed on lines which he had suggested: its religious orders claimed him as their patron; its mystics found a sympathetic tone in his teaching; its theology was consciously moulded after his doctrine; its polity was to some extent the actualisation of his picture of the Christian Church; it was in

---

is tempori aptus locus secretusque occurrerat. Erant autem, non enim vereor eos singulari benignitati tuae notos interim nominibus facere, in primis nostra mater, cujus meriti credo esse omne quod vivo; Navigius frater meus, Trygetius et Licentius, cives et discipuli mei; nec Lastidianum et Rusticum consobrinos meos, quamvis nullum vel grammaticum passi sint, deesse volui, ipsumque eorum sensum communem, ad rem quam moliebar, necessarium putavi. Erat etiam nobiscum ætate minimus omnium, sed cujus ingenium, si amore non fallor, magnum quiddam pollicetur, Adeodatus filius meus. Quibus attentis, sic cœpi. *De Beata Vita*, 6.

Post pristinum sermonem, quem in primum librum contulimus, septem fere diebus a disputando fuimus otiosi, cum tres tantum Virgilii libros post primum recenseremus, atque ut in tempore congruere videbatur, tractaremus. *Contra Acad.* II. 10. See also *De Ordine*, II. 21.

[1] *Ep.* cxlix. (*Paulino*).

its various parts a carrying out of ideas which he cherished and diffused. Nor does his influence end with the decline of mediævalism: we shall see presently how closely his language was akin to that of Descartes, who gave the first impulse to and defined the special character of modern philosophy. There are those who identify his doctrine with that of Luther, the founder of Protestantism: the controversies in which he took part were fought over again by the Jansenists in the Gallican Church, and by Calvinists and Arminians in those countries which renounced the Roman obedience: and once more in our own land when a reaction arose against rationalism and Erastianism it was to the African doctor that men turned with enthusiasm: Dr Pusey's edition of the *Confessions* was among the first-fruits of the Oxford movement. But if these facts help us to estimate the importance of S. Austin, they render it harder for us to approach him fairly. We are apt to interpret his doctrines in the form into which they were cast by others, or in the light of the applications that were made of them in subsequent ages. To some of us, it may be, the name Augustine is but the symbol for the propounder of certain so-called Augustinian theories: and our first effort must be to rid our minds of these associations. Or again, in so far as we are out of sympathy with mediæval monachism, or scholastic theology, or contemplative piety, or the ecclesiastical hierarchy, we are prejudiced against the ancient Father who did so much to encourage these developments of Christian life. But we do not judge him fairly in judging him thus: his teaching was actualised rather than realised,—applied in actual life, but not applied precisely as he would himself have wished. I shall have to point out, as these lectures proceed, several crucial instances which show that he too would have condemned much that was afterwards current in scholastic theology and mediæval practice; we want to understand what he really thought and said, and we must try not to prejudge him because of the ways in which other people carried out or modified the views he held.

Some of those who admit that scholasticism and mediævalism were exaggerated expressions of his teaching, and who do not hold him directly responsible for all that they dislike in the teaching and life of Latin Christendom, are yet inclined to contend that he was indirectly responsible for it, that his influence was exerted banefully to develop Christianity in the directions in which these evils subsequently appeared. They are ready to blame him, not for the full amount of the evil, but for fostering the conditions under which these evils appeared. But to argue thus is to forget the incalculable good which accrued from the movements which S. Austin, with all the best men of his age, favoured.

It was not possible that Christian life should remain in the undeveloped condition in which it first made its mark in the world: how chaotic and disordered it was in the days of S. Austin we may learn from many incidental remarks in his writings[1]. If Christian life was to be perpetuated in the world it was needful that it should be organised in more definite institutions: the good men and true in these times who had the preservation of the Christian Faith at heart

---

[1] Comessationes enim et ebrietates ita concessæ et licitæ putantur, ut in honorem etiam beatissimorum martyrum, non solum per dies solemnes (quod ipsum quis non lugendum videat, qui hæc non carnis oculis inspicit), sed etiam quotidie celebrentur. Quæ fœditas si tantum flagitiosa et non etiam sacrilega esset, quibuscumque tolerantiæ viribus sustentandam putaremus. Quanquam ubi est illud, quod cum multa vitia enumerasset idem apostolus, inter quæ posuit ebriosos, ita conclusit, ut diceret cum talibus nec panem edere. Sed feramus hæc in luxu et labe domestica, et eorum conviviorum quæ privatis parietibus continentur, accipiamusque cum eis corpus Christi, cum quibus panem edere prohibemur; saltem de sanctorum corporum sepulcris, saltem de locis sacramentorum, de domibus orationum tantum dedecus arceatur. *Ep.* xxii. 3. See also *Ep.* xxix. xxxiv. xxxv.

were all working on similar lines. To speak as if S. Austin were personally responsible for such changes is to overrate the possible influence of any one man: and though his power and energy were most important factors, we need not blame him solely for all the evils that eventually ensued, since we cannot ascribe to him the sole credit of so organising the teaching and work of the Church, that she was able to survive the shock of the barbarian invasions, and to bring forth a better and nobler civilisation when the dark days were done.

TRUTH, AND THE POSSIBILITY OF ATTAINING IT.

I. S. Austin's Philosophical Doctrines.

The first great controversy with which we are concerned was a discussion of the views of those who like Pilate doubted of the possibility of attaining Truth at all; for they showed that the evidence of the senses—that which seems to the plain man to give the strongest possible conviction—was not altogether beyond question. S. Austin must have come across the opinion at an earlier time, for the writings of Cicero are full of references to the Academics, and that lost dialogue which he prized so highly—the *Hortensius*—alluded to the question, if it did no more[1]. But the eloquence and imaginative power of the Manichaean teachers had carried him away in his earlier days; it was after he had left Carthage, and taken up a temporary residence in Rome[2] that the questioning habit of Academic

---

[1] Itane falsum erit, unde nec ipse (cum Academicis omnia dubia sint) Academicus ille Cicero dubitavit, qui cum vellet in Hortensio dialogo ab aliqua re certa, de qua nullus ambigeret, sumere suae disputationis exordium, *Beati certe*, inquit, *omnes esse volumus?* Absit ut hoc falsum esse dicamus. *De Trin.* XIII. 7.

[2] See Excursus II, for the *Chronology of S. Austin's Life*, p. 277.

Rationem ipse mecum habui magnamque deliberationem jam in Italia constitutus, non utrum manerem in illa secta, in quam me incidisse poenitebat, sed quonam modo verum inveniendum esset, in cujus amorem suspiria mea nulli melius quam tibi nota sunt. Saepe mihi videbatur non posse inveniri, magnique fluctus cogitationum mearum in Academicorum suffragium ferebantur. *De Util. Cred.* 20.

2—2

doubt gained a hold upon him. It may be that the isolation of the life of a stranger in a great city, along with the depressing effects of the serious illness from which he suffered, preyed upon his spirits, and predisposed him to enquire anew as to the foundation on which his convictions rested. He has himself recorded for us the course of reasoning by which he came to be sure that truth, and not mere probability, is attainable by men; he learned to hope that his own seeking would at length be rewarded by finding, and to be ready to receive the Truth as it is in Christ Jesus[1].

S. Austin's argument on these points is much affected by the nature of the doctrines he was forced to oppose.

[1] Quæ cum ita sint, accipe, mi Theodore, namque ad id quod desidero, te unum intueor, teque aptissimum semper admiror; accipe, inquam, et quod illorum trium genus hominum me tibi dederit, et quo loco mihi esse videar, et abs te cujusmodi auxilium certus exspectem. Ego ab usque undevigesimo anno ætatis meæ, postquam in schola rhetoris librum illum Ciceronis, qui Hortensius vocatur, accepi, tanto amore philosophiæ succensus sum, ut statim ad eam me transferre meditarer. Sed neque mihi nebulæ defuerunt, quibus confunderetur cursus meus; et diu, fateor, quibus in errorem ducebar, labentia in oceanum astra suspexi. Nam et superstitio quædam puerilis me ab ipsa inquisitione terrebat: et ubi factus erectior illam caliginem dispuli, mihique persuasi docentibus potius quam jubentibus esse credendum, incidi in homines, quibus lux ista, quæ oculis cernitur, inter summa et divina colenda videretur. Non assentiebar, sed putabam eos magnum aliquid tegere illis involucris, quod essent aliquando aperturi. At ubi discussos eos evasi, maxime trajecto isto mari, diu gubernacula mea repugnantia omnibus ventis in mediis fluctibus Academici tenuerunt. Deinde veni in has terras; hic septentrionem cui me crederem didici. Animadverti enim et sæpe in sacerdotis nostri, et aliquando in sermonibus tuis, cum de Deo cogitaretur, nihil omnino corporis esse cogitandum, neque cum de anima: nam id est unum in rebus proximum Deo. Sed ne in philosophiæ gremium celeriter advolarem, fateor, uxoris honorisque illecebra detinebar; ut cum hæc essem consecutus, tum demum me, quod paucis felicissimis licuit, totis velis omnibusque remis in illum sinum raperem, ibique conquiescerem. Lectis autem Platonis paucissimis libris, cujus te esse studiosissimum accepi, collataque cum eis, quantum potui, etiam illorum auctoritate qui divina mysteria tradiderunt, sic exarsi, ut omnes illas vellem anchoras rumpere, nisi me nonnullorum hominum existimatio commoveret. Quid ergo restabat aliud,

The doubt of the Academics was by no means so thorough-going as the philosophical scepticism of modern times, for they did not question the existence of things of sense, but the possibility of attaining to any certain knowledge in regard to them[1]. The search for truth was not to their minds a less worthy pursuit, because the goal lies beyond our reach; there might be probability in our opinions but how could there be certainty? Were our ordinary impressions more vivid than those of the dreamer or the man in delirium[2]? and if not why should we pin our faith to them? Does not our sight mislead us when a straight oar seems bent in the water[3]? why then should we trust it at other times? And if these simple seeming matters are thus

nisi ut immoranti mihi superfluis, tempestas quæ putabatur adversa, succurreret? Itaque tantus me arripuit pectoris dolor, ut illius professionis onus sustinere non valens, qua mihi velificabam fortasse ad Sirenas, abjicerem omnia, et optatæ tranquillitati vel quassatam navem fissamque perducerem. *De Beata Vita*, 4.

[1] On Academic doubt compare Bindemann, *Der h. Augustinus*, I. 185, or Zeller, *Stoics, Epicureans and Sceptics*, 522 f. S. Austin discusses their doctrines not only in his treatise *Contra Academicos*, but also in the *Epistolæ* iii.—xiv. to Nebridius, *De Trinitate*, XIII. 8 and xv. 21, and *De Civitate Dei*, XIX. iii.; there are frequent allusions throughout his writings.

[2] Credo enim sensus non accusari, vel quod imaginationes falsas furentes patiuntur, vel quod falsa in somnis videmus. Si enim vera vigilantibus atque sanis renuntiarunt; nihil ad eos, quid sibi animus dormientis insanientisque confingat. *Contra Academicos*, III. 25.

[3] Ergone verum est quod de remo in aqua vident? Prorsus verum. Nam causa accedente quare ita videretur, si demersus unda remus rectus appareret, magis oculos meos falsæ renuntiationis arguerem. Non enim viderent quod talibus existentibus causis videndum fuit. Quid multis opus est? Hoc de turrium motu, hoc de pinnulis avium, hoc de cæteris innumerabilibus dici potest. Ego tamen fallor, si assentiar, ait quispiam. Noli plus assentiri, quam ut ita tibi apparere persuadeas; et nulla deceptio est. *Contra Academicos*, III. 26.

Primo ipsa scientia, de qua veraciter cogitatio nostra formatur, quando quæ simus loquimur, qualis aut quanta potest homini provenire, quamlibet peritissimo atque doctissimo? Exceptis enim quæ in animum veniunt a sensibus corporis, in quibus tam multa aliter sunt quam videntur, ut eorum verisimilitudine nimium constipatus, sanus sibi esse

dubious and uncertain how can we hope to attain to true knowledge as to the ultimate nature and real causes of phænomena?

S. Austin points out that the Academics had been seeking for certainty in the wrong direction[1]: he holds that though it is easy enough to fancy we may be mistaken or mad in regard to particular things we see or feel, there is one matter about which no mistake is possible. Even though I err, still I am[2]: the fact of my self-conscious

videatur qui insanit; unde Academica philosophia sic invaluit, ut de omnibus dubitans multo miserius insaniret; his ergo exceptis quae a corporis sensibus in animum veniunt, quantum rerum remanet quod ita sciamus, sicut nos vivere scimus? in quo prorsus non metuimus, ne aliqua verisimilitudine forte fallamur, quoniam certum est etiam cum qui fallitur vivere; nec in eis visis hoc habetur, quae objiciuntur extrinsecus, ut in eo sic fallatur oculus, quemadmodum fallitur cum in aqua remus videtur infractus, et navigantibus turres moveri, et alia sexcenta quae aliter sunt quam videntur; quia nec per oculum carnis hoc cernitur. *De Trin.* XV. 21.

[1] Noli foras ire, in teipsum redi; in interiore homine habitat veritas; et si tuam naturam mutabilem inveneris, transcende et teipsum.... Omnis qui se dubitantem intelligit, verum intelligit, et de hac re quam intelligit certus est: de vero igitur certus est. Omnis igitur qui utrum sit veritas dubitat, in seipso habet verum unde non dubitet; nec ullum verum nisi veritate verum est. Non itaque oportet eum de veritate dubitare, qui potuit undecumque dubitare. *De Vera Religione*, 72, 73.

Ita omnis palma cognitioni datur et artificio et comprehensioni veritatis; ad quam nullo modo perveniunt qui foris eam quaerunt. *De Vera Rel.* 94.

Saepe mihi videbatur non posse inveniri, magnique fluctus cogitationum mearum in Academicorum suffragium ferebantur. Saepe rursus intuens, quantum poteram, mentem humanam tam vivacem, tam sagacem, tam perspicacem, non putabam latere veritatem, nisi quod in ea quaerendi modus lateret, eundemque ipsum modum ab aliqua divina auctoritate esse sumendum. *De Util. Cred.* 20.

[2] Nulla in his veris Academicorum argumenta formido, dicentium, Quid, si falleris? Si enim fallor, sum. Nam qui non est, utique nec falli potest: ac per hoc sum, si fallor. Quia ergo sum si fallor, quomodo esse me fallor, quando certum est me esse, si fallor? Quia igitur essem qui fallerer, etiamsi fallerer; procul dubio in eo quod me nosi esse, non fallor. *De Civ. Dei*, XI. XXVI. Intima scientia est qua nos vivere

existence is involved in my very doubting itself. "Attend "more carefully to the position we have laid down that "all minds know and are certain concerning themselves. "For men certainly have doubted whether the power of "living, of remembering, of understanding, of willing, of "thinking, of knowing, of judging, be of air, or of fire, or "of the brain, or of the blood, or of atoms, or besides the "usual four elements of a fifth kind of body I know not "what, or whether the combining or tempering together "of this our flesh has power to accomplish these things. "And one has attempted to establish this, and another "to establish that. Yet who ever doubts that he himself "lives, and remembers, and understands, and wills, and "thinks, and knows, and judges? Seeing that even if he "doubts, he lives; if he doubts, he remembers why he "doubts; if he doubts, he understands that he doubts; "if he doubts, he wishes to be certain; if he doubts, "he thinks; if he doubts, he knows that he does not know; "if he doubts, he judges that he ought not to assent rashly.

scimus, ubi ne illud quidem Academicus dicere potest: Fortasse dormis, et nescis, et in somnis vides. Visa quippe somniantium simillima esse visis vigilantium quis ignorat? Sed qui certus est de vitæ suæ scientia, non in ea dicit, Scio me vigilare; sed, Scio me vivere: sive ergo dormiat, sive vigilet, vivit. Nec in ea scientia per somnia falli potest; quia et dormire et in somnis videre, viventis est. Nec illud potest Academicus adversus istam scientiam dicere, Furis fortassis et nescis; quia sanorum visis simillima sunt etiam visa furentium: sed qui furit vivit; nec contra Academicos dicit, Scio me non furere; sed, Scio me vivere. Nunquam ergo falli nec mentiri potest, qui se vivere dixerit scire. Mille itaque fallacium visorum genera objiciantur ei qui dicit, Scio me vivere; nihil horum timebit, quando et qui fallitur vivit. Sed si talia sola pertinent ad humanam scientiam, perpauca sunt; nisi quia in unoquoque genere ita multiplicantur, ut non solum pauca non sint, verum etiam reperiantur per infinitum numerum tendere. Qui enim dicit, Scio me vivere, unum aliquid scire se dicit: proinde si dicat, Scio me scire me vivere; duo sunt jam; hoc vero quod scit hæc duo, tertium scire est: sic potest addere et quartum, et quintum, et innumerabilia, si sufficiat. *De Trin.* xv. 21.

"Whosoever therefore doubts about anything else, ought
"not to doubt of all these things, since if they were not he
"would not be able to doubt at all[1]." Thus self-conscious
life finds a sphere where certainty is attainable and where
doubt is impossible. Again and again S. Austin returns to
the argument in new forms[2] or with new illustrations; and

[1] Sed quoniam de natura mentis agitur, removeamus a consideratione nostra omnes notitias quae capiuntur extrinsecus per sensus corporis; et ea quae posuimus, omnes mentes de se ipsis nosse certasque esse, diligentius attendamus. Utrum enim aeris sit vis vivendi, reminiscendi, intelligendi, volendi, cogitandi, sciendi, judicandi; an ignis, an cerebri, an sanguinis, an atomorum, an praeter usitata quatuor elementa quinti nescio cujus corporis, an ipsius carnis nostrae compago vel temperamentum haec efficere valeat, dubitaverunt homines: et alius hoc, alius aliud affirmare conatus est. Vivere se tamen et meminisse, et intelligere, et velle, et cogitare, et scire, et judicare quis dubitet? Quandoquidem etiam si dubitat, vivit: si dubitat, unde dubitet meminit; si dubitat, dubitare se intelligit; si dubitat, certus esse vult; si dubitat, cogitat; si dubitat, scit se nescire; si dubitat, judicat non se temere consentire oportere. Quisquis igitur aliunde dubitat, de his omnibus dubitare non debet: quae si non essent, de ulla re dubitare non posset. *De Trin.* x. 14.

[2] Quare prius abs te quaero, ut de manifestissimis capiamus exordium; utrum tu ipse sis. An tu fortasse metuis, ne in hac interrogatione fallaris, cum utique si non esses, falli omnino non posses? E. Pergo potius ad caetera. A. Ergo quoniam manifestum est esse te, nec tibi aliter manifestum esset, nisi viveres, id quoque manifestum est, vivere te: intelligisne ista duo esse verissima? E. Prorsus intelligo. A. Ergo etiam hoc tertium manifestum est, hoc est intelligere te. E. Manifestum. *De Lib. Arb.* ii. 7.

R. Tu qui vis te nosse, scis esse te? A. Scio. R. Unde scis? A. Nescio. R. Simplicem te sentis, anne multiplicem? A. Nescio. R. Moveri te scis? A. Nescio. R. Cogitare te scis? A. Scio. R. Ergo verum est cogitare te. A. Verum. *Solil.* ii. 1.

At si tollatur assensio, fides tollitur; quia sine assensione nihil creditur. Et sunt vera quamvis non videantur, quae nisi credantur, ad vitam beatam, quae non nisi aeterna est, non potest perveniri. Cum istis vero utrum loqui debeamus ignoro, qui, non victuros in aeternum, sed in praesentia se vivere nesciunt: imo nescire se dicunt, quod nescire non possunt. Neque enim quisquam sinitur nescire se vivere: quandoquidem si non vivit, non potest aliquid vel nescire; quoniam non solum scire, verum etiam nescire viventis est. Sed videlicet non assentiendo quod vivant, cavere sibi videntur errorem: cum etiam errando convincan-

thus he states with extraordinary clearness the same proof of the possibility of indubitable certainty, which Descartes[1] was to bring forth once again, when more than a thousand years had passed away.

He points out too that there are kinds of knowledge[2] to tur vivere; quoniam non potest qui non vivit errare. Sicut ergo nos vivere non solum verum, sed etiam certum est; ita vera et certa sunt multa, quibus non assentiri, absit ut sapientia potius quam dementia nominanda sit. *Enchiridion*, xx.

Et cum dubitaret: Scisne, inquam, saltem te vivere? Scio, inquit. Scis ergo habere te vitam, siquidem vivere nemo nisi vita potest. Et hoc, inquit, scio. *De Beata Vita*, 7.

[1] *De Methodo* iv.

[2] It has been unnecessary for my immediate purpose to dwell on the use he makes of the distinction between ratio (διανοία, Verstand) and intellectus (νοῦς, Vernunft). It is carefully discussed by Storz, *Philosophie des h. A.* §§ 6, 7. It is, however, worth while to quote his own summary statement of the distinction, and one application he makes of it: Si ergo haec est sapientiae et scientiae recta distinctio, ut ad sapientiam pertineat aeternarum rerum cognitio intellectualis; ad scientiam vero, temporalium rerum cognitio rationalis: quid cui praeponendum sive postponendum sit, non est difficile judicare. Si autem alia est adhibenda discretio, qua dignoscantur haec duo, quae procul dubio distare Apostolus docet, dicens, *Alii datur quidem per Spiritum sermo sapientiae, alii sermo scientiae secundum eundem Spiritum;* tamen etiam istorum duorum quae nos posuimus evidentissima differentia est, quod alia sit intellectualis cognitio aeternarum rerum, alia rationalis temporalium, et huic illam praeponendam esse ambigit nemo. Relinquentibus itaque nobis ea quae sunt exterioris hominis, et ab eis quae communia cum pecoribus habemus introrsum ascendere cupientibus, antequam ad cognitionem rerum intelligibilium atque summarum quae sempiternae sunt veniremus, temporalium rerum cognitio rationalis occurrit. Etiam in hac igitur inveniamus, si possumus, aliquam trinitatem, sicut inveniebamus in sensibus corporis, et in iis quae per eos in animum vel spiritum nostrum imaginaliter intraverunt; ut pro corporalibus rebus quas corporeo foris positas attingimus sensu, intus corporum similitudines haberemus impressas memoriae, ex quibus cogitatio formaretur, tertia voluntate utrumque jungente: sicut formabatur foris acies oculorum, quam voluntas, ut visio fieret, adhibebat rei visibili, et utrumque jungebat, etiam illic ipsa se admovens tertiam. *De Trin.* xii. 25.

It is perhaps important to add that he does not ignore the real unity of the various mental faculties. Et sicut una caro est duorum in

which the objections that the Academics urged against the validity of the evidence of our senses do not apply. Many elements of our knowledge are obviously not merely sensible but rational[1]. The distinction of right and wrong is not given through the senses[2], and the force of a logical argument is not dependent on them[3]. We constantly enu-

masculo et femina, sic intellectum nostrum et actionem, vel consilium et exsecutionem, vel rationem et appetitum rationalem, vel si quo alio modo significantius dici possunt, una mentis natura complectitur: ut quemadmodum de illis dictum est, *Erunt duo in carne una*; sic de his dici possit, Duo in mente una." *De Trin.* XII. 3. Compare also page 97 note 1 below.

[1] Tenemus, quantum investigare potuimus, quaedam vestigia rationis in sensibus; et quod ad visum atque auditum pertinet, in ipsa etiam voluptate. Alii vero sensus non in voluptate sua, sed propter aliquid aliud solent hoc nomen exigere: id autem est rationalis animantis factum propter aliquem finem. Sed ad oculos quod pertinet, in quo congruentia partium rationabilis dicitur, pulchrum appellari solet. Quod vero ad aures, quando rationabilem concentum dicimus, cantumque numerosum rationabiliter esse compositum; suavitas vocatur proprio jam nomine. Sed neque in pulchris rebus cum nos color illicit, neque in aurium suavitate cum pulsa chorda quasi liquide sonat atque pure, rationabile illud dicere solemus. Restat ergo ut in istorum sensuum voluptate id ad rationem pertinere fateamur, ubi quaedam dimensio est atque modulatio. *De Ordine*, II. 33.

Quamvis enim alia corpore, alia mente videamus; horum tamen duorum generum ipsa discretio videtur mente, non corpore; et ea quae mente conspiciuntur, non indigent ullo corporis sensu, ut ea vera esse noverimus. Quae autem per corpus videntur, nisi mens adsit quae talia nuntiata suscipiat, nulla possunt scientia contineri; et quae nuntiata quasi suscipere perhibetur, foris ea relinquit. *Ep.* cxlvii. (*Paulinae*) 38.

[2] Haec tamen sine conclusione securissima non relinquo. Aut enim amittitur furore sapientia, et jam non erit sapiens, quem verum ignorare clamatis: aut scientia ejus manet in intellectu, etiamsi pars animi caetera id quod accepit a sensibus velut in somnis imaginetur. *Contra Acad.* III. 28.

[3] Non hic et sol lucet, et nox est. Aut vigilamus nunc, aut dormimus. Aut corpus est, quod mihi videre videor, aut non est corpus. Haec et alia multa, quae commemorare longissimum est, per istam [dialecticam] didici vera esse, quoquo modo sese habeant sensus nostri, in se ipsa vera. *Contra Acad.* III. 29.

merate sensible objects, but in apprehending unity[1] as well as in reasoning about numbers[2], we have proofs of intellectual activity. Thus our thoughts are turned towards an intellectual sphere where the illusions of sense cannot

[1] Quod si ita est (nam quis non admonitus videat, neque ullam speciem, neque ullum omnino esse corpus quod non habeat unitatis qualecumque vestigium; neque quantumvis pulcherrimum corpus, cum intervallis locorum necessario aliud alibi habeat, posse assequi eam quam sequitur unitatem?): quare si hoc ita est, flagitabo ut respondeat, ubi videat ipse unitatem hanc, aut unde videat: quam si non videret, unde cognosceret et quid imitaretur corporum species, et quid implere non posset? Nunc vero cum dicit corporibus, Vos quidem nisi aliqua unitas contineret, nihil essetis, sed rursus si vos essetis ipsa unitas, corpora non essetis; recte illi dicitur, Unde illam nosti unitatem, secundum quam judicas corpora, quam nisi videres, judicare non posses quod eam non impleant: si autem his corporeis oculis eam videres, non vere diceres, quanquam ejus vestigia teneantur, longe tamen ab ea distare? nam istis oculis corporeis non nisi corporalia vides: mente igitur eam videmus. Sed ubi videmus? *De Vera Religione*, 60.

[2] Hoc ergo, quod per omnes numeros esse immobile firmum incorruptumque conspicimus, unde conspicimus? Non enim ullus ullo sensu corporis omnes numeros attingit; innumerabiles enim sunt: unde ergo novimus per omnes hoc esse, aut qua phantasia vel phantasmate tam certa veritas numeri per innumerabilia tam fidenter, nisi in luce interiore conspicitur, quam corporalis sensus ignorat? *De Lib. Arb.* II. 23.

Sed quia dedit numeros omnibus rebus etiam infimis, et in fine rerum locatis; et corpora enim omnia, quamvis in rebus extrema sint, habent numeros suos; sapere autem non dedit corporibus, neque animis omnibus, sed tantum rationalibus, tanquam in eis sibi sedem locaverit, de qua disponat omnia illa etiam infima quibus numeros dedit: itaque quoniam de corporibus facile judicamus, tanquam de rebus quæ infra nos ordinatæ sunt, quibus impressos numeros infra nos esse cernimus, et eos propterea vilius habemus. Sed cum cœperimus tanquam sursum versus recurrere, invenimus eos etiam nostras mentes transcendere, atque incommutabiles in ipsa manere veritate. Et quia sapere pauci possunt, numerare autem etiam stultis concessum est, mirantur homines sapientiam, numerosque contemnunt. Docti autem et studiosi, quanto remotiores sunt a labe terrena, tanto magis et numerum et sapientiam in ipsa veritate contuentur, et utrumque earum habent: et in ejus veritatis comparatione non eis aurum, et argentum, et cætera de quibus homines dimicant, sed ipsi etiam vilescunt sibi. *De Lib. Arb.* II. 31. The part which numbers play in

affect us, and about which we are in complete agreement with one another. We are all ready to differ about mere sense-impressions, the pleasantness of this or that taste, the precise shade of any colour, and so forth: but all are agreed that two and two make four. Such intellectual principles are as it were a common ground which all of us enjoy together, while the senses with their impressions give to each of us their own peculiar report, which is the private property of the sentient person[1]. So too the principles of geometry[2] are intellectual principles which are exhibited and illustrated in things of sense: all such principles, but especially the contemplation of numbers, lead us to realise that there is knowledge which is not obtained from sensation, and which yet is common to all intelligents[3].

S. Austin's philosophy is very remarkable. Compare *De Ordine*, II. §§ 35—43; also his high appreciation of Pythagoras, *De Civ. Dei*, VIII. iv. This should be borne in mind in reading his mystical interpretations of the numbers in Scripture.

[1] Proprium ergo et quasi privatum intelligendum est, quod unicuique nostrum soli est, et quod in se solus sentit, quod ad suam naturam proprie pertinet: commune autem et quasi publicum, quod ab omnibus sentientibus nulla sui corruptione atque commutatione sentitur. E. Ita est. *De Lib. Arb.* II. 19.

[2] Hinc est profecta in oculorum opes, et terram coelumque collustrans, sensit nihil aliud quam pulchritudinem sibi placere, et in pulchritudine figuras, in figuris dimensiones, in dimensionibus numeros; quaesivitque ipsa secum, utrum ibi talis linea talisque rotunditas, vel quaelibet alia forma et figura esset, qualem intelligentia contineret. Longe deteriorem invenit, et nulla ex parte quod viderent oculi cum eo quod mens cerneret, comparandum. Haec quoque distincta et disposita, in disciplinam redegit, appellavitque geometriam...In his igitur omnibus disciplinis occurrebant ei omnia numerosa, quae tamen in illis dimensionibus manifestius eminebant, quas in seipsa cogitando atque volvendo intuebatur verissimas: in his autem quae sentiuntur, umbras earum potius atque vestigia recolebat. *De Ordine*, II. 42, 43.

[3] Iis et talibus multis documentis coguntur fateri, quibus disputantibus Deus donavit ingenium, et pertinacia caliginem non obducit, rationem veritatemque numerorum, et ad sensus corporis non pertinere, et invertibilem sinceramque consistere, et omnibus ratiocinantibus ad videndum esse communem. *De Lib. Arb.* II. 24.

Such in brief outline are the steps of the argument by which S. Austin rose above the quibbling objections of the Academics to a firm vantage ground from which he could establish the certainty of our intellectual principles. It would be tedious to summarise any of the other lines of reasoning he pursues when, in dealing with the ideas of Beauty[1] and the Good[2], he shows that they too testify to an intelligible order, which is not revealed to us by mere sense-impression, and which is not subject to the variableness of things of sense[3], which still is while they change and pass.

But whence can we attain to a knowledge of these unchanging realities[4]? Must it not be that just as the light of

---

[1] Quoquo enim te verteris, vestigiis quibusdam, quæ operibus suis impressit, loquitur tibi, et te in exteriora relabentem, ipsis exteriorum formis intro revocat; ut, quidquid te delectat in corpore et per corporeos illicit sensus, videas esse numerosum, et quæras unde sit, et in teipsum redeas, atque intelligas te id quod attingis sensibus corporis probare aut improbare non posse, nisi apud te habeas quasdam pulchritudinis leges, ad quas referas quæque pulchra sentis exterius. *De Lib. Arb.* II. 41.

[2] Si summum bonum omnibus unum est, oportet etiam veritatem in qua cernitur et tenetur, id est sapientiam, omnibus unam esse communem. *De Lib. Arb.* II. 27.

[3] Omne quod corporeus sensus attingit, quod et sensibile dicitur, sine ulla intermissione temporis commutatur: velut cum capilli capitis nostri crescunt, vel corpus vergit in senectutem aut in juventam efflorescit, perpetuo id fit, nec omnino intermittit fieri. Quod autem non manet, percipi non potest: illud enim percipitur quod scientia comprehenditur......Quamobrem saluberrime admonemur averti ab hoc mundo, qui profecto corporeus est et sensibilis, et ad Deum, id est veritatem, quæ intellectu et interiore mente capitur, quæ semper manet et ejusdem modi est, quæ non habet imaginem falsi a qua discerni non possit, tota alacritate converti. *De Divers. Quæst. LXXXIII.* qu. ix.

[4] This is one of the points on which he explicitly rejects a Platonic doctrine—the theory of reminiscence; though in this he was consciously or unconsciously following Plato himself.

Unde Plato ille philosophus nobilis persuadere conatus est vixisse hic animas hominum, et antequam ista corpora gererent: et hinc esse quod ea quæ discuntur, reminiscuntur potius cognita, quam cognoscuntur nova. Retulit enim puerum quemdam nescio quæ de geome-

day makes the changing things of sense visible to our differing eyes, so the light of Truth makes clear these unchanging realities to our intelligence[1]? And just as the

trica interrogatum, sic respondisse, tanquam esset illius peritissimus disciplinæ. Gradatim quippe atque artificiose interrogatus, videbat quod videndum erat, dicebatque quod viderat. Sed si recordatio hæc esset rerum antea cognitarum, non utique omnes vel pene omnes, cum illo modo interrogarentur, hoc possent: non enim omnes in priore vita geometræ fuerunt, cum tam rari sint in genere humano, ut vix possit aliquis invenire. Sed potius credendum est mentis intellectualis ita conditam esse naturam, ut rebus intelligibilibus naturali ordine, disponente Conditore, subjuncta sic ista videat in quadam luce sui generis incorporea, quemadmodum oculus carnis videt quæ in hac corporea luce circumadjacent, cujus lucis capax eique congruens est creatus. *De Trin.* XII. 24.

It appears that in his earlier days he was inclined to adopt this explanation. Compare *De Quantitate Animæ*, 34, for a passage which he subsequently criticised. In quo libro illud quod dixi, *omnes artes animum secum attulisse mihi videri; nec aliud quidquam esse id quod dicitur discere, quam reminisci ac recordari*, non sic accipiendum est, quasi ex hoc approbetur, animam vel hic in alio corpore, vel alibi sive in corpore sive extra corpus aliquando vixisse, et ea quæ interrogata respondet cum hic non didicerit, in alia vita ante didicisse. Fieri enim potest, sicut jam in hoc opere supra diximus, ut hoc ideo possit, quia natura intelligibilis est, et connectitur non solum intelligibilibus verum etiam immutabilibus rebus, eo ordine facta, ut, cum se ad eas res movet quibus connexa est vel ad seipsam, in quantum eas videt, in tantum de his vera respondeat. *Retract.* I. viii. 2. See also *Ibid.* I. iv. 4.

[1] Quæ vis magna atque mirabilis mortalibus, præter homini, animantibus nulla est: licet eorum quibusdam ad istam lucem contuendam multo quam nobis sit acrior sensus oculorum: sed lucem illam incorpoream contingere nequeunt, qua mens nostra quodammodo irradiatur, ut de his omnibus recte judicare possimus. *De Civitate Dei*, XI. xxvii. 2.

Ipsumque lumen, quo cuncta ista discernimus, in quo nobis satis apparet quid credamus incognitum, quid cognitum teneamus, quam formam corporis recordemur, quam cogitatione fingamus, quid corporis sensus attingat, quid imaginetur animus simile corpori, quid certum et omnium corporum dissimillimum intelligentia contempletur: hoc ergo lumen ubi hæc cuncta dijudicantur, non utique, sicut hujus solis et cujusque corporei luminis fulgor, per localia spatia circumquaque diffunditur, mentemque nostram quasi visibili candore illustrat, sed invisibiliter et ineffabiliter et tamen intelligibiliter lucet, tamque nobis

sun not only makes all other things to appear but is itself apparent to the eye, so is it that God who is the Truth not only makes all truths known to men, but is Himself knowable by our intelligence[1]. We may see Him since He

certum est, quam nobis efficit certa quae secundum ipsum cuncta conspicimus. *Ep.* cxx. (*Consentio*) 10.

Quod si et de coloribus lucem, et de caeteris, quae per corpus sentimus, elementa hujus mundi eademque corpora, quae sentimus, sensusque ipsos, quibus tanquam interpretibus ad talia noscenda mens utitur, de his autem, quae intelliguntur, interiorem veritatem ratione consulimus: quid dici potest unde clareat, verbis nos aliquid discere praeter ipsum qui aures percutit sonum? Namque omnia quae percipimus, aut sensu corporis aut mente percipimus. Illa sensibilia, haec intelligibilia; sive, ut more auctorum nostrorum loquar, illa carnalia, haec spiritualia nominamus........Cum vero de iis agitur quae mente conspicimus id est intellectu atque ratione, ea quidem loquimur quae praesentia contuemur in illa interiore luce veritatis, qua ipse, qui dicitur homo interior, illustratur et fruitur: sed tunc quoque noster auditor, si et ipse illa secreto ac simplici oculo videt, novit quod dico sua contemplatione, non verbis meis. *De Magistro*, 39, 40.

Istae similitudines datae sunt, ut quantum possumus intelligamus, vel, si hoc nondum possumus, sine ulla dubitatione credamus, animam rationalem non esse naturam Dei: illa quippe incommutabilis est: sed tamen eam posse participando illuminari; lucernae quippe accendi indigent, et exstingui possunt. *Ep.* cxl. (*Honorato*) 7. See also *De Trin.* xii. 24 quoted above, p. 29 n. 4.

[1] Te invoco, Deus veritas, in quo et a quo et per quem vera sunt, quae vera sunt, omnia, Deus sapientia, in quo et a quo et per quem sapiunt, quae sapiunt, omnia, Deus vera et summa vita, in quo et a quo et per quem vivunt, quae vere summeque vivunt, omnia. *Solil.* I. 3.

Nunc accipe, quantum praesens tempus exposcit, ex illa similitudine sensibilium etiam de Deo aliquid nunc me docente. Intelligibilis nempe Deus est, intelligibilia etiam illa disciplinarum spectamina; tamen plurimum differunt. Nam et terra visibilis, et lux; sed terra, nisi luce illustrata, videri non potest. Ergo et illa quae in disciplinis traduntur, quae quisquis intelligit verissima esse nulla dubitatione concedit, credendum est ea non posse intelligi, nisi ab alio quasi suo sole illustrentur. Ergo quomodo in hoc sole tria quaedam licet animadvertere; quod est, quod fulget, quod illuminat: ita in illo secretissimo Deo quem vis intelligere, tria quaedam sunt; quod est, quod intelligitur, et quod caetera facit intelligi. *Solil.* I. 15.

Quippe pro sua quisque sanitate ac firmitate comprehendit illud singulare ac verissimum bonum. Lux est quaedam ineffabilis et incom-

is the Light, and it is in His Light that all other realities become clear to us.

It is thus that S. Austin leads us from the conviction of certainty, and the kind of knowledge which is certain for all of us, to Him who is the Truth and the ground of Truth —the Light manifested and manifesting. The analogy is marvellously fruitful: it is the firm grasp which he has upon this thought in its double bearing that renders S. Austin supreme among Christian philosophers. The Divine Truth is directly borne in upon the human soul[1], as the sun

prehensibilis mentium. Lux ista vulgaris nos doceat quantum potest, quomodo se illud habeat. Nam sunt nonnulli oculi tam sani et vegeti, qui se, mox ut aperti fuerint, in ipsum solem sine ulla trepidatione convertant. His quodammodo ipsa lux sanitas est, nec doctore indigent, sed sola fortasse admonitione. Ilis credere, sperare, amare satis est. Alii vero ipso, quem videre vehementer desiderant, fulgore feriuntur, et eo non viso sæpe in tenebras cum delectatione redeunt. Quibus periculosum est, quamvis jam talibus ut sani recte dici possint, velle ostendere quod adhuc videre non valent. Ergo isti exercendi sunt prius, et eorum amor utiliter differendus atque nutriendus est. Primo enim quædam illis demonstranda sunt quæ non per se lucent, sed per lucem videri possint, ut vestis, aut paries, aut aliquid horum. Deinde quod non per se quidem, sed tamen per illam lucem pulchrius effulgeat, ut aurum argentum et similia, nec tamen ita radiatum ut oculos lædat. Tunc fortasse terrenus iste ignis modeste demonstrandus est, deinde sidera, deinde luna, deinde auroræ fulgor, et albescentis cœli nitor. In quibus seu citius seu tardius, sive per totum ordinem, sive quibusdam contemptis, pro sua quisque valetudine assuescens, sine trepidatione et cum magna voluptate solem videbit. *Solil.* I. 23.

Sed quemadmodum illi qui in luce solis eligunt quod libenter aspiciant, et eo aspectu lætificantur; in quibus si qui forte fuerint vegetioribus sanisque et fortissimis oculis præditi, nihil libentius quam ipsum solem contuentur, qui etiam cætera, quibus infirmiores oculi delectantur, illustrat: sic fortis acies mentis et vegeta cum multa vera et incommutabilia certa ratione conspexerit, dirigit se in ipsam veritatem, qua cuncta monstrantur, eique inhærens tanquam obliviscitur cætera, et in illa simul omnibus fruitur. Quidquid enim jucundum est in cæteris veris, ipsa utique veritate jucundum est. *De Lib. Arb.* II. 36

Compare also *De Gen. ad Lit.* XII. 59.

[1] Quæ [ratiocinans potentia] se quoque in me comperiens mutabilem erexit se ad intelligentiam suam; et abduxit cogitationem a consue-

is directly apparent to the human eye: here we have the mode of thought which was worked out in all the diverse forms of Christian mysticism. But S. Austin would have us remember that it is not only in such holy devotion and fixed contemplation that we can enter into the mind of God.

tudine, subtrahens se contradicentibus turbis phantasmatum, ut inveniret quo lumine aspergeretur, cum sine ulla dubitatione clamaret incommutabile præferendum esse mutabili; unde nosset ipsum incommutabile, quod nisi aliquo modo nosset, nullo modo illud mutabili certo præponeret. Et pervenit ad id quod est, in ictu trepidantis aspectus. Tunc vero invisibilia tua, per ea quæ facta sunt, intellecta conspexi; sed aciem figere non evalui: et repercussa infirmitate redditus solitis, non mecum ferebam nisi amantem memoriam, et quasi olfacta desiderantem quæ comedere nondum possem. *Conf.* VII. 23.

Sed non est nobis ullus cum eis excellentioribus philosophis in hac quæstione conflictus. Viderunt enim, suisque litteris multis modis copiosissime mandaverunt, hinc illos, unde et nos, fieri beatos, objecto quodam lumine intelligibili, quod Deus est illis, et aliud est quam illi, a quo illustrantur, ut clareant atque ejus participatione perfecti beatique subsistant. Sæpe multumque Plotinus asserit sensum Platonis explanans, ne illam quidem, quam credunt esse universitatis animam, aliunde beatam esse quam nostram: idque esse lumen quod ipsa non est, sed a quo creata est, et quo intelligibiliter illuminante intelligibiliter lucet. Dat etiam similitudinem ad illa incorporea de his cælestibus conspicuis amplisque corporibus, tanquam ille sit sol, et ipsa sit luna. Lunam quippe solis objectu illuminari putant. Dicit ergo ille magnus Platonicus, animam rationalem (sive potius intellectualis dicenda sit, ex quo genere etiam immortalium beatorumque animas esse intelligit, quos in cælestibus sedibus habitare non dubitat) non habere supra se naturam nisi Dei, qui fabricatus est mundum, a quo et ipsa facta est: nec aliunde illis supernis præberi vitam beatam et lumen intelligentiæ veritatis, quam unde præbetur et nobis; consonans Evangelio, ubi legitur, *Fuit homo missus a Deo, cui nomen erat Joannes: hic venit in testimonium ut testimonium perhiberet de lumine, ut omnes crederent per eum. Non erat ille lumen, sed ut testimonium perhiberet de lumine. Erat lumen verum, quod illuminat omnem hominem venientem in hunc mundum.* In qua differentia satis ostenditur, animam rationalem vel intellectualem, qualis erat in Joanne, sibi lumen esse non posse, sed alterius veri luminis participatione lucere. Hoc et ipse Joannes fatetur, ubi ei perhibens testimonium dicit: *Nos omnes de plenitudine ejus accepimus. De Civitate Dei,* x. ii. See also *Conf.* x. *passim.*

The ideals we cherish, the intelligible relations we all recognise, are the thoughts of the Eternal Creator—His Eternal Being manifested in space and time among things of sense[1], through which we may see Him as in a glass

[1] Sunt namque ideæ principales formæ quædam, vel rationes rerum stabiles atque incommutabiles, quæ ipsæ formatæ non sunt, ac per hoc æternæ ac semper eodem modo sese habentes, quæ in divina intelligentia continentur. Et, cum ipsæ neque oriantur neque intereant, secundum eas tamen formari dicitur omne quod oriri et interire potest, et omne quod oritur et interit......Quod si hæ rerum omnium creandarum creatarumve rationes in divina mente continentur, neque in divina mente quidquam nisi æternum atque incommutabile potest esse, atque has rerum rationes principales appellat ideas Plato: non solum sunt ideæ, sed ipsæ veræ sunt, quia æternæ sunt et ejusmodi atque incommutabiles manent. Quarum participatione fit ut sit quidquid est quoquomodo est. Sed anima rationalis, inter eas res quæ sunt a Deo conditæ, omnia superat; et Deo proxima est, quando pura est; eique in quantum caritate cohæserit, in tantum ab eo lumine illo intelligibili perfusa quodam modo et illustrata cernit, non per corporeos oculos sed per ipsius sui principale quo excellit, id est per intelligentiam suam, istas rationes, quarum visione fit beatissima. *De Divers. Quæst.* *LXXXIII.* qu. xlvi. 2.

Nemo enim dubitat quod sit ipse [Deus] primitus bonus. Multis enim modis dici res possunt similes Deo: aliæ secundum virtutem et sapientiam factæ, quia in ipso est virtus et sapientia non facta; aliæ in quantum solum vivunt, quia ille summe et primitus vivit; aliæ in quantum sunt, quia ille summe et primitus est. Et ideo quæ tantummodo sunt, nec tamen vivunt aut sapiunt, non perfecte, sed exigue sunt ad similitudinem ejus; quia et ipsa bona sunt in ordine suo, cum sit ille super omnia bonus, a quo omnia bona procedunt. Omnia vero quæ vivunt et non sapiunt, paulo amplius participant similitudinem. *De Divers. Quæst. LXXXIII.* qu. li. 2.

Religet ergo nos religio uni omnipotenti Deo; quia inter mentem nostram qua illum intelligimus Patrem, et veritatem, id est lucem interiorem per quam illum intelligimus, nulla interposita creatura est. Quare ipsam quoque Veritatem nulla ex parte dissimilem in ipso et cum ipso veneremur, quæ forma est omnium, quæ ab uno facta sunt, et ad unum nituntur. Unde apparet spiritualibus animis, per hanc formam esse facta omnia, quæ sola implet quod appetunt omnia. *De Vera Religione*, 113.

Hæc dicta sint, ne quisquam, cum de angelis apostaticis loquimur, existimet eos aliam velut ex alio principio habere potuisse naturam, nec corum naturæ auctorem Deum. Cujus erroris impietate tanto quisque

darkly. Here are the ideas which were developed in the splendid structure of the scholastic philosophy[1] and which in another form reappeared in the *Théodicée* of Leibnitz, and the *Analogy* of Butler.

These two veins of thought which have been separated and sometimes opposed in subsequent Christian teaching, are found side by side and interconnected in the writings of S. Austin: he was not merely the founder of scholasticism, because he was also the first of the Western mystics, and has thus attained his unique position in Christendom[2].

Such is the foundation on which S. Austin's teaching rests: his arguments on behalf of Christian truths are based on the nature of knowledge, on the analysis of its elements and the character of its conditions. But other Christian philosophers, with all their respect for the name of the great African doctor, have not followed him closely in this. They have sought to build up the edifice of Christian doctrine not on the nature, but on the limitations of knowledge: they have neglected the teaching which points to belief as the necessary condition of knowledge[3], and have treated it as a supplemental source of truths which may be contrasted with and opposed to knowledge. We need not follow out the weary sophistries which have come from trying to mark out two spheres of mental activity, or dwell on the futility of trying to base any positive conviction on the limitations of our powers ; but we cannot

carebit expeditius et facilius, quanto perspicacius intelligere potuerit, quod per angelum dixit Deus, quando Moysen mittebat ad filios Israel: *Ego sum, qui sum.* Cum enim Deus summa essentia sit, hoc est summe sit, et ideo immutabilis sit, rebus, quas ex nihilo creavit, esse dedit, sed non summe esse sicut ipse est; et aliis dedit esse amplius aliis minus; atque ita naturas essentiarum gradibus ordinavit. *De Civitate Dei,* XII. ii.

[1] See Excursus B. on *S. Austin's influence in the Middle Ages,* p. 142.

[2] A position which is however shared by S. Anselm and to some extent by Erigena. Compare Wiggers, *August. und Pelag.* I. 27.

[3] For an excellent discussion of this subject see Gangauf, *Metaph. Psych.* I. 31. Compare also p. 9, note 1. above and Excursus D, p. 157.

wonder that under the influence of such teaching men have come to despair of knowing with certainty aught of the nature of God.

II. The Relation of his Doctrines to those of other Thinkers.

It may possibly render this meagre sketch of S. Austin's fundamental teaching more definite, if some indication can be given of the precise points at which his doctrines diverge from those of other schools. The merest statement too may serve to show that just as S. Austin has an almost unique position in the history of Christian doctrine—as a scholastic thinker who is also a mystic, so he has a unique position in the history of philosophy. He stands alone—a central figure—the last spokesman of the wisdom of the ancient world, the first who discussed the characteristic problems of modern times. It is just because he thus stands midway as it were between the old and the new, that it is profitable, nay that it is possible, to compare his doctrines with those of the men of all other ages.

1. He gradually diverged farther from Plato in his treatment of the sensible and intelligible worlds[1]; but

[1] Gangauf, *Met. Psy.* I. 92, Ritter, *Gesch. der Philos.* VI. 237, Storz, *Phil. des h. Aug.* 71. Compare however his own remarks. Et quod duos mundos unum sensibilem alterum intelligibilem non ex Platonis vel ex Platonicorum persona sed ex mea sic commendavi, tanquam hoc etiam Dominus significare voluerit, qua non ait, Regnum meum non est de mundo; sed, *Regnum meum non est de hoc mundo*; cum possit et aliqua locutione dictum inveniri, et si alius a Domino Christo significatus est mundus, ille congruentius possit intelligi, in quo erit cœlum novum et terra nova, quando complebitur quod oramus, dicentes, *Adveniat regnum tuum*. Nec Plato quidem in hoc erravit quia esse mundum intelligibilem dixit, si non vocabulum, quod ecclesiasticæ consuetudini in re illa non usitatum est, sed ipsam rem velimus attendere. Mundum quippe ille intelligibilem nuncupavit ipsam rationem sempiternam atque incommutabilem, qua fecit Deus mundum. Quam qui esse negat, sequitur ut dicat,

the crucial difference between them is in S. Austin's thought of God. It is not enough for him to say that Truth has its ground and source in God, for it is not apart from Him, but Truth itself is God. It will not suffice S. Austin to say that God is above all being and all reason: God is the Highest Being, He is the completest Reason. And with this fuller thought of the Divine Being put before us we find ourselves in a different atmosphere. The theology of Plato has proved susceptible of various interpretations[1], it has been held by different scholars to be theistic, deistic and pantheistic in turn. But S. Austin's doctrine is unmistakably theistic: not only does he show that we must believe that God is, since otherwise the world would cease to be intelligible; we may learn to recognise what He is, and to bow before Him in reverence and worship. It is in the passionate devotion of the *Confessions* and the *Soliloquies* that we feel how far S. Austin has moved from the Platonic thought of God.

2. From the current Neo-Platonism he is most clearly separated by his teaching as to the nature of man[2]. His

---

irrationabiliter Deum fecisse quod fecit, aut cum faceret, vel antequam faceret, nescisse quid faceret; si apud eum ratio faciendi non erat; si vero erat, sicut erat, ipsam videtur Plato vocasse intelligibilem mundum. *Retract.* I. iii. 2.

Sed animal esse istum mundum, sicut Plato sensit, aliique philosophi quam plurimi, nec ratione certa indagare potui, nec divinarum Scripturarum auctoritate persuaderi posse cognovi. *Retract.* I. xi. 4.

[1] Gangauf, *Met. Psy.* I. 78. Hegel, *Gesch. Phil.* III. 47.
[2] Ritter, VI. 230, 235.

Sed philosophi, contra quorum calumnias defendimus civitatem Dei, hoc est ejus Ecclesiam, sapienter sibi videntur irridere quod dicimus, animae a corpore separationem inter poenas ejus esse deputandam: quia videlicet ejus perfectam beatitudinem tunc illi fieri existimant, cum omni prorsus corpore exuta ad Deum simplex et sola et quodammodo nuda redierit.......Hoc tantum contra istos commemorandum putavi, qui se Platonicos vocari vel esse gloriantur, cujus superbia nominis erubescunt esse Christiani, ne commune illis cum vulgo vocabulum vilem faciat palliatorum tanto magis inflatam quanto magis exiguam paucitatem: et quaerentes quid in doctrina Christiana reprehendant, exagitant

strong sense of human personality prevents him from sharing in the aspiration for mere absorption into God. His regard for every-day experience forces him to believe that the human soul is so linked to the human body that they react on one another, that the souls which God has given may be changed for the worse by deeds done in the body. And thus he has light to give us on our every-day duties—truth not merely for the hermit in his cell, or the scholar in unperturbed and cultured leisure, but for the market and the street, for man as he jostles with man in the struggles of daily life.

3. The Schoolmen[1], who treasured his words with such reverence, did not altogether retain the spirit of his teaching; they spoke of God and of His work in the world in the same sort of language as they used of the things that He has created and made. In their admiration for Aristotle and the clearness with which he discussed the phænomena around us, they sought to force our knowledge of God into the same shell, and express it in the same terms. S. Austin had given a note of warning against this error. He had applied the Aristotelian logic to the thought of God and learned to confess, "It was falsehood I conceived of "Thee, not truth; fictions of my misery not the realities of "Thy Blessedness[2]." And from this profounder view of the

æternitatem corporum, tanquam hæc sint inter se contraria, ut et beatitudinem quæramus animæ, et eam semper esse velimus in corpore, velut ærumnoso vinculo colligatam: cum eorum auctor et magister Plato, donum a Deo summo diis ab illo factis dicat esse concessum, ne aliquando moriantur, id est a corporibus, quibus eos connexuit, separentur. *De Civitate Dei*, XIII. xvi.

[1] See Excursus B, p. 152. Compare also the criticism of S. Austin in C. van Endert's *Gottesbeweis*, 176 n.

[2] *Conf.* IV. 28, 29. Compare also the following more detailed statement: Ut sic intelligamus Deum, si possumus quantum possumus, sine qualitate bonum, sine quantitate magnum, sine indigentia creatorem, sine situ præsidentem, sine habitu omnia continentem, sine loco ubique totum, sine tempore sempiternum, sine ulla sui mutatione mutabilia

nature of God, and of the extent to which our thoughts and conceptions are applicable to it, he was able, as the mediæval thinkers were not, to protest against the crudeness of much popular theology and the grossness of popular superstitions. "One class of men," he said, "endeavour to "transfer to things incorporeal and spiritual the facts they "have learned about things corporeal, whether through ex- "perience of the bodily senses, or by natural human wit and "diligent quickness, so as to seek to measure and conceive of "the former by the latter. Others again frame whatever "idea they have of God after the pattern of the nature "and affections of the human mind: and through this error, "in disputing concerning God, they argue by distorted and "fallacious rules. While yet a third class do indeed strive "to transcend the whole creation, which doubtless is change- "able, and so to raise their thought to the unchangeable "substance, which is God; but being weighed down with "the burden of mortality, whilst they both would seem to "know what they do not, and cannot know what they "would, they shut against themselves the path of under- "standing by an overbold affirmation of the assumptions of "their own judgment[1]." We certainly cannot charge against him the defects which have been alleged against the scholastic theology.

4. And if we turn to that other thinker who sought to pass through every phase of doubt that he might attain certainty at last, we cannot but feel that though the *cogito ergo sum* of Descartes repeats the *si enim fallor, sum* of S. Austin, there is yet something far nobler in the use the ancient Father made of his principle. Descartes' train of thought was so individualistic that one may say he never

---

facientem, nihilque patientem. Quisquis Deum ita cogitat, etsi nondum potest omni modo invenire quid sit; pie tamen cavet, quantum potest, aliquid de eo sentire quod non sit. *De Trin.* v. 2.

[1] *De Trin.* 1. 1.

advanced beyond subjective certainty[1] : he felt that the existence of God was clear to his own mind, and to any other mind that followed his process, but S. Austin recognises throughout that there are intellectual elements which are common to all intelligents, and forces his way to objective knowledge, to knowledge of the truth. S. Austin's arguments on the reliability of the evidence of the senses[2]

[1] See my *Descartes and Metaphysical Speculation in England*, p. 50.

[2] Quod autem attinet ad illam differentiam, quam de Academicis novis Varro adhibuit, quibus incerta sunt omnia, omnino civitas Dei talem dubitationem tanquam dementiam detestatur, habens de rebus, quas mente atque ratione comprehendit, etiamsi parvam propter corpus corruptibile quod aggravat animam, (quoniam sicut dicit Apostolus, *Ex parte scimus,*) tamen certissimam scientiam: creditque sensibus in rei cujusque evidentia, quibus per corpus animus utitur: quoniam miserabilius fallitur, qui nunquam putat eis esse credendum. *De Civitate Dei*, XIX. xviii.

Cum enim duo sint genera rerum quæ sciuntur, unum earum quæ per sensus corporis percipit animus, alterum earum quæ per se ipsum, multa illi philosophi garrierunt contra corporis sensus, animi autem quasdam firmissimas per se ipsum perceptiones rerum verarum, quale illud est quod dixi Scio me vivere, nequaquam in dubium vocare potuerunt. Sed absit a nobis ut ea quæ per sensus corporis didicimus, vera esse dubitemus: per eos quippe didicimus cœlum et terram et ea quæ in eis nota sunt nobis, quantum ille, qui et nos et ipsa condidit, innotescere nobis voluit. Absit etiam ut scire nos negemus, quæ testimonio didicimus aliorum: alioquin esse nescimus Oceanum; nescimus esse terras atque urbes, quas celeberrima fama commendat; nescimus fuisse homines et opera eorum, quæ historica lectione didicimus; nescimus quæ quotidie undecumque nuntiantur et indiciis consonis contestantibusque firmantur; postremo nescimus in quibus locis, vel ex quibus hominibus fuerimus exorti; quia hæc omnia testimoniis credidimus aliorum. *De Trin.* xv. 21.

Deinde paulatim tu, Domine, manu mitissima et misericordissima pertractans et componens cor meum, consideranti quam innumerabilia crederem quæ non viderem, neque cum gererentur adfuissem: sicut tam multa in historia gentium, tam multa de locis atque urbibus quæ non videram, tam multa amicis, tam multa medicis, tam multa hominibus aliis atque aliis, quæ nisi crederentur, omnino in hac vita nihil ageremus: postremo, quam inconcusse fixum fide retinerem, de quibus

appear even more striking when we contrast them with the rough and ready process by which Descartes reassured himself on this point[1].

If I thus claim a very high place for S. Austin among the greatest thinkers the world has ever seen, I do not forget the defects of his writings. Philosophy was not the main business of his life, and perhaps it chiefly interested him because in his own case it had served as a guide to prepare his heart to receive the Christian Faith. He fell on evil days when the pressing needs of active controversy kept him too busy to pursue philosophical enquiries with heart and soul. Nor need anyone suppose that he was before his time in the sense of answering questions which no one had asked or settling issues that had never been raised. He has not said the last word on any of the problems of philosophy; but even if we look at the most recent advances the human mind has made in the search for truth, we may yet feel that it was the principle he announced which became fruitful in after times.

But to judge of him fully we must stand above him: shall we not rather do well to look up to him as a teacher from whom we fain would learn? There is a wonderful interest about such a man as he—the last of the thinkers of the old world, trained in the wisdom of his age, interested in the subtleties of its logic, fascinated by the

parentibus ortus essem, quod scire non possem, nisi audiendo credidissem. *Conf.* VI. 7.

[1] S. Austin is content to treat the evidence of the senses and oral communications as giving us probable evidence, while Descartes attempts to deduce the validity of empirical knowledge directly from the veracity of the Perfect Being who has created us.

Ratio enim nobis non dictat ea quae sic videmus vel imaginamur, idcirco revera existere. Sed plane nobis dictat, omnes nostras Ideas sive notiones aliquid in se veritatis continere; alioqui enim fieri non posset ut Deus qui summe perfectus et verax est, illas in nobis posuisset. *De Methodo,* IV.

strange speculations which India and Persia had given to the Western world, wearied by doubt, and reassured in conviction as he pondered over the thoughts[1] of Plato, and who yet turned at last to enter the kingdom of God as a little child, and offer himself to be Christ's faithful soldier and servant to his life's end.

[1] Procurasti mihi per quemdam hominem immanissimo typho turgidum quosdam Platonicorum libros ex græca lingua in latinam versos: et ibi legi, non quidem his verbis, sed hoc idem omnino multis et multiplicibus suaderi rationibus, quod in principio erat Verbum, et Verbum erat apud Deum, et Deus erat Verbum. *Conf.* VII. 13. See Excursus C, on *S. Austin's knowledge of Greek*, p. 154.

LECTURE II.

The sting of death is sin. 1 Cor. xv. 56.

THE ORIGIN OF EVIL AND THE PUNISHMENT OF SIN.

I. THE MANICHÆANS AND THE NATURE OF EVIL.

THE firstfruits of S. Austin's regenerate zeal were shown in the energy with which he threw himself into the contest with the followers of Mani. He had been so long under the spell of their teaching that he was specially fitted to expose as erroneous the opinions which he had cherished through his early manhood : and when he once more found himself in Rome on his way to his native land, circumstances arose which seemed to call on him to take a part in the controversy. It gives us some idea of the intellectual ferment which was then going on in the capital of the world, when we remember that it was in Rome that S. Austin had come in close contact with the doctrines of the Academics and that it was again "when in Rome after his "baptism that," as he tells[1] us, "he could not bear in silence "the vaunting of the Manichæans about their pretended "continence...in which to deceive the inexperienced, they "claim superiority over true Christians to whom they are "not to be compared." He then wrote two short treatises on the subject.

But when he reached his old home, and when after a time he was ordained to be a priest and appointed to the care of the Christian flock in Hippo, he found himself forced in

[1] *Retract.* I. vii. 1.

the interest of the souls which were committed to his charge[1] to attack the false doctrine in every way, in his sermons, tracts and letters, as well as by public disputations. These public disputations were much in favour with the Manichæans: and were perhaps a practice which indicated their Eastern origin: the first teacher of their tenets had suffered a violent death as the consequence of being worsted in one of those contests which gave the courts of Eastern monarchs their pretensions to learning[2]. In his public controversy with Fortunatus, S. Austin was so successful as to turn the tide of popular opinion at Hippo in favour of the orthodox faith[3]: and when the practical issue was thus decided in his own church, he ceased to take such a keen interest in the matter, though he had occasionally to return to the controversy during his episcopate[4]. But it is not out of place to note that the nature of these discussions affects the form of his principal treatise against the Manichæans: in the work against Faustus there are statements and counter-statements,—statements which are one of the chief sources of our knowledge of Manichæan teaching and which seem to be fairly made. It is no longer, as in his Academic dialogues, the report of a conversation where friends were engaged in helping each other in the search for truth, it is a written controversy in which the two opponents each try to establish their own case and to weaken the position of their adversary in the eyes of the public.

It may appear at first sight that there can be little permanent interest for us in the religious disputations of the fourth century. Public discussions have gone out of

[1] Bindemann, *Der h. Aug.* II. 342.
[2] Beausobre, *Histoire critique de Manichée et du manichéisme*, I. 202.
[3] *Vita S. Augustini*, III. vii. 3.
[4] Bindemann, III. 122.

fashion; the courtly argument and pre-arranged conversions of the sixteenth century were more decorous but not more weighty than the public wranglings over the mysteries of faith which attracted popular audiences in the last generation. But at any rate the controversies in which S. Austin took part have an historical interest for us,—for he had to face the last, the final struggle of heathenism to absorb a measure of Christian truth, and thus to persuade men to sacrifice the distinctive and vital elements of the Christian Faith. There was a place for Christ among the gods of Rome, but Rome was pagan for this very reason that He was only one among her many gods: and there was a place for Christ in the system of Mani, but that system was heathen still. The best of heathen aspiration,—to lose oneself in God, the best of heathen morality—to destroy the fleshly passions which fetter the spirit, and no small measure of heathen art and heathen eloquence, were all arrayed against the Church of Christ—but not to prevail. And if we have found an interest in seeing how S. Austin received a noble heritage of pre-Christian thought and built it into the edifice of Christian philosophy—may we not also pause for a while to note how he came in contact with the best of heathen aspiration and morality and worship, and showed how meagre and imperfect they are, at their best?

Mani was indeed a religious reformer: deeply impregnated with the belief and practice which Buddhist monks were spreading in the East[1], he tried with some success to reform the religion of Zoroaster in Persia—his native land. While his fundamental doctrine, the root of his system, was of Persian origin, and he figured the universe to himself as if it were given over to one unending struggle between the Powers of Light and Darkness, in regard to discipline

[1] On the Buddhist elements in Manichæism compare F. C. Baur, *Das manichäische Religionssystem,* 424, 434, 445.

his system very closely resembles that founded by Buddha; the *elect* of the Manichæans correspond to the Buddhist *monks*; the precepts about abstinence from meat and things of sense are, if not borrowed from the rules Gotama gave for the conduct of his followers, the outcome of the same principles about the nature of man. But if Mani thus sought to reform one of the noblest non-Christian religions through the influence of another, he did not rise above heathenism. He still set the problem of religion as it occurs to heathen minds; man is but a part of the world of phænomena, to be explained as other phænomena are[1]: the dualism of his doctrine did not render it wholly incompatible with popular polytheism[2], and its contempt for heathen modes of worship did not really raise it above heathen modes of thought, although there were portions of New Testament story and teaching which could be easily assimilated to the rest of his teaching. In S. Austin's controversy with the Manichæans then we may find no ordinary theological polemic: it gives us the record of the last struggle of heathenism, and of its defeat.

But it may have more than a merely historical interest for us. Heathenism was defeated; for the future, learning and science and philosophy were to be cast in Christian not in heathen moulds, Christian not heathen modes of thought were to enter into all the affairs of life among the peoples which formed the van of human progress. But heathenism is not extinct: Buddhism is still supreme in Ceylon; the doctrine of Zoroaster is cherished by the Parsis in Bombay; and the belief of the crowds who flock to the lovely shrines on the Girnar and at Mount Abu[3] shows still closer affinities to the teaching of Mani. The vitality of the primæval theology is shown by the attraction

[1] Baur, *D. man. Rel.* 345.
[2] *Ibid.* 340.
[3] On its affinities with the Jain religion see Baur, *D. man. Rel.* 449.

it exercises over Western minds: when we are told of the grandeur of Theosophy or the depths of Esoteric Buddhism we cannot but see that we may be called on to enter on the old controversy in some new form among our fellow-subjects or even in our own land; and if such a day shall come for any of us, we may feel that it is no small gain that the weapons S. Austin used are ready to our hands.

The vantage ground from which he attacked their position was furnished by his studies in Greek philosophy. "We all," he says, "desire to live happily;...but the title "happy cannot in my opinion belong either to him who has "not what he loves, whatever it may be, or to him who has "what he loves, if it is hurtful, or to him who does not love "what he has although it is good in perfection....There is "a fourth case where the happy life exists, when that which "is man's chief good is both loved and possessed[1]." He goes on to show that there is but one worthy object of love through Whom we may attain true happiness. It is "God, "in following after Whom we live well, and in reaching "Whom we live both well and happily[2]." "Following after "God is the desire of happiness, to reach God is happiness "itself. We follow after God by loving Him: we reach "Him, not by becoming entirely what He is, but in near- "ness to Him, and in wonderful and spiritual contact with "Him, and in being thoroughly illuminated and embraced "by His truth and holiness. For He is light itself: but we "too may receive light from Him....And if nothing can "separate us from His love must not this be surer as well as "better than any other good[3]?"

This is the true good and source of happiness, and it is one which external things cannot mar. "Present troubles "do not separate us, for we feel their burden the less the

---

[1] *De Moribus Eccl.* 4.   [2] *Ibid.* 10.   [3] *Ibid.* 18.

"closer we cling to Him from Whom they try to sever us[1]." God alone is to be loved, and all this world, that is, sensible things are to be despised—while however they are to be used as this life requires.

The old question, as to how far external goods were necessary to the life of virtue and therefore to true happiness, presents little difficulty to S. Austin. All earthly things work for the good of those who love God. The very passions which disturb the even tenour of life may be rightly directed and offer occasions for self-discipline[2]. Pain, sickness, suffering and all else may be disciplinary, and in so far as they serve for our training and improvement they cannot be really evil; since even the poisons and mischiefs in the physical universe, harmonise into a whole that is truly good[3].

[1] *De Moribus Eccl.* 19.
[2] Denique in disciplina nostra non tam quæritur utrum pius animus irascatur, sed quare irascatur; nec utrum sit tristis, sed unde sit tristis; nec utrum timeat, sed quid timeat. Irasci enim peccanti, ut corrigatur; contristari pro afflicto, ut liberetur; timere periclitanti, ne pereat; nescio utrum quisquam sana consideratione reprehendat. Nam et misericordiam Stoicorum est solere culpare: sed quanto honestius ille Stoicus misericordia perturbaretur hominis liberandi, quam timore naufragii! *De Civitate Dei,* IX. v.
[3] Quemadmodum nec bonis imputatur, quod ipsis prodesse volentibus nocetur alicui, sed bono animo benevolentiæ præmium tribuitur: ita etiam cætera creatura pro meritis animarum rationalium vel sentitur vel latet, vel molesta vel commoda est. Summo enim Deo cuncta bene administrante quæ fecit, nihil inordinatum in universo, nihilque injustum est, sive scientibus sive nescientibus nobis. *De Divers. Quæs.* *LXXXIII.* qu. xxvii.

Quibus recte consideratis atque perspectis, attende utrum aliquid mali acciderit fidelibus et piis, quod eis non in bonum verteretur. *De Civitate Dei,* I. x. 1.

Nec attendunt, quam vel in suis locis naturisque vigeant, pulchroque ordine disponantur; quantumque universitati rerum pro suis portionibus decoris tanquam in communem rempublicam conferant, vel nobis ipsis, si eis congruenter atque scienter utamur, commoditatis attribuant; ita ut venena ipsa, quæ per inconvenientiam perniciosa sunt, convenienter adhibita in salubria medicamenta vertantur: quamque a contrario etiam hæc quibus delectantur, sicut cibus et potus et

There are diverse ways in which the good things God bestows subserve the highest good; some cannot be misused, while others can[1]. But all that God gives us is still in its own nature good, as the Creator at first pronounced it to be. And thus in the full view of all the evil in the world, physical and moral, all the suffering and all the sin, S. Austin maintains the old Platonic doctrine[2], that evil is not an absolute, positive factor in the universe[3], but that it is only the priva-

ista lux, immoderato et inopportuno usu noxia sentiantur. Unde nos admonet divina providentia, non res insipienter vituperare, sed utilitatem rerum diligenter inquirere; et ubi nostrum ingenium vel infirmitas deficit, ita credere occultam, sicut erant quaedam quae vix potuimus invenire: quia et ipsa utilitatis occultatio, aut humilitatis exercitatio est, aut elationis attritio; cum omnino natura nulla sit malum, nomenque hoc non sit nisi privationis boni: sed a terrenis usque ad cœlestia, et a visibilibus usque ad invisibilia sunt aliis alia bona meliora; ad hoc inaequalia, ut essent omnia. *De Civitate Dei*, XI. xxii. Compare also *De Vera Religione*, 74—78.

[1] Ista ergo magna bona sunt: sed meminisse te oportet, non solum magna, sed etiam minima bona non esse posse, nisi ab illo a quo sunt omnia bona, hoc est Deo. Id enim superior disputatio persuasit, cui toties tamque lætus assensus es. Virtutes igitur quibus recte vivitur, magna bona sunt: species autem quorumlibet corporum, sine quibus recte vivi potest, minima bona sunt: potentiæ vero animi sine quibus recte vivi non potest, media bona sunt. Virtutibus nemo male utitur: cæteris autem bonis, id est, mediis et minimis, non solum bene, sed etiam male quisque uti potest. *De Lib. Arb.* II. 50.

[2] It was accepted by several of the Fathers. Origen (*Comment. in Evan. Joan.* II. 7). Athanasius (*Orat. contra Gentes*, 4). Greg. Nyss. (*Or. Cat.* v. vi. vii.).

[3] Peccatum nihil est, et nihil fiunt homines cum peccant. *Tract. I. in Ev. Joan.* 13.

Omne igitur quod est, sine aliqua specie non est. Ubi autem aliqua species, necessario est aliquis modus: et modus aliquid boni est: summum ergo malum nullum modum habet; caret enim omni bono. Non est igitur; quia nulla specie continetur, totumque hoc nomen mali de speciei privatione repertum est. *De Divers. Quæst. LXXXIII.* qu. vi.

Unde res mira conficitur, ut, quia omnis natura in quantum natura est bonum est, nihil aliud dici videatur, cum vitiosa natura mala esse natura dicitur, nisi malum esse quod bonum est: nec malum esse, nisi quod bonum est; quoniam omnis natura bonum est, nec res aliqua mala

tion of good[1]: there is no existence apart from the good[2],—
esset, si res ipsa quae mala est, natura non esset. Non igitur potest esse malum, nisi aliquod bonum. *Enchiridion*, xiii.
Malumque illud quod quaerebam unde esset, non est substantia, quia si substantia esset, bonum esset. *Conf.* vii. 12.

[1] Quid est autem aliud quod malum dicitur, nisi privatio boni? Nam sicut corporibus animalium nihil est aliud morbis et vulneribus affici, quam sanitate privari (neque enim id agitur, cum adhibetur curatio, ut mala ista quae inerant, id est, morbi ac vulnera recedant hinc, et alibi sint; sed utique ut non sint. Non enim ulla substantia, sed carnalis substantiae vitium est vulnus aut morbus: cum caro sit ipsa substantia, profecto aliquod bonum cui accidunt ista mala, id est privationes ejus boni quod dicitur sanitas); ita et animorum quaecumque sunt vitia, naturalium sunt privationes bonorum: quae cum sanantur, non aliquo transferuntur; sed ea quae ibi erant, nusquam erunt, quando in illa sanitate non erunt. *Enchiridion*, xi.

Mali enim nulla natura est; sed amissio boni mali nomen accepit. *De Civitate Dei*, xi. ix.

Quaeram ergo tertio quid sit malum. Respondebitis fortasse, Corruptio. Quis et hoc negaverit generale malum esse? Nam hoc est contra naturam, hoc est quod nocet. Sed corruptio non est in seipsa, sed in aliqua substantia quam corrumpit: non enim substantia est ipsa corruptio. Ea igitur res quam corrumpit, corruptio non est, malum non est. Quod enim corrumpitur, integritate et sinceritate privatur. *De Mor. Manich.* 7.

[2] Dicimus itaque incommutabile bonum non esse, nisi unum verum beatum Deum: ea vero quae fecit, bona quidem esse, quod ab illo; verumtamen mutabilia, quod non de illo, sed de nihilo facta sunt. Quanquam ergo summa non sint; quibus est Deus majus bonum: magna sunt tamen ea mutabilia bona, quae adhaerere possunt ut beata sint, immutabili bono; quod usque adeo bonum eorum est, ut sine illo misera esse necesse sit. Nec ideo caetera in hac creaturae universitate meliora sunt, quia misera esse non possunt. Neque enim caetera membra corporis nostri ideo dicendum est oculis esse meliora, quia caeca esse non possunt. Sicut autem melior est natura sentiens et cum dolet, quam lapis qui dolore nullo modo potest: ita rationalis natura praestantior est etiam misera, quam illa quae rationis vel sensus est expers, et ideo in eam non cadit miseria. Quod cum ita sit, huic naturae, quae in tanta excellentia creata est, ut licet ipsa sit mutabilis, inhaerendo tamen incommutabili bono, id est summo Deo, beatitudinem consequatur, nec expleat indigentiam suam nisi utique beata sit, cique explendae non sufficiat nisi Deus, profecto non illi adhaerere, vitium est. Omne autem vitium naturae nocet, ac per hoc contra naturam est. Ab illa igitur quae adhaeret Deo, non natura differt ista, sed vitio: quo tamen etiam vitio

the most corrupted nature has good in it or it could not be[1].

By thus insisting on the unreality of evil, on its unsubstantiality and nothingness, S. Austin is able to strike a blow at the very foundation of the Manichæan system. Evil no longer appears an eternal power ever opposing God, nor are we forced like the Manichæans to think of God as one whose will is limited, whose power is thwarted by evil, for He ever brings good out of it: He so orders all things that fail that they may exist where their existence is most suitable[2]. On no other supposition can we think worthily of God, as unchanging, eternal, incorruptible, for if God is not thus supreme in all that is, but merely a Soul that is in every human soul, then does it seem that the corruptions of human souls must be corruptions of that God of which they form the parts[3].

valde magna multumque laudabilis ostenditur ipsa natura. Cujus enim recte vituperatur vitium, procul dubio natura laudatur. Nam recta vitii vituperatio est, quod illo dehonestatur natura laudabilis. *De Civ. Dei*, XII. i. 3. On S. Austin's philosophy of Nature see the excellent remarks in Dr Konrad Sc:pio's *Des A. A. Metaphysik in Rahmen seiner Lehre vom Uebel*, p. 31.

[1] Quia nec ipse diabolus a potestate Omnipotentis alienus est, sicut neque a bonitate. Nam et maligni angeli unde qualicumque subsisterent vita, nisi per eum qui vivificat omnia? *De Trin.* XIII. 16.

[2] Sed Dei bonitas eo rem perduci non sinit, et omnia deficientia sic ordinat, ut ibi sint ubi congruentissime possint esse, donec ordinatis motibus ad id recurrant unde defecerunt. Itaque etiam animas rationales, in quibus est potentissimum liberum arbitrium, deficientes a se, in inferioribus creaturæ gradibus ordinat, ubi tales esse decet. *De Mor. Manich.* 9.

Ita nec præter ordinem sunt mala, quæ non diligit Deus, et ipsum tamen ordinem diligit: hoc ipsum enim diligit, diligere bona et non diligere mala; quod est magni ordinis et divinæ dispositionis. Qui ordo atque dispositio quia universitatis congruentiam ipsa distinctione custodit, fit ut mala etiam esse necesse sit. Ita quasi ex antithetis quodammodo, quod nobis etiam in oratione jucundum est, id est ex contrariis, omnium simul rerum pulchritudo fignatur. *De Ordine*, I. 18. See also *De Lib. Arb.* III. 35.

[3] Deus igitur vobis auctoribus, siquidem pars Dei est Deus, et

II. THE ORIGIN OF EVIL.

The question as to the nature of evil is to S. Austin a far more important one than the issue which the Manichæans constantly raised as to its origin. They challenged their opponents on this point; if evil is not, they argued, a substantial element in the universe, it is incumbent upon you to show us whence it comes: and S. Austin took up the challenge; he proceeds to show how the origin of evil is possible, how it might appear among the works of an unchanging God Who is all good.

The answer I shall give in the words in which he himself summarises it. "All things that exist, therefore, seeing "that the Creator of them all is supremely good, are them-"selves good. But because they are not like their Creator "supremely and unchangeably good, their good may be "diminished and increased[1]...and the cause of evil is the fall-"ing away from the unchangeable good, of a being made good "but changeable[2]....This is the first evil that befell the in-"telligent creation—that is, its first privation of good. Fol-"lowing upon this crept in, and now even in opposition to "man's will, ignorance of duty, and lust after what is hurt-"ful, and these brought in their train error and suffering...

stultitia corrumpitur, et cadendo mutatus est, et amissa perfectione violatus, et opis indiget, et debilis morbo, et oppressus miseria, et servitute turpatus est. Quod si Dei pars Deus non est; nec incorruptus potest esse, in cujus parte corruptio est; nec incommutatus, qui ex aliqua parte mutatus est ; nec inviolatus, qui non ex omni parte perfectus; neque non indigens, qui sedulo agit ut sibi restituat partem suam; nec omnino sanus, qui aliqua parte imbecillus est; nec beatissimus, qui habet aliquam partem subjectam miseriæ ; nec omnino liber, cujus pars aliqua premitur servitute. Hæc omnia cogimini dicere, cum animam, quam tantis obrutam calamitatibus cernitis, partem Dei esse perhibetis. *De Mor. Manich.* 22, 23.

[1] *Enchiridion*, xii.
[2] *Ibid.* xxiii.

"From these fountains of evil which spring out of defect rather than superfluity, flows every form of misery that besets a rational nature[1]."

It is thus through the defect of will—the negligence of a changeful will—that the origin of evil is possible. "For as a snake does not creep on with open steps, but by the very minutest efforts of its several scales, so the slippery motion of falling away from what is good, takes possession of the negligent only gradually, and beginning from a perverted straining after the likeness of God, arrives in the end at the likeness of beasts[2]." Such is S. Austin's argument to show that the possibility of the origin of evil was conceivable, when its true nature was understood, and that it was unnecessary to assume with the Manichaeans that evil like good was a substantial and permanent reality.

Had S. Austin left the matter here, little exception could have been taken to his treatment of this difficult problem: but he went on to discuss the farther point as to the actual origin of sin in this world. How did evil actually and as a matter of fact come to take possession of human hearts?

It is of course clear that this is a question of actual history; and it is also pretty clear that the Bible,—the only history to which we should be likely to turn—does not give us an account of actual occurrences. The allegory of the

[1] *Enchiridion* xxiv. Compare also another statement of the same doctrine, Nemo igitur quaerat efficientem causam malae voluntatis: non enim est efficiens, sed deficiens; quia nec illa effectio est, sed defectio. Deficere namque ab eo quod summe est, ad id quod minus est, hoc est incipere habere voluntatem malam. Causas porro defectionum istarum, cum efficientes non sint, ut dixi, sed deficientes, velle invenire, tale est ac si quisquam velit videre tenebras, vel audire silentium: quod tamen utrumque nobis notum est; neque illud nisi per oculos, neque hoc nisi per aures; non sane in specie, sed in speciei privatione. *De Civitate Dei*, xii. vii.

[2] *De Trinitate*, xii. 16.

Fall puts clearly before our minds the important truths that evil is not the work of God—that it arises through the defect of will of a changeful creature, that its punishment follows in consciousness of guilt, and separation from God. It was in parables that our Lord taught the gospel of the kingdom of God, and it was in an allegory that the truth about creation and the origin of sin was divinely set before human minds. Christian teachers like Origen and S. Ambrose laid stress almost entirely upon the allegorical interpretation: and had S. Austin been careful to take a line which should be perfectly consistent with other portions of his teaching, he would not have insisted on interpreting this chapter of *Genesis* as a history of actual facts. It was of course clear to him that the first chapter of *Genesis* was purely allegorical, for it is obvious that the coming into being of Time could not take place in periods of time[1]: but the third chapter he regards as actual history, and it may not be uninstructive, both with respect to the man[2] and his times, if we dwell briefly on the cir-

---

[1] Cum igitur Deus, in cujus æternitate nulla est omnino mutatio, creator sit temporum et ordinator, quomodo dicatur post temporum spatia mundum creasse, non video; nisi dicatur ante mundum jam aliquam fuisse creaturam, cujus motibus tempora currerent. Porro si Litteræ sacræ maximeque veraces ita dicunt, in principio fecisse Deum cœlum et terram, ut nihil antea fecisse intelligatur, quia hoc potius in principio fecisse diceretur, si quid fecisset ante cætera cuncta quæ fecit; procul dubio non est mundus factus in tempore, sed cum tempore. Quod enim fit in tempore, et post aliquod fit, et ante aliquod tempus; post id quod præteritum est, ante id quod futurum est: nullum autem posset esse præteritum; quia nulla erat creatura, cujus mutabilibus motibus ageretur. Cum tempore autem factus est mundus, si in ejus conditione factus est mutabilis motus, sicut videtur se habere etiam ordo ille primorum sex vel septem dierum, in quibus et mane et vespera nominantur, donec omnia quæ his diebus Deus fecit, sexto perficiantur die, septimoque in magno mysterio Dei vacatio commendetur. Qui dies cujusmodi sint, aut perdifficile nobis, aut etiam impossibile est cogitare; quanto magis dicere? *De Civitate Dei*, XI. vi.

[2] See Excursus D, p. 157.

cumstances which may have induced him to prefer this interpretation.

The Manichæan controversy incidentally raised many questions as to the interpretation of Scripture to an importance which they had never previously possessed. That system being as it was a heathenism, though a pure heathenism, was utterly opposed to the genius of the religion of Israel[1], and thus attacks were constantly directed against the sacred scriptures of the Jews. There was a debased form of Christianity which the Manichæans extracted from the New Testament, and though they seemed to orthodox Christians to play fast and loose with the Gospels and Epistles, they did not reject these altogether as they did the books of the Old Testament, which they were accustomed to criticise with unmeasured scorn. S. Austin defended the Old Testament from their attacks by asserting the fundamental harmony which existed between it and the New: while he also wrote elaborate commentaries in which he replies to the objections they urged against particular passages—objections which are repeated in very similar form by Secularists in the present day. The story of the Fall was especially a stumbling-block to the Manichæan, who denied the possibility of evil originating and asserted its substantial character; there was accordingly a great temptation to a controversialist to attempt not only to prove that evil could arise, but to make the most of an account that purported to describe how it had arisen as a matter of fact.

There was another influence which affected S. Austin too: there is a considerable difference between the allegorising of such a preacher as S. Ambrose and the elucidations which S. Austin gives: the very cast of his mind forced him to treat many things as plain matters of fact, which others had chiefly valued for some spiritual interpretation.

[1] Baur, D. man. Rel. 356.

He seems to have accepted some such canon as this—to treat all Scriptural narratives as not only revelations of matters of faith about the unseen, but also as statements of actual fact, unless they were obviously allegorical[1]. Now in the times when he wrote, and with the knowledge of natural history and cognate studies which he could draw— say from the pages of Pliny—there was no real ground for regarding the Biblical account of the Fall as inconsistent with human experience, and he would not consent to sacrifice a shred of the possible meaning of the written word.

One may add as a third point, that the reference which S. Paul makes in the *Epistle to the Romans* to death coming into the world through the fall of Adam, seems to give apostolic sanction to the opinion that the Biblical story is a relation of actual matters of fact.

The exigencies of the Manichæan controversy no longer weigh upon us directly; but it is worth while to notice how far we are removed from S. Austin's position in other respects. For there is a point in which the Biblical narrative conflicts with our knowledge of man's physical nature and the phenomena of animal life. We know that physical death had entered the world long before man appeared, and that generation after generation of living beings had already passed away: we know too that man, the noblest of created things, was not so different from the others in physical organism that he could subsist for ever, that no decay awaited him, and that he was free from the claim which death asserts over all that lives on the earth[2]. Yet

---

[1] *Sermo* lxxxix. 4, 5, 6. *De Doctrina Christiana*, III. 14. See Excursus D, § 5, p. 165.

[2] Posse non mori. The doctrine of a minor immortality appears to imply a belief in the earth as everlasting: but S. Austin insists on the possibility of a deathless translation to the true immortality, mori non posse. *Op. imp. contra Jul.* VI. xxx. The belief that divine Grace was so given to Adam that he was preserved from physical decay and that during his sinless life a supernatural harmony reigned throughout the

the third chapter of *Genesis* seems to imply that the animate creation enjoyed the possibility of an immortal life upon earth, before man's sin brought on it the penalty of physical death.

We then, with our greater experience of the facts of life, shall, if we regard human intelligence as reverently as S. Austin did[1], be satisfied with grasping the spiritual truth which is conveyed in the story of the Fall, without insisting on it as an account of an historical event in the world. There may be some of us, however, who have been habituated to regard it as recounting an actual event, and to whom it may seem that in taking it as symbolical we deprive S. Paul's argument on death and the resurrection of all its force, since he too writes as if death had been newly imposed on created beings as a penalty on fallen man.

But assuredly to fallen man—to man who by defect of will has allowed evil to enter his heart—death is a new thing; parting from life is not the same thing to him as it is to a mere animal: for the Fall of man—through whatever event it actually occurred—was an awakening to a knowledge of good and evil, to a new consciousness of himself—and thus has given death new terrors. For in the Fall, the

---

earth, is not contradicted by evidence of any kind but it is unverified by our empirical knowledge. On the relation between the words of Scripture and empirical knowledge see Excursus D, § 4, p. 162.

[1] Nam quo intellectu Deum capit homo, qui ipsum intellectum suum quo eum vult capere nondum capit? Si autem hunc jam capit, attendat diligenter nihil eo esse in sua natura melius, et videat utrum ibi videat ulla lineamenta formarum, nitores colorum, spatiosam granditatem, partium distantiam, molis distensionem, aliquas per locorum intervalla motiones, vel quid ejusmodi. Nihil certe istorum invenimus in eo, quo in natura nostra nihil melius invenimus, id est, in nostro intellectu, quo sapientiam capimus quantum capaces sumus. Quod ergo non invenimus in meliore nostro, non debemus in illo quaerere, quod longe melius est meliore nostro: ut sic intelligamus Deum, si possumus, quantum possumus. *De Trin.* v. 2. See above p. 10 and Excursus A, p. 137.

awakening to a consciousness that the human heart is out of harmony with the Powers above us, man comes to feel that at death he has to face the moral realities which he has tried, it may be, to ignore and forget in life. It is thus that sin is the sting of death; to the mere animal, death may be painful but it has no sting; while for man, a moral being, conscious that he is part of a moral order, an order which prevails apart from the things of sense, death has a sting; he may hardly fancy there is a future life before him, he may figure it in the dimmest way, and yet it is thus that death—apart from the pain of dying—comes to be dreadful. Physical death comes to have a new meaning, through the Fall, to the awakened moral consciousness of man, who has begun to have a sense that he is apart from God.

If we thus fix our thoughts as S. Austin bids us do[1], on the character of evil, rather than merely on its origin, we may feel that the whole springs from the defect of a mutable will—be it angelic or be it human, be the will a sudden creation, be it evolved through a long series of ages. The accidents of time and place do not affect the truth of a story which sets these deep realities before us; the investigation of physical phenomena, and the new lights which may be given us on the development of man, do not render the old account of the nature of evil, and its manifestation in the world less striking; still it puts before us the really important elements which are true for all time—the defect of will, the awakening of moral consciousness—the dread of a moral ruler and severance from Him[2]. None the

---

[1] *De Duabus Animabus*, 10. *Contra Epistolam Manichæi*, 38.

[2] Evitando vivit anima, quæ appetendo moritur. Continete vos ab immani feritate superbiæ, ab inerti voluptate luxuriæ, et a fallaci nomine scientiæ; ut sint bestiæ mansuetæ, et pecora edomita, et innoxii serpentes. Motus enim animæ sunt isti in allegoria: sed fastus elationis, et delectatio libidinis, et venenum curiositatis motus sunt animæ mortuæ; quia non ita moritur, ut omni motu careat, quoniam

less may we regret that S. Austin, who set the teaching of the story in its clearest light, should have supposed it had a double meaning—not only as a manifestation of everlasting truths, but as a record of actual occurrences as well.

III. THE PUNISHMENT OF SIN.

The train of thought which we have followed thus far leads us naturally to the consideration of the punishment of sin. There were those in S. Austin's times as well as in ours who held that all punishment is remedial in character and that it is for the sake of correcting the evil doer that punishment can be justified. "Some Platonists there are "who though they assign a punishment to every sin, yet "hold that all such inflictions, be they human or divine, in "this life or the next, tend only to the purgation of the "soul from enormities[1]." But it would be hard indeed to plead for the infliction of punishment, if it were only justified by its corrective influence. Punishment is requisite on other grounds: for it is the assertion of the moral order which crime has disturbed; be it heavy or be it light, it is the way in which the moral order necessarily reasserts itself. Some punishments come in the ordinary course of nature, when vice is stigmatised by marks of suffering.

discedendo a fonte vitæ, moritur, atque ita suscipitur a prætereunto sæculo, et conformatur ei. *Conf.* XIII. 30.
Nulla vita est quæ non sit ex Deo, quia Deus utique summa vita est et ipse fons vitæ, nec aliqua vita in quantum vita est, malum est, sed in quantum vergit ad mortem: mors autem vitæ non est, nisi nequitia, quæ ab eo quod ne quidquam sit, dicta est; et ideo nequissimi homines, nihili homines appellantur. Vita ergo voluntario defectu deficiens ab eo qui eam fecit, et cujus essentia fruebatur, et volens contra Dei legem frui corporibus, quibus eam Deus præfecit, vergit ad nihilum; et hæc est nequitia: non quia corpus jam nihilum est. *De Vera Religione*, 21. See also *De Trinitate*, XII. 13.

[1] *De Civitate Dei*, XXI. xiii.

There are other punishments which men inflict on those who break the law of the land; the criminal has defied the law, he has set himself in opposition to it, and it reasserts itself in the punishment which declares what is right, by depriving him of his goods or confining his person, even perhaps by taking away his life[1].

Punishment thus is the vindication of right, the suppression of wrong[2], whether done in full consciousness or not. The best manner of punishment is an entirely different question: if a punishment is a corrective discipline as well as a vindication of right so much the better; if it proves exemplary and warns others lest they sin, so much the better also; but it is not the usual characteristic of punishment that it corrects the evil doer. It is a matter of every day knowledge that the punishments of our code are not remedial; capital punishment is not; sending boys to jail may only serve to corrupt them; and flogging is commonly said to be brutalising. And neither are the divine punishments in themselves corrective; whether they take the form of bodily sufferings, or consist in the increased blindness of error, and subjection to lust and passion. Assuredly those who realise how truly such punishment follows sin, and cuts the sinner off from righteous life, and from the true freedom of true manliness will never suppose that divine punishments were meant to be corrective. For had it been so, had the Law with its penalties sufficed to restore human nature, to what purpose had the Son of God come forth to

---

[1] Bradley, *Ethical Studies*, 26, G. W. F. Hegel, *Phil. d. Rechts*, 132.

[2] Nos vero etiam in hac quidem mortali vita esse quasdam pœnas purgatorias confitemur, non quibus affliguntur quorum vita vel non inde fit melior, vel potius inde fit pejor; sed illis sunt purgatoriæ, qui eis coerciti corriguntur. Cæteræ omnes pœnæ, sive temporariæ, sive sempiternæ, sicut unusquisque divina providentia tractandus est, inferuntur, vel pro peccatis sive præteritis, sive in quibus adhuc vivit ille qui plectitur, vel pro exercendis declarandisque virtutibus, per homines et angelos, seu bonos seu malos. *De Civitate Dei*, XXI. xiii.

redeem us? It is not by punishment that man is saved, not by the bare assertion of right upon him and in him, not by the Cain-like brand that cuts him off from God and man, but by the love that goes forth to seek and to save those who have sinned and come short of the glory of God.

The nature of the inevitable punishment of sin is well worthy of consideration; physical evil may or may not follow; the body which has been the instrument of sin may or may not bear a part in its punishment; but there is a far more terrible penalty which is certain and inevitable. "It is the "most just punishment of sin, that everyone should lose "that which he would not use well, when he might have "done so without any difficulty if he had wished: that is to "say that he who knows what is right and does not do it "should lose the knowledge of what is right; and that he "who will not do right when he might should lose the "power of doing it. For in actual fact ignorance and inca- "pacity are two penalties that befall every soul that sins[1]." Punishment leaves its mark on the soul in increased prone- ness to choose evil, and increased weakness in striving after

[1] *De Lib. Arb.* III. 52.
Non enim sicut peccatum in ejus potestate est, ita etiam pœna peccati. Magna quippe res est ipsa anima, nec ad opprimendos lascivos motus suos idonea sibi remanet. Valentior enim peccat, et post peccatum divina lege facta imbecillior, minus potens est auferre quod fecit. *De Musica,* VI. 14.

Verum hic admonendus es, quid de hoc unde nunc agimus, sapere debeas, pœnam scilicet et præmium, intuenda inter se esse contraria, et alia duo contraria his contrariis adhærere; sic ergo in pœna est non posse recte agere, sicut erit in præmio non posse peccare. *Operis imp. contra Jul.* VI. X.

Cæcitas igitur cordis, qua nescitur quid justitia vetet, et violentia concupiscentiæ, qua vincitur etiam qui scit unde debeat abstinere, non tantum peccata, sed pœnæ sunt etiam peccatorum. *Operis imp. contra Jul.* VI. XVII.

Ac per hoc, nisi prius homo faceret peccando quod vellet, non pateretur concupiscendo quod nollet. *Operis imp. contra Jul.* VI. XIV. See also *De Utilitate Jejunii,* IV. *Contra Adv. Leg. et Proph.* I. 18. *Enarr. in Ps.* XXXVII. 15.

right: this is the mark of wrong-doing, the punishment of sin, a punishment which serves directly to set before us the truth that it is only as our life is lived in close communion with the source of life that it is true life worthy the name at all. The weakness of a changeful creature and defect of will were the causes of evil, but its punishment is found in the bands which the sinner has forged for himself—the bands of sins by frailty committed—and which in their turn force him into deeper sin, and more complete alienation from God.

Perhaps it was his sense of the terribleness of the punishment of sin, of the way in which it drags us farther and farther from God, that tended to give S. Austin such a deep horror of sin—a feeling which comes out again and again in his writings. It might be supposed that because he holds that evil is a defect and unreality, which merely exists as a parasite on goodness, he would attach little importance to it as an actual phenomenon in the world and in our hearts; but his sense of the actual power of lust and sin distinguishes him markedly from many modern writers. This striking difference comes out most clearly in his treatment of incontinence—he insists on continence as a virtue for all, in every state of life, and exhorts to what many regard now as impossible virtue; while he tries to show how it may be cultivated. And just because this form of self-indulgence seems to many a necessity, we may find in it the clearest evidence of the power of sin to darken and weaken our nature. But while we in modern times are tempted only to exclaim against its violent excesses, and to try to set up one feeble barrier or another which shall confine, and serve to regulate lust, he will have no compromise with it whatever. The raging of human lust may indeed carry man to the lowest depths of fiendish cruelty, as S. Austin saw in his day, as we have heard in ours. But he knew only too well—as we all may know—

that this same lust was in him, that he dared not yield to it at all, or tolerate its slightest promptings: he knew the futility of trying to raise the social standard, unless he could dare to denounce the evil of lust under what guise soever it sought to hide itself. We in this day, even if we strive to salve our consciences by denouncing its grosser forms, are not thus intolerant of the evil itself: there are many men who make a profession of Christianity, and who think lightly of incontinence in married life[1]: there are others perhaps who make no such profession who yet treat the incontinence of the married as an excuse for their own fornication; and thus each sinner strives to palliate his own crime by pointing at the self-indulgence of others. Let us not deceive ourselves in this matter: it is not the suffering caused by fiendish lust that renders self-indulgence an evil —that only exhibits how evil it is. The consent of partners in guilt does not render self-indulgence less guilty; nor is it innocent because it does not overstep the bounds set by the institutions of society. Self-indulgence is an evil at all times, and there is no condition of life in which those who yield to it do not suffer the penalty of sin—in the darkening of the eye whereby we see the right, in the weakening of the power to do it.

S. Austin's decided utterances on this point cost him dear during his life, and have in our own days served to cast a shadow on his reputation[2]. It was said that the old leaven of Manichæan teaching still affected his doctrine; because he had a strong sense of the actual power of sin in the human heart he seemed to regard it as an original part of the constitution of our nature, to figure it to himself as a mighty opponent of God. To those who are not convinced

---

[1] See Excursus E, *On Continence in married life*, p. 168.
[2] Milman, *Latin Christianity* (1872), I. 152. Neander (*History of the Christian Religion*, IV. 280) does him complete justice in this particular.

by the language in which he himself repudiated the charge[1] it is perhaps hopeless to try to say more, but whether we fix our attention on his teaching as to the real nature of evil or the duties he inculcated, we may see that he was fundamentally opposed to the Manichæan. To him the things of sense are not evil but good, though good which may be abused: it is not in avoiding matter[2], as the Manichæan vainly tried, but in the right use of the things which God has pronounced good that we attain to virtue. Nor could his authority be fairly appealed to by those mediæval reformers who insisted on celibacy as a duty, and condemned

---

[1] *De Nuptiis*, II. iii. quoted in Excursus E, p. 171.

[2] Non enim parva sunt haec interim duo, quae salubriter sua incarnatione monstravit, nec carne posse contaminari veram divinitatem, nec ideo putandos dæmones nobis esse meliores, quia non habent carnem. *De Civitate Dei*, IX. xvii.

His own practice in regard to eating and drinking was entirely free from those Manichæan elements which occasionally reappear both in Teetotalism and Vegetarianism. Possidius (*Vita* xxii.) describes his habits thus, Vestes ejus et calceamenta vel lectualia ex moderato et competenti habitu erant, nec nitida nimium, nec abjecta plurimum: quia his plerumque vel jactare se insolenter homines solent, vel abjicere; ex utroque non quae Jesu Christi, sed quae sua sunt iidem quaerentes: at iste, ut dixi, medium tenebat, neque in dexteram, neque in sinistram declinans. Mensa usus est frugali et parca, quae quidem inter olera et legumina, etiam carnes aliquando propter hospites, vel quosque infirmiores, semper autem vinum habebat. Quia noverat, et docebat, ut Apostolus dicit, quod *omnis creatura Dei bona si*!, *et nihil abjiciendum, quod cum gratiarum actione percipitur; sanctificatur enim per verbum Dei et orationem.* Et, ut idem Augustinus sanctus in suis Confessionum libris posuit, dicens: *Non ego immunditiam obsonii timeo, sed immunditiam cupiditatis.* Scio Noe omne genus carnis quod cibo esset usui, manducare permissum; Eliam cibo carnis refectum; Joannem mirabili abstinentia præditum, animalibus, hoc est locustis, in escam cedentibus non fuisse pollutum. Scio et Esau lenticulæ concupiscentia deceptum; et David propter aquæ desiderium a se ipso reprehensum; et Regem nostrum, non de carne, sed de pane esse tentatum. Ideoque et populus in eremo, non quia carnes desideravit, sed quia escæ desiderio contra Deum murmuravit, meruit improbari (*Confess.* x. 46). De vino autem sumendo Apostoli exstat sententia ad Timotheum scribentis,

marriage as little if any better than fornication. He knew that the celibate might fall into other sins, as truly evil as that he abjured; while marriage was not in itself evil, but a good instituted by God, though not as S. Austin thought the most excellent way of life to choose, since it was a path beset by many temptations.

Thus far we have endeavoured to follow out S. Austin's view as to the nature of punishment—it is assertory, and as to the kind of punishment which follows sin—ignorance and incapacity. But we cannot pass away from the topic without dwelling on one other point: How far are the divine punishments proportionate to the sin? The opinion put forth by some Christian teachers that since all human sin is infinitely guilty all alike demands an infinite punishment, has given a great shock to the ordinary sense of justice, and has done much to discredit Christianity in the eyes of men of deep moral feeling who do not accept its teaching. But though the tone of S. Austin's discussion of this subject is sure to jar on many ears now-a-days, when his teaching is taken as a whole it is seen that it is far less likely to cause offence in this matter than that of many more recent writers. He insists that in those words where our Lord lifts the veil and tells us something of the judgment to come, He does set that judgment before us as a real decision[1], and He speaks of it as a just one where penalty is proportioned to guilt, since some are to be beaten with few stripes and some with many. There are present punishments of the soul and of the body, there will be future

ac dicentis: *Noli usque adhuc aquam bibere, sed vino modico utere propter stomachum et frequentes tuas infirmitates.* Cochlearibus tantum argenteis utens, caetera vasa quibus mensae inferebantur cibi, vel testea, vel lignea, vel marmorea fuerunt: non tamen necessitatis inopia, sed proposito voluntatis. Sed et hospitalitatem semper exhibuit. Et in ipsa mensa magis lectionem vel disputationem, quam epulationem potationemque diligebat.

[1] *De Civitate Dei*, xx. v.

punishments as well, but much of that in the future as in the present is temporary[1] punishment. He inserts an interesting discussion[2] on the possibility of proportioning the duration of punishment to guilt in treating of punishment which has no end, and which seems necessarily disproportioned to any act in time, though even this may differ in degree if not in duration[3].

There is another matter in regard to which he speaks with less uncertainty[4] and again adopts an opinion, grounded on the literal sense of Scripture and exemplified as he be-

[1] Sed temporarias poenas alii in hac vita tantum, alii post mortem, alii et nunc et tunc, verumtamen ante judicium illud severissimum novissimumque patiuntur. Non autem omnes veniunt in sempiternas poenas, quae post illud judicium sunt futurae, qui post mortem sustinent temporales. Nam quibusdam, quod in isto non remittitur, remitti in futuro saeculo, id est, ne futuri saeculi aeterno supplicio puniantur. *De Civitate Dei*, XXI. xiii.

[2] Sic autem quidam eorum, contra quos defendimus civitatem Dei, injustum putant, ut pro peccatis quamlibet magnis, parvo scilicet tempore perpetratis, poena quisque damnetur aeterna; quasi ullius id unquam justitia legis attendat, ut tanta mora temporis quisque puniatur, quanta mora temporis unde puniretur admisit. Octo genera poenarum in legibus esse scribit Tullius, damnum, vincula, verbera, talionem, ignominiam, exsilium, mortem, servitutem. Quid horum est quod in breve tempus pro cujusque peccati celeritate coarctetur, ut tanta vindicetur morula, quanta deprehenditur perpetratum, nisi forte talio? *De Civitate Dei*, XXI. xi.

[3] *De Civitate Dei*, XXI. xvi.

[4] Utrumque autem horum, ignem scilicet atque vermem, qui volunt ad animi poenas, non ad corporis pertinere, dicunt etiam uri dolore animi sero atque infructuose poenitentis eos qui fuerint a regno Dei separati: et ideo ignem pro isto dolore urente non incongrue poni potuisse contendunt, unde illud Apostoli est, *Quis scandalizatur, et ego non uror?* Eumdem etiam vermem putant intelligendum esse. Nam scriptum est, inquiunt, *Sicut tinea vestimentum et vermis lignum, sic maeror excruciat cor viri*. Qui vero poenas et animi et corporis in illo supplicio futuras esse non dubitant, igne uri corpus, animum autem rodi quodammodo verme moeroris affirmant. Quod etsi credibilius dicitur; quia utique absurdum est, ibi dolorem aut corporis aut animi defuturum : ego tamen facilius est ut ad corpus dicam utrumque pertinere, quam neutrum. *De Civitate Dei*, XXI. ix.

lieved by actual experience[1], that the punishment after death is material, as well as spiritual. His whole philosophy of punishment and its nature shows that the true punishment of sin is spiritual, and he recognises that the punishment of the evil angels is only spiritual; but in his anxiety not to sacrifice a shred of the meaning that can be fairly drawn from Holy Writ he insists on taking the literal interpretation as well[2]. In thus insisting on the literal as well as the allegorical sense of the Scriptural language, he forces himself into a position which was one of great difficulty in his own time, and the difficulty of which has been considerably increased in ours. For in figuring the future life to himself as a physical state[3], he was inclined to view it too exclusively as subject to the same conditions of place and

[1] *De Civitate Dei*, XXI. iv.

[2] There is however some recognition of the difficulties in *Enarr. in Ps. l.c.c.c.* 17, 18. In 21 and 24 the eternal life is interpreted in a purely spiritual sense as the vision of God. See also the discussion in *De Gen. ad Lit.* XII. xxxii., xxxiii., xxxiv. The difficulty in which S. Austin's literalism places him here is very similar to that noted above—seeing he is forced to maintain an everlasting continuance of certain physical conditions, and thus to put forward an opinion in regard to phenomena in space and time which at all events transcends all our experience. But though this is hardly in accordance with his own principles of Scriptural interpretation, his doctrine is not self-contradictory; he never admits that the existence of evil is a blot on God's universe, or that its everlasting continuance can in any sense affect the real carrying out of the Divine purpose. Erigena attempted to reconcile Origen and S. Austin; he ultimately repudiated the belief in material punishment, while holding that the effects of sin on the spiritual nature were everlasting. See Excursus B, § 5, p. 146.

[3] Si autem quaeritur, cum anima de corpore exierit, utrum ad aliqua loca corporalia feratur, an ad incorporalia corporalibus similia, an vero nec ad ipsa, sed ad illud quod et corporibus et similitudinibus corporum est excellentius: cito quidem responderim, ad corporalia loca eam vel non ferri nisi cum aliquo corpore, vel non localiter ferri. Jam utrum habeat aliquod corpus, cum de hoc corpore exierit, ostendat qui potest; ego autem non puto: spiritualem enim arbitror esse, non corporalem. Ad spiritualia vero pro meritis fertur, aut ad loca poenalia similia corporibus. *De Gen. ad Lit.* XII. 60.

time as our life here, and to regard the life of the world to come as extended through an indefinite protraction of time. Had he sought to realise his own conception of the eternal and blessed life, and to frame a corresponding thought of a life of defect and misery, he might not have so readily dismissed Origen's doctrine of the final salvation of all[1]. As apprehended by S. Austin that doctrine was fanciful, and it did not seem to harmonise readily with the plain language of our Lord. But even if we confine ourselves to S. Austin's own teaching as to the real nature of the punishment of sin —in want of knowledge and of capacity, we may set the problem before ourselves in a different light. Punishment is bitter to bear,—a misery rooted in an undying spirit, it is the assertion of the Eternal Righteousness of God, in and through those who have set Him at nought—it is the vengeance of Eternal Fire[2]. But the question of final salvation, of deliverance from this punishment, is not a question of time, as if it were a physical state from which the sufferer could be withdrawn, but rather we must ask whether such defect and corruption as this can be healed at all? If there is to be a deliverance from this eternal punishment, it is not the mere cessation of the duration of suffering that is needed, but the restoration and healing of the blinded and diseased spirit. This always, and nought but this, is the passage from death unto life, both in this world and in the world to come. If then we ponder whether there is a deliverance from punishment in the world to come, we need not ask the irrelevant and inapplicable questions, at what time, after what years it may take place? but we shall turn our thoughts to such considerations as these—Is there

[1] *De Civitate Dei*, XXI. xvii.
[2] Obliviscendo autem Deum, tanquam obliviscendo vitam suam, conversæ fuerant in mortem, hoc est, in infernum. Commemoratæ vero convertuntur ad Dominum, tanquam reviviscentes reminiscendo vitam suam, cujus eas habebat oblivio. *De Trin.* xiv. 17.

any corruption of spirit so deeply seated, that the grace of God cannot heal it[1]? Can man succeed in his effort to hold himself aloof from God?

There are many who are inclined to answer these questions unhesitatingly in the negative: it seems to them that if evil should anywhere maintain itself ultimately, it must be because God's work had failed, because the opposition of the rebels who held out against Him had triumphed. But this difficulty did not press on the mind of S. Austin; he would have resented the implied Manichæism of the argument. To him evil was not a real substantial existence opposing God, it was a defect in things otherwise good, and which despite these defects still made a harmonious whole: in so far as a being persists it is because it has elements of goodness; and thus as he believed the whole of existence continues to afford a changed but perfect harmony. To most of us it is hard so to look at things *sub specie æternitatis* that we can see that God is glorified in all His works: and for those who cannot see it in earthly things[2], it is indeed hard to believe it as S. Austin did, of the life beyond the grave[3]. And if we cherish another hope, if we think that S. Paul's pæan points to another form of Divine tri-

---

[1] S. Austin's opinion on this point is expressed in an entirely different connexion, but is perfectly decided.

Cum ergo alius sic, alius autem sic moveatur ad fidem, eademque res sæpe alio modo dicta moveat, alio modo dicta non moveat; aliumque moveat, alium non moveat; quis audeat dicere defuisse Deo modum vocandi, quo etiam Esau ad eam fidem mentem applicaret voluntatemque conjungeret, in qua Jacob justificatus est? Quod si tanta quoque potest esse obstinatio voluntatis, ut contra omnes modos vocationis obdurescat mentis aversio; quæritur utrum de divina pœna sit ipsa duritia, cum Deus deserit non sic vocando, quomodo ad fidem moveri potest. Quis enim dicat modum quo ei persuaderetur ut crederet, etiam Omnipotenti defuisse? *De Divers. Quæst. ad Simpli.* I. qu. ii. 14.

[2] See above, p. 50, note 3. Also below p. 99.

[3] Sed in parte offenditur anima peccatrix: tamen quia pro meritis ibi est ubi talem esse decet, et ea patitur quæ talem pati æquum est,

umph, and trust to see, not only a harmonious whole, but every individual part restored to the fullest measure of existence of which it is capable[1], let us at least also remember the plain words of our Lord as to the sin for which there is no forgiveness in the world to come and the language of the *Epistle to the Hebrews* concerning the reprobate; let us beware how we diminish aught of the force which these warnings ought to have for ourselves. We cannot doubt of the power of the grace of God to win the ignorant who have never known His love, who have never

universum regnum Dei nulla sua fœditate deformat. De *Diversis Quæst. LXXXIII.* qu. xxvii.

Deus igitur summus et verus lege inviolabili et incorrupta, qua omne quod condidit regit, subjicit animæ corpus, animam sibi, et sic omnia sibi: neque in ullo actu eam deserit, sive pœna, sive præmio. Id enim judicavit esse pulcherrimum, ut esset quidquid est quomodo est, et ita naturæ gradibus ordinaretur, ut considerantes universitatem nulla offenderet ex ulla parte deformitas, omnisque animæ pœna et omne præmium conferret semper aliquid proportione justæ pulchritudini dispositionique rerum omnium. *De Quantitate Animæ*, 80.

Non igitur numeri, qui sunt infra rationem et in suo genere pulchri sunt, sed amor inferioris pulchritudinis animam polluit: quæ cum in illa non modo æqualitatem, de qua pro suscepto opere satis dictum est, sed etiam ordinem diligat, amisit ipsa ordinem suum; nec tamen excessit ordinem rerum, quandoquidem ibi est et ita est, ubi esse et quomodo esse tales ordinatissimum est. Aliud enim est tenere ordinem, aliud ordine teneri. *De Musica*, VI. 46.

Quoniam igitur vitium animæ non natura ejus sed contra naturam ejus est, nihilque aliud est quam peccatum et pœna peccati; inde intelligitur nullam naturam, vel, si melius ita dicitur, nullam substantiam sive essentiam malum esse. Neque de peccatis pœnisque ejus animæ efficitur, ut universitas ulla deformitate turpetur. Quia rationalis substantia, quæ ab omni peccato munda est, Deo subjecta, subjectis sibi cæteris dominatur. Ea vero quæ peccavit, ibi ordinata est, ubi esse tales decet, ut Deo conditore atque rectore universitatis decora sint omnia. Et est pulchritudo universæ creaturæ per hæc tria inculpabilis; damnationem peccatorum, exercitationem justorum, perfectionem beatorum. *De Vera Religione*, 44.

[1] For some interesting criticism of S. Austin's doctrine of the harmony of the Kosmos, and its bearing on the personal problem of individual suffering, see Scipio *Des A. A. Metaphysik*, 106.

heard His call and have never turned from it: sinful they are and have been, fit subjects for punishment, yet for them the stripes are few. But for those who have been received into the membership of Christ's Church, sealed with His Spirit, and strengthened by His Life—by what stronger pleading shall He win them if they turn from the Grace of God? Wherefore let him that thinketh he standeth take heed lest he fall: let him keep under his body and bring it into subjection.

And if while these terrible warnings come home to our hearts in their full significance—that those who have tasted the grace of God may yet so alienate themselves from Him that His grace does not restore them to their true life—we still strive to hold to a hope of triumphant goodness; if the puzzle seems too hard for us let us not despair, though S. Austin's attempt to reconcile the opposing truths shall fail to satisfy us. For we have studied him to little purpose if we cherish a hope of obtaining light by merely going to his books, or any books, for teaching; rather let us follow his example. The views we can gather from his writings will not suffice us, for it is not the reading of the Fathers, but Faith that is the source of knowledge. It was by turning to God for light, that he attained the measure of truth which cheered his heart and showed him the path of action; it is by turning to God now that we too may each obtain a new measure of truth for ourselves.

LECTURE III.

If the Son therefore shall make you free, ye shall be free indeed. S. John viii. 36.

HUMAN FREEDOM AND THE DIVINE WILL.

I. The Pelagian Controversy.

The part which S. Austin had taken in the controversy with the Manichæans as to the nature of evil had attracted attention far beyond his own diocese; the works he had written on the subject had been circulated over a wide area and had met with general approval; but a Welsh monk living in Rome into whose hands they fell took decided exception to an expression he used in the *Confessions*[1]. This was the occasion which gave rise to the Pelagian controversy—to which I now wish to turn, leaving the Donatist controversy—the next in biographical order— for incidental mention next lecture; for it is convenient to treat some of the issues raised by Pelagius as an appendage to the contest with the Manichæans, rather than to sketch, even in the briefest way, the course of the argument with Pelagius and his followers. For the fact that this was a controversy within the Church gave it a different character from those we have already tried to review. The opposing

---

[1] Quid autem meorum opusculorum frequentius et delectabilius innotescere potuit, quam libri Confessionum mearum? Cum et ipsos ediderim antequam Pelagiana hæresis exstitisset; in eis certo dixi Deo nostro, et sæpe dixi: Da quod jubes, et jube quod vis (x. 40, 44, 60). Quæ mea verba Pelagius Romæ, cum a quodam fratre et coepiscopo meo fuissent eo præsente commemorata, ferre non potuit, et contradicens aliquanto commotius, pene cum eo qui illa commemoraverat litigavit. *De Dono Perser.* 53.

parties appealed to the judgment of the leaders in the Christian Church in all parts of the world; petty personal questions of honesty of conviction and fairness in discussion came to assume an immense temporary importance and to confuse the fundamental issues. Perhaps we shall do wisely therefore to try and fix our minds on the difficulty which came to the front at that time, and which after centuries of discussion may be set in clearer light than when it was first forced on the attention of the Church.

But there is after all something significant in the form of this new controversy. It was no question as to the possibility of knowledge to be solved by strict analysis of self-consciousness in a little circle of friends; it was not the defence of the faith of his own flock from the attacks of the open but insidious enemies who lived among them in Africa; it was a question which was of interest to every Christian man, as to his personal need of the salvation which was offered in Christ; it was a question which was of interest to the whole Church, as to the kind of corruption in the hearts of unregenerate men to whom she offered a deliverance from evil. And hence it came to be one of those great theological discussions which seem to be so unnecessarily embittered by personal feeling, which seem to refine themselves into mere exercises of hair-splitting ingenuity, but which are not barren, since it is through them that the minds of God's faithful people are taught to discern some truth more clearly, to see at least some error they will do well to avoid. For the outcome of it all was a real gain, a gain for which all subsequent generations of Christians are deeply indebted to S. Austin. Not that Christian experience has fully endorsed all the positive teaching of S. Austin; neither at Orange[1] nor at Trent was

---

[1] Bright, *Antipelagian Treatises*, lxiv. 384. I cannot however see that either of these Councils departed from S. Austin's standpoint, in the way that is commonly supposed.

his language adopted, though his doctrine was retained and restated; but Christian experience has condemned the explicit teaching which he deemed so dangerous and against which he furnished the strongest defences.

And thus on entering this new field we seem to find ourselves engaged on a very different task—not looking back to the old world and its great philosophers,—not tracing the final struggle of heathenism in its effort to pervert the message of the Cross, but marking the lists within which modern combatants were to engage and noting the issues for which they would contend. S. Austin no longer appears in the guise of the last of ancient philosophers, nor as the latest of the apologists who resisted the attacks of paganism, but as a thinker whose principles have gone far to determine the direction of the thoughts of many later students and the discussions of subsequent ages.

Those who do not fully appreciate the gain which came from his treatment of the subject have sometimes been inclined to blame S. Austin as if he had been personally responsible for raising a hopeless problem which he could not settle. Greek Philosophy had troubled itself but little about the question of Free Will: and the controversy never took much of a hold upon the Eastern Church—why could he not let it alone as they did? But it would be more profitable to try and account for the fact that this controversy was not raised before or elsewhere, rather than to amuse ourselves with the fancy that S. Austin was personally responsible for awakening an intellectual monster which would otherwise have rested undisturbed. It may be enough to say that their less perfect understanding of personality prevented the Greeks from dwelling on the subject, and that the irresponsiveness of the East was perhaps a symptom of the inactivity which was even then beginning to spread over the Church under Byzantine influence. But a question which had been debated by Cicero, and which underlay the whole structure of Christian doctrine, could not remain for ever outside the pale of discussion: it was sure to be raised sooner or later. And it was most natural that, when the issue was raised by Pelagius, S. Austin should take a leading part in the fray[1].

For the doctrine of Pelagius was specially distasteful to S. Austin since it was so completely inconsistent with his own religious experience. His extraordinary care for the facts of the case—as he understood them—is very noticeable in all his philosophical writings. The earnestness with which he has described his own religious experience has made the *Confessions* a precious possession to thousands of seekers after God: we can read there how he interpreted his own religious experience[2], how it seemed to him that he was always turning from God but that God's Love sought him and prevailed within him,—overpowering his habits, altering all his aspirations—giving him a new peace in life. He could do nothing good of himself, his will had not been able to choose the right till through God's grace a new light and a new strength came upon him.

And it was natural too that one who had not only had this religious experience, but had been eagerly engaged in a contest with the Manichaeans should take up this new controversy. For it is no mere accident that connects the two; when we find the innermost core of each we

[1] His doctrine however was definitely formulated before the controversy with Pelagius arose, and was less affected by exigencies of polemics than is usually supposed. Neander, *History of Christian Religion*, IV. 298. See Excursus F, § 3, p. 175.

[2] Et in eisdem etiam libris quod de mea conversione narravi, Deo me convertente ad eam fidem, quam miserrima et furiosissima loquacitate vastabam, nonne ita narratum esse meministis, ut ostenderem me fidelibus et quotidianis matris meae lacrimis ne perirem fuisse concessum? Ubi utique praedicavi, non solum aversas a recta fide, sed adversas etiam rectae fidei, Deum sua gratia ad eam convertere hominum voluntates. *De Dono Persev.* 53.

feel that they are different aspects of the same problem. The dispute with the Manichæans centred in the *metaphysical* question as to the nature of evil in the universe, and as to its first manifestation in the world. The dispute with Pelagius was chiefly concerned with the *psychological* question as to the nature of evil in the heart of man and as to the depth of the corruption of his fallen nature. We have again to deal with a subject very similar to that which was before our minds last lecture, but now in its psychological and not in its metaphysical aspect.

II. COMMONLY RECOGNISED FACTS OF HUMAN NATURE.

It may serve to set the matter in the clearest light if we note two or three of the facts in regard to human nature which are commonly recognised in the present day, and note S. Austin's opinion on each of these points in turn.

1. Observations have been made in recent years which have rendered the depravity of man as born into the world, even in his earliest years, more obvious than was formerly the case. Attention has been called to the extraordinary influence of heredity, and we are all ready to note inherited tendencies as going far to account for the conduct of many criminals. Evil dispositions appear to be clearly born in us, and physical tendencies to evil are handed on from one generation to another. We all feel the absurdity of the doctrines which were promulgated about the beginning of the century by a school of thinkers who argued that evil was not planted in every human heart, but that it was really maintained by the corrupting institutions of society, and that if the individual intellect had only free play it would shake off these mischievous influences and attain to a perfectly rational and comfortable condition of life. But though we may sometimes hear isolated opinions expressed

which can only be justified on such principles as these, the principles themselves are no longer accepted as tenable[1]. It is generally recognised that as a matter of fact children are born with dispositions which incline them more or less decidedly towards evil.

S. Austin's doctrine of the origin of evil and of its first manifestation in the world has already claimed our attention; and the plain fact, as I think one may call it, of the transmission of evil from one generation to another is the other element which is combined to give us his doctrine of *original sin*, of human depravity commencing in a fall and transmitted to all future generations—a depravity which according to his view consists of a double defect in a nature which remains otherwise good—a defect in the power of seeing what is right and a defect in the power of doing it.

And here a brief digression is necessary to enable us to appreciate S. Austin's doctrine fairly. We have seen already how he has suffered at the hands of those who professed to follow him. His theology has been recast by the scholastics; his asceticism has been exaggerated by mediæval rules of life; and now we may see how much his doctrine of the nature of man has suffered by being presented to us in the form of Calvinism; it is therefore necessary if we are to weigh S. Austin's teaching fairly that we should note how at point after point Calvin failed to follow the doctrine of the African doctor. It has been so often said[2] and believed that the

---

[1] Somewhat similar principles in regard to life according to nature had been advocated by the Stoics.

[2] Calvin, *Institutes*, III. xxii. 8. "Were we disposed to frame an entire volume out of Augustine it were easy to show the reader that I have no occasion to use any other words than his."

A very full demonstration of the differences which really separated the two writers and of which Calvin was so completely unconscious may be found in the excellent *Antithesis Augustini et Calvini* by F. J[ean] F[onteau], C[anon]. R[egularis] S.T.P. A[cad]. P[aris]. C[ancellarius]. (Paris, 1651). See also F. Hewit, *Studies in S. Augustine* i. (New York; 1868). Gangauf, *Met. Psych.* p. 345.

doctrines of these two teachers are precisely similar that it is necessary to try and exhibit how widely they really fall apart.

There is a fundamental difference of opinion in regard to the subject before us. Calvin and his followers have asserted that human nature is totally depraved: of the innocent infants which have committed no actual sin he says, "their whole nature is, as it were, a seed-bed of sin, and therefore cannot but be odious and abominable to God[1]." Now this doctrine, whatever there may be to be said for it, is not the doctrine of S. Austin: he held that sin is the defect of a good nature, which retains elements of goodness even in its most diseased and corrupted state, and he gives no countenance whatever to this modern opinion of total depravity[2].

[1] *Institutes*, II. i. 8, see also II. v. 19. "Let it stand, therefore, as an indubitable truth, which no engines can shake, that the mind of man is so entirely alienated from the righteousness of God that he cannot conceive, desire or design anything but what is wicked, distorted, foul, impure and iniquitous; that his heart is so thoroughly environed by sin that it can breathe out nothing but corruption and rottenness; that if some men occasionally make a show of goodness, their mind is ever interwoven with hypocrisy and deceit, their soul inwardly bound with the fetters of wickedness."

[2] Tamen si etiam ipsa peccaret, sufficeret Dei potestas ineffabilis potentiæ ad regendam istam universitatem, ut omnibus congrua et condigna retribuens nihil in toto imperio suo turpe atque indecorum esse permitteret. *De Lib. Arb.* III. 35.

Quid enim majus in creaturis quam vita intelligens, aut quid minus potest esse quam corpus? Quæ quantumlibet deficiant et eo tendant ut non sint, tamen aliquid formæ illis remanet, ut quoquo modo sint. Quidquid autem formæ cuipiam rei deficienti remanet, ex illa forma est quæ nescit deficere motusque ipsos rerum deficientium vel proficientium excedere numerorum suorum leges non sinit. *De Lib. Arb.* II. 46.

Quapropter natura est, in qua nullum malum est, vel etiam in qua nullum potest esse malum : esse autem natura, in qua nullum bonum sit, non potest. Proinde nec ipsius diaboli natura, in quantum natura est, malum est: sed perversitas eam malam facit. *De Civitate*

2. To pass once more to current opinion in the present day. In spite of heredity, and all other excuses which can be made for the criminal, we feel that he deserves to be punished. The disposition may have been planted at his birth, it may have been fostered by circumstances, but it is in him, an element in his character, and it is at each moment with his consent that it ripens into action. He has been willing to carry out the promptings of evil actions—he has made them his own, and he is responsible for them. We may analyse the motives for action as we like, but the play of motive is part of my deepest conscious life; the decision under whatever pressure is mine—this is certain with the deepest measure of certainty to which we can attain,—I will therefore I am[1]. What I do is my doing, it is in my mind that the various motives have been at work, it is through my determination that they issue in action, and for this act and its results I am responsible[2]. This is the common opinion in the present day: the amount of temptation may affect the fair amount of punishment, but it can never render a rational being wholly irresponsible for his actions.

This doctrine of personal responsibility is strongly insisted on by S. Austin: his whole treatment of the will, though difficult to follow from the defectiveness of the current terminology, is a marvel of skilful ana-

---

Dei, XIX. xiii. 2. Illa vero quae facta sunt, ejus bono indigent, summo scilicet bono, id est summa essentia. Minus autem sunt quam erant, cum per animae peccatum minus ad illum moventur: nec tamen penitus separantur; nam omnino nulla essent. *De Vera Religione*, 28.

Nec moveat quod *naturaliter* eos dixit, *quae legis sunt facere*, non spiritu Dei, non fide, non gratia. Hoc enim agit spiritus gratiae, ut imaginem Dei, in qua naturaliter facti sumus, instauret in nobis. Vitium quippe contra naturam est, quod utique sanat gratia. *De Spiritu et Lit.* 47.

[1] See above, p. 23.
[2] Bradley, *Ethical Studies*, Essay I.

lysis and weighty judgment[1]: but he is clear that evil deeds cannot be justly punished unless they are done voluntarily[2].

And here again Calvin fails to follow on the lines of the Father he so frequently quotes. Although he prefers his treatment of the subject to that of any other Father or Schoolman he does not accept it[3], he does not appear to see the importance of voluntariness in our action as bearing on responsibility, and he uses language which seems to make the Divine control over the human consciousness so complete as to remove the decision in cases of sin from the mind of man to the mind of God—as when he notes without any attempt at qualification how God "directs men's coun-"sels, and excites their wills, and regulates their efforts as He

[1] See Excursus F, p. 171.
[2] Non igitur nisi voluntate peccatur. Nobis autem voluntas nostra notissima est: neque enim scirem me velle, si quid sit voluntas ipsa nescirem. Definitur itaque isto modo; Voluntas est animi motus, cogente nullo, ad aliquid vel non amittendum, vel adipiscendum. Cur ergo ita tunc definire non possem? An erat difficile videre invitum volenti esse contrarium, ita ut contrarium sinistrum dextro esse dicimus, non ut nigrum albo? Nam eadem res simul et nigra et alba esse non potest: duorum autem in medio quisque positus, ad alterum sinister est, ad alterum dexter; simul quidem utrumque unus homo, sed simul utrumque ad unum hominem nullo modo. Ita quidem invitus et volens unus animus simul esse potest; sed unum atque idem nolle simul et velle non potest. Cum enim quisque invitus aliquid facit, si eum roges utrum id facere velit, nolle se dicit: item si roges utrum id velit non facere, velle respondet. Ita invitum ad faciendum, ad non faciendum autem volentem reperies: id est enim unum animum uno tempore habentem utrumque, sed aliud atque aliud ad singula referentem. Cur haec dico? Quia si rursum quaeramus quam ob causam id invitus faciat, cogi se dicet. Nam et omnis invitus faciens cogitur; et omnis qui cogitur, si facit, nonnisi invitus facit. Restat ut volens a cogente sit liber, etiamsi se quisquam cogi putet. Et hoc enim modo omnis qui volens facit, non cogitur; et omnis qui non cogitur, aut volens facit, aut non facit. *De Duabus Animabus*, 14.

Qua propter peccatum sine voluntate esse non posse verissimum est. *Retract.* I. xv. 3.
[3] *Institutes*, II. ii. 7.

"pleases[1]." It is difficult to reconcile such language with any sort of human responsibility: but S. Austin is careful to attempt to harmonise the belief in God's omnipotence with human responsibility in speaking of these very passages of the Old Testament on which Calvin relied for the proof of his doctrine. "They both came of their own will, and "yet the Lord stirred up their spirit: and this may with "equal truth be stated the other way, The Lord stirred up "their spirit and yet they came of their own will[2]." He here tries to show that the play of motive and the human decision are not illusory, and that the deepest convictions of our inner consciousness are sound. And thus whatever may be the tendency of the teaching of Calvin, the doctrine of S. Austin is carefully guarded so as not to diminish the sense of real human responsibility for evil deeds.

On these two fundamental points as to the nature of man Calvin's doctrine diverges considerably from that of S. Austin, who did not hold that man, though sinful, was totally depraved, and who was careful to maintain that men are fully responsible for their actions.

3. There is another view which is not so commonly expressed perhaps, but which certainly is very generally held at present, as to the hopelessness of finding a remedy for existing evils. Evidence has already been adduced which goes to show that punishment is rarely remedial, and the recognition of this fact along with the depressing conviction which is forced on many men who accept the teaching of some Malthusians as to the overwhelming strength of animal impulses, goes far to induce the hopelessness as to reformation, which is by no means uncommon. There are some of

---

[1] *Institutes*, II. iv. 3. Similar expressions (*De Gratia et Lib. Arb.* 41), which Calvin subsequently quotes (iv. 7.) are used by S. Austin to illustrate the view that voluntas humana non tollitur sed ex mala mutatur in bonam by Divine grace. See also *Institutes*, II. v. 5.

[2] *De Gratia et Lib. Arb.* 42.

course who still pin their faith to national education[1] as a panacea, but the evidence drawn either from other countries or our own[2] can hardly inspire us with much confidence in its effects in destroying crime. And in the presence of all these miserable phenomena of immediate and growing evil which is handed down to future generations we cannot wonder that there are so many who are forced into some sort of Pessimism,—or at least into a cynical indifference to the fate of a world that is in a hopeless case. As we ponder on it we may feel as if the cry which has risen in all ages that the world is becoming worse and worse, was simply the confirmation of a fact which might have been established by more general reasoning and which becomes more appalling when viewed in the light of a belief in a life beyond the grave—a life of ever-increasing wickedness and misery. Here we have a doctrine which is assuredly terrible enough, but which, be it observed, is perfectly self-consistent, and which, though it seems to neglect some important facts[3], presents no serious difficulty to many acute minds in the present day.

This self-consistent doctrine as to the growing and ineradicable power of evil is in brief the doctrine of S. Austin; but in his writings, and as he holds it, it does give rise to a very serious difficulty—a difficulty which is created by the Christian view[4] of God. Men might patiently accept the horror of a life in which they were condemned to evil, and in which the evil tended to increase continually, but the mind begins to revolt against such pessimistic teaching when it is assured that this world—now existing under this

[1] The arguments on behalf of national education are sometimes put in such a form that they seem to imply the perfectional principles alluded to above.
[2] *Statistical Society's Journal*, XLVI. 343.
[3] The facts of religious experience and successful struggling with evil.
[4] The theology of the Mohammedan is fatalistic, but it does not give such teaching in regard to the character of God as to raise this difficulty.

terrible blight—has been created by an all-loving God, omnipotent, and omniscient. It is then and only then that the terrible facts of the undying power of evil in the world come into an apparently irreconcilable conflict with what we are told of the character of God.

There are many who are tempted to solve the dilemma at once, by rejecting the Christian revelation which has created the difficulty. But at least let us remember that if they thus get rid of the intellectual inconsistency, they also get rid of every element of hope. The problem of evil with its increasing horror is still before us unsolved when we have said in our hearts that there is no God. We may brace ourselves to struggle against it—to alleviate it, as far as in us lies; or we may turn our backs upon it and try to forget it; but if our faith is vain the misery of sin and evil is still appalling—the horror of a great darkness overshadowing us still. But if we are not ready thus to sever the knot, if we would fain solve the problem let us look at it as S. Austin does: and take each separate difficulty in turn.

III. Divine Foreknowledge.

There are difficulties which arise from our belief in God's foreknowledge.

(A) How is it possible to say that man is really responsible for all the evil in the world,—the first sin that manifested it, and the many sins that have perpetuated it,— if God the Creator foreknew it all? But as S. Austin argues, even though all things happen as God foreknew them, this does not remove the responsibility of those who commit any crime, for we may think of Him as foreseeing what they would decide, not as controlling their decision. To assert His foreknowledge does not imply that the human beings whose conduct He foresaw were not really responsible, and that no real play of motive and decision took place

DIVINE FOREKNOWLEDGE.

in their minds[1]. It is only a matter of knowledge, not of control, for, to use his own illustration, "as the memory

[1] Certe enim hoc te movet et hoc miraris, quomodo non sint contraria et repugnantia, ut et Deus praescius sit omnium futurorum, et nos non necessitate sed voluntate peccemus. Si enim praescius est Deus, inquis, peccaturum esse hominem, necesse est ut peccet: si autem necesse est, non ergo est in peccando voluntatis arbitrium, sed potius inevitabilis et fixa necessitas. Qua ratiocinatione hoc videlicet ne conficiatur times, ut aut Deus futurorum omnium praescius impie negetur, aut si hoc negare non possumus, fateamur non voluntate sed necessitate peccari: an aliquid aliud te movet? E. Nihil interim aliud. A. Res ergo universas, quarum Deus est praescius, non voluntate sed necessitate fieri putas. E. Omnino ita puto. A. Expergiscere tandem, teque ipsum paululum intuere, et dic mihi, si potes, qualem sis habiturus cras voluntatem, utrum peccandi, an recte faciendi. E. Nescio. A. Quid? Deum itidem nescire hoc putas? E. Nullo modo id putaverim. A. Si ergo voluntatem tuam crastinam novit, et omnium hominum, sive qui sunt sive qui futuri sunt, futuras praevidet voluntates, multo magis praevidet quid de justis impiisque facturus sit. E. Prorsus si meorum operum praescium Deum dico, multo fidentius cum dixerim praescire opera sua, et quid sit facturus certissime praevidere. A. Nonne igitur caves ne tibi dicatur etiam ipsum quaecumque facturus est non voluntate sed necessitate facturum, si omnia quorum Deus praescius est necessitate fiunt, non voluntate? E. Ego cum dicerem necessitato universa fieri quae Deus futura praescivit, ea sola intuebar quae in creatura ejus fiunt, non autem quae in ipso: non enim ea fiunt, sed sunt sempiterna.......Non enim posses aliud sentire esse in potestate nostra, nisi quod cum volumus facimus. Quapropter nihil tam in nostra potestate quam ipsa voluntas est. Ea enim prorsus nullo intervallo mox ut volumus praesto est. Et ideo recte possumus dicere, Non voluntate senescimus, sed necessitate; aut, non voluntate morimur, sed necessitate; et si quid aliud hujusmodi: non voluntate autem volumus, quis vel delirus audeat dicere? Quamobrem, quamvis praesciat Deus nostras voluntates futuras, non ex eo tamen conficitur ut non voluntate aliquid velimus.......Attende enim, quaeso, quanta caecitate dicatur, Si praescivit Deus futuram voluntatem meam, quoniam nihil aliter potest fieri quam praescivit, necesse est ut velim quod ille praescivit: si autem necesse est, non jam voluntate, sed necessitate id me velle fatendum est.......Quod si fieri non potest ut dum volumus non velimus, adest utique voluntas volentibus; nec aliud quidquam est in potestate, nisi quod volentibus adest. Voluntas igitur nostra nec voluntas esset, nisi esset in nostra potestate. Porro, quia est in potestate, libera est nobis. Non enim est nobis liberum, quod in potestate non habemus, aut potest non esse

"does not compel those deeds of yours which are past, so
"the foreknowledge of God does not compel that those
"things which are in the future should be done[1]."

Here we may again notice how different is the doctrine
of Calvin; and on this point we are not left to gather
the difference by comparing the statements of the later
writer with those of the doctor he professed to follow, for
he explicitly rejects the distinction thus drawn. "Even
"Augustine," he says, "was not always free from this super-
"stition, as when he says that blinding and hardening[2]
"have not reference to the operation of God, but to pre-
"science. But this subtilty is repudiated by many passages
"of Scripture, which clearly show that the Divine interference
"amounts to something more than prescience[3]." And thus
we may once more be warned against taking popular Calvinism as a fair representation of the teaching of S. Austin.

But even though, so far as this distinction can be maintained[4], the reality of human responsibility is kept in sight,

quod habemus. Ita fit ut et Deum non negemus esse præscium omnium
futurorum, et nos tamen velimus quod volumus. Cum enim sit præscius
voluntatis nostræ, cujus est præscius ipsa erit. Voluntas ergo erit, quia
voluntatis est præscius. Nec voluntas esse poterit, si in potestate non
erit. Ergo et potestatis est præscius. Non igitur per ejus præscien-
tiam mihi potestas adimitur, quæ propterea mihi certior aderit, quia
ille cujus præscientia non fallitur, adfuturam mihi esse præscivit. E.
Ecce jam non nego ita necesse esse fieri quæcumque præscivit Deus, et
ita cum peccata nostra præscire, ut maneat tamen nobis voluntas libera,
atque in nostra posita potestate. *De Lib. Arb.* III. 6, 7, 8.

[1] *De Lib. Arb.* III. 11.

[2] Ac per hoc quando legitis in litteris veritatis, a Deo seduci homines, aut obtundi vel obdurari corda eorum, nolite dubitare præcessisse
mala merita eorum ut juste ita paterentur. *De Gratia et Lib. Arb.* 43.

It is of course true that an increase of wickedness is the penalty
imposed on sin in the order of God's Universe; but it is a self-inflicted
penalty.

[3] *Institutes*, II. iv. 3.

[4] Calvin appears to think that S. Austin altered his opinion on this
point, but the passage to which he refers does not appear at all conclusive. There was apparently some modification (Neander, *History of*

it may yet appear as if all the misery and sin were really due to the fact that man had been created with the nature he possesses. Since he was created with a Will, which was in some sense free, was it not by the very fact of its freedom impelled to resist the guiding and direction which might conceivably have kept men in a state of innocence, —if they had not thus been endued with free will?

But to S. Austin's mind this implied a confusion as to the real nature of freedom. A rational being is only free when delivered from those penalties of sin which distort and blind his true nature. To be free from the preying anxieties and cares which press on those who cannot trust God's discipline for them here, to be free from the weight that may press on the conscience which has never sought

Christian Religion, IV. 295), but he continued to draw the distinction between foreseeing and predetermining even in his latest writings; though it is exceedingly difficult to grasp the precise meaning which it had for him.

At first sight it would seem as if the distinction implied that the Eternal purpose of God is something that has followed upon foreseen events in time: but S. Austin has no such meaning. Omnia itaque Dei dona quæ in eodem opere sive optavi, sive laudavi, quis, non dicam negare, sed dubitare saltem audeat Deum daturum se esse præscisse, et quibus daturus fuerit, nunquam potuisse nescire? Hæc est prædestinatio manifesta et certa sanctorum. *De Dono Persev.* 53. But the severance of knowledge from will seems to lose all meaning in regard to the Eternal Mind.

The distinction presents less difficulty in regard to the evil than to the good. Since evil is due to man, a defect not caused by God, it is easy to say that He foresees their evil thoughts and deeds as the ground of His decision. But of the good it is different: they have been called by God, but on what grounds have they been called and the others left to themselves? What is it that is foreseen, and the knowledge of which determines the Divine will? It is not according to S. Austin because of the right deeds (*De Divers. Quæst. ad Simpl.*, I. qu. ii. 2), nor because of the faith (*ibid.* 5) of men, as God foresees it, that they are chosen by God to be the recipients of His grace; nor because of the opportunities of hearing His message (*ibid.* 14). To assert any of these would be either implicitly to deny that faith and goodness are the gift of God (*ibid.* 21), or to deny the power of God's grace to win any heart (*ibid.* 14). The

God's pardoning mercy; to be free from the dread of going forth alone to face the eternal realities, this is a true freedom, the true life of the wise man, the real field for rational self-development. "There is no true liberty but that of "those who are blessed and who keep the eternal law[1]." Self-conscious life is the thought from which all his reasoning starts, the realisation of this life apart from all the deliraments of sense and passion is, as he paints it, the blessedness to which men may attain, it is the true Freedom. At all times, under any condition, in a primæval

passage is very strong, and seems to leave the human will so little part in cooperating with God, that all human action seems to be determined rather than merely foreseen by God. But we must bear in mind that the purpose of this argument is to show that it is not any merit on the part of the recipient that determines the gift of grace.

At the same time it must be borne in mind that according to S. Austin the effect of God's grace is to free the will from the slavery of sin, and that thus man's will is set free to cooperate with God's in working out his salvation. See below p. 93 note 1. As then evil is not from God, and the will of those who are called is set free by grace, it cannot be said that the course of either the evil or the good is absolutely and directly controlled by God, and there is room for a distinction between prescience and predetermination. So with regard to the argument just quoted, the freed will is *given* by God, but it is given by Him to man to use. Again He *might* draw the vilest by His love, and therefore it is no mark of goodness to turn at His call, but yet His call is given through means and institutions which He has ordained—it is mediate. Hence, once again we may see that S. Austin does not figure the Divine will as immediately and directly determining, and that there is room for a prescience which is not predetermination. See below p. 127 note.

[1] *De Lib. Arb.* I. 32. Compare also a more expanded statement.

Nec ideo liberum arbitrium non habebunt, quia peccata eos delectare non poterunt. Magis quippe erit liberum, a delectatione peccandi usque ad delectationem non peccandi indeclinabilem liberatum........ Certe Deus ipse numquid, quoniam peccare non potest, ideo liberum arbitrium habere negandus est? Erit ergo illius civitatis et una in omnibus et inseparabilis in singulis voluntas libera, ab omni malo liberata, et impleta omni bono, fruens indeficienter æternorum jucunditate gaudiorum, oblita culparum, oblita pœnarum; nec tamen ideo suæ liberationis oblita, ut liberatori suo non sit grata. *De Civitate Dei*, XXII. XXX. 3.

paradise[1], in the world here, in the world to come, this is the nature of Freedom, the condition of the exercise of a will that is truly free, like the Will of God.

We can have little difficulty in distinguishing such freedom as this from the liberty of indifference, or scope for the exercise of caprice for which Pelagius contended long ago[2], and which is claimed by many to-day. If the true freedom is attained there must be perfect harmony

---

[1] Sic enim oportebat prius hominem fieri, ut et bene velle posset, et male; nec gratis, si bene; nec impune, si male: postea vero sic erit, ut male velle non possit; nec ideo libero carebit arbitrio. Multo quippe liberius erit arbitrium, quod omnino non poterit servire peccato. *Enchiridion*, cv.

This gives a clue to the interpretation of all the passages about Grace rendering the will free: they have been very generally misapprehended.

Liberum ergo arbitrium evacuamus per gratiam? Absit: sed magis liberum arbitrium statuimus. Sicut enim lex per fidem sic liberum arbitrium per gratiam non evacuatur, sed statuitur. Neque enim lex impletur nisi libero arbitrio: sed per legem cognitio peccati, per fidem impetratio gratiae contra peccatum, per gratiam sanatio animae a vitio peccati, per animae sanitatem libertas arbitrii, per liberum arbitrium justitiae dilectio, per justitiae dilectionem legis operatio. Ac per hoc, sicut lex non evacuatur sed statuitur per fidem, quia fides impetrat gratiam qua lex impleatur: ita liberum arbitrium non evacuatur per gratiam, sed statuitur, quia gratia sanat voluntatem, qua justitia libere diligatur. Omnia haec, quae velut catenatim connexi, habent voces suas in Scripturis sanctis. Lex dicit: *Non concupisces*. Fides dicit: *Sana animam meam, quoniam peccavi tibi*. Gratia dicit: *Ecce sanus factus es, jam noli peccare, ne quid tibi deterius contingat*. Sanitas dicit: *Domine Deus meus, exclamavi ad te, et sanasti me*. Liberum arbitrium dicit: *Voluntarie sacrificabo tibi*. *De Spir. et Lit.* 52.

Haec enim voluntas libera tanto erit liberior quanto sanior: tanto autem sanior, quanto divinae misericordiae gratiaeque subjectior. Ipsa enim fideliter orat et dicit: *Itinera mea dirige secundum verbum tuum, et ne dominetur mihi omnis iniquitas*. Quomodo enim libera est, cui dominatur iniquitas? *Ep.* cxlvii. (*Hilario*), 8.

Compare especially the admirable note in Gangauf's *Speculative Lehre*, 421.

[2] Liberum arbitrium non est aliud quam possibilitas peccandi et non peccandi. *Op. Imp. contra Jul.* VI. ix.

Libertas arbitrii, qua a Deo emancipatus homo est, in admittendi

with other beings who attain it too. The caprice of one man may conflict with the caprice of another—since it is the self-seeking of a sensuous being: but the free play of a rational nature need involve no conflict with those who are rational too in their decisions and aims: there may be the fullest enjoyment of true freedom by each without encroachment on one another. And thus, it is when man finds his true freedom, the freedom of his rational nature from sense and passion, that he can at length live in complete harmony with the Will of God.

Human freedom then, so far as it is realised here below, is in complete harmony with the Will of God. It is the soul that is not free, that is in bondage to lust, that is deceived by the devil, that is at enmity with God. It is when by God's grace man is delivered from these bonds that he becomes free from the slavery of sin[1]. The question which peccati et abstinendi a peccato possibilitate consistit. *Ibid.* I. lxxviii. See also lxxxii.

To this S. Austin answers: Si liberum non est nisi quod duo potest velle, id est et bonum et malum; liber Deus non est, qui malum non potest velle. *Ibid.* I. c.

[1] Proinde bonus etiamsi serviat, liber est: malus autem etiamsi regnet, servus est; nec unius hominis, sed quod est gravius, tot dominorum, quot vitiorum. De quibus vitiis cum ageret Scriptura divina, *A quo enim quis,* inquit, *devictus est, huic et servus addictus est.* De *Civitate Dei,* IV. iii.

Hae sunt duo illa, libertas et cupiditas laudis humanae, quae ad facta compulere miranda Romanos. Si ergo pro libertate moriturorum et cupiditate laudum, quae a mortalibus expetuntur, occidi filii a patre potuerunt; quid magnum est, si pro vera libertate, quae nos ab iniquitatis et mortis et diaboli dominatu liberos facit, nec cupiditate humanarum laudum, sed caritate liberandorum hominum, non a Tarquinio rege, sed a daemonibus et daemonum principe, non filii occiduntur, sed Christi pauperes inter filios computantur? De *Civitate Dei,* v. xviii. 1.

Arbitrium igitur voluntatis tunc est vere liberum, cum vitiis peccatisque non servit. Tale datum est a Deo: quod amissum proprio vitio, nisi a quo dari potuit, reddi non potest. Unde Veritas dicit, *Si vos Filius liberaverit, tunc vere liberi eritis.* De *Civitate Dei,* XIV. xi. 1.

Quem ergo delectat libertas, ab amore mutabilium rerum liber esse appetat. De *Vera Religione,* 93.

has agitated moral philosophers in England as to the scope for human caprice is not the one which is of chief interest for S. Austin: he would be at one with the modern defenders of Free Choice in firmly upholding human responsibility, but freedom for the exercise of caprice was not a liberty which he greatly cared about. It did not seem to him a very precious boon, for he held that the saints of God have no freedom to sin[1]: he held too that unregenerate man is so bound by lust that he is not "free" to do right. His whole mode of stating and discussing the question differs from that which is current in ordinary English discussion, for the only freedom he cares about and discusses is rational freedom, freedom from sin: in this sense, unregenerate man is not free, though through the Grace of God he may at length attain to Freedom. Thus in its true nature, as created, and as delivered from the disease of sin, the will is in complete harmony with the will of God: evil was not necessarily involved in the act of creating beings

[1] Posset enim perseverare si vellet: quod ut nollet, de libero descendit arbitrio; quod tunc ita liberum erat, ut et bene velle posset et male. Quid erit autem liberius libero arbitrio, quando non poterit servire peccato, quae futura erat et homini, sicut facta est Angelis sanctis, merces meriti? Nunc autem per peccatum perdito bono merito, in his qui liberantur factum est donum gratiae, quae merces meriti futura erat. Quapropter, bina ista quid inter se differant, diligenter et vigilanter intuendum est; posse non peccare, et non posse peccare, posse non mori, et non posse mori, bonum posse non deserere, et bonum non posse deserere.......Prima ergo libertas voluntatis erat, posse non peccare; novissima erit multo major, non posse peccare: prima immortalitas erat, posse non mori; novissima erit multo major, non posse mori: prima erat perseverantiae potestas, bonum posse non deserere; novissima erit felicitas perseverantiae, bonum non posse deserere. *De Corrept. et Grat.* 32, 33.

Ipsa enim sanitas est vera libertas, quae non perisset, si bona permansisset voluntas. Quia vero peccavit voluntas, secuta est peccantem peccatum habendi dura necessitas, donec tota sanetur infirmitas, et accipiatur tanta libertas, in qua sicut necesse est permaneat beate vivendi voluntas, ita ut sit etiam bene vivendi et nunquam peccandi voluntaria felixque necessitas. *De Perf. Just. Hom.* 9.

endowed with a Free Will. For between the will of the Divine nature, which is set on the good of His creatures, and the will of true human nature there is no necessary conflict; the depraved will, blinded by passion and enslaved by lust, does indeed rebel against God: but not so the will of the man who has attained to Freedom: he has come to see things as God sees them, and to will as God wills; just for the very reason that he is at length free, the discord between the human will and the divine is at an end, since the two natures are reconciled[1].

A few words may be added to point out the nature of the fallacy which S. Austin has avoided, but by which later writers and Calvin among them have been entangled. There is a temptation to separate the Will of God from the Nature of God, and to discuss His Will and His Power without taking His Character into account as well. In the same way men are ready to separate man's will from man's nature; and then proceed to try and discuss the relation between such an unreal divine Will, and an unreal human will. If we have two capricious wills in close connexion with each other, there can be no doubt that a conflict must arise, and that the struggle between a capricious divine Will and a capricious human will, could only mean the subjection of the human will, whatever free play for its caprice it may appear to have.

We must thus be forced into some form of determinism, for the play of such a human will, in the presence of such a divine Will must be an illusion. But S. Austin does not follow this train of thought: he does not try to separate the Will and the Nature of God. He is the supreme

[1] Beato autem, quales se esse omnes volunt, non recte nec vere dicitur, Non potest fieri quod vis. Si enim beatus est, quidquid vult fieri potest; quia non vult quod fieri non potest. Sed non est mortalitatis hujus hæc vita, nec erit nisi quando et immortalitas erit. Quæ si nullo modo dari homini posset, frustra etiam beatitudo quæreretur; quia sine immortalitate non potest esse. *De Trin.* XIII. 10.

Reason, free from change, the Eternal Thought. His Will is not capricious or changeful, but the Will of a Loving Nature: it is ever working out His Eternal Purpose, and willing not the death of a sinner, but rather that he should be converted and live. S. Austin could not treat the Divine Will as mere Absolute Caprice, acting apart from the Divine Nature as revealed to us, for he knew that conscious life cannot be thus severed into isolated parts[1].

(B) A second difficulty arises however, from our belief in God's foreknowledge: did He not foresee that as a matter of fact, the created will would become depraved, that all the sin and misery would ensue? was not the very creation of man accomplished in full view of all the infinite misery which would follow from it? Can God be good when He has done this?

There are three points on which S. Austin lays stress: to which attention may be recalled.

1. For one thing, at the utmost it can only be said that evil is divinely permitted[2] but it is really due to human

[1] Atque ita fit illa trinitas ex memoria, et interna visione, et quae utrumque copulat voluntate. Quae tria cum in unum coguntur, ab ipso coactu cogitatio dicitur. Nec jam in his tribus diversa substantia est. *De Trin.* XI. 6.

Ego per omnia illa tria memini, ego intelligo, ego diligo, qui nec memoria sum, nec intelligentia, nec dilectio, sed haec habeo. *De Trin.* XV. 42.

Haec igitur tria, memoria, intelligentia, voluntas, quoniam non sunt tres vitae, sed una vita; nec tres mentes, sed una mens: consequenter utique nec tres substantiae sunt, sed una substantia. Memoria quippe, quae vita et mens et substantia dicitur, ad se ipsam dicitur: quod vero memoria dicitur, ad aliquid relative dicitur. Hoc de intelligentia quoque et de voluntate dixerim: et intelligentia quippe et voluntas ad aliquid dicuntur. Vita est autem unaquaeque ad se ipsam, et mens, et essentia. Quocirca tria haec eo sunt unum, quo una vita, una mens, una essentia: et quidquid aliud ad se ipsa singula dicuntur, etiam simul, non pluraliter, sed singulariter dicuntur. *De Trin.* x. 18.

[2] Quocirca cum in Catholica dicitur, omnium naturarum atque substantiarum esse auctorem Deum, simul intelligitur ab eis qui hoc possunt intelligere, non esse Deum auctorem mali. (Quomodo enim

action: it is not divinely caused, it has come about through man's act with God's permission. We dare not say that His purpose in creation has failed unless evil had attained an absolute mastery which we cannot ascribe to it. For,

2. After all, despite its depravity, the power of will is a noble power[1]. Creation is not so utterly spoiled by

potest ille, qui omnium quae sunt causa est ut sint, causa esse rursus ut non sint, id est, ut ab essentia deficiant et ad non esse tendant? quod malum generale esse clamat verissima ratio. *De Moribus Man.* 3.

Quisquis omnium quae sunt auctor est, et ad cujus bonitatem id tantum pertinet ut sit omne quod est, non esse ad eum pertinere nullo pacto potest. Omne autem quod deficit, ab eo quod est esse deficit, et tendit in non esse. Esse autem et in nullo deficere bonum est, et malum est deficere. At ille, ad quem non esse non pertinet, non est causa deficiendi, id est, tendendi ad non esse; quia, ut ita dicam, essendi causa est. Boni igitur tantummodo causa est: et propterea ipse summum bonum est. Quocirca mali auctor non est, qui omnium quae sunt auctor est: quia in quantum sunt, in tantum bona sunt. *De Divers. Quaest. LXXXIII.* qu. xxi.

Sicut ergo tu dicis, Cur permittit ista, si displicent? ita ego dico, Cur punit ista, si placent? Ac per hoc sicut ego confiteor quod omnino ista non fierent, nisi ab Omnipotente permitterentur; ita tu confitere facienda non esse quae a justo puniantur: ut non faciendo quae punit mereamur ab eo discere cur permittit esse quae puniat. *Perfectorum est* enim, sicut scriptum est, *solidus cibus*: in quo hi qui bene profecerunt, jam intelligunt ad omnipotentiam Dei potius id pertinuisse, ut ex libero arbitrio voluntatis venientia mala esse permitteret. Tanta quippe est omnipotens ejus bonitas, ut etiam de malis possit facere bona, sive ignoscendo, sive sanando, sive ad utilitates piorum coaptando atque vertendo, sive etiam justissime vindicando. *De Continentia,* 15.

Here again Calvin rejects S. Austin's opinion:

"It seems absurd that man should be blinded by the will and command of God, and yet be forthwith punished for his blindness. Hence, recourse is had to the evasion that this is done only by the permission and not also by the will of God. He himself, however, openly declaring that He does this, repudiates the evasion." *Institutes*, I. xviii. 1.

[1] Fecit et hominem ad imaginem suam; ut quemadmodum ipse per omnipotentiam suam praeest universae creaturae, sic homo per intelligentiam suam, qua etiam Creatorem suum cognoscit et colit, praeesset omnibus terrenis animalibus.......Praesciebat autem Deus eos transgressuros: sed tamen quia conditor est et effector omnis boni, magis eos

sin[1] through all its length and breadth, that it were better it had never been, or that it should be altogether blotted out. God's creation is still good, though marred.

3. And again, we cannot see all the aspects of evil[2]: misery and pain may be disciplinary, and as such may be not evil but good: only if we could see the end from the beginning, could be sure that good is not brought out of the evil, is not exhibited through evil, only then could we dare to be sure that the very permission of evil had not been justified by the ultimate triumph of good.

These considerations are not urged with the view of demonstrating to natural reason that the Governor of the universe is good, after the manner of eighteenth century theologians: S. Austin had no hope of attaining to knowledge of God by direct inductions from the experience of the man of ordinary intelligence and honesty. For him the goodness of God, a supernatural reality, had been manifested in the person of our Lord; it had been declared by

fecit, quando fecit et bestias, ut impleret terram bonis terrenis. Et utique melior est homo etiam peccator, quam bestia.......Qui enim hominibus dedit liberum arbitrium, ut non servili necessitate, sed ingenua voluntate Deum colerent. *De Cat. Rud.* 29, 30.

Nam Deus hominem inexterminabilem fecit, et ei liberum voluntatis arbitrium dedit. Non enim esset optimus, si Dei præceptis necessitate, non voluntate serviret. *De Agone Christ.* 11.

[1] Neque enim Deus ullum, non dico Angelorum, sed vel hominum crearet, quem malum futurum esse præscisset, nisi pariter nosset quibus eos bonorum usibus commodaret, atque ita ordinem sæculorum tanquam pulcherrimum carmen ex quibusdam quasi antithetis honestaret. *De Civitate Dei*, XI. xviii.

[2] Talia, credo, sunt omnia; sed oculos quærunt. Solœcismos et barbarismos quos vocant, poetæ adamaverunt; quæ schemata et metaplasmos mutatis appellare nominibus, quam manifesta vitia fugere maluerunt. Detrahe tamen ista carminibus, suavissima condimenta desiderabimus. Congere multa in unum locum, totum acre, putidum, rancidum fastidibo. Transfer in liberam forensemque dictionem, quis non eam fugere atque in theatra secedere jubebit? Ordo igitur ea gubernans et moderans, nec apud se nimia, nec ubilibet aliena esse patietur. *De Ordine*, II. 13. Compare p. 71, note 3.

the Incarnate Word. To him the belief in the goodness of God had been confirmed as time after time the Spirit bore witness with his spirit: he held to this belief. Nor was his belief shaken by the objection drawn from the misery in the world which God has made, since that misery is not so utter, the good is not so wholly extinguished, as to exclude a belief in the goodness of God, despite it all.

And if that belief, based on God's revealed love, be firmly held, it may become more than a mere belief, it may prove to be the key of knowledge. The strange medley of human life is not self-interpreting: is it all an evil dream, purposeless and vain, are we the sport of malign and capricious influences, or is there a dismal fate which drags us slowly to lower depths of misery and sin? It often seems as if it must be so, and we cannot find a clue to unravel the mystery fully. It is beyond our ken: our experience fails us, but we need not ponder in doubt over the depths which our eyes cannot scan, if grace is given us to believe that our Father is good. We cannot know that the suffering of this present time is not worthy to be compared to the glory which shall be revealed, but we may believe. It is this belief and this belief alone which can harmonise all our conflicting experiences and render them intelligible; such a belief does not conflict with knowledge; it systematises it; it renders the various parts of our knowledge self-consistent: it is to many minds an intellectual necessity, since our life seems to be an unintelligible contradiction unless we can look at it in the light of the belief in the goodness of God. The belief does not enable us to understand it all, but it renders knowledge possible, it makes us see that there is a meaning in our life here which we may find out at length. And when an objection is urged which strikes, not at any particular opinion but at the very possibility of knowledge at all, we are bound to subject it to the closest scrutiny.

For the belief in the goodness of God, and this belief alone, renders our knowledge harmonious with itself. We know that sorrow and suffering are a discipline which may work for good; we know that "men may rise on stepping-"stones of their dead selves to higher things," yet how can we reconcile these facts[1] with the evidences before us of the power of evil? The world must remain a mystery, the scene of a strangely swaying struggle between opposing principles. And to hold that this warfare wages unceasingly with no vantage gained, as a confused mêlée, is to treat the history of the world as a purposeless contradiction; it is to hold that it is not merely hard to explain, but that it is in itself unintelligible.

It is hard indeed to hold fast to the belief in the goodness of the Creator in presence of the agony of pain, or the bitterness of death or the horrors of sin and passion and crime,—to believe that the God Who has permitted it all is good: yet it is harder still to cast away that belief, and with it all hope of ever reading the riddle—to see all the misery in the world, all the pain and all the evil and to say that there is no purpose in it at all, no triumph of good accomplishing itself through it all, but that it is an evil dream from which there is no awaking.

And thus, though we cannot see far enough to solve the terrible questions which the misery of the world forces upon us, cannot demonstrate from experience that God is good, we may yet feel that the difficulty when scrutinised has no force to rob us of our belief—a belief which we may hold not merely as a comfortable opinion which we wish to be true despite the conflicting evidence, but as an intellectual necessity which is forced upon us in the effort to harmonise our knowledge, and to find a meaning in human life. The argument from the limitation of our range of

[1] Which have become a matter of common experience through the influence of Christianity.

vision which is falsely applied to throw doubt on our knowledge of the Unseen and Eternal, is really valid against those who would treat our earthly experience as so complete and convincing that we are able to criticise the Divine purpose and its modes of operation.

IV. DIVINE OMNIPOTENCE.

There are other difficulties which arise from our belief in the omnipotence of God. It seems (A) derogatory to omnipotence to stoop to the use of means at all, to work by the gradual evolution of good, instead of at once and for ever destroying evil and accomplishing the triumph of good; while it may also (B) be felt that the particular means provided in the Gospel are proving themselves so limited as not to cover the whole field, and it almost seems, inadequate to cope with the power of evil. The second of these questions will occupy our attention in the last lecture, in a somewhat different form, but we may now say that so far as there is in the use of means an apparent conflict with the Divine Omnipotence, we may once more remember the limitation to our knowledge, and that it is not for us to decide what the Omnipotent can, and what He cannot do. I say advisedly what the Omnipotent cannot do; for just as we cannot separate God's Will from His Character, so we cannot separate His Omnipotence from His Nature. It is impossible to think of His Omnipotence as a power of defying Himself, of setting His own Purpose at nought, of disregarding His own Will. It was said of old that there are things the gods cannot do, that they cannot alter the past: and there are things God cannot do: He cannot change: the eternal purpose of Love which as we believe was uttered at first in creation is working itself to its completion. The Eternal Wisdom has manifested itself in all His works, its power is felt over all, it is omnipotent; but in that Will there is no variableness, nor shadow of turning, no undoing and no hasting. The omnipotence of the Divine Will is shown not in the sudden accomplishment of a purpose, but in the marvellous control of all the unruly elements[1] till by their interaction the end is at length attained.

So long as we think of God as arbitrary, so long will the belief in His omnipotence suggest one insuperable difficulty after another: but to say that He is arbitrary is to neglect the revelation of Himself which He gave to His ancient people, to ignore the perfect manifestation of His character in the Incarnate Word. Let us not be wise above what is written, or venture, from the hope of exalting Him in the eyes of men, to depict His purpose as unintelligible in its nature, or to think of His Will as arbitrary. It has been by thus falsely honouring God that Calvinism has done so much to alienate men's minds from His service. Mere

[1] Tanta quippe est omnipotens ejus bonitas, ut etiam de malis possit facere bona, sive ignoscendo, sive sanando, sive ad utilitates piorum coaptando atque vertendo, sive etiam justissime vindicando. Omnia namque ista bona sunt, et Deo bono atque omnipotente dignissima: nec tamen fiunt nisi de malis. Quid igitur melius, quid omnipotentius eo qui cum mali nihil faciat, bene etiam de malis facit? Clamant ad eum qui male fecerunt, *Dimitte nobis debita nostra:* exaudit, ignoscit. Nocuerunt sua mala peccantibus: subvenit eorum medeturque languoribus. Saeviunt suorum hostes: de illorum saevitia facit martyres. *De Continentia,* 15.

Omnipotens enim Deus qui operatur bona etiam de nostris malis, qualia dabit bona, cum liberaverit ab omnibus malis? *De Continentia,* 16.

Utrum enim non potest facere ut resurgat caro, et vivat in aeternum; an propterea credendum non est id eum esse facturum, quia malum est atque indignum Deo? Sed de omnipotentia ejus, quae tot et tanta facit incredibilia, jam multa diximus. Si volunt invenire quod omnipotens non potest, habent prorsus: ego dicam, Mentiri non potest. Credamus ergo quod potest, non credendo quod non potest. Non itaque credentes quod mentiri possit, credant esse facturum quod se facturum esse promisit. *De Civitate Dei,* XXII. xxv.

Qui certe non ob aliud vocatur omnipotens, nisi quoniam quidquid vult potest. *De Civitate Dei,* XXI. vii. 1.

Compare other passages quoted and discussed by Gangauf, *Speculative Lehre von Gott,* 167.

Power apart from Reason, mere Might apart from Love, is not that which we have learned to worship; and Calvin in asserting the absolute and apparently arbitrary power of the Divine Will[1], has once more taken up a position which was not that of S. Austin.

It thus appears that the really distinctive and fundamental doctrine in S. Austin's teaching in this controversy, is in regard to the nature of Will. Will is free when it is

[1] *Institutes*, III. xxi. 1. "It is plainly owing to the mere pleasure of God that salvation is spontaneously offered to some, while others have no access to it....It is not right that man should with impunity pry into things which the Lord has been pleased to conceal within Himself and scan that eternal wisdom which it is His pleasure that we should not apprehend but adore, that therein also His perfection may appear."

S. Austin is careful to point out that even if the Divine decisions are inscrutable and mysterious now, they are not arbitrary but rest on reasons we shall eventually understand. *De Gratia et Lib. Arb.* 45.

Calvin of course attributes the Highest Reason to the Divine Being, but he seems to use the term in a non-natural sense. For S. Austin man is really a partaker of the Divine Reason, while with Calvin human reason appears to be different in kind, not only limited in range and power. It is in a "way superior to human judgment" that we become convinced of the worth of the Scriptures. "We ask not for proofs or probabilities on which to rest our judgment, but we subject our intellect and judgment to it as too transcendent for us to estimate.......Such then is a conviction which asks not for reasons, such a knowledge which accords with the highest reason, namely knowledge in which the mind rests more firmly and securely than in any reasons.......This singular privilege God bestows on the elect only whom He separates from the rest of mankind...God having been pleased to reserve the treasure of intelligence for His children, no wonder that so much ignorance and stupidity is seen in the rest of mankind." (*Institutes*, I. vii. 5.) On these principles it is clear that "purpose," "wisdom," "reason" &c. when spoken of God are used in an esoteric sense, and do not mean purpose, wisdom, reason such as are found in the men who are made in the image of God. When we remember how S. Austin's doctrine of God is all built upon the certainty of our intellectual conceptions, and the necessary conditions for such conceptions, we see that Calvin's doctrine of the knowledge of God differs entirely from that of S. Austin: it seems to vacillate between a deism which is satisfied to seek for God in His Works, and a superstitious credulity about the Bible which refuses to advance to knowledge.

rational, and the will of man here in this world is not entirely free: he cannot as the Pelagians maintained be good if he likes; he has not the liberty of indifference. But when we go farther to ask, Why is he not thus free to do as he likes? we find that the answer of S. Austin is very different to that of Calvin. Man is not free to do good if he likes, because he is enslaved by lust and blinded by passion, because his resolution is weak; he cannot do the good he would:—such is the plain matter of fact. Calvin on the other hand holds that man is not free to do good if he likes because his course here in this world has been determined for him by the arbitrary decree of an Omnipotent power—a doctrine which at once transcends our experience and conflicts with the whole teaching of revelation as to the Nature and Character of God.

Had he written on no other subject than this, his treatment of it would serve to place S. Austin in the front rank of philosophers. Just as it is true that he may well be compared with Descartes in regard to the problem of the certainty of knowledge, so is it true that he seems to have anticipated Kant[1] in proclaiming the true Freedom of the Will. But the doctrine, so subtle and so profound, has never been cordially accepted throughout Christendom: it might indeed be almost said to be the distinctive mark of the English Church that so many of her leaders have sought to reproduce and perpetuate the very teaching of the African Doctor. In the days when Pelagian opinion seemed everywhere to have triumphed in Christendom[2], when the recognised authorities in theology were affected

[1] It has also been maintained that he anticipated Kant in another important point—the anthropological argument for the existence of God. Gangauf, *Speculative Lehre*, 94.

[2] Sicut olim contra unicum Dei prophetam octingenti et quinquaginta prophetae Baal, et similes sunt reperti, quibus et innumerabilis populus adhaerebat; ita et hodie in hac causa... Totus etenim paene mundus post Pelagium abiit in errorem. Bradwardine, *De Causa Dei*, preface.

by it, there was one man who stood forth to oppose it—the most learned student, the deepest thinker, the holiest Christian of his time—the one man whom king and monks and pope alike agreed was fittest to rule the see of Canterbury[1]—the Englishman who in our Chaucer's eyes was worthy to have his name coupled with "the holy doctor" S. Austin[2]. Thomas Bradwardine too was a man of the deepest personal religious experience; he too had learned in his communing with God[3], that all the good that was in him was of Him; and having thus learned for himself as it were the falseness of Pelagian teaching[4], he set himself to attack it on the ground where it fancied itself impregnable[5]. With

[1] Fuller, *Church History*, II. 305. Compare however Collier, *Eccl. Hist.* III. 108.

[2] Chaucer, *Nun's Priest's Tale*.

[3] Verum talia mihi supplicanti diutius et anxius deprecanti, ecce nuper in cujusdam noctis silentio, postquam coram Domino praecordia mea fudi, soporatus didici et inveni, quod ipse est qui post tempestatem facit tranquillum, et post lachrymationem exultationem infundit, ac omnibus invocantibus cum veraciter prope adest. Bradwardine, *De Causa Dei*, preface.

[4] Ego autem stultus a scientia Dei et vanus, quando Philosophicis literis intendebam, errore contrario seducebar. Quandoque enim audivi Theologos istam tractare materiam, et pars Pelagii mihi verior videbatur. In Scholis enim Philosophorum, raro solebam quicquam audire de gratiâ, nisi aequivoce forsan dicta; sed tota die audivi, quod nos sumus Domini nostrorum actuum liberorum, et quod in nostra potestate est, operari bene vel male, habere virtutes vel vitia, cum similibus suis multis. Et si quandoque in Ecclesia audivi lectionem Apostoli gratiam extollentem, et liberum deprimentem arbitrium, cujusmodi est illud ad Rom. IX. *Non volentis atque currentis, sed miserentis est Dei*, et multa similia, ingrato mihi gratiae displicebat... Postea vero adhuc nondum Theologiae factus auditor, praedicto argumento velut quodam gratiae radio visitatus, sub quadam tenui veritatis imagine, videbar mihi videre a longe gratiam Dei omnia bona merita praecedentem tempore et natura, scilicet gratam Dei voluntatem, qui prius utroque modo vult merentem salvari et prius naturaliter operatur meritum ejus in eo, quam ipse, sicut est in omnibus motibus primus Motor; unde et ei gratias refero qui mihi hanc gratiam gratis dedit. Bradwardine, *De Causa Dei*, 308.

[5] Audivi namque quosdam advocatos Pelagii, licet multum provectos in sacris apicibus, affirmantes Pelagium nusquam potuisse convinci per naturalem et philosophicam rationem; sed vix arguebatur utcumque per

a fervent admiration for S. Austin personally he had also an extraordinary familiarity with his works, for there is hardly a single treatise of the Bishop of Hippo's to which reference is not made in the *De Causa Dei*[1]; while the whole plan of the book, the prominence that is given to the question as to the nature of Will[2] and the masterly argument on the subject[3], alike seem to show how accurately he apprehended, how fully he sympathised with the doctrine of S. Austin.

And in after days, when Christendom no longer appeared to be at one, when it was rent in pieces, and the discord had robbed every land and every city of all appearance of peace, one branch of the Church was still faithful to the ancient teacher. While Calvinism, with all its exaggerations, was fixing its hold in France and Switzerland and Scotland, the English Church[4] was not carried away by any novel definition of orthodoxy—not because the leaders were successful in cunningly framing some meaningless compromise which all parties could accept, but because they would not desert the old paths; and alike in re-arranging our services, in setting forth Christian truth in homilies, and in the framing of the Articles, they were constantly and consciously influenced by S. Austin.

quasdam auctoritates Theologicas satis nudas, maxime autem per auctoritatem Ecclesiae, quae Satrapis non placebat. Quapropter per rationes et auctoritates philosophicas ipsos disposui reformare. Bradwardino, *De Causa Dei*, preface.

[1] Lechler, *De Thoma Bradwardino*, 17.

[2] Dr Mozley has unfortunately followed a different order of treatment, and discussed predestination without a sufficient preliminary examination of the nature of the will.

[3] The keynote is given in the *De Causa*, 444. Ex his autem evidenter apparet, quod liberum arbitrium, seu potius arbitrium liberum potest definiri seu describi hoc modo, Quod ipsum est potentia Rationalis rationaliter judicandi, et voluntarie exequendi.

[4] See Excursus G, § 3, p. 182.

LECTURE IV.

By grace are ye saved, through faith. Eph. ii. 8.

THE KINGDOM OF GOD AND THE MEANS OF GRACE.

I. THE CITY OF GOD.

THERE is one point in which the life of S. Austin contrasts strikingly with those of many of the other bishops of his time. Alike at Antioch and Alexandria, at Constantinople and Rome, political troubles and political partisanship often interfered with the due discharge of strictly episcopal duties, and the bishop might be forced to take an important part in affairs of state. But in the obscurity of his own little city, S. Austin was but little affected by palace intrigues or political cares; and though he eagerly watched the course of affairs, and corresponded with one at least of the leading courtiers at Ravenna[1], his work was not interrupted, nor was he disturbed in pursuing the even tenour of his way.

But there was at length an event which sent a shock through the length and breadth of the known world. Rome had fallen from her high estate; her last great soldier had been basely destroyed, and she fell a prey to the plundering army of Alaric. History has drawn a veil[2] over the horrors of that unexampled catastrophe; we know of it chiefly from the sensation it caused in distant places—such as is reported

[1] Olympius. *Ep.*, xcvi, xcvii.
[2] The sixth book of Zosimus is incomplete. S. Austin, like other writers at a distance, only preserved such details as served his immediate purpose.

in the writings of S. Jerome. But many of the fugitives who escaped the slaughter and destruction took refuge in Africa,—a province which seemed for the time to be protected from the barbarian hordes; though it too had terrible days in store[1], it served to shelter the Italian refugees from immediate danger. And thus it came about that in S. Austin's diocese there were many, many exiles who had lost all but their lives; and while some were Christians who were able to thank God that they had escaped when so many had perished, there were not a few heathens among them who constantly maintained that Rome had perished because she had begun to follow the doctrine of Christ, that since she had forsaken her ancient gods, the gods had forsaken her and suffered her glory to perish.

It was under these circumstances that S. Austin was led to begin his book on the *City of God*. He insists that all the mitigations of the horror were due to Christian influence, and that the very men who blasphemed the name of Christ had themselves profited by the protection which it gave from earthly death. "Now in their ungrateful pride, and "ungodly madness, they stand against that Name (in per-"verseness of heart and to their punishment in eternal "darkness) to which they fled even with lying lips that "they might enjoy the light of this present world[2]."

As an argument against these heathen exiles it was fair to maintain that Christ had been their protector against temporal evil; but it was clear enough that the Christians too had suffered terribly. They lost all their possessions[3]: the extremity of famine destroyed them[4], and the dead were left

---

[1] From the invasion of the Vandals. See *Ep.* ccxxviii. (*Honorato*), in which he decides the principles which should determine a bishop on remaining with or leaving his flock in such troubled times.
[2] *De Civitate Dei*, I. i.
[3] *De Civitate Dei*, I. x. 1.
[4] *De Civitate Dei*, I. x. 4.

unburied[1]: others were led into captivity and suffered violence[2] that was worse than death itself. And yet with all this misery before his eyes, with the wail of it ringing in his ears[3], S. Austin did not lose his faith in the goodness of the God who had permitted it all. "Tell me now," he says[4], "in all this desolation what one thing did the Christians "endure that upon due consideration might not turn to "their edification?" "For as for temporal goods and evils, "God had intended them for the common use both of good "and bad; that the goods of this world should not be too "eagerly desired, when even the wicked are seen to partake "them; and that the evils of this world should not be too "cowardly avoided, wherewith the good are sometimes "visited....For neither do these temporal goods exalt a "good man, nor do the evil deject him....Whatever affliction "good and bad men suffer together in this life it doth not "prove the persons to be the same, because they jointly "endure like pains. For as under one flail the straw is "bruised and the ear cleansed, and as the lees and the oil "are not confused because they are both pressed in one press, "so likewise one and the same violence of affliction proves, "purifies and melts the good, and condemneth, wasteth "and casteth out the bad. And thus in one and the same "distress do the wicked offend God by hate and blasphemy, "and the good glorify Him by prayer and praise."

Starting thus from the personal experience of these terrible sufferings, he goes on to discuss the two explanations which were being currently given of that marvellous event—the fall of the city of Rome. To say as many did that the destruction of the city had come about because she had forsaken her gods was, he argued, absurd, for these

---

[1] *De Civitate Dei*, I. xii. 1.
[2] *De Civitate Dei*, I. xiv. xvi.
[3] *De Urbis Excidio*, 3.
[4] *De Civitate Dei*, I. ix. viii.

very gods had failed to protect her in old days: they were really powerless to avert any evil[1]. Rather was it the case that all this evil was permitted by God, so that in the course of His Providence, His great purpose might be accomplished, and the City of God might be established among men. And thus he turns away from the sorrows and misery that had come on his own generation to review God's dealings with His chosen people, and to use the clue thus furnished to unravel the intricate story of His dealings with the other races of men, with mankind as a whole. And so he sets before us a philosophy of History,—the continuous evolution of the Divine Purpose in human society: he contrasts the earthly polities which change and pass with the eternal City of God which is being manifested in the world: he shows how these two are intermingled, interacting now, but how different they are in their real nature: one is of the earth, centred only in earthly things, while the other, because it has its chief regard fixed on that which is Eternal, gives us the best rule for the things of time. The earthly city which aimed only at earthly prosperity failed to attain even that, while the Heavenly City, aiming at an Eternal Peace, supplies the best conditions for earthly good as well. It is in the hope of the final triumph of the City of God, that the course of the world becomes intelligible, for then we may see that the rise and fall of earthly empires, the glories of ancient civilisation, the sufferings of men in their ruin, have not been unmeaning or in vain; for they have served to prepare for the coming of the kingdom of God.

Thus it is that for S. Austin, faith in the Holy Catholic

[1] Si igitur Virgilius tales deos et victos dicit, et, ut vel victi quoquo modo evaderent, homini commendatos; quae dementia est existimare his tutoribus Romam sapienter fuisse commissam, et nisi eos amisisset, non potuisse vastari? Imo vero victos deos tanquam praesides ac defensores colere, quid est aliud quam tenere non numina bona, sed omnia mala. *De Civitate Dei*, I. iii.

Church serves to render History intelligible: this faith was the key of knowledge, for it gave the first philosophy of history worthy the name. His work was indeed a masterly argument on the pressing practical difficulty in his own diocese, but it was far more than this; and if to some of us the train of thought is commonplace and obvious, that is because the world in which we have been brought up has been permeated with such teaching as his. But to those who imagined that the affairs of men were swayed by the mere caprices of many gods, or subject to the inscrutable decrees of fate, this philosophy of History was by no means commonplace. And indeed if we examine it more carefully even now we shall be amply rewarded. We may find new reasons to admire S. Austin,—the discrimination he occasionally displays in the use of evidence[1], the marvellous power of combining many isolated facts into a connected system, even though here and there he puts forward opinions which are hard to reconcile with his general position. But we may find greater merits than these: we may turn from the grandest modern account of the evolution of human progress—turn from Hegel himself—to S. Austin and feel that the historical system of the ancient father is more perfect and complete; inasmuch as he had a clearer conception of the beginning, and a more definite perception of the final end[2] towards which the whole Creation moves.

There are other ways in which many of us may learn from him. We are so often ready to cherish a hope in the kingdom of God as something in the far future, and justify the troubles of the present by reference to this dim far-off event. Or if we think of the kingdom of God as in the present, evil world, we profess that we cannot discern it, that it is a spiritual reality invisible[3] to the human eye,

---

[1] Reinkens, *Die Geschichtsphilosophie des h. A.* 37.
[2] Reinkens, *Die Geschichtsphilosophie des h. A.* 40.
[3] " When in the Creed we profess to believe the Church, reference is

unperceivable by the human mind. But for S. Austin the kingdom of God was not a mere hope, but a present reality, not a mere name for a divine idea, but an institution, duly organised among men, subsisting from one generation to another; closely inter-connected with earthly rule[1], with definite guidance to give, and a definite part to take in all the affairs of actual life. To him the kingdom of God was an actual Polity, just as the Roman Empire was a Polity too: it was 'visible' in just the same way as the earthly State, for it was a real institution with definite organisation, with a recognised constitution, with a code of laws and means of enforcing them, with property for its uses, and officers to direct it.

Some of us may perhaps fancy that in the time of S. Austin it was easy enough to identify the divine ideal of the kingdom of God with the actual institution,—the Church throughout the world. In those early days of purity it may seem that there was no room for the dissensions which have marred the Church in our day, or the schisms which have severed so many from it. Which body of professing Christians is the true Church? one is often

---

made not only to the visible Church of which we are now treating, but also to all the elect of God, including in the number even those who have departed this life. And, accordingly, the word used is 'believe,' because oftentimes no difference can be observed between the children of God and the profane, between His proper flock and the untamed herd....Hence, regard must be had both to the secret election and to the internal calling of God, because He alone 'knoweth them that are His'; and as Paul expresses it, holds them as it were enclosed under His seal, although, at the same time, they wear His insignia, and are thus distinguished from the reprobate. But as they are a small and despised number, concealed in an immense crowd, like a few grains of wheat buried among a heap of chaff, to God alone must be left the knowledge of His Church, of which His secret election forms the foundation." Calvin, *Institutes*, IV. i. 2.

[1] On S. Austin's political teaching compare Dubief, *Essai sur les idées politiques de Saint Augustin* (1859): also Excursus G, § 6, p. 192.

asked, or if we are unwilling to 'unchurch'[1] any set of professing Christians, how can we discern a unity in the Church now? But if we suppose that this difficulty did not occur in the fourth and fifth centuries—that the Church throughout the world was then one, undisturbed by dissension, unrent by schism—we shall do well to consider the times of S. Austin and the difficulties with which he had to contend in his own diocese. The Donatists in his day held aloof from communion with the Church throughout the

[1] One may notice in passing that those who deny the name of "Church" to any of the protestant sects, are not in any way guilty of intolerance, since they are perfectly willing to admit of the members of these bodies what they claim for themselves. The Independent who denies that there is a visible Catholic and Apostolic Church, and applies the word either to the invisible aggregate of the elect, or to his own congregation, can hardly be hurt when those who do believe in a visible Catholic and Apostolic Church decline to assert that his congregation is a part of that body the very existence of which he himself denies. So too, according to Zwinglian doctrine, the Lord's Supper offers an opportunity for self-recollectedness and quiet thought about our Lord's death. That an opportunity for the exercise of such pious dispositions is good and profitable can never be denied. But there are those who treasure the faith that the Sacrament of the Lord's Body and Blood is more than this, that the benefit accrues through That which is divinely bestowed, not merely in the quickened fervency of our own thoughts. This is not one of the points on which Calvinism departs from the Augustinian doctrine. Edward Irving, in the preface to his edition of the Scotch Articles of 1560, writes on the fifth of them, "It was this article which delivered me from the infidelity of evangelicalism, which denies any gift of God either in the work of Christ, or in the sacraments, or anywhere, until we experience it to be within ourselves, making God a mere promiser, until we become receivers; making His bounty and beneficence nought but words, till we make it reality by accepting thereof; in one word making religion only subjective in the believer, and not elective in God,—objective in Christ, in order that it may be subjective in the believer; a religion of moods, and not of purposes and facts; having its reality in the creature, its proposal of reality only in God." (*Confessions of Faith*, 1831, p. xcix.) Those who treasure a faith in the Sacraments are not necessarily arrogant, because they are dissatisfied with Zwinglian doctrine, and deny that the rites which embody it are an adequate fulfilling of our Lord's dying command.

world; they professed to enforce a stricter sort of Church discipline than that which was elsewhere current, and to attach more importance to personal holiness,—while some of them certainly showed a vehement earnestness about matters of religion. And S. Austin never denied that their Christian teaching, their Christian ordinances were valid as means of grace for the soul[1]. He thus was confronted with the same difficulty as we find to-day, in the real Christian faith of many, who are yet organised into distinct and separate and it may be rival bodies of worshippers.

And his treatment of this real difficulty may prove instructive now: he does not deny the efficacy of Christian teaching or Christian ordinances for personal salvation, but he notes whence and how the efficacy of these ordinances has been derived: the sectaries had indeed cut themselves off from the full enjoyment of Church life, but in so far as they retained Gospel truth, or sacramental privileges, they were to just this extent partakers in the life of the One Church. "There is one Church which alone is called "Catholic, and whenever it finds any element of itself, in "these communions of different bodies which are separate "from itself, it is by means of this element so found that "the Church regenerates and not the separated communion. "It is certainly not their separation which regenerates but "that element which they have received from the Church. "...The regeneration, then, in each case proceeds from the "Church, and from the retention of its sacraments, for from "them alone can such regeneration proceed,—although not "all who are thus regenerate, belong to that unity which "shall save those who persevere even to the end. Nor "again are they alone outside that unity who are openly "guilty of the manifest sacrilege of schism, but also those

[1] *De Baptismo*, I. 22.

"who, being outwardly joined to its unity, are yet separated "by a life of sin[1]."

The last sentence shows that it was not only through schism that the Church Life of the Fifth Century fell short of the ideal: persecution had not always served to purify. It had sometimes helped to relax the discipline, or to disorganise the government of the Church; and when the days of trial were over it sometimes happened that numbers of heathen were attracted to seek baptism, and were admitted to membership before they were fully instructed, or while they were still inclined to retain immoral habits and superstitious practices. The Church of the Fifth Century was not united, and it was not pure: many of its members were a disgrace to their profession, their lives were an open disavowal of their baptismal promises: and if any of us cherish the fancy that the Early Church was perfectly pure, we may be as completely disillusioned by reading the letters of S. Austin as by studying those of S. Paul. For from the first Christ's kingdom has been in the world, has been composed of men who are still struggling with sin, not of saints wholly free from its power: and from the first Christ's Church has been torn with dissension and rent with schism: and it has ever been by faith, not by sight, that men have recognised that the Church though in the world is not of it; it is through faith they have learned that though her children err and wander she yet is the pillar and ground of the truth; by faith they have come to know that through the things of nature and here in time she exercises an influence which is supernatural and eternal.

[1] *De Baptismo*, I. 14. Compare also 23. Si ergo potest dare aliquid quia aliquid habet, manifestum est posse dare hæreticos Baptismum, quia cum ab Ecclesia recedunt, habent lavacri Sacramentum quod ibi acceperant: nam redeuntes non recipiunt, quia non amiserant cum recesserunt. *De Bapt.* VII. 57.

II. THE DONATIST CONTROVERSY.

S. Austin's doctrine on all matters of Church organisation and Church life comes out most clearly not in the *City of God*, but in the controversy with the Donatists. The schism was no new thing like the teaching of Pelagius, for it had lasted for eighty years before S. Austin was ordained at Hippo, and it necessarily engaged his attention during the whole of his ministry: but his chief treatises on the subject appeared soon after his consecration. Controversial treatises however were not the only nor indeed the chief means by which he exposed the evil of the schism: it was only by his writings that he could reach the distant cities where Pelagius was diffusing his doctrine: but the Donatists were close at hand: they were not unwilling to listen to his discourses from the pulpit. The Manichæans had been met and confuted in public discussion, and it was by his preaching that S. Austin produced the greatest effect upon the schismatics[1]. They came to listen to his words, and were often deeply impressed with the power of his pleading for unity.

There were two points on which he dwelt; not only does

---

[1] Bindemann, III. 198. A few remarks on preaching by such a master of the art are worth quoting.

Sed quod ad tuam proprie considerationem pertinet, nolim te moveri ex eo quod saepe tibi abjectum sermonem fastidiosumque habere visus es. Fieri enim potest ut ei quem instruebas non ita sit visum, sed quia tu aliquid melius audiri desiderabas, eo tibi quod dicebas videretur indignum auribus aliorum. Nam et mihi prope semper sermo meus displicet. Melioris enim avidus sum, quo saepe fruor interius, antequam cum explicare verbis sonantibus coepero: quod ubi minus quam mihi notus est evaluero, contristor linguam meam cordi meo non potuisse sufficere. Totum enim quod intelligo, volo ut qui me audit intelligat; et sentio me non ita loqui, ut hoc efficiam: maxime quia ille intellectus quasi rapida coruscatione perfundit animum; illa autem locutio tarda et longa est, longeque dissimilis. *De Cat. Rud.* 3.

he show that they had, by their separation, broken the true unity of the Church, but he proves that they had departed from the ordinary custom of the Church by the practice on which they insisted in regard to Baptism[1]. If the Church existed before this schism, and "had not perished through a "breach of continuity, but was on the contrary holding its "ground and receiving increase, surely it is the safest plan to "abide by this same custom which then embraced good and "bad alike in unity[2]." If the Church before that schism were contaminated and unworthy, whence had the schismatic bishop made his appearance, "from what land did he spring? "or from what sea did he emerge? or from what sky did he "fall?" There was a continuity in the life of the Church, while the innovators had broken with the past, and were condemning their own fathers in Christ.

And this leads naturally to his main point. The schismatics were so self-opinionated: they had struck out their own line, that was a trifling thing, but they were so enamoured of their own opinions that they separated themselves from all who would not accept their way of thinking. It was in this respect that they differed from S. Cyprian— the renowned prelate under whose name they sought to shelter themselves. He held their view it is true, but yet "his pious humility in guarding the peace of the Church "was most noticeable." For when a bishop of so "important "a church, himself a man of so great merit and virtue, "endowed with such excellence of heart and power of elo- "quence, entertained an opinion about baptism different "from that which was to be confirmed by a more diligent "searching into the truth, though many of his colleagues

---

[1] Verumtamen quae soleret esse Ecclesiae consuetudo, satis idem Cyprianus ostendit, qui ait, in praeteritum de haeresi ad Ecclesiam venientes sine Baptismo admissos. *De Baptismo*, III. 7. Compare also s. 9, 10, 11, 12.

[2] *De Baptismo*, III. 3.

"held what was not yet made manifest by authority but
"was sanctioned by the past custom of the Church, and
"afterwards embraced by the whole Catholic world, he did
"not sever himself, by refusal of communion, from the
"others who thought differently, and indeed never ceased
"to urge on the others that they should forbear one an-
"other in love, endeavouring to keep the unity of the Spirit
"in the bond of peace[1]." Even then if they were of the
same opinion as Cyprian, their self-opinionated conduct
was condemned by his humility and charity.

The very nature of the point on which the whole controversy turned shows that error had made a deep mark
on the Church life of the Fourth Century. All agreed that
in Baptism men received forgiveness of sins and became
citizens of the kingdom of Heaven,—but could it be said
that Baptism by heretics was efficacious? was it really valid?
To some of us here the question may appear to be of greater
interest when we remember that it was a very anxious personal question with Frederick Maurice. He had been baptized as an infant by his father, who was a Unitarian minister,
but in later life he determined to seek re-baptism[2], thus it
would appear following the opinion of Cyprian and rejecting
the doctrine of S. Austin. The Donatists argued that right
belief and true faith on the part of the priest was a necessary condition, and that, without it, baptism had no efficacy.
They therefore insisted on re-baptizing those who had received the rite at the hands of heretics, and emphasised in
this practical form their conviction that baptism by heretics
was no baptism at all.

Put in its most general form the question was this—is
the worthiness of the minister, the rightness of his belief
and the purity of his life, an essential condition without

---

[1] *De Baptismo*, I. 28.

[2] *Life of F. D. Maurice*, I. 122. The precise reasons for this step are not quite clear though of course the two cases are not identical.

which Baptism is not valid? To this S. Austin answers with an emphatic No, which is re-echoed in our xxvith Article. "The baptism of Christ consecrated by the words of the "Gospel is necessarily holy, however polluted and unclean "its ministers may be: because its inherent sanctity cannot "be polluted, and its divine excellence abides in the sacra- "ment whether to the salvation of those who use it aright "or to the destruction of those who use it wrong....If we "turn our thoughts to the visible materials themselves, "which are to us the medium of the sacraments, everyone "must know that they admit of corruption. But if we "think on that which they convey to us, who can fail to see "that it is incorruptible, however much the men through "whose ministry it is conveyed are either being rewarded "or punished for the character of their lives?[1]" The effect of Christ's ordinance is not taken away by their wickedness[2]; and who that remembers how Moses and Isaiah protested their own unworthiness to bear a message from God, and how S. Peter felt his own sinfulness and shrank from the presence of his Lord, shall dare to say that the ministers of Christ's Church can ever be personally worthy to exercise their high vocation?

III. THE MEANS OF GRACE.

Perhaps however it may be more instructive for us to dwell on the point on which the disputants were agreed, on which the whole Church was at one and which had been held from time immemorial, as to the benefit which was bestowed in baptism when valid, rather than to linger on the controverted point, as to the primary conditions under which baptism was valid.

---

[1] *De Baptismo*, III. 15.
[2] Article XXVI.

In Baptism, God bestows forgiveness of sins[1]: the sacrament does not constitute a fully formed religious life—it does not take the place of repentance, though repentance is easier to him who realises the meaning of Baptism: it has no magic power of instantaneously creating a well-instructed fully-disciplined Christian[2]. "Certainly this "renewal does not take place in the single moment of "conversion itself, as that renewal in baptism takes place "by the remission of all sins; for not one, be it ever so "small, remains unremitted. But as it is one thing to be "free from fever and another to grow strong again from "the infirmity which the fever produced, and again one "thing to pluck out of the body a weapon thrust into it "and another to heal the wound thereby made by a pro-"sperous cure, so the first care is to remove the cause of "infirmity, and that is wrought by the forgiving of all sins: "but the second care is to heal the infirmity itself, and this "takes place gradually by making progress in the renewal

---

[1] Ac per hoc non solum peccata omnia, quorum nunc remissio fit in Baptismo, quæ reos faciunt, dum desideriis vitiosis consentitur atque peccatur ; verum etiam ipsa desideria vitiosa, quibus si non consentitur, nullus peccati reatus contrahitur, quæ non in ista, sed in alia vita nulla erunt, eodem lavacro Baptismatis universa purgantur. *De Pec. Or.* 44.

[2] Ex quo itaque sumus adhuc filii hujus sæculi, exterior homo noster corrumpitur, ex hoc et hujus sæculi filii generantur, nec filii Dei nisi regenerentur fiunt : sed ex quo sumus filii Dei, interior de die in diem renovatur. Quamvis et ipse exterior per lavacrum regenerationis sanctificatus sit, et spem futuræ incorruptionis acceperit, propter quod et templum Dei merito dicitur: *Corpora vestra*, inquit Apostolus, *templum in vobis Spiritus sancti est, quem habetis a Deo: et non estis vestri; empti enim estis pretio magno. Glorificate ergo et portate Deum in corpore vestro.* Hoc totum non solum propter præsentem sanctificationem, sed maxime propter illam spem dictum est, de qua idem alio loco dicit: *Sed et nos ipsi primitias Spiritus habentes, et ipsi in nobismetipsis ingemiscimus, adoptionem exspectantes, redemptionem corporis nostri.* Si ergo redemptio corporis nostri, secundum Apostolum, exspectatur; profecto quod exspectatur, adhuc speratur, nondum tenetur. *De Nuptiis et Concup.* I. 20.

See also *De Pec. Mer.* I. 39, II. 45 : compare Dorner *Augustinus*, 198.

"of the image, which two things are plainly shown in the "psalm where we read *Who forgiveth all thine iniquities*, "which takes place in Baptism, and then follows, *and heal-* "*eth all thine infirmities*, and this takes place by daily "additions, while this image is being renewed[1]."

It is true that God is the Father of all men, but this relationship which has its ground in God's great love does not really hold good as effective and operative unless the man knows of it. A relationship cannot exist with one term only: so long as by the depravity of his nature, man is blinded to God's Love, it does not exist for him. And hence the evidence of that Love declared in Baptism constitutes the relationship for him: it is the Divine message of love specially declared to him and none other, by sign and word; to eye and ear the comforting assurance is given. It is hard for the human heart to rest on general declarations of the love of God—to believe that Love extends to such a sinner as he feels himself to be, and that the message of salvation is for him. But Baptism has given this assurance to each individual person: he may have been neglected in his early years and grown up in ignorance of God, but he is the child of God, the love has been extended to him.

But besides this, Baptism makes us members of Christ, parts of His body the Church: the little child has been regenerated; he is not merely an earthly being with needs that must be satisfied and ambitions to be fulfilled; he has a real part in a higher, better life. Besides the sense of earthly ties of father and mother and home, there is awakened a gradual consciousness of the deeper ties in which he too has a part; vaguely and dimly they may be understood it is true, but none the less they may be felt as real. The conscious sense may come to the child in earliest years that God is a Father, that he himself is that Father's

[1] *De Trin.* xiv. 23.

child; he may come to know that the Church is an army, and that he himself is a soldier who marches with the rest; he may come to have the hope of a Blessed Life which shall be his when Death shall have laid him cold and still. And thus the child need never think of himself as merely earthly, with merely an earthly life, and merely an earthly home. His mind as it awakens, and as he comes to realise what he is, may begin to understand that he has, in his Baptism, become something more than he appears.

While S. Austin did not hold, as the Donatists did, that the worthiness of the minister was so essential that, without it the Divine power was inoperative, he did recognise that there are other conditions which do limit the operation of God's grace.

(*a*) It is not every heart that is reached by the Grace of God. The knowledge of God's Love is given through human lips, the assurance of it is conveyed by human hands, and those to whom that Love remains unknown, cannot be touched by it: it is hid from them. The knowledge of the Lord shall cover the earth as the waters cover the sea, but it is through human agencies that the knowledge is spread, and if those to whom that charge is committed are slothful and listless there must be many who remain in ignorance of the salvation that has appeared. God has not shed this light miraculously on all; He has committed the torch to human hands that they may bear it to the ends of the earth.

It is at this point that we may see most clearly the nature of S. Austin's doctrine of Predestination. God who foresees all things sees also that there are some who never receive the message of grace, and some to whom it is brought. He has provided the means of salvation, He foresees how far these shall be rendered accessible to any generation, how far each man shall avail himself of them, and thus there are some who are predestined to salvation since God knows from the first that they will work out their own salvation with fear and trembling. The effort to preach the Gospel is a real effort, the struggle to persevere is a real struggle, not the mere rehearsing of a decision taken before the world was. It is because God foresees what man will do, that He predestines; and thus it is by the use of the means of grace that human beings accomplish the destiny which He has foreseen[1]. The doctrine of Calvin however by ignoring the distinction between foreknowledge and predetermining seems to take all reality out of the ordinances of Christian Life: why should I listen to preaching if I am predestined to damnation? why should I seek to discipline my body or to seek God in prayer if I am predestined to salvation? It is thus that the doctrine of Predestination may give an excuse for Antinomianism, if it be regarded as an arbitrary decree, not a foreknowledge which has its ground in the divine prevision of the actual occurrences in time. It is because S. Austin holds so firmly to the real efficacy of the sacraments as means of accomplishing God's Purpose of Love towards the world that he

[1] Haec est praedestinatio sanctorum, nihil aliud : praescientia scilicet, et praeparatio beneficiorum Dei, quibus certissime liberantur, quicumque liberantur. *De Dono Persev.* 35.
Electi sunt itaque ante mundi constitutionem ea praedestinatione, in qua Deus sua futura facta praescivit : electi sunt autem de mundo ea vocatione, qua Deus, id quod praedestinavit, implevit. *De Praedest. Sanct.* 34.
The prescience here spoken of is not a prescience of human deserts, but of the divine operation through the instituted means. He thus even in his latest writings adheres to the distinction between prescience and predetermination, and guards against the appearance of anything arbitrary in what God does. Thus it may be said that God's purpose is to win a willing service from man, and that to this *end*, He has established certain *means:* in regard to the whole world we may recognise *why* this is His Will (see page 90, note 4). In regard to individuals we may recognise that He foresees *how* the ordained means operate. From this point of view there is no *arbitrariness* in the bestowal of grace on one and not on another.

does not regard predestination as a mere arbitrary decree, but as prescience of the actual course of the ministration of divine grace through a defective human agency.

(*b*) Again, there is another limit to the operation of God's Grace: not only in the energy and earnestness of those to whom the ministry is committed, but in the fact that some hearts are more hardened than others, not all are equally ready to enter the kingdom of God, or willing to live as its citizens. Inherited dispositions and deeply-rooted habits, if nothing else, make them to differ as subjects for the operation of God's Grace. This was the point which Pelagianism ignored: insisting as it did on the indifference of the human will, its perfect ability to choose this or that, to be good by its own apprehension of the Divine truth manifested to it, it ignored the truth that man is in bondage to sin: that he must be divinely set free from that bondage by Divine forgiveness, that he must be kept free from that bondage by partaking of the strength of Christ, or he cannot choose his true good, he cannot make a start on the path of life. From this it necessarily follows that Pelagianism is inclined to overvalue preaching as the most important means of grace[1], since it sets before the man good and evil and leaves it to him to choose on the representation set before him.

(*c*) But those who feel that they were not thus free to choose, that it was because Christ came to the world that the world was enabled to turn to God, because they were brought to Christ that He blessed them, will have no pride in the saintliest life, in the best work for God: they will recognise with S. Paul that it all comes from the Grace of God; that it is through God's purpose of Love that they have attained any measure of good: they will thank the goodness and the grace which have smiled on their birth, and thus the meditation on this Divine power may save us

[1] *De Gratia Christi*, 45.

from the spiritual pride of fancying we have done aught for ourselves[1].

Or if we seem to be falling away from God, if we feel that we have turned from Him and grieved His Spirit, and the terrible thought haunts us that He has not predestined us to life, let us lay firm hold of the knowledge that He has given grace, that He has called us in His providence and by the ministry of the word and sacraments: that if we fall from Him it is not because of His decree, but because of the sloth and negligence which He foresaw in us, that we would not come to Him for Life. He has forgiven our sins, He has called us to membership in His Church; He will give His Holy Spirit to them that ask Him. We may conquer our sloth and negligence if we will use the means of life He has provided. Let us not dare to lay the blame of our own backwardness on Him. We need not fear that any decree of His loving heart is holding us back from Him.

Perhaps the whole doctrine of the means of grace may come into clearer light, if we try to note one or two points which distinguish S. Austin's doctrine from that of more recent schools of thought.

(*a*) The sacraments are the means of grace but after all only means. Baptism does not restore the primæval condition of those who have not sinned[2], but the grace conveyed through it delivers from the power of sin, enlightens the eye and strengthens the resolution, while it removes the burden of guilt. Precious as we may find them to be they are only the means of grace, not things which by their mere operation deliver from evil. In so far as any have come to think of the sacraments as magical means, committed to human hands, of turning to good and delivering from evil, they have departed from the doctrine of S. Austin: they go to the channels through which God's

---

[1] Article XVII. See also Excursus G, § 3, p. 182.
[2] See p. 124, note 2.

Love may reach us most fully, and mistake them for God's Love itself. Thus to exalt the sacraments, and the human agency in administering or receiving them, may lead to many grievous errors: but it is enough for us to note in passing that it lends itself to the entry of Pelagianism, under a new and more subtle form.

(*b*) Farther, the sacraments are not the sole means of grace, they are the divinely appointed means, the means by which God's Grace may most easily reach the human heart, the means by which God's Love may most fully embrace it, but they are not the sole means. For just because God's Love works so powerfully through them,—through water and bread and wine,—we may know that it can work through things of sense, that all that He has created and made may have a sacramental Power, if we can perceive Him in it. The stream of God's Love wells forth to the world and overflows the channels He has provided for it: on hearing the word the grace of Repentance is given to many, and the Faith which comes through hearing. The hearts of those who are strangers to God's revelation of Himself may yet receive some message from Him, for the centurion Cornelius was devout and earnest, and his faithful struggle was rewarded by full Christian privileges[1].

It was the full recognition of this truth which gave their power to Whitfield[2], the followers of the Wesleys, and to all

---

[1] Neque enim et Cornelii gentilis hominis orationes non sunt exauditæ, aut eleemosynæ non sunt acceptæ: imo et angelum ad se mitti, et missum meruit intueri, per quem posset utique sine hominis alicujus accessu cuncta necessaria discere. Sed quoniam quidquid boni in orationibus et eleemosynis habebat, prodesse illi non poterat, nisi per vinculum christianæ societatis et pacis incorporaretur Ecclesiæ; jubetur mittere ad Petrum, et per illum discit Christum; per illum etiam baptizatus, christiano populo consortio quoque communionis adjungitur, cui sola bonorum operum similitudine jungebatur. *De Bapt.* I. 10.

[2] Sermon on *The Nature and Necessity of the New Birth in Christ Jesus*, preached in S. Mary, Redcliffe, 1738. John Wesley's own

who since their day have spoken of conversion as the true beginning of the Christian life. They have felt and known the power of God in converting the hearts of those who listened to His messages though they had never been regenerated in Baptism, or, if baptized, had been brought up in total ignorance and neglect of their Christian privileges. They have seen that Baptism did not create Christian habits of life, and they have thus been apt to prove inattentive to the importance of the sacraments as real means of grace. But while we may fully recognise the vast importance of the truth they hold so dear,— a truth which had perhaps been suffered to fall into neglect,—a truth which must be the foundation of all missionary effort and the fuller recognition of which has called forth unexampled missionary energy—we may yet note that it is but a part of the truth about the manifestation of God's Love to the world, and that if we treat it as the sole truth we may fall into dangerous modes of thought, and serious errors of life.

(i) For by laying stress on this special mode of the manifestation of God's Love—on a sudden awakening to

teaching was of an entirely different type and harmonised with that of S. Austin. "By baptism we who were 'by nature children of wrath' are made the children of God. And this regeneration which our Church in so many places ascribes to baptism is more than barely being admitted into the church though commonly connected therewith; being grafted into the Body of Christ's church, we are made the children of God by adoption and grace. This is grounded on the plain words of our Lord: 'Except a man be born again of water and of the Spirit, he cannot enter into the kingdom of God' (John iii. 5). By water then, as a means, the water of baptism we are regenerated or born again, whence it is also called by the Apostle, 'the washing of regeneration.' Our Church therefore ascribes no greater virtue to Baptism than Christ Himself has done. Nor does she ascribe it to the outward washing, but to the inward grace, which, added thereto, makes it a sacrament. Herein a principle of grace is infused, which will not be wholly taken away, unless we quench the Holy Spirit of God by long-continued wickedness." *A Treatise on Baptism. Works* (1836) x. 184.

the sense of sin, or a conscious realising of complete deliverance from its guilt and power—we are apt to frame to ourselves a misleading thought of God. To look for His chief manifestations of Himself only in special times of excitement, to see His power only in strange and unwonted occurrences, to find an answer to prayer only in unexpected events. But it has been by constant and daily communing with God, that His saints have come most truly to abide in Him; they have seen His hand in all the events of life, in all the course of His providence, in all the order of His Universe; they have found an answer to their cry for strength to bear His Will when the cup was not taken away, and the adversary beset them still. It is indeed a terrible thing if we come to think of God's grace and love and purpose as only given in exceptional ways, and never advance to realise that it embraces and suffuses the whole of human life at all times, not only at every time of need.

(ii) And just because there is this danger of a false theology, there is a danger too of inattention to the use of these means by which God strengthens His life within us. The prayers and alms of Cornelius were accepted and blessed, for God brought him within the fold of the Church, where he might taste more fully of the grace of God. It is indeed a terrible error if any of us shall be satisfied with having known the love of God, with having tasted of the powers of the world to come, and shall undervalue the means by which that Power may free our wills from weakness and form in us a fuller knowledge of God[1].

(iii) And in such teaching S. Austin would once more have detected the taint of Pelagianism. He would have seen that it tended to the overvaluing of preaching—of effective oratory, and touching appeals, and the personal power of the speaker as a man,—not as the mere mouthpiece for the utterance of a Divine message. In so far as

[1] On S. Austin's doctrine of the Eucharist see Excursus G, § 9, p. 198 f.

we come to trusting to the power of the preacher to stir the emotions, we begin to lose our firm hold of the truth that it is only God Who can touch the heart. Or again, if we venture to neglect the Divine offers of strength and grace, if we are so satisfied that our life is a true life given by God, that we are not careful to use those means whereby it may grow, we may come to trust to our own experience, or the depth of our feelings, or the fervency of our utterances, to ourselves, and not to Him.

(c) It is perhaps unnecessary to add that S. Austin would have strongly repudiated the doctrine which found its fullest expression in the usages of the Society of Friends, that the sacraments have no efficacy and may be ignored—and that God works directly in the human heart without the intervention of any means. For it seems as if the Omnipotent did indeed always work in this world by means, even if we cannot always detect the means through which He works,—through which He clears the eye for a brighter vision of Himself. He has Himself instituted the means of grace which He is ever ready to bless; and those who choose to disdain what He has appointed do not thereby escape the necessity of using means, they are only compelled to institute new means of grace for themselves, whether it be the sitting still in silence of the Quakers, or the violent excitement of the Shakers' dancing. It is true that there may be an excuse for such self-willed devotion, in the superstition which lurks in all our hearts, and treats the preaching of the word or the administration of the sacraments as though they could bestow goodness, not as the means by which God gives His grace. But if there is danger of self-deception in thus misusing the means of grace, there is still deeper danger of self-deception in neglecting them altogether. Those who claim to live in the Spirit and who yet forsake the assembling of themselves together and reject bodily self-discipline, may fall away unwittingly, "as the snake moves," into a strange carelessness about the things of God. For a religion that is thus spiritual, just because it has its hold merely on the spirit, may fade away and disappear without any noticeable signs of decline to arrest attention and awaken vigilance.

The importance which S. Austin attaches to the means of grace has prevented him from falling into the difficulties which have beset later writers. If the Divine life is formed in the human heart by the mere direct action of God's Spirit, then the election of those who are to be saved does not depend on the energy with which men work for God, foreseen by His wisdom, but is the immediate result of His own decree, a decree which we can only characterise as arbitrary. Here once more we find that the difficulties arise from thinking of God's Will, apart from His Character: 'election' comes to be the bare decision of a will which is depicted as merely capricious, as having no intelligible ground of determination. As too there is no outward sign by which those who are thus elected can be distinguished from others, the Church of God can no longer be conceived, as the body of Christ, apparent and working in the world, bearing His name though unworthily, but as a band of individuals with no definite marks of fellowship, unknown and unrecognisable by all but God alone. And apart from all the danger which may ensue from neglecting the discipline of mind and body that S. Austin prized, those who rely on the direct action of God's love on the human soul, or on His more powerful aid through other means, can attach little real import to the sacraments, and must either neglect them altogether, or retain them as harmless if empty ceremonies.

But any of us who feel how weak after all is our faith in God's Love extended through His sacraments, how little we realise the privileges of the Baptized, how dimly we discern the Lord's Body, will have little heart to try and measure the distance which others have gone in disparaging the means of Grace. Some perhaps trust to God's omnipotent Love, constraining without limit; some dwell on His Omnipotent Will decreeing without grounds; and others on His all-powerful Spirit working without means. Let us then each beware how we come to reverence the mere abstraction of some one divine attribute, instead of the Living God, revealed to us in Jesus Christ and working in the world through definite ordinances by His Spirit. Let us pray that God, Who has given us grace by the confession of a true faith to acknowledge the glory of the Eternal Trinity, to keep us stedfast in that faith. Let us beware of ever resting satisfied with meagre thoughts of God, remembering how many have been turned away from seeking Him, because they could not really reverence One Who is said to be arbitrary, even though He be omnipotent. And if our lives have been darkened by a sense of this horror, and we would fain see God as He has revealed Himself, and not as men have described Him, let us go to the Bible, but not to the Bible only, lest we find there a mere echo of the discords in our own hearts. Let us turn too to the Fathers of the Church and see what Christianity was to them, let us take the Prayer-book and learn what Christ may be to us, and how He will meet us; above all, let us discipline our minds and bodies, let us offer ourselves, our souls and bodies to Him, as we kneel to plead the memorial of the one atoning sacrifice.

EXCURSUS A.

S. Austin and the Observation of Nature, pp. 10, 14, 59.

THERE are many allusions which enable us to see that S. Austin was keenly interested in the observation of nature, and attached great importance to empirical investigations. We may remark it even in the aptness of his illustrations,—such as that taken from the gliding of a snake (*De Trinitate*, XII. 16), the description of a cock-fight (*De Ordine*, I. 25), the olive and oleaster (*Ep.* cxciv. 44), and the nightingale's song (*De Ver. Rel.* 79). Throughout his writing one feels that all the pictures are true to nature and drawn by one who had a keen eye for what was happening around him.

But he was not a mere observer, he was inclined to speculate on the reasons of things. The cock-fight gives him a considerable fund for speculation; his difficulty about the oleaster is propounded to the husbandman; and in another passage (*De Civ. Dei*, XXI. vii. 2) he mentions a whole series of perplexities in regard to natural phenomena that had come under his own observation, as well as others of which he had been credibly informed.

The most interesting of his observations and remarks are those which are connected with animal life, and the relation of soul and body. In this respect one may notice especially the long discussion (*De Quantitate Animae*, 62—68) which arose from his seeing that a little reptile, which had been cut in two, continued to move, and to be sensitive in both the dismembered parts. He refers too to questions as to the memory of swallows in returning to their old nests, and bases a part of his argument in regard to the true nature of different human faculties upon these and similar facts (*Contra Ep. Manich.* 20). In another passage he gives us the facts from which he had gathered that fishes also were possessed of memory (*De Genes. ad Lit.* III. 12). Equally noteworthy are his remarks on the consciousness of an infant, and its interest in seeing a light (*De Trin.* XIV. 7), and again on the nature of vision (*De Trin.* XI. 4).

Though these psychological inquiries appear to have had a special attraction for him we have also interesting remarks on other phenomena as well: an empty jar is really full of air, and it has a considerable power of resistance (*De Anima et Orig. ejus*, IV. 18). The physical science of his day had comparatively little to do with observation and experiment, and he refers to it again and again with considerable and not undeserved scorn: but his whole attitude is not unlike that in which a modern might speak of the methods of fourth century physicists. He is specially scornful of the calculations of the magicians and astrologers. Adversus eos autem qui nunc appellantur mathematici, volentes actus nostros corporibus cœlestibus subdere, et nos vendere stellis, ipsumque pretium, quo vendimur, a nobis accipere, nihil verius et brevius dici potest, quam eos non respondere, nisi acceptis constellationibus. In constellationibus autem notari partes, quales trecentas sexaginta dicunt habere signiferum circulum: motum autem cœli per unam horam fieri in quindecim partibus, ut tanta mora quindecim partes oriantur, quantam tenet una hora. Quæ partes singulæ sexaginta minutas habere dicuntur. Minutas autem minutarum jam in constellationibus, de quibus futura prædicere se dicunt, non inveniunt; conceptus autem geminorum quoniam uno concubitu efficitur, attestantibus medicis, quorum disciplina multo est certior atque manifestior, tam parvo puncto temporis contingit, ut in duas minutas minutarum non tendatur. Unde ergo in geminis tanta diversitas actionum, et eventuum, et voluntatum, quos necesse est eamdem constellationem conceptionalem habere, et amborum unam constellationem dari mathematico, tanquam unius hominis? (*De Divers. Quæst. LXXXIII.* qu. xlv.). Ad hoc genus pertinent omnes etiam ligaturæ atque remedia, quæ medicorum quoque disciplina condemnat, sive in præcantationibus, sive in quibusdam notis quos characteres vocant, sive in quibusque rebus suspendendis atque illigandis, vel etiam aptandis quodammodo, non ad temperationem corporum, sed ad quasdam significationes aut occultas, aut etiam manifestas; quae mitiore nomine physica vocant, ut quasi non superstitione implicare, sed natura prodesse videantur: sicut sunt inaures in summo aurium singularum, aut de struthionum ossibus ansulae in digitis, aut cum tibi dicitur singultienti, ut dextera manu sinistrum pollicem teneas (*De Doctrina Christ.* II. 30). The superstition of the 'mathematicians' was on the one hand akin to mere fatalism, and repellent to one who was fully alive to the reality of human responsibility; and on the other hand ministered to an idle curiosity which was gratified by the marvels of spectacular exhibitions, and served no useful end[1] (*Conf.* X. 55).

There is indeed one speculation, which he condemns, which later days have completely established; but even in regard to the antipodes the position which he takes is genuinely scientific. He

[1] Ritter (*Geschichte*, VI. 200) quotes this passage without reference to its context, and argues that S. Austin was in the latter part of his life inclined to disparage mere secular studies. But it is clear that he is condemning inquiries which modern science also completely discards. In so far as the passage in *De Trin.* XIV. 3 depreciates knowledge, it clearly applies to these superstitions, as the whole Chapter argues for the prosecution of rational knowledge, in which the faithful were too often deficient. The remaining passage to which Ritter refers (*Enchiridion*, IX.), asserts that a knowledge of the things that concern his salvation suffices for the Christian man and that it is unnecessary for him to penetrate the mysteries of nature in regard to which students often differ, and about which they attain to opinion rather than rational knowledge. It is difficult to see any evidence here of a disparagement of scientific investigation, in the face of the evidence of his own continued interest, and the strong expressions he uses as to its value. Et quoniam de auctoritatis beneficentia, quantum in praesentia satis visum est, locuti sumus; videamus quatenus ratio possit progredi a visibilibus ad invisibilia, et a temporalibus ad aeterna conscendens. Non enim frustra et inaniter intueri oportet pulchritudinem coeli, ordinem siderum, candorem lucis, dierum et noctium vicissitudines, lunae menstrua curricula, anni quadrifariam temperationem, quadripartitis clementis congruentem, tantam vim seminum species numerosque gignentium, et omnia in suo genere modum proprium naturamque servantia. In quorum consideratione non vana et peritura curiositas exercenda est, sed gradus ad immortalia et semper manentia faciendus (*De Ver. Rel.* 52).

does not attempt to prejudge the empirical enquiry by Scriptural assertions: and in a matter of this kind we need pay far less attention to the results he obtained than to the steps by which he reached them. The real measure of the intelligence of a fourth century writer lies in the grounds on which he based his opinion not in the actual opinion itself. S. Austin did not believe in the existence of human beings at the antipodes,—not because he denied the rotundity of the earth, but because he denied that even if the earth were round it was necessarily inhabited by men, and because he regarded it as inconceivable that the descendants of the first pair should have travelled there. He holds that the Scriptural astronomy is confirmed, but he argues the question on empirical grounds, in exactly the same way as men might now discuss the existence of inhabitants in the moon, or in Jupiter[1]. His view in regard to the whole matter is stated at length in the treatise in which he discusses various branches of human knowledge and shows their bearing on the interpretation of Scripture. It brings out very clearly the nature

[1] He does assume that mankind sprang from a single pair as Scripture asserts. Quod vero et Antipodas esse fabulantur, id est, homines a contraria parte terræ, ubi sol oritur, quando occidit nobis, adversa pedibus nostris calcare vestigia, nulla ratione credendum est. Neque hoc ulla historica cognitione didicisse se affirmant, sed quasi ratiocinando conjectant, eo quod intra convexa cœli terra suspensa sit, eumdemque locum mundus habeat, et infimum, et medium: et ex hoc opinantur alteram terræ partem, quæ infra est, habitatione hominum carere non posse. Nec attendunt, etiamsi figura conglobata et rotunda mundus esse credatur, sive aliqua ratione monstretur: non tamen esse consequens, ut etiam ex illa parte ab aquarum congerie nuda sit terra: deinde etiamsi nuda sit, neque hoc statim necesse esse, ut homines habeat. Quoniam nullo modo Scriptura ista mentitur, quæ narratis præteritis facit fidem, eo quod ejus prædicta complentur: nimisque absurdum est, ut dicatur aliquos homines ex hac in illam partem, Oceani immensitate trajecta, navigare ac pervenire potuisse, ut etiam illic ex uno illo primo homine genus institueretur humanum. Quapropter inter illos tunc hominum populos, qui per septuaginta duas gentes et totidem linguas colliguntur fuisse divisi, quæramus, si possumus invenire illam in terris peregrinantem civitatem Dei, quæ usque ad diluvium arcamque perducta est, atque in filiis Noe per eorum benedictiones perseverasse monstratur, maxime in maximo, qui est appellatus Sem: quandoquidem Japheth ita benedictus est, ut in ejusdem fratris sui domibus habitaret. *Civ. Dei*, xvi. ix. Compare Plin. *Hist. Nat.* ii. 65. Lactantius, *Instit.* iii. 24.

of the science falsely so called against which he protested, and the value he attached to the genuine study of natural science[1], as well as to the masterpieces of classical literature[2].

[1] Siderum autem cognoscendorum non narratio, sed demonstratio est, quorum perpauca Scriptura commemorat. Sicut autem plurimis notus est lunæ cursus, qui etiam ad passionem Domini anniversarie celebrandam solemniter adhibetur; sic paucissimis cæterorum quoque siderum vel ortus, vel occasus, vel alia quælibet momenta sine ullo sunt errore notissima. Quæ per seipsam cognitio, quanquam superstitione non alliget, non multum tamen ac prope nihil adjuvat tractationem divinarum Scripturarum, et infructuosa intentione plus impedit; et quia familiaris est perniciosissimo errori fatua fata cantantium, commodius honestiusque contemnitur. Habet autem præter demonstrationem præsentium, etiam præteritorum narrationi simile aliquid, quod a præsenti positione, motuque siderum, et in præterita eorum vestigia regulariter licet recurrere. Habet etiam futurorum regulares conjecturas, non suspiciosas et ominosas, sed ratas et certas; non ut ex eis aliquid trahere in nostra facta et eventa tentemus, qualia genethliacorum deliramenta sunt, sed quantum ad ipsa pertinet sidera. Nam sicut is qui computat lunam, cum hodie inspexerit quota sit, et ante quotlibet annos quota fuerit, et post quotlibet annos quota futura sit potest dicere; sic de unoquoque siderum, qui ea perite computant, respondere consueverunt. De qua tota cognitione, quantum ad usum ejus attinet, quid mihi videretur aperui. *De Doct. Christ.* II. 46.

[2] Sed sive ita se habeat quod Varro retulit, sive non ita; nos tamen non propter superstitionem profanorum debemus musicam fugere, si quid inde utile ad intelligendas sanctas Scripturas rapere potuerimus; nec ad illorum theatricas nugas converti, si aliquid de citharis et de organis, quod ad spiritualia capienda valeat, disputemus. Neque enim et litteras discere non debuimus, quia earum repertorem dicunt esse Mercurium; aut quia justitiæ virtutique templa dedicarunt, et quæ corde gestanda sunt in lapidibus adorare maluerunt, propterea nobis justitia virtusque fugienda est: imo vero quisquis bonus verusque christianus est, Domini sui esse intelligat, ubicumque invenerit veritatem, quam confitens et agnoscens, etiam in Litteris sacris superstitiosa figmenta repudiet; doleatque homines atque caveat, qui cognoscentes Deum, non ut Deum glorificaverunt, aut gratias egerunt, sed evanuerunt in cogitationibus suis, et obscuratum est cor insipiens eorum: dicentes enim se esse sapientes, stulti facti sunt, et immutaverunt gloriam incorruptibilis Dei in similitudinem imaginis corruptibilis hominis, et volucrum, et quadrupedum, et serpentium. *De Doct. Christ.* II. 28.

EXCURSUS B.

S. Austin's influence in the Middle Ages. pp. 10, 35, 60.

1. Mode of testing it.
2. The system of Study.
3. Erigena on Reason and Authority.
4. Erigena on Prescience and Predestination.
5. Erigena on Eternal Punishment.
6. S. Anselm.
7. The decline of his influence.

1. It is unfortunate that no serious attempt has yet been made by students of scholastic philosophy to examine the precise nature of the influence which S. Austin exercised in the middle ages. I can only attempt to indicate one or two points which seem to show that both the extent and the value of the influence he exercised have commonly been underrated.

It has been too much the habit to treat the beginnings of literary effort in the ninth century as the real starting point from which the developments of mediaeval thought can be properly traced. But though a revival of learning becomes apparent then, we must go much earlier to find the spring in which the hidden stream really had its source. The schools of Charlemagne may mark the beginnings of Scholasticism[1], but the revived interest in study was not the immediate occasion of a fresh start in philosophical investigation: it does not mark a real turning point in the history of Thought. The whole range of study was dominated by the influence of the great bishop of Hippo, and the thinkers of the ninth and tenth centuries may be appropriately described as the school of S. Austin. That his name carried great weight has of course been abundantly recognised, and it would be idle to accumulate evidence on the point. But it would be worth while to put the question in another form and ask, How far did the early mediaeval writers consciously discard him, and

---

[1] Hauréau, *Histoire de la Phil. Scol.* I. 36.

strike out some original vein? How far does their positive teaching show the influence of any school of thought that is not congruent with his doctrine? It is no part of my purpose to attempt to answer this question fully, and it must suffice for the present to take one or two alleged cases of independence and examine them briefly.

2. There is no more difficult question in regard to early mediaeval studies than that as to the origin of the common division of the Arts and Sciences. It has been ascribed to S. Austin, but on mistaken grounds, for the *Dialectic* in which M. Barthélemy Saint-Hilaire traced it, was not from his pen. But for all that, without ascribing to him the first suggestion of this famous division, one may at least say that the founders of an educational system in the dark ages might well feel that the arrangement was in complete accordance with his views. Hauréau[1] dismisses the question of the Augustinian recognition of this distinction with the hasty discussion of a phrase[2] to which Brucker[3] had called attention, but it would have been worth while to examine the careful discussion of the different sciences which occupies the latter chapters of the second book *De Ordine*. Grammar, Dialectic and Rhetoric are treated of first of all: the author then proceeds to extol the higher sciences, which afterwards formed the Quadrivium. Music, Geometry, and Astronomy are treated in turn, and though Arithmetic is not enumerated with the others, it is by no means ignored in his discussion of liberal studies: for S. Austin it is the very type of intellectual knowledge, and as such was discussed in another portion of the same book, while at every turn stress is laid on the close connexion between numbers and each of the special branches of knowledge. Whether founded on it or not, the mediaeval scheme of education is in complete harmony with the Augustinian classification of knowledge.

3. Johannes Scotus Erigena is the most striking figure, the most learned and independent of all ninth century authors, and

---

[1] *Histoire de la Phil. Scol.* I. 22.
[2] Cum enim artes illae omnes liberales, partim ad usum vitae, partim ad cognitionem rerum contemplationemque discantur. *De Ordine*, II. 44.
[3] *Hist. Crit. Phil.* III. 957.

his relations to S. Austin will therefore well repay a brief examination in connexion with the special point before us. Modern writers have been inclined to bestow on him a somewhat indiscriminate praise. "C'était un penseur libre et original, celui qui osait dire : L'autorité est dérivée de la raison, nullement la raison de l'autorité[1]." But even here he was only following the suggestions thrown out by S. Austin, who was to almost the same extent un libre penseur du monde nouveau, and who gave us the phrase, Tempore auctoritas, re autem ratio prior est[2]. Erigena does indeed sometimes express the ideas which are common to both more tersely and forcibly, and sum up in a sentence the result of a paragraph of S. Austin's, but in the whole treatment of reason and authority there is comparatively little difference between the two.

Reuter[3] recognises the Augustinian influence on Erigena far more fully than most recent writers, but he singles out[4] one sentence as distinctly original. Vera enim auctoritas rectæ rationi non obsistit, neque recta ratio veræ auctoritati. Ambo siquidem ex uno fonte, divina videlicet sapientia, manare dubium non est[5]. But though there is nothing so epigrammatic in S. Austin's treatment of the subject, he really expressed the same opinion as to the complete harmony and similar origin of reason and authority.

Nulli autem dubium est gemino pondere nos impelli ad discendum, auctoritatis atque rationis. Mihi autem certum est usquam prorsus a Christi auctoritate discedere : non enim reperio valentiorem. Quod autem subtilissima ratione persequendum est; ita enim jam sum affectus, ut quid sit verum, non

[1] Rousselot. *Phil. dans le moyen âge*, I. 44.
[2] *De Ordine*, II. 26.
Unde igitur exordiar? ab auctoritate, an a ratione? Naturæ quidem ordo ita se habet, ut cum aliquid discimus, rationem præcedat auctoritas. Nam infirma ratio videri potest, quæ cum reddita fuerit, auctoritatem postea, per quam firmetur, assumit. Sed qnia caligantes hominum mentes consuetudine tenebrarum, quibus in nocte peccatorum vitiorumque velantur, perspicuitati sinceritatique rationis aspectum idoneum intendere nequeunt; saluberrime comparatum est, ut in lucem veritatis aciem titubantem veluti ramis humanitatis opacata inducat auctoritas. *De Moribus Eccl.* 3.
[3] *Geschichte der religiösen Aufklärung im Mittelalter*, I. 41 and 277, note 2.
[4] *Ibid.* 52.   [5] *De Divis. Naturæ*, I. 66 (Migne, CXXII. 511).

credendo solum, sed etiam intelligendo apprehendere impatienter desiderem ; apud Platonicos me interim quod sacris nostris non repugnet reperturum esse confido. *Contra Acad.* III. 43.

Duplex enim est via quam sequimur, cum rerum nos obscuritas movet ; aut rationem, aut certe auctoritatem. Philosophia rationem promittit, et vix paucissimos liberat : quos tamen non modo non contemnere illa mysteria, sed sola intelligere, ut intelligenda sunt, cogit. Nullumque aliud habet negotium, quæ vera, et, ut ita dicam, germana philosophia est, quam ut doceat quod sit omnium rerum principium sine principio, quantusque in eo maneat intellectus, quidve inde in nostram salutem sine ulla degeneratione manaverit : quem unum Deum omnipotentem cumque tripotentem, Patrem, et Filium, et Spiritum sanctum, docent veneranda mysteria, quæ fide sincera et inconcussa populos liberant. *De Ordine*, II. 16.

Quanquam pudet imbecillitatis, cum rationi roborandæ hominum auctoritas quæritur, cum ipsius rationis ac veritatis auctoritate, quæ profecto est omni homine melior, nihil deberet esse præstantius. *De Musica*, v. 10.

The sole point of difference appeared to arise when Erigena went further and not only proclaimed the harmony of true reason and true authority but the identity of religion and philosophy : and even for this he supported himself by a reference to S. Austin's *De Vera Religione*. For this view he was taken to task by Prudentius[1] and it need not now be discussed : it is sufficiently obvious, as S. Austin contends more than once, that the two are so far distinct that truth in the form of religious teaching may be apprehended by those who cannot grasp it in the form of philosophical discussions.

4. In regard to the vexed question of predestination, in which he followed S. Austin's *De Libero Arbitrio* very closely, there is one important divergence. As the Benedictine editors note[2], he taught that predestination and prescience were one and the same, thus ignoring the distinction examined above (p. 90, note 4). He reached this result in a somewhat curious way. He accepts

[1] In Maguin, *Veterum Auctorum*, I. *De Prædest. contra J. Scot.* 1.
[2] Migne, CXXII. 348.

from Dionysius the doctrine that all things exist in the divine mind, that things are, in so far as God thinks them; Divinus itaque animus nullum malum nullamque malitiam novit. Nam si nosset, substantialiter extitissent neque causa carerent. Jam vero et causa carent, ac per hoc in numero conditarum naturarum essentialiter non sunt, ideoque omnino divina alienantur notitia[1]. The unreality of evil is asserted in a new and more startling form.

Since then God cannot know evil men and angels, and the transgressors of divine law, He cannot design or think their increasing evil and punishment[2]; there can be no divine reprobation, but only predestination to life. His argument against Gotteschalk really turns on this point; that from the very constitution of the divine nature there cannot be a double, but only one true and sole divine predestination[3]. Condemnation thus occurs without divine design, because without divine knowledge. It is unnecessary to show that this is not an Augustinian doctrine: it really came from Greek writers, whose influence on Erigena was so strikingly marked[4].

5. There is one other point on which Erigena appears to break away from S. Austin altogether: he again follows Greek writers, and is commonly referred to as one who pronounced against the eternity of future punishment[5]. He did indeed differ from S. Austin in this matter, but not to the extent that has been generally asserted. The question was not as to the eternity but the materiality of future pain: in the work on *Predestination* (c. xi.) his language is somewhat undecided, though even here Prudentius saw that he argued for an undying feeling rather than an indestructible substance[6], and thus departed from the original sense of the passages which he quoted from S. Austin. In the

---

[1] *De Divis. Naturæ*, v. 27 (Migne, cxxii. 925).

[2] O miranda, imo dolenda cæcitas eorum qui e contrario intelligere nolunt, si quando in divina, seu humana legerint auctoritate, Deum præsciisse vel prædestinasse peccata, mortem, supplicia, quæ penitus nihil sunt, quia defectus sunt. *De Prædest.* xi. 5 (Migne, 396, 7).

[3] *De Prædestinatione*, cc. ii, iii, iv.

[4] Baur, *Die christliche Lehre von der Dreieinigkeit*, ii. 203, 263.

[5] R. L. Poole, *Illustrations of the History of Mediæval Thought*, 60, 71.

[6] Maguin, *Veterum Auctorum*, i. 545.

last book of the *De Divisione Naturæ*, however, the subject is treated much more explicitly. He discards entirely the idea of materiality in future punishment[1],—a point in regard to which S. Austin showed some hesitation, but was decided by his desire not to depart unnecessarily from the letter of Scripture. But Erigena does hold that the defect which sin introduces into the nature of men and angels will continue eternally. Differences will eternally subsist: all attain to paradise but not all to the enjoyment of the true life, which is Christ[2]. Thus there may be extreme differences among those who are together in the place of the dead.

Beati sunt, qui adyta intrant sapientiæ, quæ est Christus ;

---

[1] Hæc enim omnia tormentorum nomina figurate in sacra Scriptura posita sunt, sancto Ambrosio attestante, græcisque vocabulis, quæ, ut prædiximus, expressius informant, quid divina Scriptura inferni nomine insinuat. Ἀιδης quippe dicitur, hoc est, ut paulo superius expositum, absque deliciis, vel absque voluptatibus, vel insuavitas. Item λύπη vocatur cujus interpretatio est tristitia, vel mæror vel luctus. Ἄχος quoque solet appellari, hoc est desperationis gravitas, quæ demersas oppressasque malas cupiditates, egestate temporalium rerum, quas in hac vita intemperanter concupiverant, afflictas veluti in profundissimam quandam voraginem, inque vanarum phantasiarum rerum sensibilium caligines in quibus cruciantur, obruit, divinæque sententiæ incommutabili mole perpetualiter calcatas et irrevocabiliter contemptas. Quæ cunctæ significationes apud Græcos infernum cum omnibus suis suppliciis non esse localem vel temporalem vel sensibilem, seu in aliqua parte quattuor elementorum, quibus mundus iste constituitur, neque in toto ipsius constitutum, sed quiddam lugubre lacrimabileque, gravemque, desperationis plenum inevitabilemque carcerem, omniumque bonorum egestatem in phantasticis vanissimisque visionibus incunctanter pronunciant. *De Divis. Nat.* v. 36 (Migne 971).

[2] Aliud enim est in paradisum redire, aliud de ligno vitæ comedere. Legimus quippe, primum hominem, ad imaginem et similitudinem Dei factum, in paradiso positum fuisse, sed non legimus eum de ligno vitæ comedisse. Esus siquidem prohibiti ligni præoccupatus, dulcedine ligni vitæ est expulsus : futurum quippe erat ei de ligno vitæ edere, si divinis præceptis voluisset parere : feliciter tamen vixisset, etiam priusquam de ligno vitæ comederet, si absque mora, postquam creatus est, non peccaret. Ubi datur intelligi, quod tota nostra natura, quæ generaliter vocabulo hominis ad imaginem et similitudinem Dei facti significatur, in paradisum, hoc est, in pristinam conditionis suæ dignitatem reversura sit, in his autem solummodo, qui deificatione digni sunt, ligni vitæ fructum participabit. Ligni autem vitæ quod est Christus, fructus est beata vita, pax æterna in contemplatione veritatis quæ proprie dicitur deificatio. *De Divis. Nat.* v. 36 (Migne, 979).

qui accedunt in obscurissimas tenebras excellentissimæ lucis, in qua simul in causis suis vident omnia, ubi non locorum vel temporum intervalla bonos a malis, sed meritorum distantia segregat; non quantitas et pulchritudo corporum, sed honestas et magnitudo virtutum laudatur; non personarum, sed morum dignitas et nobilitas quæritur: una omnibus communis natura, diversa autem gratia; ubi omnes simul sunt, et simul non sunt, simul sunt similitudine substantiarum, simul non sunt dissimilitudine affectuum. Simul erant dives et Abraham, in spiritualibus substantiis, quas una eademque humana colligit et inseparabiliter jungit essentia, sed non simul erant per differentiam spiritualium qualitatum. Chasma magnum inter eos erat: Abraham quippe in æterna quiete gaudebat, dives in flumine inextinguibili lugebat: propterea vidit dives de longe Abraham. Quis verbis potest exprimere, quantum interstitii est inter lætitiam et tristitiam, etiam in hac vita, quanto magis in altera, in qua nulla tristitia sequetur justorum lætitiam, neque ulla lætitia sequetur impiorum tristitiam, divina sententia dignas singulis incommutabiliter attribuente retributiones! Et hoc est chasma magnum et impermeabilis hiatus, dividens inter præmia et supplicia. Dives tamen non de longe sed juxta ad Abraham loquebatur, ut intelligas, eum non natura segregatum fuisse ab Abraham, sed culpa. Una siquidem essentia jungit, quos meritum dissimile dividit. Paulo priusquam Dominus pateretur simul in uno cœnaculo Judas Iscariotes et Simon Petrus cum Christo cœnabant, sed unus juxta Christum, alter longe erat a Christo. Unus qui cum Christo intingebat manum in paropsidem, humanitatis Christi erat traditor, alter qui non legitur intinxisse manum cum Christo in paropsidem, divinitatis Christi erat contemplator; unus avarus vendidit hominem Deum, alter theologus cognovit Deum hominem, unus osculo corporis corpus tradidit, alter osculo mentis divinam mentem dilexit. Hoc autem dico, ut cognoscas, quod non locorum intervalla, sed meritorum qualitates faciunt hominem appropinquare Christo, aut ab eo elongari. Hinc datur intelligi, omnes homines unius ejusdemque naturæ, quæ in Christo redempta est omnique servitute, sub qua adhuc congemiscit et dolet, liberata, participes esse, et in ea unum omnes subsistere: meritorum vero qualitates et quantitates, hoc est, bonorum actuum malorumque differentias, quibus unusquisque in hac vita bene vixit adjutus Deo per gratiam, seu male desertus Deo per justitiam, longe a se invicem et multipliciter et in infinitum disparari, omnia autem hæc in illa una et amplissima domo ordinari et comprehendi, in qua respublica universitatis a Deo et in Deo conditæ per multas diversasque dispensatur mansiones, hoc est, meritorum et gratiarum ordinationes. *De Divis. Nat.* v. 36 (Migne 983).

This passage is quoted from the long discussion as to how far the doctrine of eternal punishment is consistent with that belief in the restoration of all things on which Erigena also strongly insists. Jam video undique me captum, nullamque rationem reperire, qua possim astruere, malitiam mortemque ac miseriam in humanitate aut in tota aut in aliqua parte ejus dominaturam perpetuoque permansuram, quoniam in Verbo Dei, quod eam totam in unitatem suæ substantiæ suscepit, universaliter et redempta et liberata est; ac per hoc rectæ ratiocinationis virtute superatus cogor fateri, totam humanitatem in omnibus eam participantibus liberandam, omnibusque malitiæ vinculis mortisque atque miseriæ absolvendam, quando in suas causas, quæ in suo Salvatore subsistunt, reversura est. *De Divis. Nat.* v. 27 (Migne 927). Those who assert that he gave up the doctrine of the eternity of punishment rely on this and similar passages; but apparently in Erigena's view *mors* and *miseria* were evil, but *tristitia* was not. There may be a godly sorrow; such sorrow is not an evil, and its continuance is according to his doctrine quite consistent with the restoration of all things. This doctrine is at least easy to grasp as compared with S. Austin's doctrine of the persisting harmony and perfection of the universe, both now, and in the future.

It is of course clear that he here departs from the doctrine of S. Austin; though he defends himself against the charge of doing so with ingenious special pleading[1]. On one other point also he discards him—as to the nature of humanity before the Fall[2]. But in neither instance can he be said to disregard the authority of this father, but only to try and reconcile his doctrine with that of S. Ambrose or S. Gregory in regard to points where they differed. The positive influence of S. Austin is apparent on almost

---

[1] *De Divis. Nat.* v. 37 (Migne 991).
[2] *De Divis. Nat.* IV. 14 (Migne 801).

every page, though recent commentators have failed to recognise it. The striking sentence, Clare perspicis Deum nullam creaturam, quam fecit, punire * * sed quod non fecit in omnibus punit¹, is ascribed by himself to Augustinian² influence, not as by Christlieb to that of Dionysius. The same writer is almost equally bold in claiming for Erigena³ an independent discovery of Descartes' doctrine of certainty, or S. Anselm's credo ut intelligam, when both are so frequently found in the writings of S. Austin.

6. The influence of S. Austin is perhaps most perfectly reflected in the writings of S. Anselm[4], though here again there are considerable differences in the form of expression. S. Austin wrote with a practical bearing, stating a principle and hurrying on to its application, almost regardless of the form of his argument, with interruptions and repetitions. But S. Anselm had to set himself to give oral instruction in its clearest form to the brethren of his order; and thus his treatment is careful and systematic throughout. We may remember too that the dialectic art was carefully studied in his time by a master, and we shall see at once that it was necessary for his purpose and in his day that the old truths should be presented in a new form. And one may readily admit that in many cases the old truths gained by being re-cast; if there is much interest in noticing the occasional character of S. Austin's writings there can be little doubt that his doctrine loses something in force and in clearness from the various modes of expression he adopted at different times and from the want of system in his treatment. S. Anselm was far more systematic in the mode of expression, but it is the old doctrine after all that reappears—the old doctrine in all its completeness. We have once more the union of scholastic and mystic lines of thought—the scholastic argument of the *Cur Deus Homo*, and the mysticism of the *Proslogion*.

The ontological proof of the Divine existence has often been claimed as an original effort of the genius of S. Anselm, but Hasse[5] who has urged this most strongly can hardly have

[1] *De Divis. Nat.* v. 27 (Migne, 927).   [2] *De Gen. ad Lit.* xi. 28.
[3] *Leben und Lehre des J. S. Erig.*, pp. 287, 418, 436.
[4] The 'alter Augustinus' of the middle ages. Hasse, ii. 32.
[5] *Anselm v. Canterbury*, ii. 240.

compared those passages to which S. Anselm refers in urging that his *Monologion* is not new, and has overlooked the extent to which ontological elements are present in S. Austin's various statements on this subject. S. Anselm has separated out the cosmological argument in the *Monologion* from the ontological in the *Proslogion*, and by so doing has rendered both clearer: the hours of pious contemplation which he devoted to setting forth this train of thought have indeed conferred a priceless boon on subsequent ages of Christian thought. But the ontological argument, from our thought of God to His Existence is completely implied in passages of that book *De Trinitate*[1] which S. Anselm specially studied[2] as well as in others of S. Austin's writings[3]. It would be beside the mark to enter here on any discussion as to the precise validity of this proof: but one may note in passing that since it is an argument from my idea of God, its force must greatly depend on the nature of the idea I have. For the mere deist it will have none; he must first be convinced as S. Anselm tries to show, that his thought of God is inadequate[4]; and then the proof ceases to be a mere paralogism[5].

While then S. Anselm was not entirely original in the substance of his argument, though his way of putting it is entirely his own, there is another point of theology in regard to which he does seem to have struck out an independent line. S. Austin only once, I believe, uses the word satisfacere in connexion with human sin (*Sermo* cccli. 12), and there he insists that it is necessary that the sinner should not only change his mode of life, but 'make amends' to God by the grief of penitence, by the sigh of humility, by the sacrifice of a contrite heart, accompanied by almsgiving. This is an entirely different conception of satisfaction from that which occurs throughout the

---

[1] Bk viii. Cf. van Endert, *Gottesbeweis*, 153.

[2] Quapropter, si cui videbitur quod in eodem opusculo aliquid protulerim, quod aut nimis novum sit, aut a veritate dissentiat, rogo ne statim me aut praesumptorem novitatum, aut falsitatis assertorem exclamet; sed prius libros praefati doctoris Augustini de Triuitate diligenter perspiciat, deinde secundum eos opusculum meum dijudicet. *Monologion*, Preface.

[3] *Lib. Arb.* ii. 11—39. Ritter, vi. 280 n. Gangauf, *Spec. Lehre*, 81.

[4] *Proslogion*, cc. ii. iv.

[5] Hegel, *Phil. der Rel.* ii. 209. For an excellent and brief statement on the subject see Caird, *Phil. of Rel.* 153.

Cur Deus Homo. How far S. Anselm was adopting the ordinary legal language of the time, we need not pause to consider, but the doctrine of the atonement as it was shaped by him and commonly held since his day, was not the doctrine of S. Austin.

7. These are the chief points in regard to which it has been argued that any writer of the early middle ages had broken away from the Augustinian tradition: but more careful consideration seems to show that for seven hundred years his modes of thought, and the opinions he held were not so much dominant as supreme. A few words may be added with regard to the decline of his influence.

The subject of dialectic had undoubtedly proved advantageous in enabling men to write in more systematic form,—as we have seen in the case of S. Anselm, but it was eventually pursued with more zeal than discretion. It is curious to note how from holding a subordinate place in the *trivium*, the dialectic art came to attract a chief share of intellectual activity till in the twelfth century it absorbed all other interests. John of Salisbury complains when revisiting his former class-fellows at S. Genevieve "that whereas dialectic furthers other studies, so if it remain by itself it lies bloodless and barren, nor does it quicken the soul to yield fruit of philosophy, except the same conceive from elsewhere[1]." But barren though it might prove, dialectic set the form in which the problems of philosophy were then raised. The great question was no longer as to the reality of that which I know, but as to the nature of that which I use in discussion and exposition.

This was the beginning of the reaction against the dominance of S. Austin: he ceased to command attention by his philosophy. The problem of certainty, which he had discussed, did not attract much interest; and on the nature of universals he had little if any light to give. Before this dialectical fervour arose, the great problems of nature and the world presented themselves in forms in which he could help to give a solution, but on the special problem of the Scholastic philosophy he had little to say: his language had an affinity with the views of the realists, but he could furnish them with few weapons, and the nominalists dis-

---

[1] Quoted by R. L. Poole, *Illustrations*, 212.

carded him altogether. He thus ceased to dominate in mediæval philosophy and his place as an authority was taken by Aristotle.

There are two most important points of a theological doctrine[1] which were undoubtedly affected by this change. Scholastic Aristotelianism furnished those conceptions of Substance and Accident, which lent themselves to supply a metaphysical explanation of the doctrine of the real presence: and it framed a doctrine of the will which laid stress on mere indifferentism rather than rational freedom. Neither of these doctrines are Augustinian, but both of them came to be incorporated in the orthodox doctrine of the Latin Church. In the time of S. Thomas Aquinas, the philosophy of Aristotle was once more asserting its sway: debased and disguised as it was by translators and commentators it yet gave the form in which theological doctrine was cast. There were some in England who held aloof: Roger Bacon, Robert of Lincoln, and Thomas Bradwardine were not carried away by this enthusiasm, but on the Continent and at length in England the new philosophy was completely triumphant. S. Austin was still studied and quoted; but he only furnished extracts to deck out the peripatetic scholasticism, not the whole body of doctrine. His opinions were forced by the schoolman into a setting which he had distinctly disavowed. There was indeed one English theologian who more than any of the other doctors of his time influenced popular thought: though Wyclif was a Thomist and familiar with the current philosophy of his time, he became more and more attached to the study of theology and of the theology of S. Austin. His doctrines of the Being of God, and of the Incarnation are both according to Mr Shirley[2] definitely Augustinian: the same careful editor finds that the doctrine of Dominion, when stripped of its paradoxical form, is also completely congruous with S. Austin's teaching[3]; and apparently the same

---

[1] For divergences on other theological points see van Endert.

[2] Shirley's Introduction to *Zizaniorum Fasciculi*, LIV. His adversaries endeavoured to prove that Wyclif's doctrine was not based on that of the fathers, but on Plotinus, Hermes Trismegistus and other non-Christian writers. This of itself shows that he was more in sympathy with S. Austin's Platonism than most contemporary Thomists could possibly be. Thom. Waldensis, *Doctrinale*, I. xxxiv.

[3] See below Excursus G, § 6, p. 193.

might be said of the doctrine of the Eucharist. Considering the extraordinary influence which was exercised at home and abroad by one whom his disciples spoke of as specially Augustinian[1], it is interesting to remember from what source his inspiration was drawn.

The unqualified condemnation of Wyclif, however far it may have been justified on political and other grounds, could hardly have taken place unless the current philosophy had undermined the influence of S. Austin. The spirit of the age too demanded other changes—not only the discussion of the special philosophical problem of these days, but social and political life was very different from that in which S. Austin had lived. The political doctrine of S. Thomas and of Wyclif alike is strongly affected by feudal conceptions; new orders, new rites, new aspirations had come into being, and in the fourteenth and fifteenth centuries the teaching of the Bishop of Hippo seems to have fallen more and more into the background: his works furnished a quarry from which fragments could be drawn, but he was no longer the great master spirit who presided over the whole structure.

EXCURSUS C.

Knowledge of Greek, p. 42.

THE frequent references to Greek words and phrases, as well as the considerable knowledge of Greek philosophical writers which one finds in S. Austin's writings, seem at first sight difficult to reconcile with the statement in the *Confessions*, as to his unwillingness to learn that language. Cur ergo græcam etiam grammaticam oderam talia cantantem? Nam et Homerus peritus texere tales fabellas, et dulcissime vanus est, et mihi tamen amarus erat puero. Credo etiam græcis pueris Virgilius

---

[1] Et forsan hac audaci pompa confisi sui discipuli vocabant eum famoso et elato nomine JOANNEM AUGUSTINI. Thom. Waldensis, *Doctrinale*, I. xxxiv. § 5.

ita sit, cum eum sic discere coguntur, ut ego illum. Videlicet difficultas, omnino ediscendæ peregrinæ linguæ, quasi felle aspergebat omnes suavitates græcas fabulosarum narrationum. Nulla enim verba illa noveram, et sævis terroribus ac pœnis ut nossem instabatur mihi vehementer. *Conf.* I. 23. But there are several passages which show that though he was afterwards able to understand and use the Greek language, he was never thoroughly familiar with it. Quod si ea quæ legimus de his rebus, sufficienter edita in latino sermone aut non sunt, aut non inveniuntur, aut certe difficile a nobis inveniri queunt, græcæ autem linguæ non sit nobis tantus habitus, ut talium rerum libris legendis et intelligendis ullo modo reperiamur idonei, quo genere litterarum ex iis quæ nobis pauca interpretata sunt, non dubito cuncta quæ utiliter quærere possumus contineri. *De Trin.* III. 1. We need not therefore be surprised to find that he preferred to use translations out of Greek when he had the opportunity of doing so. Compare the *Confessions*, VII. 13, quoted above, page 42 note. Petimus ergo, et nobiscum petit omnis Africanarum Ecclesiarum studiosa societas, ut interpretandis eorum libris, qui græce Scripturas nostras quam optime tractaverunt, curam atque operam impendere non graveris. Potes enim efficere ut nos quoque habeamus tales illos viros, et unum potissimum, quem tu libentius in tuis litteris sonas. *Ep.* xxviii. (*Hieronymo*), 2.

It is sufficiently clear therefore that his knowledge of Greek Philosophy (see especially *De Civ. Dei*, VIII., X.) was chiefly obtained through translations; for Plato he relied on Victorinus.

But it would be a mistake to assume too hastily that because he preferred to use translations he was as entirely ignorant of Greek as he appears to have been of Hebrew. Clausen has investigated the matter with care (*A. A. Hippo. S. Script. Interpres*, 1826, pp. 30—40) on the only satisfactory method, by examining the actual use he makes of Greek in his writings. He comes to a conclusion which is quite in accordance with S. Austin's own language, that though he was not an accurate scholar he had a working knowledge of Greek. One may note a single instance to show that he attempted to carry on critical studies. Verum Scripturarum sanctarum multiplicem copiam scrutatus, invenio scriptum esse in libro Job, eodem sancto viro loquente: *Ecce pietas est sapientia; abstinere autem a malis est scientia*

(Job XXVIII. 28). In hac differentia intelligendum est ad contemplationem sapientiam, ad actionem scientiam pertinere. Pietatem quippe hoc loco posuit Dei cultum, quæ græce dicitur θεοσέβεια. Nam hoc verbum habet ista sententia in codicibus græcis. *De Trin.* XII. 22. At any rate he fully recognised the value of such scholarship. Tum vero, facta quadam familiaritate cum ipsa lingua divinarum Scripturarum, in ea quæ obscura sunt aperienda et discutienda pergendum est, ut ad obscuriores locutiones illustrandas de manifestioribus sumantur exempla, et quædam certarum sententiarum testimonia dubitationem incertis auferant....Nunc de incognitis agimus, quorum duæ formæ sunt, quantum ad verba pertinet. Namque aut ignotum verbum facit hærere lectorem, aut ignota locutio. Quæ si ex alienis linguis veniunt, aut quærenda sunt ab earum linguarum hominibus, aut eædem linguæ, si et otium est et ingenium, ediscendæ, aut plurium interpretum consulenda collatio est. Si autem ipsius linguæ nostræ aliqua verba locutionesque ignoramus, legendi consuetudine audiendique innotescunt. Nulla sane sunt magis mandanda memoriæ, quam illa verborum locutionumque genera quæ ignoramus; ut cum vel peritior occurrerit de quo quæri possint, vel talis lectio quæ vel ex præcedentibus vel consequentibus vel utrisque ostendat quam vim habeat, quidve significet quod ignoramus, facile adjuvante memoria possimus advertere et discere. Quanquam tanta est vis consuetudinis etiam ad discendum, ut qui in Scripturis sanctis quodammodo nutriti educatique sunt, magis alias locutiones mirentur, easque minus latinas putent, quam illas quas in Scripturis didicerunt, neque in latinæ linguæ auctoribus reperiuntur. Plurimum hic quoque juvat interpretum numerositas collatis codicibus inspecta atque discussa; tantum absit falsitas: nam codicibus emendandis primitus debet invigilare solertia eorum qui Scripturas divinas nosse desiderant, ut emendatis non emendati cedant, ex uno duntaxat interpretationis genere venientes. *De Doct. Christ.* II. 14, 21.

EXCURSUS D.

The Authority and Interpretation of Scripture, pp. 10, 35, 56, 58.

1. Eternal Truth.
2. The Bible and the Church.
3. How is a conflict between 'Reason' and 'Authority' possible?
4. False pretensions to Authority and the limits of Empirical Opinion.
5. The Interpretation of Authority.
6. The conditions for apprehending Bible Truth.

1. It is exceedingly difficult to appraise the precise authority which S. Austin attributed to Holy Scripture; but it may at least be worth while to state a few of the questions which are involved and thus get an approximation to his view, even though we cannot hope to do more than this.

We may of course take for granted that he recognised in the Bible a revelation of truth, not the Truth itself. The Eternal Unchanging Reality, Truth, God, is manifested through the changing phenomena of time[1], and has expressed His will in the word, but all such expressions bring us within the realm of sense, and away from the Truth itself. The whole argument as to certainty, and the reality of the divine existence, shows us that he treats Truth, or Intellectual Principles as the supreme reality. This is re-iterated as the introduction to an interesting passage where he discusses the grounds of the Christian faith : Distribuitur enim [animæ medicina] in auctoritatem atque rationem. Auctoritas fidem flagitat, et rationi præparat hominem. Quanquam neque auctoritatem ratio penitus deserit, cum consideratur cui sit credendum ; et certe summa est ipsius jam cognitæ atque perspicuæ veritatis auctoritas. Sed quia in temporalia devenimus, et eorum amore ab æternis impedimur, quædam temporalis medicina, quæ non scientes, sed credentes ad salutem vocat, non naturæ et excellentiæ sed ipsius temporis ordine prior est. *De Ver. Rel.* 45. (Compare also *De Utilitate Credendi*, 34.) These

---

[1] *De Civ. Dei*, VIII. vi. *De Trin.* xv. 7. *De Vera Religione*, 57, 58.

distinctions are pre-supposed in his whole philosophy; and reappear explicitly in the schoolmen who systematised his teaching. Not only in Erigena[1] with his proof that Reason is first in Nature and that all Authority must depend on Reason, or when S. Anselm wrote his *Proslogion* in the expectation that those who believed the true faith might be led by understanding the reason of the hope that was in them to the fuller contemplation of God: for it is at least illustrated by S. Thomas Aquinas when he distinguishes the Eternal Law, from the Law of Nature, and from Divinely Revealed Law. Truth is the supreme reality which is manifested in Holy Writ, as well as in other ways: authority is the means by which we may attain to reason. Vide ergo secundum hæc verba tua, ne potius debeas, maxime de hac re in qua præcipue fides nostra consistit, solam sanctorum auctoritatem sequi, nec ejus intelligentiæ a me quærere rationem. Neque enim cum cœpero te in tanti hujus secreti intelligentiam utcumque introducere (quod nisi Deus intus adjuverit, omnino non potero), aliud disserendo facturus sum, quam rationem ut potero redditurus: quam si a me, vel a quolibet doctore non irrationabiliter flagitas, ut quod credis intelligas, corrige definitionem tuam, non ut fidem respuas, sed ut ea, quæ fidei firmitate jam tenes, etiam rationis luce conspicias. Absit namque ut hoc in nobis Deus oderit, in quo nos reliquis animantibus excellentiores creavit. Absit, inquam, ut ideo credamus, ne rationem accipiamus sive quæramus; cum etiam credere non possemus, nisi rationales animas haberemus. Ut ergo in quibusdam rebus ad doctrinam salutarem pertinentibus, quas ratione nondum percipere valemus sed aliquando valebimus, fides præcedat rationem, qua cor mundetur, ut magnæ rationis capiat et perferat lucem, hoc utique rationis est. Et ideo rationabiliter dictum est per prophetam : *Nisi credideritis, non intelligetis* (Isai. VII. 9 *sec*. LXX). Ubi procul dubio discrevit hæc duo, deditque consilium quo prius credamus, ut id quod credimus intelligere valeamus. Proinde ut fides præcedat rationem, rationabiliter visum est. Nam si hoc præceptum rationabile non est, ergo irrationabile est : absit. Si igitur rationabile est ut ad magna quædam, quæ capi nondum possunt,

---

[1] *De Divis. Nat.* I. 69 (Migne 513). This is also explicitly stated by S. Austin, Tempore auctoritas, re autem ratio prior est. *De Ordine*, II. 26.

fides præcedat rationem, procul dubio quantulacumque ratio quæ hoc persuadet, etiam ipsa antecedit fidem. Propterea monet apostolus Petrus, paratos nos esse debere ad responsionem omni poscenti nos rationem de fide et spe nostra: quoniam si a me infidelis rationem poscit fidei et spei meæ, et video quod antequam credat capere non potest, hanc ipsam ei reddo rationem in qua, si fieri potest, videat quam præpostere ante fidem poscat rationem earum rerum quas capere non potest. Si autem jam fidelis rationem poscat, ut quod credit intelligat, capacitas ejus intuenda est, ut secundum eam ratione reddita sumat fidei suæ quantam potest intelligentiam; majorem, si plus capit; minorem, si minus: dum tamen, quousque ad plenitudinem cognitionis perfectionemque perveniat, ab itinere fidei non recedat. Hinc est quod dicit Apostolus: *Et tamen si quid aliter sapitis, id quoque vobis Deus revelabit; verumtamen in quod pervenimus, in eo ambulemus.* Jam ergo si fideles sumus, ad fidei viam pervenimus, quam si non dimiserimus, non solum ad tantam intelligentiam rerum incorporearum et incommutabilium, quanta in hac vita capi non ab omnibus potest, verum etiam ad summitatem contemplationis, quam dicit Apostolus, *facie ad faciem,* sine dubitatione perveniemus. Nam quidam etiam minimi, et tamen in via fidei perseverantissime gradientes, ad illam beatissimam contemplationem perveniunt: quidam vero quid sit natura invisibilis, incommutabilis, incorporea, utcumque jam scientes, et viam quæ ducit ad tantæ beatitudinis mansionem, quoniam stulta illis videtur, quod est Christus crucifixus, tenere recusantes, ad quietis ipsius penetrale, cujus jam luce mens eorum velut in longinqua radiante perstringitur, pervenire non possunt. *Ep.* cxx. (*Consentio*) § 2, 3, 4.

2. That this Truth is not explicitly manifested, according to his view in the Bible, becomes apparent from other considerations: the authority of the Bible is so directly dependent upon the Church, and men may make grievous errors in interpreting it. The book did not spring into being by a sudden miracle, complete as we have it; still less is it self-interpreting. And thus both in regard to the formation of the Canon and the interpretation of Scripture, we are forced back from the authority of the Bible to the authority of the Church, and the singleheartedness of the reader. Even in the authority of the Church however there is

no final resting place : not only is truth progressive and rendered clearer by the opposition of heretics and the experience and discussions of the faithful, but even the decision of a General Council of the Church may require subsequent modification[1]: we must be ready to test the decisions of Councils by the language of Scripture, and check the one by the other. Just as we have seen from the nature of Truth that it cannot be perfectly expressed through phenomena, so we may see from S. Austin's view as to the possibility of error on either hand, that he does not recognise any absolutely infallible authority either in the Bible or the Church. And if this is the case with authority, it is still more obviously true that ordinary human reason does not give us a complete solution of all the problems in the universe : there are but few if any who can attain to a great measure of insight by this light alone[2]. Thus S. Austin will not let either stand in the place of God, the Eternal Reason, and hence we have the constant attempt, which is repeated by S. Anselm, to advance beyond the mere acceptance of truth from some authority, to the fuller light in which we may know, even as also we are known.

3. But if authority and reason are thus fundamentally at one—different stages in the progress of knowledge—how can a conflict arise ?

It may be due on one hand to false pretensions to authority or to the misuse and misinterpretation of an authority that rightly demands our respect. Manichæans and others produced their pretended revelations, and Donatists quoted miracles on behalf of their doctrines : but S. Austin meets them by contemptuous criticism[3]. He urged that it was foolish to seek for authority where we have the light of reason to guide us. (Compare

---

[1] [Quis autem nesciat] et ipsa concilia quæ per singulas regiones vel provincias fiunt, plenariorum conciliorum auctoritati, quæ fiunt ex universo orbe christiano, sine ullis ambagibus cedere : ipsaque plenaria sæpe priora posterioribus emendari ; cum aliquo experimento rerum aperitur quod clausum erat, et cognoscitur quod latebat ; sine ullo typho sacrilegæ superbiæ, sine ulla inflata cervice arrogantiæ, sine ulla contentione lividæ invidiæ, cum sancta humilitate, cum pace catholica, cum charitate christiana? *De Bapt. contr. Donat.* II. 4.

[2] *De Util. Cred.* 24.

[3] *In Joan. Evan. Tract.* XIII. 17.

Excursus B, § 3.) The existence of these false pretenders to authority must put us on our guard whom we trust, but need not lead us to abandon authority altogether: Itaque ut inter studentem alicujus rei et omnino studiosum, rursumque inter curam habentem atque curiosum, ita inter credentem et credulum plurimum interest. *De Util. Cred.* 22. False pretenders do serve however to show one of the grounds for the apparent opposition between authority and reason. Another which lies in misinterpretation of a genuine authority need only be noticed here, as it is discussed below in § 5.

But the opposition is also partly caused by the defective character of human intelligence: mere empirical opinion so often mistakes itself for 'knowledge' and 'reason.' Opinari autem duas ob res turpissimum est: quod et discere non potest, qui sibi jam se scire persuasit, si modo illud disci potest; et per se ipsa temeritas non bene affecti animi signum est. Nam etiamsi hoc ipsum quod de Cicerone dixi, scire se quisquam arbitratur, quanquam nihil cum impediat a discendo, quia res ipsa nulla scientia teneri potest: tamen quod non intelligit multum interesse, utrum aliquid mentis certa ratione teneatur, quod intelligere dicimus, an famæ vel litteris credendum posteris utiliter commendetur; profecto errat, neque quisquam error turpitudine caret. Quod intelligimus igitur, debemus rationi: quod credimus, auctoritati: quod opinamur, errori. Sed intelligens omnis etiam credit, credit omnis et qui opinatur: non omnis qui credit intelligit; nullus qui opinatur intelligit. *De Util. Cred.* 25. Quia cum ordinem suum peragit pulchra mutabilitas temporum, deserit amantem species concupita, et per cruciatum sentientis discedit a sensibus, et erroribus agitat; ut hanc esse primam speciem putet, quæ omnium infima est, naturæ scilicet corporeæ, quam per lubricos sensus caro male delectata nuntiaverit, ut cum aliquid cogitat, intelligere se credat, umbris illusus phantasmatum. Si quando autem non tenens integram divinæ providentiæ disciplinam, sed tenere se arbitrans, carni resistere conatur; usque ad visibilium rerum imagines pervenit, et lucis hujus quam certis terminis circumscriptam videt, immensa spatia cogitatione format inaniter: et hanc speciem sibi futuræ habitationis pollicetur; nesciens oculorum concupiscentiam se trahere, et cum hoc mundo ire velle extra mundum; quem propterea ipsum esse non putat, quia ejus

clariorem partem per infinitum falsa cogitatione distendit. *De Vera Relig.* 40. Compare also *Ep. xiii.* (*Nebridio*) § 2. Our first crude opinion is of course that the impressions of our senses give us the fullest knowledge we can possess : it is needless to repeat here the arguments by which the Academics, and modern agnostics, have destroyed this claim. The phenomena of colour blindness prove that we do not see things as they really are : the reliance each man places on the reports of his senses is after all belief, and not knowledge. In the combining of these impressions too there are opportunities for error, and thus while true authority harmonises with reason, it may yet be opposed by mere empirical opinion. And thus we reach the result that while authority and reason are at one, there is ample room for conflict between these different factors,—pretended authority or falsely interpreted authority and reason, and between true authority and mere empirical opinion.

4. If we start from the belief that authority and reason are really at one we may find that in the case of an apparent conflict it is necessary either to test the weight, or the interpretation of our authority, or to correct our empirical opinions. From the hints that S. Austin has thrown out here and there, as well as from his practice, it seems that he would have tried to solve the difficulty of an apparent conflict in different ways, according to the circumstances of the case.

If it were a question about the constitution of the world of phenomena there can I think be little doubt that he would have preferred the results of human experience. The Bible is not meant to be an easy substitute for investigation and discovery and we dare not use it as such. The literal statements of the Bible on the phenomena around us, must give way to the more careful results of empirical investigation where they come in conflict. S. Austin was careful not to pre-judge any empirical investigation by scriptural assertions. This comes out most clearly in his treatment of the subject of the Antipodes[1].

When we come however to consider the possibility of the occurrence of particular events which conflict with our experience, it

---

[1] Compare Excursus A, p. 140.

AUTHORITY AND INTERPRETATION OF SCRIPTURE. 163

is a different matter: for our experience is not exhaustive. The first question must of course be, what is the evidence for the marvel? And in regard to alleged contemporary miracles S. Austin shows himself extremely critical[1]. The Donatists maintained that miracles had been done by their founder. This S. Austin disputes, but he also holds that the power of working miracles is not necessarily a proof of the truth of the opinion of those who perform such wonders: he would not have rested his belief in the Apostles' doctrine on the ground that they did mighty works[2]. He distinguishes 'faith' in past events, from faith in the eternal reality. Temporal faith is propædeutic to faith in the eternal, and this may rise to the full knowledge of God. All other knowledge of things of sense, and even of God's dealings with men is of true value in so far as it leads to this complete vision[3].

The evidence for the miracles recorded in Scripture is to his mind infinitely stronger; and he has no hesitation in taking the

[1] He holds that the age of miracles had passed lest we should be enthralled by things of sense. *De Vera Rel.* 47. On the whole subject compare *A.'s Lehre vom Wunder*, by F. Nitzsch, 1865.

[2] Though this might be the occasion of belief. Tenet auctoritas miraculis inchoata, spe nutrita, caritate aucta, vetustate firmata. *Contra Ep. Manich.* 5.

[3] De [humana scientia] volumine tertio decimo disputavi, non utique quidquid sciri ab homine potest in rebus humanis, ubi plurimum supervacaneæ vanitatis et noxiæ curiositatis est, huic scientiæ tribuens, sed illud tantummodo quo fides saluberrima, quæ ad veram beatitudinem ducit, gignitur, nutritur, defenditur, roboratur: qua scientia non pollent fideles plurimi, quamvis polleant ipsa fide plurimum. Aliud est enim scire tantummodo quid homo credere debeat propter adipiscendam vitam beatam, quæ non nisi æterna est; aliud autem scire quemadmodum hoc ipsum et piis opituletur et contra impios defendatur, quam proprio appellare vocabulo scientiam videtur Apostolus. De qua prius cum loquerer, ipsam præcipue fidem commendare curavi, a temporalibus æterna breviter ante distinguens, atque ibi de temporalibus disserens: æterna vero in hunc librum differens, etiam de rebus æternis fidem temporalem quidem, et temporaliter in credentium cordibus habitare, necessariam tamen propter adipiscenda ipsa æterna esse monstravi. Fidem quoque de temporalibus rebus, quas pro nobis æternus fecit et passus est in homine, quem temporaliter gessit atque ad æterna provexit, ad eamdem æternorum adeptionem prodesse disserui: virtutesque ipsas, quibus in hac temporali mortalitate prudenter, fortiter, temperanter, et juste vivitur, nisi ad eamdem, licet temporalem fidem, quæ tamen ad æterna perducit, referantur, veras non esse virtutes. *De Trin.* XIV. 3. See also *De Consensu Evangel.* I. 53.

11—2

Gospel narrative as a record of facts. He is of course aware that the account of the Resurrection conflicts with all our other experience, and from his high regard for empirical knowledge we might have supposed that like Hume he would have regarded any human testimony however good as insufficient to outweigh the conclusions of our organised experience. Just because he had, as Hume had not, rational grounds for his reverence for empirical knowledge, he did not unduly magnify its worth. To his mind empirical knowledge was incomplete and it was not the most certain part of our knowledge: it has to do with mere changing phenomena, not with the Eternal Reality. Just as we must not rule empirical knowledge out of court because of some scriptural assertion, so we must not rule a narrated miracle out of court because we have no experience of such occurrences; for though exceptional, they may still be rational, and in complete accordance with the Eternal Reason[1].

They may be rational as manifesting a truth which ordinary phenomena do not exhibit: the victory of the Divine Life over Death and Sin was manifested by the Resurrection of our Lord: from the very nature of the truth thus exhibited it could not be conveyed in normal experiences. It is in the import of the miracle that we may find its rational justification.

At times indeed it may take place as a mere portent to attract human attention, and awaken attention to a divine message that is being given in some other form. For this purpose an occurrence that goes beyond our knowledge of nature may possibly serve as truly as a real miracle, or actual departure from the normal course of phenomena.

It is thus that he conceives miracles hold a place in the Divine Order and have therefore a rational justification, as serving to manifest Eternal Truth in time, though in ways that are inconsistent with the normal course of events as well as inconsistent with our empirical knowledge. They have their ground in the

---

[1] Et universa Dei miracula ideo ab infidelibus non creduntur, quia eorum ratio non videtur. Et revera sunt de quibus ratio reddi non potest, non tamen non est: quid enim est in rerum natura, quod irrationabiliter fecerit Deus? Sed quorumdam mirabilium operum ejus, etiam expedit tantisper occultam esse rationem, ne apud animos fastidio languidos ejusdem rationis cognitione vilescant. *Ep. cxx.* (*Consentio*) 5.

Divine Will[1], as the divinely appointed means of effecting the Divine Purpose for the world.

5. So far cases have been considered where the solution is reached by noting the false pretensions of authority, or the true limits within which empirical opinion may be relied on. There are other cases however where we must reconsider our interpretation[2] of an authority which we rightly revere, and where, as in the case of the Scriptural account of Creation, we are compelled to discard it, in its literal sense.

For S. Austin it is not less truly the word of God, but we have failed to interpret it aright. There is a threefold reference in most of the Psalms or Prophecies—some refer to the earthly Jerusalem, some to the Heavenly City, and some apply both to one and the other[3]. He denies that the Scripture is merely allegorical, and also rejects the views of those who treat it as merely literal[4], while he cannot see, as some maintained, that

---

[1] Not an arbitrary changing Will, but an Eternal Will which is not limited by the normal course of phenomena, but is none the less unchanging.

[2] *De Util. Credendi*, 10.

[3] On the fourfold interpretation see *De Utilitate Cred.* 5. Omnis igitur Scriptura, quae Testamentum Vetus vocatur, diligenter eam nosse cupientibus quadrifaria traditur; secundum historiam, secundum aetiologiam, secundum analogiam, secundum allegoriam.***Secundum historiam ergo traditur, cum docetur quid scriptum, aut quid gestum sit, quid non gestum sed tantummodo scriptum quasi gestum sit. Secundum aetiologiam, cum ostenditur quid qua de causa vel factum vel dictum sit. Secundum analogiam, cum demonstratur non sibi adversari duo Testamenta, Vetus et Novum. Secundum allegoriam, cum docetur non ad litteram esse accipienda quaedam quae scripta sunt, sed figurate intelligenda.

[4] Nam in principio cavendum est ne figuratam locutionem ad litteram accipias. Et ad hoc enim pertinet quod ait Apostolus: *Littera occidit, spiritus autem vivificat*. Cum enim figurate dictum sic accipitur, tanquam proprie dictum sit, carnaliter sapitur. Neque ulla mors animae congruentius appellatur, quam cum id etiam quod in ea bestiis antecellit, hoc est, intelligentia carni subjicitur sequendo litteram. Qui enim sequitur litteram, translata verba sicut propria tenet, neque illud quod proprio verbo significatur, refert ad aliam significationem: sed si Sabbatum audierit, verbi gratia, non intelligit nisi unum diem de septem, qui continuo volumine repetuntur; et cum audierit Sacrificium, non excedit cogitatione illud quod fieri de victimis pecorum terrenisque fructibus solet. Ea demum

every passage has a double bearing. So long as the literal reference is not sacrificed, he has little objection[1] to finding profit in additional senses. In some cases, e.g. in the song of Hannah, he feels that the occasion is too paltry for such an outburst of devotion and that a spiritual reference is certainly implied[2]. The laxity which he thus allows himself produces most curious results: he is able to regard the Septuagint and Hebrew text as equally inspired despite their differences and inconsistencies, for there is a reference to some part of the work of Christ—to His Resurrection or to the Great Forty Days—whether we take three days or forty days as one reading in the *Book of Jonah*[3]. The variety of the lessons which could be drawn from Holy Writ on such principles as these is practically infinite, and we may see that mediæval theologians found ample authority in S. Austin for pursuing their method of study. "The sense of the divine utterances," said Erigena[4], "is manifold and infinite."

6. If we admit such laxity and variety of interpretation, it almost seems as if the Bible must cease to be an authority in any real sense of the word. And so it would if we could admit the right of the individual to handle it as he pleased: and do not limit the freedom of interpretation by insisting that the sense drawn from it shall be for *edification*. Whatever appears derogatory to God must be taken figuratively, what does not incite to charity is not a true interpretation of Scripture. Non autem præcipit Scriptura nisi caritatem, nec culpat nisi cupiditatem; et eo modo informat mores hominum. Item si animum præoccupavit alicujus erroris opinio, quidquid aliter asseruerit Scriptura, figuratum homines arbitrantur. Non autem asserit nisi catholicam fidem, rebus præteritis, et futuris, et præsentibus. Præteritorum narratio est, futurorum prænuntiatio, præsentium demonstratio: sed omnia hæc ad eamdem caritatem nutriendam atque corroborandam, et cupiditatem vincendam atque exstinguendam valent. *De Doct. Christ.* III. 15.

est miserabilis animæ servitus, signa pro rebus accipere; et supra creaturam corpoream oculum mentis ad hauriendum æternum lumen levare non posse. *De Doct. Christ.* III. 9.

[1] *Civ. Dei*, XVII. iv.
[2] *Civ. Dei*, XVIII. xliv.
[3] *De Doct. Christ.* II. 17.
[4] *De Divis. Nat.* IV. 5 (Migne, 749).

So too, the right of putting an interpretation on Scripture is affected by the state of mind in which the reader approaches the study (*De Doct. Christ.* I. 44, II. 62). The Manichæans contended for an unconditioned right of private judgment, and it was S. Austin's part to expose the falseness of such pretensions. It is by faith that we discern the things of the Spirit, it is as the individual partakes in this Spirit that he really finds the Scripture profitable: to the unbelieving it is of no avail. It is as faith is wakened and maintained through the ordinances and ministry of Christ's Church, that the individual is able to receive nourishment from the word: but to the faithful it supplies all the knowledge of the things of God that he needs.

The Bible is thus an authority in things of faith to the faithful, for it is a source from which they learn the Will of God: it is His message to them; let them learn to receive it in all humility and search the Scriptures for the light God gives in them. But just because it only profits when it thus speaks authoritatively, it must be commended to those who read it—commended by the living faith of the Church or the personal power of a teacher, such as S. Ambrose had been[1].

Great evil has accrued in modern times from the neglect of these personal qualifications for the apprehension of God's truth in the Scriptures. Protestants often seem[2] to regard Scripture as possessed of some magical efficacy, and have neglected the conditions on which its authority depends. The indiscriminate scattering of the Bible, with no real instruction, with no Church life to commend it[3], would not, so far as one can judge have had the approval of S. Austin: for his own personal experience was against it. Ego vero Evangelio non crederem nisi me catholicæ Ecclesiæ commoveret auctoritas (*Contra Epist. Manichæi* 6). Nor would he have been surprised that one[4] who discarded all previous opinions and set out to study the Bible by the light of his own judgment should make but little progress in apprehending the

---

[1] *De Util. Cred.* 20.
[2] "Scripture bears upon the face of it as clear evidence of its truth, as white and black do of their colour, sweet and bitter of their taste." Calvin, *Institutes*, I. vii. 2.
[3] *De Doct. Christ.* I. 43, 44.
[4] Locke, *Reasonableness of Christianity*, 1.

Christian faith[1]. The spread of Christianity must come by leading men to accept it—not as a system which is proved congruent with our empirical knowledge,—but as an authority which conducts us to a higher and more enduring knowledge, and through the reverent study of which we may enter into the mind of God.

EXCURSUS E.

Continence in Married Life, p. 65.

It seems to be the common impression in England in the present day that continence is not a thing to be aimed at by married people, and that if aimed at it cannot be attained; that the desires of the flesh are too strong to submit to any check. And those who have either before or after marriage resigned themselves to the complete indulgence of their desires for any length of time must certainly find it terribly hard to recover a mastery over the passions to which they had given full rein. "Sunt item viri usque adeo incontinentes, ut conjugibus nec gravidis parcant" (*De Bono Conjugali*, 5). But the results of such incontinence are plain enough to those who will consider the matter; not only in the physical effects on the offspring, but in the cruel suffering and serious weakness to which wives are often condemned, and under which they may sink before their time. If these things attract little attention in ordinary society, they are noted by those who are rebelling against its institutions. There are some who, like Robert Owen, are so repelled by the misuse of marriage that they are led to inveigh against the institution itself, and to declare in favour of some form of free love, as the less objectionable practice. And those who are eager

---

[1] Compare *De Util. Cred.* 31. At scriptura omnis, si nova et inaudita proferatur, vel commendetur a paucis, nulla confirmante ratione, non ei, sed illis qui eam proferunt, creditur. Quamobrem scripturas istas si vos profertis, tam pauci et incogniti, non libet credere. Simul etiam contra promissum facitis, fidem potius imperando, quam reddendo rationem.

to retain the institution of marriage and who regard the family as necessary to the well-being of the State, would do well to refute the attacks which are made upon it by using every endeavour to render marriage pure and matrimony a truly holy state.

The Christian view of the subject is clearly stated in the Marriage Service in the Prayer-book; the preliminary address follows S. Austin's teaching so closely that it is unnecessary to seek to frame a better exposition of his views.

Marriage was ordained *for the procreation of children to be brought up in the fear and nurture of the Lord and to the praise of His holy name.* And carnal connection with this end in view is amply justified; the human race is to be perpetuated that God may be glorified by men throughout all times (*De Nuptiis et Concup.* II. 25). But carnal connection which has not this end in view is mere self-indulgence and tends to sin; though over-indulgence in the married state is venial and a far less serious evil than the sin of those who are guilty of fornication or adultery (*De Bono Conjugali*, 5, 12). Thus continence is a virtue after which the Christian should make a life-long struggle, and for the sake of which he should use such self-discipline in matters of diet and exercise as may render the practice more possible.

Such is the broad principle which governs Christian marriage; but those who after serious effort fail to attain such complete mastery over themselves are not to be condemned, though they can never be exonerated from the duty of farther effort. Hence follows the second reason why marriage was ordained, *as a remedy against sin and to avoid fornication.* It may be that one of the partners in marriage is willing and able to live in continence, but to do so may be inconsistent with conjugal duty. Each has power over the body of the other, and each must render to the other due benevolence; if either so refused conjugal duty, from whatever motive, as to drive the other into fornication, marriage would cease to be preventive of serious sin. The rendering of conjugal duty is a remedy against sin, in that one partner is thus able to aid the other in avoiding fornication (*De Bono Conjugali*, 6).

That which the Prayer-book puts last is regarded by S. Austin as the main object for which marriage was ordained: it was *for the mutual society, help, and comfort that one ought to have of the other* that Eve was given to Adam, and this (*De Bono Conjugali*, 1) is the main element in marriage. Those who agree together to live in continence by no means break the marriage bond; "imo firmius erit, quo magis ea pacta secum inierint, quæ carius concordiusque servanda sunt non voluptariis nexibus corporum sed voluntariis affectibus animorum" (*De Nuptiis et Concup.* I. 12).

Even during his life it was alleged against S. Austin that he unduly disparaged marriage, and that he had not wholly shaken himself free from the Manichæan errors of his youth; the charge has been repeated by Dean Milman in the most popular Church history of modern times, but it is difficult to see on what grounds it is based. S. Austin's language gives no excuse for that exaggerated depreciation of the married state which became common in Christendom at a later date. The conduct which Bede commends so highly in S. Etheldreda would possibly have seemed to him an unwarrantable reluctance to fulfil the duty to which she was bound by her marriage vows. The language in which he enforces the objection to the election of digamous bishops (*De Bono Conjugali*, 21) affords no palliation for the persistence shown by mediæval reformers, in imposing celibacy on the clergy of the English Church. He altogether repudiates the principles which were implied in the practice of later ecclesiastics. Non ergo duo mala sunt connubium et fornicatio quorum alterum pejus, sed duo bona sunt continentia et connubium quorum alterum est melius (*De Bono Conjugali*, 8). Bodily health and sickness are not two evils of which one is worse, but bodily health and immortality are each good, though one is better than the other. Like knowledge, the married state shall pass away, but continence, like charity, endures for ever, and hence the celibate life is the better of the two. But those who enter on this life may fall into sins which are as truly evil as incontinence, into luxury and pride and the habits of busybodies (*De Bono Conjugali*, 14).

Such teaching as this is entirely free from the exaggerations of a later age; but his doctrine is rendered clearer in the defence which may be found in the second book of his *De Nuptiis*, where he replies to the charge which had been brought against him by

Julianus, that in his antagonism to the Pelagian and Cœlestine heresies he had adopted the views of Manichæans, especially as to the transmission of sin to the offspring of carnal connexion. His detailed vindication of himself against the misrepresentations in a lost treatise are of little interest (see, however, xii.); but it is worth while to quote his summary on the main point at issue. Audi ergo breviter, quid in ista quæstione versetur. Catholici dicunt humanam naturam a creatore Deo bono conditam bonam, sed peccato vitiatam medico Christo indigere. Manichæi dicunt humanam naturam, non a Deo conditam bonam peccatoque vitiatam, sed ab æternarum principe tenebrarum de commixtione duarum naturarum, quæ semper fuerunt una bona et una mala, hominem creatum. Pelagiani et Cœlestini dicunt humanam naturam a bono Deo conditam bonam sed ita esse in nascentibus parvulis sanam, ut Christi non habeant necessariam in illa ætate medicinam (II. 9).

EXCURSUS F.

The Freedom of the Will, pp. 14, 80, 85.

1. The Will and Rational Freedom.
2. S. Austin's originality.
3. The asserted modification of his views.

1. WIGGERS complains (*August. u. Pelagian.* II. 383) that S. Austin confuses freedom as a moral condition with freedom as the faculty of a rational being, and the objection has been popularised by Neander (*History of Christian Religion,* IV. 371) and Professor Bain (*Mental and Moral Science,* 409). This widely diffused opinion amply deserves the caustic criticism it has called forth from Gangauf (*Metaph. Psych.* 325, 412). For it is difficult to see that S. Austin has been guilty of any confusion here: it would be more correct to say that the originality of his doctrine lies in his attempt to discriminate these two things, and to show how the exercise of *freedom as a faculty* is affected by *differences of moral condition.*

According to S. Austin, will is the power of determination without external compulsion, and rational beings are distinguished from things by the possession of this characteristic. Whether I determine to do what I like or what I dislike, it is by my will that the decision is taken. Non igitur nisi voluntate peccatur. Nobis autem voluntas nostra notissima est: neque enim scirem me velle, si quid sit voluntas ipsa nescirem. Definitur itaque isto modo: Voluntas est animi motus, cogente nullo, ad aliquid vel non amittendum, vel adipiscendum. Cur ergo ita tunc definire non possem? An erat difficile videre invitum volenti esse contrarium ita ut contrarium sinistrum dextro esse dicimus, non ut nigrum albo? Nam eadem res simul et nigra et alba esse non potest: duorum autem in medio quisque positus, ad alterum sinister est, ad alterum dexter; simul quidem utrumque unus homo, sed simul utrumque ad unum hominem nullo modo. Ita quidem invitus et volens unus animus simul esse potest; sed unum atque idem nolle simul et velle non potest. Cum enim quisque invitus aliquid facit, si eum roges utrum id facere velit, nolle se dicit: item si roges utrum id velit non facere, velle respondet (*De duab. Animabus* 14). Si autem nolunt, non utique coguntur ut non faciant, sed voluntate sua nolunt (*De Act. cum Fel. Man.* II. v.).

But the exercise of this faculty must be affected by the different conditions in which rational beings have existed. To the first man there was a real liberty of indifference, a complete "free choice." Sic et hominem fecit cum libero arbitrio, et quamvis sui futuri casus ignarum, tamen ideo beatum, quia et non mori et miserum non fieri in sua potestate esse sentiebat (*De Correp. et Grat.* 28). Denique ille [Adam] et terrente nullo, et insuper contra Dei terrentis imperium, libero usus arbitrio, non stetit in tanta felicitate, in tanta non peccandi facilitate (*De Correp. et Grat.* 35). Peccavit anima, et ideo misera est. Liberum arbitrium accepit; usa est libero arbitrio quemadmodum voluit: lapsa est, ejecta de beatitudine, implicata est miseriis (*Contra Fortunatum Disput.* II. 25).

Fallen man is enslaved by lust; separated from God he has no longer the power to keep himself free from sin. Man has not lost the power of will, but he has fallen from the state of freedom where he could exercise that power by avoiding sin. His act is still determined by his will, but it is a base and "servile freedom" of following his lower nature willingly. Nam et animæ in ipsis peccatis suis non nisi quamdam similitudinem Dei, superba et præpostera, et, ut ita dicam, servili libertate sectantur (*De Trinitate* XI. 8). But he need not rest satisfied with this low estate, for a better freedom than freedom to sin, or even than mere free choice, is held out to him: he may ultimately attain through Christ to a complete victory over sin, and thus to a divine freedom from evil in which it shall be impossible to sin. Sic enim oportebat prius hominem fieri, ut et bene velle posset et male; nec gratis, si bene; nec impune, si male: postea vero sic erit, ut male velle non possit; nec ideo libero carebit arbitrio. Multo quippe liberius erit arbitrium, quod omnino non poterit servire peccato (*Enchir.* cv.). Nam et ipsa libertas credentibus a liberatore promittitur. *Si vos*, inquit, *Filius liberaverit, tunc vere liberi eritis.* Victa enim vitio in quod cecidit voluntate, caruit libertate natura. Hinc alia Scriptura dicit, *A quo enim quis devictus est, huic et servus addictus est.* Sicut ergo non est opus sanis medicus, sed male habentibus: ita non est opus liberis liberator, sed servis; ut ei dicat gratulatio libertatis, *Salvam fecisti de necessitatibus animam meam* (Psal. xxx. 8). Ipsa enim sanitas est vera libertas, quæ non perisset, si bona permansisset voluntas. Quia vero peccavit voluntas, secuta est peccantem peccatum habendi dura necessitas, donec tota sanetur infirmitas, et accipiatur tanta libertas, in qua sicut necesse est permaneat beate vivendi voluntas, ita ut sit etiam bene vivendi et nunquam peccandi voluntaria felixque necessitas (*De Perfect. Just.* rat. 9). Nec ideo liberum arbitrium non habebunt, quia peccata eos delectare non poterunt. Magis quippe erit liberum, a delectatione peccandi usque ad delectationem non peccandi indeclinabilem liberatum. Nam primum liberum arbitrium, quod homini datum est, quando primum creatus est rectus, potuit non peccare, sed potuit et peccare: hoc autem novissimum eo potentius erit, quo peccare non poterit, verum hoc quoque Dei munere, non suæ possibilitate naturæ. Aliud est enim, esse Deum; aliud, participem Dei. Deus natura peccare non potest; particeps vero Dei ab illo accipit, ut peccare non possit. Servandi autem gradus erant divini muneris, ut primum daretur liberum arbitrium, quo non peccare posset homo; novissimum, quo peccare non posset: atque illud ad comparandum meritum, hoc ad recipiendum præmium pertineret. Sed quia peccavit ista natura cum peccare potuit, largiore gratia liberatur, ut ad eam perducatur libertatem, in qua peccare non possit (*De Civit. Dei*, XXII. xxx. 3).

It may render the whole clearer if we note that Pelagius ascribed to fallen man the same free choice which S. Austin regarded as the possession of Adam but forfeited by him. Libertas arbitrii, possibilitas est vel admittendi vel vitandi peccati, expers cogentis necessitatis (*Op. imp. contr. Julian.* I. lxxxii., also lxxviii., VI. x.). The Pelagians argued that if there were no such liberty of indifference, there could be no justification for the punishment of the sins of individuals now, but S. Austin held that as sin is committed "voluntarily" or willingly it does deserve punishment: while by maintaining that Adam really had free choice he avoided the position of the Manichæans.

2. It would be easy enough to show that there was no originality in any part of S. Austin's doctrine : it is chiefly remarkable for the subtle combination of views that had never been placed in such interconnexion before. Rational freedom as an ideal moral condition, freedom from sense and passion, had been the aim of many philosophers, both Oriental and Grecian. Free choice and the limits of its exercise was not a new subject of debate. The great body of Christian writers had undoubtedly spoken of it in terms which seemed to harmonise with the views of Pelagius in regard to human nature, for this was inevitable in consequence of the special character of the controversies of their time. Certe enim si de divinarum Scripturarum tractatoribus qui fuerunt ante nos, proferrem defensionem hujusce sententiæ, quam nunc solito diligentius atque copiosius contra novum Pelagianorum defendere urgemur errorem ; hoc est, gratiam Dei non secundum merita nostra dari, et gratis dari cui datur ; quia neque volentis, neque currentis, sed miserentis est Dei ; justo autem judicio non dari cui non datur, quia non est iniquitas apud Deum : si hujus ergo sententiæ defensionem ex divinorum eloquiorum nos præcedentibus catholicis tractatoribus promerem ; profecto hi fratres, pro quibus nunc agimus, acquiescerent : hoc enim significastis litteris vestris. Quid igitur opus est

ut eorum scrutemur opuscula, qui priusquam ista hæresis oriretur, non habuerunt necessitatem in hac difficili ad solvendum quæstione versari? quod procul dubio facerent, si respondere talibus cogerentur. Unde factum est ut de gratia Dei quid sentirent, breviter quibusdam scriptorum suorum locis et transeunter attingerent: immorarentur vero in eis quæ adversus inimicos Ecclesiæ disputabant, et in exhortationibus ad quasque virtutes, quibus Deo vivo et vero pro adipiscenda vita æterna et vera felicitate servitur (*De Prædest. Ss.* 27). But S. Austin's doctrine of the voluntary nature of the actions of fallen man—as well as his admission of an initial free choice—takes account of the phenomena on which they insisted. On the other hand, by dwelling as he does on the bondage of man to lust and passion, he calls attention to those phenomena on which the Stoics and other determinists rested their case.

It is perhaps all the more remarkable that he reached this deep and subtle doctrine by a simple endeavour to follow out the teaching of Scripture: here as always his philosophy is based on revelation, faith is the key to knowledge. He accepted the Bible account of the creation of man and his fall, and thus had new data on which to build his doctrine of the true character of the human will, and the conditions of its exercise. He accepted the Gospel message of a deliverance from sin, and thus was able to cherish the hope that man may attain to a condition of the truest freedom at length. It was in the light of the story of the fall and the hope of salvation that he could attempt to harmonise the one-sided and conflicting or isolated doctrines of preceding philosophers.

3. Much learned discussion has taken place on the question of a supposed modification in S. Austin's doctrine of the will; it has had reference specially to the date at which the alteration may be noted. It is commonly said that the exigencies of the Pelagian controversy forced him to express himself differently (Bright, *Anti-Pelagian Treatises*, li.). On the other hand Neander maintains (*History of Christian Religion*, IV. 298) that the change took place before his Episcopate; and that it would be more true to say that the exaggerated development of his doctrine called forth the Pelagian opposition than that the controversy with

Pelagius forced him to adopt extreme views. This difficulty is set in a new light by Gangauf, who argues with much acumen (*Metaph. Psych.* 325) that S. Austin's view did not undergo any real modification at all; but that he was forced to accentuate different sides of his opinion in the earlier and later controversies. S. Austin was as a rule by no means self-complacent when criticising his own work. Qui primo ratiocinationum contortione atque brevitate sic obscurus est, ut fatiget, cum legitur, etiam intentionem meam, vixque intelligatur a meipso (*Retract.* I. v. 1). Item de Mendacio scripsi librum, qui etsi cum aliquo labore intelligitur, habet tamen non inutilem ingenii et mentis exercitationem, magisque moribus ad veriloquium diligendum proficit. Hunc quoque auferre statueram de opusculis meis, quia et obscurus et anfractuosus, et omnino molestus mihi videbatur, propter quod eum nec edideram (*Retract.* I. xxvii.). But the question was raised in his own time, and he maintains that on this point he has not changed at all. Speaking of his books on *Free Will* he says, Ecce tam longe antequam Pelagiana hæresis exstitisset, sic disputavimus velut jam contra illos disputaremus (*Retr.* I. ix. 6). There is certainly a presumption that he understood his own opinion and could note a modification better than modern readers can hope to do: and an examination of the passages on which his critics rely confirms the impression that if his earlier and later statements appear to be inconsistent, it is because the view which he steadily maintained is one that is difficult to apprehend.

S. Austin's doctrine of the Will must however be understood before it is possible to enter on any discussion as to his opinion regarding the mode and effectiveness of the operation of divine grace on the human will. On this it must suffice to refer to Gangauf's excellent remarks (*Speculative Lehre*, 421). But the greater number of those who have appealed to S. Austin's authority, or criticised citations from his writings in regard to grace, have failed to grasp his position about the will. It is this which renders it unnecessary to discuss S. Austin's influence in connexion with the controversy between Calvinists and Armenians or Jesuits and Jansenists. Attempts were made to graft his theological views on to a doctrine of will which was not his; to try and find a clue by which to unravel the confusions that ensued would be a weary task which cannot be attempted here.

EXCURSUS G.

The influence of S. Austin on the English Church,
pp. 107, 129, 132.

1. The negative and positive proofs of his influence.
2. Its duration.
3. The *Prayer Book* and *Articles*.
4. The Brownists.
5. Penal Laws against Dissenters.
6. Passive Obedience.
7. Popular Influence in the XVIIth Century.
8. The XVIIIth Century.
9. His Eucharistic doctrine.

1. THE influence of S. Austin on the English Church is shown in two ways, negatively and positively. There is no point in which she has departed from his principles: there is no doctrine or practice of his which she has disavowed or condemned: no doctrine which she has defined in terms which he could not have accepted. On the other hand, Calvinism in all lands has discarded as superstitious many things he loved, and has recast his theological teaching in several points of vital importance.

His positive influence is shown in the fact that so many leading English theologians have consciously and avowedly been his disciples. S. Anselm, and Bradwardine, Cranmer and Laud were all consciously guided by him in regard to the points for which they were severally called to witness. Nor was it merely the heads of the hierarchy who looked to the Doctor who had done much to strengthen the episcopal order in his own day; King Alfred translated a portion of the *Soliloquies* for his people, and some of the leaders of popular religious movements within our Church have been his followers; for Wyclif quoted his authority, and Wesley was familiar with the patristic teaching which so closely resembled his own. The details which follow may help to show how greatly the English Church has been indebted to S. Austin in modern as well as in mediæval times.

2. It is a familiar fact that in the countries which acknowledged the authority of the Roman See through the middle ages there was far greater scope for diversity of opinion than has been permitted by the papacy since the sixteenth century. The decrees of the Council of Trent formulated with some slight modifications the theological doctrine which had been generally current in the immediately preceding centuries; but by the mere formulating of these doctrines, and through the action of the papacy in insisting on their acceptance as final, the opportunity for divergence of opinion was taken away. There was little enthusiasm anywhere for the new exposition of Latin orthodoxy, but it was in the Gallican Church that the opposition was most pronounced. At this juncture, the scope for the exercise of opinion on points of theology was distinctly narrowed, and the success of the Jesuits did something to enforce this uniformity; but in pre-Tridentine days, the tone of Christian thought in one land might differ considerably from that which was current in another. In a preceding section (Excursus B, § 6) there has been occasion to notice that the most perfect representative of S. Austin's school was found in the person of an English Archbishop: and that even after the time of S. Anselm, Thomas Bradwardine, and some of the most popular ecclesiastical writers which mediæval England produced followed on similar lines. Thus we find that while the world at large was divided between the Aristotelian Thomists, and Scotists with at least affinities to Pelagianism, the genuine Augustinian tradition was at any rate well represented among the leaders of English theology, in an age when it was much neglected elsewhere. The Franciscans who enjoyed such extraordinary popularity in England, doubtless diffused semi-Pelagian views among the people here and elsewhere in Europe. It is difficult to know how far the doctrine of the Archbishops and Bishops penetrated among their clergy, or permeated popular consciousness, but the mere fact that she produced writers and thinkers, who did so much to present the doctrine of S. Austin in its purity, does very distinctly mark the English Church from the rest of mediæval Christendom.

It might have been supposed that the violent reaction against mediæval usages which took place in the sixteenth century would have made a marked change in the treatment which his teaching received. Especially might this have been the case as he was at all events a patron of that mode of exposition which the first reformers at Oxford had denounced as futile and misleading. It is therefore curious to note that while Duns found his way to Bocardo, and the scholastic philosophy and canon law were discarded and forgotten, S. Austin retained his place as an authority in theology. He was perhaps more thoroughly read than had been the case for some generations, and rather gained than lost importance and influence.

This was undoubtedly partly due to the line which was taken by Molina and the Jesuits, as it seemed possible to convict them of departing from the teaching of one of the great doctors of the Latin Church[1]. Indeed polemical fervour carried men much farther than this: in so far as Lutheran and Calvinist writers ventured to appeal to Christian antiquity at all they sheltered themselves under the name of S. Austin. Luther and Calvin had dismissed the fathers generally with scant courtesy; but they made a partial exception in favour of the Bishop of Hippo. It thus came about that the works of S. Austin furnished a commonly recognised authority to which writers of every possible school appealed; and a good deal of controversy ensued of a most inconclusive sort between Romanists and their opponents. A priest named John Brerely published a work entitled *S. Austin's religion*, which I have not seen[2]: it called forth a vigorous Calvinistic reply by Mr William Crompton of Brazenose College, Oxford, and Preacher of the Word of God at Little Kymbell in Buckinghamshire. This is called *Saint Austin's religion: wherein is manifestly proved out of the Workes of that Learned Father who lived near twelve hundred years before the time of Luther, that he dissented from Poperie, and agreed with*

[1] Compare *True Idea of Jansenisme* by T(homas) G(ale), 1669, pp. 3—5.
[2] On the same side may be noticed the preface by Sir Tobias Matthew to his translation of the *Confessions* published in 1620, pp. 45—89. This work of the son of an English Archbishop who had been received into the Church of Rome called forth an angry rejoinder from Sutcliffe, the Dean of Exeter, which he entitled *The Unmasking of a Masse-monger, who in the counterfeit Habit of S. Augustine hath cunningly crept into the closets of many English Ladies. Or the Vindication of Saint Augustine's Confessions from the calumniations of a late noted Apostate*, 1626.

the religion of the Protestants in all the maine points of faith and doctrine, contrary to the impudent, erronious, and slanderous Position of the bragging Papists of our times who falsely affirme wee had no Religion before the Times of Luther and Calvaine. Whereunto is newly added, Saint Austin's Summes, in answer to Mr John Breerley Priest (1625). It is a work of considerable ingenuity, but is a mere patchwork of excerpts from different parts of S. Austin's writings: it was easy enough to quote isolated statements to show a certain affinity to Calvinistic doctrine, but the treatise cannot have been convincing to anyone[1]. It was easy for Romanists and Calvinists alike to show that their opponents had departed from the lines of doctrine and practice laid down by S. Austin, but it was impossible for either to demonstrate that their own system would have met his approval. Other writers appealed to him on particular issues; but just as he had exercised a special influence over English thought in the middle ages, so he continued to dominate as the greatest of Christian Doctors throughout the seventeenth century; and hence we find a very distinct continuity of doctrine through the leading English theologians from the time of S. Anselm to the beginning of the eighteenth century: though it seems as if his writings ceased to be generally studied during the Georgian era, when the philosophy of Locke had come to have its full effect on theological opinions in England.

3. The most striking change which took place under Henry VIII. and Edward VI. was the disuse of many pious rites which had undoubtedly been abused, but which were endeared to many

---

[1] Mr C. H. Collette's *Saint Augustine* puts the argument in regard to the departure of the Church of Rome from the teaching and practice of S. Austin in its strongest form—with special regard to recent definitions and developments of doctrine. Father Hewit, in his *Studies in S. Augustine*, has given a trenchant criticism on Calvinism. On the whole controversy it is worth while to remember the judgment of Julius Müller, "This must be openly admitted, by every unprejudiced historical investigation, that not merely the ecclesiastical theology of the middle ages, but even the Patristic theology of the fourth, fifth and sixth centuries, are upon every point that is a matter of dispute between Catholicism and Protestantism, more on the side of the former than of the latter." (Quoted by Döllinger, *Church and Churches*, 208.)

hearts by long association. But there were good grounds for saying that these changes were in accordance with the tone of S. Austin's teaching and would have had his approval. In the preface to the Prayer Book we read *Of Ceremonies:*

"Some are put away, because the great excess and multitude of them hath so increased in these latter days, that the burden of them was intolerable; whereof Saint *Augustine* in his time complained, that they were grown to such a number, that the estate of Christian people was in worse case concerning that matter, than were the Jews. And he counselled that such yoke and burden should be taken away[1], as time would serve quietly to do it. But what would Saint *Augustine* have said, if he had seen the Ceremonies of late days used among us; whereunto the multitude used in his time was not to be compared?"

It may not unfairly be said that the general principles of the revision of the services of the English Church under Cranmer in 1549, were in complete accordance with the principles expressed in S. Austin's letters to Januarius. The above quoted declaration on the subject appears as an appendix in the First Prayer Book of King Edward VI. Cranmer and the first reformers were consciously and avowedly following his instructions in this matter. This is confirmed by a comparison of the ritual explicitly retained and enjoined in that Prayer Book with these letters, as there is a close accordance between the religious usages that were there enjoined and those which S. Austin had practised. Complete coincidences in detail we hardly hope to find: the address in the

---

[1] Omnia itaque talia, quæ neque sanctarum Scripturarum auctoritatibus continentur, nec in conciliis episcoporum statuta inveniuntur, nec consuetudine universæ Ecclesiæ roborata sunt, sed pro diversorum locorum diversis moribus innumerabiliter variantur, ita ut vix aut omnino nunquam inveniri possint causæ, quas in eis instituendis homines secuti sunt, ubi facultas tribuitur, sine ulla dubitatione resecanda existimo. Quamvis enim neque hoc inveniri possit, quomodo contra fidem sint; ipsam tamen religionem, quam paucissimis et manifestissimis celebrationum sacramentis misericordia Dei esse liberam voluit, servilibus oneribus premunt, ut tolerabilior sit conditio Judæorum, qui etiamsi tempus libertatis non agnoverunt, legalibus tamen sarcinis, non humanis præsumptionibus subjiciuntur. Sed Ecclesia Dei inter multam paleam multaque zizania constituta, multa tolerat, et tamen quæ sunt contra fidem vel bonam vitam non approbat, nec tacet, nec facit. *Ep.* lv. 35. See also *Ep.* liv.

Marriage Service to which reference has been made above (Excursus E) was apparently drawn from the *Consultatio* of Archbishop Hermann of Cologne, and was not directly borrowed from the African Bishop. On the other hand, in the *Homilies* which date from the same period, the references to S. Austin are not infrequent. There are far fewer signs of his direct influence on the *Articles*, although they are not inconsistent with his teaching. The seventeenth Article appears to be Calvinistic; but it has no reference to predestination to evil, except as an opinion that may drive the "curious" to "desperation": it deals with predestination to life, and certainly implies the important distinction between prescience and predestination. "It is evident," wrote Dean Fogg, "that although the Hypothetical Prescience which we have said must be understood in this Doctrine of Predestination is not Mention'd in *express Words* in this Article, yet it must necessarily be supposed, because the Article affirms God to have firmly decreed from Eternity, to have delivered those whom he had Chosen in Christ, and by certain means bring them to Salvation; for it is necessary that he should Fore-see those to be Created, and in the Rank of Creatures indowed with Freedom of Choice, to be ready to abuse their Freedom, yea, to be lapsed, that he should, I say, foresee them, at least Hypothetically, and Antecedently (according to our Capacity of Understanding in Matters of this Nature) before he decreed anything concerning their Deliverance. Therefore we have only uttered, that something more Explicitly, which is *Necessarily* supposed and Concisely suggested in the Article[1]."

That the Articles, though Augustinian, are not Calvinistic is farther brought out by the refusal of the Hampton Court Conference to accept the gloss which the Puritans desired to incorporate into Article XVI., so as to introduce the Calvinistic doctrine of perseverance. But in protesting against this change, and retaining the Article in the same form as before, the Conference was really maintaining the doctrine of S. Austin, as is clearly shown by Thorndike[2]. It thus appears that the Church of England refused to incorporate definitely Calvinistic doctrines

---

[1] *God's Infinite Grace in Election*, by Lawrence Fogg (1713), p. 43.
[2] *Epilogue to the Tragedy of the Church of England*, II. xxxi. §§ 48, 51.

even in that portion of her formularies where Genevan influence showed itself most strongly: she still continues to maintain the doctrine of S. Austin.

4. Passing now from these changes in the services of the Church and the new formularies to the principles on which action was taken in the seventeenth century, we find the same constant appeal to S. Austin. The pressing question as to the treatment of Brownists, and Puritan Dissenters generally, presented a striking parallel to the difficulties connected with the Donatist schism. The subject is worked out with much acuteness by George Gyffard, Minister at Maldon, a writer with Genevan sympathies, in a work entitled *A Plaine Declaration that our Brownists be full Donatists*. Some paragraphs may be quoted as showing the method by which he endeavoured to establish his thesis.

"We see that the Donatists departed disorderlie out of the Church, condemning it not for any point of doctrine (for therein they did not disagree) but for that many, which in the time of persecution dissembled, many which revolted, and to save their lives did sacrifice to the Idolls: many which delivered the bookes of holie Scripture to bee burned, and betraied the names of the brethren: when the storme was over, and there was a sodaine calme, the Emperor Constantine being become Christian, such joy in all Christian lands, Christianitie magnified with such honour: for that (I say) many such returned to professe the Gospel againe as members of the Church, and were received. For, saide the Donatists, the Church is holie, consisting of such as he called foorth and separated from the impure and wicked world: and therefore no separation being made, but such villanous traitors, so vile Idolaters and their children being communicated with all, all your assemblies through this mixture are none other before God, but heapes of abominable unclean persons. Your teachers are the sons of Apostates and traitors, and no Ministers of Christ. Now look upon the Donatists of England: Antichrist hath been exalted according to the prophesie of S. Paul, he hath sate in the Temple of God, boasting himselfe as God, persecuting and murthering God's true worshippers. He is disclosed by the glorious light of the Gospell: his damnable doctrine, cursed Idolatrie, and usurped tyrannie are cast foorth of this land by the holie sacred power of our dread Souveraigne Ladie Queene Elizabeth, whom God hath placed and settled upon the Throne of this noble Kingdome. The true doctrine of faith is published and penalties are by lawes appoynted for such as shall stubbernlie despise the same. Our Donatists crie out, that our assemblies (as ye may see in their printed bookes) and that the people were all by constraint received immediatlie from Idolatrie into our Church without preaching of the Gospell, by the sound of a Trumpet at the Coronation of the Queene, that they be confused assemblies, without any separation of the good from the bad. They affirme also that our Ministers have their discent and ordination, and power, from Antichrist, and so are his marked servants. Hereupon, not understanding the manifest Scripture, that the Apostasie having invaded the Church, it continued still even then the temple of God in which Antichrist did sit, and that the verie Idolaters were within the Church, were sealed with the signe of baptisme, professed Christ in some points rightlie, their children from ancient discent being within the covenant of God, and of right to bee baptized, the Ministerie of Christ so farre remaining, as that it was the authentick seale which was delivered by the same ; in a mad furie, like blind hypocrites they condemne the reformation by civill power, and purging God's Temple by the authoritie of Princes, because the Church of Christ is founded and built by the doctrine of the Gospell. Herein they are deceived, that they imagine the Princes take upon them to compell those to bee a Church which were none before : whereas indeed they do but compell those within their kingdom over whome the Lord hath set them, which have received the signe of the covenant, and professe themselves to bee members of the Church, accordinglie to renounce and forsake all false worship, and to imbrace the doctrine of salvation. What other thing did Josias and other holie Kings of Juda, when they compelled the multitude of Idolaters, which were the seed of Abraham, and circumcised, to forsake their Idolatrie and to worship the Lord ? It is most cleare also, that where the reformation of the Kings was not perfect, (as appeareth in the bookes of the Kings and Chronicles) yet all the foulest things being abolished, and the substance of trueth brought in, they were reputed godlie

Churches, where many were false brethren and open offenders. The Brownists blinded with their swelling pride, and not seeing the evident matters of the Scriptures, without all order of that holie discipline of Christ, accuse, condemne and forsake our Churches, under the appearance of fervent zeale, and rigorous severitie against all sinne, not inferiour to the Donatists: as if they were the onely men that stood for Christ and his kingdome, they crie out aloude and proclaime all the Ministers of our Churches to be Antichristian, the sonnes of the Pope, false Prophets, Baal's Priests that prophesie in Baal, and plead for Baal, persecutors of the just, bearing the marke, the power and life of the beast, because they say our ordeiners bee such. They say wee have no word of God, no Sacraments nor true Church, but that all is utterlie polluted and become abominable: our assemblies they call the very Synagogs of Antichrist, utterlie fallen from the Covenant of God, and all that joyne with them, through the pollution of open sinners which are not cast foorth: and therefore they have separated themselves, and crie aloud unto others to doo the same if they will be saved. What rule of discipline have they observed in this: Have these things been brought foorth, scanned, discussed, and judged in the Synods of the learned Pastors and teachers of the Churches? Nay, but even as Augustine saith of the other, *furor, dolus, et tumultus*, furie, deceit and tumult, do beare the sway. Then I conclude, that in this poynt of accusing, condemning, and manner of separating themselves from the Church, the Donatists and the Brownists doo agree and are alike.

* * * * * *

"Thus have I laide open, that the Church in olde time was full of open wicked men both of ministers and people: That the Donatists under the colour of zeale and severitie against sinne did separate themselves, affirming that all were polluted and fallen from the covenant, which did communicate in the worship of God and Sacraments with such notorious evill men. All men may see by that which I have noted, that the Donatists did maintaine this their opinion with the same Scriptures and arguments that the Brownists doe maintain it withall nowe: And received the same answers to confute them, which we make nowe to confute the Brownists. This was the maine point of Donatisme and as it were the pith and substance thereof: and it is one of the foure chiefe pillers of Brownisme. Yea but now the Brownists doe separate themselves from a worship which is Idolatrous, full of blasphemies and abominations: The Donatists did rend themselves from an holy and true worship. Indeede where the worship is idolatrous and blasphemous, a man is to separate himself. But there are many and great corruptions before it come to that: for it is the true worship of God where the foundation is layd and standeth sure. If there be timber, Hay, and stubble built upon the foundation, the fault is great, such things are not to bee approved: But yet there is Gods true worship. And now to come to the verie poynt of the matter: I doe affirm and will stand to justifie that there were greater corruptions in the worship of God, even in those Churches from which the Donatists did seperate themselves, than be at this day in the worship of the Church of England. So that if Brownisme be anything to be excused in that, the Donatisme may as justly therein be defended. For if wee consider matters which concerne doctrine what can any man shew so corrupt in this our Church, as in the publike worship to pray for the soules of the dead, and to offer oblations for the dead? This corruption was generall in the Church then, yea long before the days of Augustine, as it appeareth in Cyprian and by Tertullian which was before him, and nearer to the time of the Apostles: who in his booke De Monogamia reasoning against second marriage (for hee was fallen into that error) woulde persuade any woman that had buried her husband not to marie againe, because, he being separated from her in peace and not divorced, she was to pray for his soule and yearely to offer oblation for him: thus he writeth, *Et pro anima ejus oret, et refrigerium interim adpostulet ei et in prima resurrectione consortium: et offerat annuis diebus dormitionis ejus.* That is, And let her pray for his soule and crave refreshing for him nowe in the mean time, and his felowship in the first resurrection, and let her offer yearely upon the day of his departure. It will be said by some ignorant man, that this was but the minde and practice of some few which were corrupt and superstitious. I answere it was the practice of the Church in generall, and the corruption so anncient, that the same Tertullian in his booke *De corona militis*, speaking of it and certain other things saith they were observed by tradition from the Apostles, they were observed so generally in the Churches and no scripture to warrant them. These bee his wordes, *Oblationes pro defunctis, annua die facimus.* Wee make oblations for the dead on the yeerely day. The doctrine of Purgatory, and the doctrine of Free will were crept in also[1], besides divers other grosse errors

[1] Gyffard's argument would have been more conclusive if he could have shown that either the Donatists or S. Austin disapproved of these practices. As to S. Austin's views, the English priests abroad endeavoured to keep their countrymen fully informed in various works, but especially in a little volume, *Saint Austin's care for the dead*, which was issued in 1636. Calvin and his followers endeavoured to explain away his language as if it were a mere accommodation to popular superstitions which he was not at the trouble to rebuke. "We ought not," says Calvin, "to indulge our love so far as to set up a perverse mode of prayer in the Church. Surely every person possessed of the least prudence easily perceives, that whatever we meet with on this subject in ancient writers, was in deference to public custom and the ignorance of the vulgar. I admit they were themselves also carried away into error, the usual effect of rash credulity being to destroy the judgment. Meanwhile the passages themselves show, that when they recommended prayer for the dead it was with hesitation. Augustine relates in his *Confessions* that his mother, Monica, earnestly entreated to be remembered when the solemn rites at the altar were performed; doubtless an old woman's wish, which her son did not bring to the test of Scripture, but from natural affection wished others to approve. His book *de Cura pro mortuis agenda* is so full of doubt, that its coldness may well extinguish the heat of a foolish zeal." *Institutes* III. v. 10.

It is however sufficiently clear that S. Austin himself attached a high value to the practice of offering the Eucharist on behalf of the dead, and to prayers for the dead. Besides those in the tract on which Calvin pronounced such a strange criticism there are many other references to the subject in his writings.

The chief passages on the state of the dead are, *Conf.* IX. 6, *Enarratio in Ps.* xxxvi. 1, 10, *Enchiridion*, cix. As to the offering the Eucharist on behalf of the dead his language is very clear. Orationibus vero sanctæ Ecclesiæ, et sacrificio salutari et eleemosynis, quæ pro eorum spiritibus erogantur, non est dubitandum mortuis adjuvari ut cum eis misericordius agatur a Domino, quam eorum peccata meruerunt. Hoc enim a patribus traditum, universa observat Ecclesia, ut pro eis qui in corporis et sanguinis Christi communione defuncti sunt, cum ad ipsum Sacrificium loco suo commemorantur, oretur ac pro illis quoque id offerre commemoretur. *Sermo* CLXXII. 2, compare also *Conf.* IX. 27, 32. Of course to S. Austin's mind universal custom and tradition of the fathers implied apostolic authority. In Macha-

which sundrie of the chief teachers held, some in one poynt some in another. Touching Ceremonies not for order and comlynes, but with signification, the libertie was exceeding which men tooke and the corruption greevous, which was not espied but of few. Tertullian for his time nameth these, which he saith were received by tradition and had no scripture to warrant them. First in baptism having shewed what they professed, and the three times dipping into the water, hee addeth, *Inde suscepti lactis et mellis concordiam*

bæorum libris legimus oblatum pro mortuis sacrificium (II. *Mac.* XII. 43). Sed et si nusquam in Scripturis veteribus omnino legeretur, non parva est universæ Ecclesiæ, quæ in hac consuetudine claret, auctoritas, ubi in precibus sacerdotis quæ Domino Dei ad ejus altare funduntur, locum suum habet etiam commendatio mortuorum. *De Cura pro Mortuis*, 3. It is also clear from S. Austin's own prayer for his mother in *Conf.* IX. 35 and from *Enchiridion*, cx. that he believed that the defilements of sin which God's saints carry with them from this world are expiable in the place of the dead.

At the same time it is pretty clear that, whether it is a legitimate development of his view or not, he did not hold the Roman doctrine of purgatory, as popularly understood in the present day. On this as in so many other points his position is adequately represented by the doctrines of our Reformers as represented in the First Prayer Book of Edward VI., especially in the Burial Service: nor does *Article* XXII. condemn his practice in this matter, so far as we can gather it from his writings. The whole subject, both as regards Scriptural and patristic authority and the opinion of English theologians, was thoroughly discussed by the Hon. Archibald Campbell, in his book on *The Doctrines of a Middle State* (1721), a work which called forth the following judgment from Dean Hickes: "And it were much to be wished that in those Churches (both of the East and West) where it is still kept up it were perfectly reformed according to the true Primitive Model, from all Superstitions and Abuses of every kind; and that in those where for the sake of these it hath been removed out of the Public Service, it might be restored again in its first Integrity, according to the best and most ancient forms which we have extant. This though it be a Real, yet I can by no means look upon as an essential defect in a Church; and especially where the same is barely omitted, not positively condemned or anathematised: And therefore I cannot but esteem it very unwarrantable and absurd for anyone to leave a Communion on that Account and go over to another where the same is retained, but not without most gross Superstition, were there even nothing else to be considered in the Change of Communions. So far is the Primitive Practice of Prayers and Oblations for the Souls of the Faithful Departed from either inferring the Purgatory of the Modern Church of Rome, or from disposing any one to seek for refuge in a Church so greatly departed from her first Faith and Practice." Campbell's *Doctrines of a Middle State*, 202.

prægustamus. Exque ea die lavacro quotidiano per totam hebdomadam abstinemus. That is Taken from thence (hee meaneth from the water) wee first taste the concord of milke and hony, and from that day we abstaine from the dayly washing a whole week. *Die dominico jejunium nefas ducimus vel de geniculis adorare: Eadem immunitate a die paschæ in Pentecostem usque gaudemus.* That is We account it an heynous matter to fast on the Lord's day or to worship upon the knees: by the same freedome, from Easter unto Pentecost we rejoyce. And by and by after hee saith *Ad omnem progressum atque promotum, ad omnem aditum et exitum, ad vestitum, ad calciamentum, ad lavacra, ad mensas, ad lumina, ad cubilia, ad sedilia, quacunque nos conversatio exercet, frontem crucis signaculo terimus.* That is, At everie setting forward and moving, at everie coming to or going foorth, at our appareling and putting on our shoes, at washing, at table, at lighting the candle, at bed, at sitting, whatsoever wee are busied about, we weare our forehead with the signe of the Crosse. These superstitious observations were crept into the Church, and in the days of Tertullian who lived not much more than two hundred yeares after our Saviour Christ, receaved so generallie, that hee saieth they were by tradition from the Apostles. Augustine unto Januarius complaineth that there was such a multitude of rites or ceremonies in the Church. But what should I labour in this point: If the Brownists will affirme that there be as great corruptions in the worship of the Church of England, if we respect either doctrine or ceremonies, as were in the Churches from which the Donatists did separate themselves, they shall be convinced of grosse ignorance. And if they stande in it, they shall shew themselves shameless: let the reader in the meantime, but looke upon the Epistle of Master Beza before the new Testament, and see what he affirmeth in this matter, how corrupt the Churches were. Then I conclude that the Donatists separating themselves from Churches more corrupt than the Churche of England in the worship of God, as I dare stand to maintain against them; if they denie it, may as well bee excused as the Brownists, and so hetherto they bee even bretheren with them or their naturall Children, no difference to bee found at all" (pp. 6 f., 37 f.).

5. It was not only in the early days of Puritanism that it

was confronted by the authority of the Bishop of Hippo: he was also summoned to justify the civil proceedings which were subsequently taken against non-conformists. When after the temporary triumph of Presbyterianism, the State stepped in to enforce penalties against non-conformists and dissenters, there was once more a parallel to be found in the similar action of the Christian Emperors. In neither case had the Church initiated the movement for penal legislation[1], in neither case did the penalties compare in severity with the treatment which Churchmen had already suffered at the hands of schismatics when they had the power of working their will[2]: but it was obvious that the violence of the sectaries could never give any real justification for violent reprisals, and it was doubtful whether such civil penalties could be fairly accepted by the Church as a support to her Master's cause. Such a question of political duty, depending as it did on the political conditions of the time, could not of course be decided by an appeal to the opinion of a bygone age, but the opinion of S. Austin on the corresponding difficulty in his own day might certainly be of use in helping men to a sound judgment on the expediency of imposing civil disabilities upon schismatics. It was specially convincing perhaps because S. Austin had himself changed his opinion on the point[3]; experience of the working of the penal laws had led him to renounce the opinions he had once held,—that no man ought to be compelled to the unity of Christ, and that this was to be done only by argument

---

[1] Ranke's *History of England*, III. 367.

[2] Walker's *Sufferings of the Clergy*, pp. 59, 73.

[3] Si trahimur ad Christum, ergo inviti credimus; ergo violentia adhibetur, non voluntas excitatur. Intrare quisquam ecclesiam potest nolens, accedere ad altare potest nolens, accipere Sacramentum potest nolens: credere non potest nisi volens. Si corpore crederetur, fieret in nolentibus: sed non corpore creditur. Apostolum audi: *Corde creditur ad justitiam. Et quid sequitur? Ore autem confessio fit ad salutem.* De radice cordis surgit ista confessio. Aliquando audis confitentem, et nescis credentem. Sed nec debes vocare confitentem, quem judicas non credentem. Hoc est enim confiteri, dicere quod habes in corde: si autem aliud in corde habes, aliud dicis; loqueris, non confiteris. Cum ergo in Christum corde credatur, quod nemo utique facit invitus, qui autem trahitur, tanquam invitus cogi videtur; quomodo istam solvimus quæstionem, *Nemo venit ad me nisi Pater qui misit me traxerit eum?* In Joan. Ev. Tract. XXVI. 2.

and the force of disputation, and that men were to be convinced by reason and not compelled by laws,—and to approve of the edict of Constantine (*Ep.* xciii. 17, *Vincentio*). The anonymous translator who reprinted this *Judgment of the learned and pious S. Augustine concerning penal lawes against Conventicles* in 1670, introduces it with an interesting preface in which he says that he publishes this epistle "because of the Great Esteem which this Holy and Learned Prelate hath always had in the Church of Christ, and especially in that part of it which hath accounted itself the most Reformed, and we see that most Men are more led by the Authority of the Writer than the Strength of the Argument. Besides when those who have written amongst us are charged by the Adverse Party to be partial, by reason of their interest in the Present Controversie; This cannot be laid to the charge of Him who dyed many hundred years before Our Present Debate." But the translator did not notice that it was this very fact of distance of time and diversity of circumstances which made S. Austin's experience irrelevant to the precise issue. The general opinion in the present day, based on the experience of the last two centuries, would certainly be against reliance on penal laws in such a cause. This was very strongly put by Peter Bayle in the third part of his *Commentaire philosophique sur ces paroles de Jesus Christ, Contrain les d'entrer* which was published at Canterbury in 1687, where there is some caustic criticism of S. Austin's reasoning.

Perhaps the chief interest in the matter lies in the side light which it throws on the working of S. Austin's mind, and his persistent reliance on experience (see above, Excursus A). For the rest it is easy to show that he had attained to a far truer ideal of toleration than was at all common among those who denounced the Clarendon Code at the time of the Revolution. Locke was satisfied to prove in his *Essay on Toleration* that the State might be indifferent to any form of religious opinion (except Atheism) because they had all a sufficiently similar bearing upon civil duty. S. Austin goes far deeper: he has such confidence in the prevailing power of Truth that he can listen calmly to the most hostile opinion. Nullus enim reprehensor formidandus est amatori veritatis. Etenim aut inimicus reprehensurus est, aut amicus. Si ergo inimicus insultat, ferendus est: amicus autem si errat, docendus; si docet, audiendus (*De Trin.* II. 1).

6. Far more interesting than his apology for penal measures is the question as to the political principles which he upheld. There were in the seventeenth century two very opposite opinions which were held and acted upon by professing Christians: we have on the one hand the active desire to obey God's will as understood, and to oppose to the death any authority which dared to intervene: this was the standpoint of Puritanism generally, but it is seen most clearly in the persons of the Covenanters, and constantly led them into rebellion against existing authority. At the opposite pole was the doctrine of those who seemed to carry compliance to the extreme of subservience, and insisted on the duty of obedience to constituted authority. Their doctrine was that of passive obedience: that it was the duty of the subject to do the commands of the ruler in everything which did not conflict with the revealed will of God; and that in cases where this active obedience was inconsistent with Christian duty, as in the time of the Christian emperors, they were still to submit themselves to the will of the earthly ruler by bearing the punishments he imposed patiently, i.e. by passive obedience. A most striking instance of the effort to maintain these principles may also be drawn from Scotland, in the story of the Episcopate there since the Revolution.

English Churchmen and Scotchmen who remained in communion with them, were in advocating the duty of passive obedience sufficiently distinguished from Jesuits on the one hand and Puritans on the other; but they were also maintaining precisely the Christian view of civil duty as it had been understood and set forth by S. Austin. It may even be said that his teaching in political matters came into greater prominence in England in the XVIIth century than in any other land, or at any previous time. It is of course true, that the whole form of the political institutions of the middle ages was an actualisation of ideas that he set forth, and that he exercised an extraordinary political influence even then. But it is also true that the feudal forms which moulded society in so many ways did not readily lend themselves to the application of his doctrines;

while in the later middle ages the influence of Aristotle and the example of the free citizenship of ancient pagan times impressed the schoolmen more deeply than the isolated hints in S. Austin. These two elements are very noticeable in Wyclif's doctrine of *Dominion;* it is permeated by feudal analogies, and specially by analogies with the English feudalism of 1085, when each tenant received his land directly from the king. But in the XVIIth century all this was changed and the influence of S. Austin was more directly and fully felt. There are two points on which it is worth while to note his opinion. He does not conceal his preference for the monarchy of the Empire in discussing the fortunes of the Roman Republic (*De Civ. Dei,* III. xxi.); and his criticism of its injustice and cruelty leads him to speak of the God who is the supreme Governor of the whole universe (*De Civ. Dei,* XIX. xxi). But on the whole his preference for monarchical institutions is not so decided as it was among XVIIth century English Churchmen, as he considers that under some circumstances one, and under others another form of polity may be preferable (*De Lib. Arb.* 1. 14), though royalty as opposed to faction is the type of well-ordered rule (*De Bono Conjug.* 16). Civil authority has however grown up with the divine sanction—it was not, as in Filmer, part of the primal grant to man—and it will pass away when its purpose is served (*De Civ. Dei,* XIX. xv). Still he insists on the Christian duty of obedience to the civil power, while he carefully draws a line as to the limits of its authority. Quod autem ait, *Omnis anima potestatibus sublimioribus subdita sit: non est enim potestas nisi a Deo,* rectissime jam monet, ne quis ex eo quod a Domino suo in libertatem vocatus est, factusque christianus, extollatur in superbiam, et non arbitretur in hujus vitæ itinere servandum esse ordinem suum, et potestatibus sublimioribus, quibus pro tempore rerum temporalium gubernatio tradita est, putet non se esse subdendum. Cum enim constemus ex anima et corpore, et quamdiu in hac vita temporali sumus, etiam rebus temporalibus ad subsidium degendæ hujus vitæ utamur; oportet nos ex ea parte, quæ ad hanc vitam pertinet, subditos esse potestatibus, id est, hominibus res humanas cum aliquo honore administrantibus. Ex illa vero parte qua credimus Deo, et in regnum ejus vocamur, non nos oportet esse subditos cuiquam homini, idipsum in nobis evertere cupienti, quod Deus ad vitam æternam donare dignatus est. Si quis ergo putat quoniam christianus est, non sibi esse vectigal reddendum, aut tributum, aut non esse exhibendum honorem debitum eis quæ hæc curant potestatibus; in magno errore versatur. Item si quis sic se putat esse subdendum, ut etiam in suam fidem habere potestatem arbitretur cum qui temporalibus administrandis aliqua sublimitate præcellit; in majorem errorem labitur. Sed modus iste servandus est, quem Dominus ipse præscribit, ut reddamus Cæsari quæ Cæsaris sunt, et Deo quæ Dei sunt. Quanquam enim ad illud regnum vocemur ubi nulla erit potestas hujusmodi, in hoc tamen itinere dum agimus, donec perveniamus ad illud sæculum ubi fit evacuatio omnis principatus et potestatis, conditionem nostram pro ipso rerum humanarum ordine toleremus, nihil simulate facientes, et in eo ipso non tam hominibus quam Deo, qui hæc jubet, obtemperantes. *Quarumdam Prop. ex Epist. ad Rom., Expositio* LXXII.

Very interesting too is his doctrine as to the true basis of civil law, not in mere human convention or expediency, but in the Divine Will. Simul etiam te videre arbitror in illa temporali [lege] nihil esse justum atque legitimum quod non ex hac æterna sibi homines derivarint. *De Lib. Arb.* I. 15. Compare also *De Civitate Dei*, XIX. xxi, *De Vera Religione*, 58.

These are the elements which were compounded into the doctrine of the divine right of kings, as we find it in the pages of Jacobean and Caroline writers. The doctrine of passive obedience is more explicitly stated in a passage to which Archbishop Laud referred in his defence of the Canon of 1640 (*Works*, III. 36). It runs thus: Si Dominus cœli et terræ, per quem facta sunt omnia, servivit indignis, rogavit pro sævientibus et furentibus, et tanquam medicum se exhibuit adveniens (nam et medici et arte et sanitate meliores serviunt ægrotis); quanto magis non debet dedignari homo, ex toto animo, et ex tota bona voluntate, cum tota dilectione servire domino etiam malo? Ecce servit melior deteriori, sed ad tempus. Quod autem dixi de domino et servo, hoc intelligite de potestatibus et regibus, de omnibus culminibus hujus sæculi. Aliquando enim potestates bonæ sunt, et timent Deum; aliquando non timent Deum. Julianus exstitit infidelis imperator, exstitit apostata, iniquus, idololatra: milites christiani servierunt imperatori infideli; ubi veniebatur ad causam Christi, non agnoscebant nisi illum qui in cœlo erat. Si quando volebat ut idola colerent, ut thurificarent, præponebant illi Deum: quando autem dicebat, Producite aciem, ite contra illam gentem, statim obtemperabant. Distinguebant dominum æternum a domino temporali; et tamen subditi erant propter dominum æternum etiam domino temporali. *Enarr. in Ps.* cxxiv. 7. This passage is also noticeable as it not impossibly suggested to Wyclif the famous paradox in which he expressed his doctrine of dominion. There is indeed a curious irony in noticing that it is at all events possible that the revolutionary doctrines of John Ball may be traced through a misunderstanding of Wyclif's idealism to the very sentences which served as the chief patristic authority for the passive obedience of the Caroline divines. However that may be there can be no doubt that the doctrine of civil obedience which was adopted by the clergy of the seventeenth century was consciously based on the teaching of the fathers, and in particular of S. Austin. For other sides of his political teaching it is well worth while to consult M. L. Dubief's *Essai sur les idées politiques de Saint Augustin* (1859).

7. We have other evidence of the influence which his name exercised during the seventeenth century. When the authorised version of the English Bible was first put forth the translators compiled a most interesting preface which is too little known in the present day. They were anxious to remove certain objections to their undertaking, and to the way in which they had executed their task, and it is very remarkable to notice how time after time they attempt to justify themselves by an apt quotation from S. Austin. They of course appeal to other patristic authority as well, but the frequency of their references to the Bishop of Hippo in regard to one point after another shows that if they did not rely on him exclusively, they believed that their readers would especially value his opinion.

There were several other matters too in which appeal was made to his authority: it was obviously the opinion of seventeenth century writers that S. Austin's words would carry greater weight with the public than anything they could say themselves. Thus Sir Henry Spelman appends to his *De Non Temerandis Ecclesiis* (1613) a translation of a supposititious sermon of S. Austin's, *De*

Reddendis Decimis (Appendix, *Sermo* CCLXXVII.), for the genuineness of which he contends.

Matthew Scrivener fell into a similar error, when he translated two sermons (Appendix, *Sermo* CCXLIV., CCXLV.) with the view of better "encountering so grand an Enemy and over-grown a Monster as the vice of Drunkenness in this present Age" (*A treatise Against Drunkennesse*, 1685).

One other attempt of a similar kind may be noticed. Dr Stillingfleet had published in his *Vindication* of the protestant grounds of faith some rather disparaging criticism of miracles attributed to S. Francis Xavier and other Jesuits. This called forth the *Digitus Dei*, an anonymous pamphlet without date or place of publication, which consists of a translation of the *De Civitate*, XXII. viii, and is followed by some *Reflexions*, in which the argument from the continuance of miraculous gifts is used in a way which S. Austin would hardly have endorsed. It is perhaps most interesting where the appeal is made to moral certainty—a conception which is carefully defined, and which was destined to play an important part in the great controversy with the Deists, that must have been beginning about that time: though some verbal criticism is directed more especially against Stillingfleet, the full force of the argument is turned against those who held deistical opinions. Thus through the whole of the seventeenth century we find indirect evidence from the use that was made of S. Austin's works as to the weight which his opinion appeared to have with the English public.

8. The eighteenth century witnessed a revival of the controversy in regard to Predestination and Free Will: it was called forth by the writings of President Edwards, but the references to S. Austin's doctrine are comparatively few, and writers on each side seemed to assume that it was identical with that of Calvin. The philosophy of Locke, and indirectly the discoveries of Newton, had come to exercise an enormous influence over the English public; and for good or evil, they rendered disputants more inclined to argue out questions as they appeared to their own individual minds, and less disposed to attach importance to the opinions of bygone ages. Even among the Oxford methodists with their strong attachment to the authority of the Church, and

determination to live by a strict rule, personal experience was the basis of their whole doctrine. When we consider the interesting parallels which might be drawn between the story of S. Austin and that of John Wesley,—the similarity in the combination of a dialectical and mystical vein in both,—the close affinity on many points of doctrine—it is most extraordinary that the African father should be so little regarded. It is of course true that Wesley was acquainted with S. Austin's writings, and refers to him not infrequently: he knew him better than most of his contemporaries, for he was clear that he could not be treated as a thorough-going supporter of Calvinistic doctrine (*Works*, x. 255). There are frequent references to different treatises in his *Roman Catechism and a Reply to it*, and Augustinian phrases occur here and there in his sermons. He dwelt with approval on the account of S. Austin's conversion in his *Confessions*, VII. 10. But Wesley felt no enthusiasm for the African Doctor and pronounced a judgment on him which is very unsympathetic (*Works*, VI. 310). Nor did the founder of Methodism attribute any of his own spiritual progress to the influence of S. Austin's writings; while he did not include any of them among the numerous abridgments which he issued for the use of the English public.

Nor is it only in this connexion that the absence of eighteenth century references to S. Austin is noteworthy, for it marks a startling change in the habits of English thought when we find pamphlet after pamphlet treating of the claims of authority and reason, in which there is hardly a passing reference to the father who had dealt so thoroughly with the subject. Berkeley's *Alciphron*, both in its form, and in its dependence on Plato, may serve to recall the *Contra Academicos* and other dialogues, but there is no reason to believe that Berkeley[1] had been much influenced by these writings. The teaching of S. Austin had at last ceased to be a matter of living interest to English theologians.

9. There was however one important exception, for it is in the eighteenth century that we have the most thorough English

[1] He mentions the *De Civitate* in his Fifth Dialogue and the *Tract. in Evan. Joannis* in *Siris*: but they are merely incidental references.

discussion of S. Austin's Eucharistic doctrine. It is of course obvious that he held firmly to a doctrine of the Real Presence: but in what sense did he hold it? It would be generally admitted that his writings do not contain the doctrine of Transubstantiation: that attempt at explaining the manner of Christ's presence was due to a philosophical doctrine which had not been formulated in his day. The doctrine of Transubstantiation is a scholastic explanation of that which S. Austin believed, but it is not his own explanation, and there is at all events room for much argument as to whether he could have approved this Aristotelian statement of his faith. Dr Waterland, who was then Archdeacon of Middlesex, had made the doctrine of the Eucharist the subject of a charge[1] to the clergy of that Archdeaconry at S. Clement Danes in 1738. He had then quoted S. Austin as an authority for the Calvinistic doctrine of a Real but purely Spiritual Presence. The reply which this statement called forth from a divine of the University of Cambridge who is identified by Lathbury with a non-juring clergyman named George Smith is a lengthy discussion of S. Austin's doctrine on this important subject. It is so full and careful that I have ventured to reprint in its entirety a tract which is rare and practically unknown. It seems to show that the Calvinistic doctrine of the Real Presence does not contain the full sense of S. Austin's language, just as Bishop Hamilton's charge[2] has proved that the Genevan teaching is not an adequate expression of the opinion which the Reformers embodied in the services of our Church. There is perhaps an additional interest in the matter when we remember that shortly before this discussion took place John Wesley was resident at Oxford, in full knowledge of the theological controversies of the day. These facts, connected with the time at which he wrote, must be remembered before we venture to explain as mere poetical licence those Eucharistic hymns which have done so much to maintain and diffuse a doctrine precisely similar to that which was expressed by S. Austin.

[1] *The Christian Sacrifice Explained.* He remarks, "The sacrament of the Eucharist has for some time been the subject of debate among us, and appears to be so still in some measure" (p. 1).
[2] *A Charge at his Triennial Visitation, in May* 1867, by Walter Kerr, Bishop of Salisbury (1885), 51.

AN

EPISTOLARY DISSERTATION

Addressed to the

CLERGY *of Middlesex*,

WHEREIN THE

Doctrine of St. AUSTIN,

CONCERNING THE

CHRISTIAN SACRIFICE,

Is set in a true Light:

By Way of REPLY to

DR WATERLAND'S late Charge to them.

By a Divine of the University of Cambridge.

In nullum autem nomen religionis, seu verum, seu falsum, coagulari homines possunt, nisi aliquo signaculorum vel sacramentorum visibilium consortio colligentur: quorum sacramentorum vis inenarrabiliter valet plurimum, & ideo contemta sacrilegos facit. Impie quippe contemnitur, sine qua non potest perfici pietas. S. Aug. cont. Faust. lib. XIX. c. 11.

LONDON:
Printed by J. BETTENHAM, *and sold by*
J. ROBERTS IN *Warwick Lane*
M.DCC.XXXIX.

AN

EPISTOLARY DISSERTATION

Addressed to the

Clergy of Middlesex, ETC.

REVEREND BRETHREN,

I HAVE read your learned *Archdeacon's* Charge concerning the Christian Sacrifice, but must confess I have not received the Satisfaction I usually found in his other excellent Writings. I question not but those of your venerable Body, whom he is pleased to distinguish by the Name of *Materialists*, think of this Piece as I do. And I fancy the Reverend Mr. *Wheatley* for Instance, who perhaps might be in the Number of his Auditors, will scarce upon the Perusal of it, now it is printed, retract what he has said in his admirable Commentary upon the Liturgy. Our Doctrine of the Sacrifice was, in the Dispute between the late Dr. Hickes and his Opponents, formerly cried down as *Popish*: Of this Imputation Dr. *Waterland* has been so just as to clear it, for which we cannot but return him our Thanks. I say so just; because it is evident it is entirely inconsistent with the *Popish*, and quite overthrows it; there being as much Difference between it and the *Romish*, as between the Substance of Bread and Wine, and the Substance of our blessed Saviour's Body and Blood. And this the *Papists* are so sensible of, that they endeavour all they can to render our notion of a Sacrifice contemptible; and they have by their Wiles decoy'd some Protestants, not sufficiently attending to the primitive Doctrines, to join with them in this. But tho' the

Archdeacon has wip'd off the Scandal of its being *Popish*, yet he has laid another on, that it is *Jewish*; which it cannot be, unless it could be proved the Christian Sacraments are *Jewish*; a thing I dare say he will never attempt. We are exhorted to return to the old Definitions, and to regard nothing else but what some have been pleased to confine the Name of spiritual Sacrifice to: as if our material Sacrifice, considered as what Christ by his holy Institution has made it, is not as much at least a spiritual Oblation, an unbloody, reasonable, holy and lively Sacrifice unto God, a Sacrifice of Praise and Thanksgiving, as any vocal Service can possibly be. We have St. *Austin's* Definition produced against us, as if that was absolutely inconsistent with a visible or material Sacrifice; whereas I hope to prove to every Person, even of the meanest Capacity, that St. *Austin* intended to contain the visible Sacrifice under his general Definition, and that this holy Father's Sense is altogether mistaken.

In order to this I will first set down St. *Austin's* Definition of a true Sacrifice: "Verum Sacrificium est omne opus quod agitur, "ut sancta Societate inhæreamus Deo, relatum scilicet ad illum "finem boni, quo veraciter beati esse possimus: A true Sacrifice "is every Work which is performed to unite us with God, and to "keep up a holy Covenant and Communion with him; having a "Respect to that great End and sovereign Good, by which we may

5. "be truly happy." This is St. *Austin's* general Definition, which you see is very extensive, and will comprehend a great many various Works and Sacrifices under it. Every Work, whether the Subject of the Operation be something internal or external; be invisible, or visible and material; if it be done with a view to God and his Glory, to unite us to God, and to maintain our Fellowship and Communion with him, and in the End to bring us to everlasting Life, is a true and proper Sacrifice. But to consider the Particulars a little more minutely.

And 1. This Definition contains the internal or mental Sacrifices, such Works as are done or performed within us by our Thoughts only, out of a true and sincere Love to God, and out of a pure Heart and a good Conscience, and a Faith unfeigned; of which Works no one is conscious but God and the Doer of them. Among these we may reckon, 1. Mental Prayers and Praises, as they are considered abstractedly from vocal ones, and as they proceed from a pure Mind. 2. The Sacrifice of a penitent and contrite Heart. 3. The Sacrifice of our selves, our Souls and Bodies, by which is meant, as it is an inward Sacrifice, a firm and unfeigned Resolution and Engagement to God to persevere in all religious Duties which concern either our Souls or Bodies, and to perform all sorts of good Works : And this Sacrifice supposes, that our Hearts will actually concur with our inward Actions in the Performance of those Duties, and that we intentionally refer them all to the Honour of God. Now these internal Sacrifices, or if there be any other of the like Nature, of sincere Piety, Charity, and Obedience, are the Oblations of Christians as Members of the invisible Church, and are no Part of the external Sacrifice of the visible Church, which the Priest in a solemn Manner offers at the Altar. For the Priest cannot offer that c. which he is entirely ignorant of, and is known only to God and the Conscience of the Offerer. Such invisible Sacrifices can only be offered^a by the Souls of devout and holy Men themselves, and by Christ the invisible High-Priest, as^b St. *Austin* informs us : The visible Priest offering them not really, but vocally and by Signs and Symbols. These invisible Sacrifices then ought not to be brought into the Debate. And tho' it be granted they are not only true and proper Sacrifices, but also the most ^cperfect, excellent and acceptable to God, (and without which the external Sacrifices are so far from being beneficial, that they are indeed hurtful to the Offerers,) and may and ought to be offered, tho' invisibly, at the Eucharist both by Priest and People ; yet they are manifestly besides the Question, which relates only to the publick and visible Ministration of the blessed Sacrament ; unless Sacrifices can be visible and invisible at the same Time, which seems to me a Contradiction.

[a] Ei sacrificamus hostiam humilitatis & laudis in ara cordis igne fervidæ caritatis. De civ. Dei, lib. x. c. 3, § 2. Cum ad illum sursum est, ejus est altare cor nostrum. Ibid.

[b] Ejus unigenito cum sacerdote placamus. Ibid. & cap. 6. Cum igitur vera Sacrificia opera sint misericordiæ...opera vero misericordiæ non ob aliud fiant, nisi ut a miseria liberemur—profecto efficitur, ut tota ipsa redempta Civitas, hoc est, congregatio societasq ; sanctorum, universale sacrificium offeratur Deo per sacerdotem magnum—

[c] Hujus autem præclarissimum atq ; optimum sacrificium nos ipsi sumus, hoc est Civitas ejus—Ib. lib. xix. c. 23, § 5.

2. BESIDES these invisible Sacrifices, which are only the inward Operations of the Soul, and which therefore in the strictest Sense are spiritual Sacrifices, Sacrifices of the Heart, or Soul and Spirit; there is another Sacrifice, formerly visible when offered, but now invisible to us, and that is the Sacrifice of the Death of Christ, the all-sufficient and truly meritorious Atonement which Christ made in Person upon the Cross for the Sins of the whole World. This was a Work which only our blessed Saviour himself, being God as well as Man, could perform. And since this Sacrifice could be but once offered, it cannot now be often repeated, but can only be commemorated and represented in the Way our Lord has appointed. 'Tis this Sacrifice once offered, which alone is in itself and in its own Nature propitiatory and expiatory: This great Work of Mercy is the Foundation of the Covenant God made with Mankind, and purchased for us all those Benefits which will undoubtedly make us everlastingly happy: And from this one Oblation all other Sacrifices whatever derive their whole Efficacy and Virtue.

3. HAVING thus treated of the internal and of the invisible Sacrifices, which the visible Priest or sacerdotal Officer can't perform; I come now to speak of the external Sacrifices, the Oblation of which is his proper and sole Business. And we may, I think, rightly enough divide these into two Sorts, viz. *Vocal* and *Material*.

And 1. OF the Vocal, which consist of Forms of Prayer, Praise, and Commemoration offered to God by the Tongue of the Priest. Now these are commonly called spiritual Sacrifices, because the Priest presents them to God in the Name of the whole Congregation, as supposed to be expressive both of his own and of their Sentiments, which are the Acts of the Soul or Spirit of Man. But I must beg Leave to observe, that these are not strictly speaking spiritual Sacrifices, because tho' they may seem to signify and declare the real inward Sense of the whole Congregation, yet this is too frequently not the Truth of the Matter. For both Priest and People may be very wicked, and they may ᵈcome near to God with their Lips, while their Hearts

---

ᵈ St. *Cyprian* intimates something to this Purpose in these Words: Obrepit adversarius frequenter & penetrat, & subtiliter fallens preces nostras a Deo avocat, ut aliud habeamus in corde, aliud in voce, quando intentione

are far from him. And in such a Case, tho' the Matter of Prayers, Praises and Commemorations be very good and holy in itself, yet they are not spiritual and reasonable, but mere Lip-Service with Regard to those who pay it; and therefore their paying it is an Abomination, for which God will severely punish them. Suppose in an Assembly there are a great many, as too often happens, who in their Hearts believe nothing of the Christian Religion; or, if they do believe it, do it in so slight and superficial a Manner, which their wicked and debauched Lives do notoriously testify, that they may as well, perhaps better, not believe it at all. Now these may come to Church for Form's Sake, and give their assent to the Words of the Prayers; but it by no Means follows that those Prayers express the inward Thoughts of their Hearts. The Sacrifice of the Priest therefore, as he is as it were the Mouth of the Assembly, is merely external and vocal : And those who are the good Members of the Congregation, whether the Priest or any of the People, joining their true inward and properly spiritual Sacrifices to the publick Ministration of the Priest do their whole Duty. But in this Affair every Man is his own Priest, because, as I hinted above, he alone can invisibly offer such a spiritual Sacrifice. And if he unfeignedly, without Guile and Hypocrisy in his Mind and Heart, goes along with the Words the Priest utters, the outward Celebration will become to him a spiritual Sacrifice, because through the Mediation of Christ God will certainly hear the Prayers with Regard to him, and confer upon him those spiritual Blessings, which are the Reward of all true and sincere Worshippers. To prove farther, that the Office of the Priest is merely external, let me put the Case with ᵉSt. *Austin*, that one who merely counterfeits a Belief in Christ should come to receive

---

sincera Dominum debeat non vocis sonus, sed animus & sensus orare. De oratione Dominica, p. 152.

ᵉ Quid si ad ipsum baptismum fictus accessit, dimissa sunt peccata, annon sint dimissa?—Si dixerint, non esse dimissa; quaero, si postea fictionem suam corde concusso & vero dolore fateretur, denuo baptizandus judicaretur? Quod si dementissimum est dicere; fateantur vero baptismo Christi baptizari posse hominem, & tamen cor ejus in malitia vel sacrilegio perseverans peccatorum abolitionem non sinere fieri. De Baptismo, lib. 1 § 18.

Baptism, and the Priest thereupon performs the outward Rite; no Body will deny that he receives true Baptism, tho' he remains still unconverted. The Priest then does not here offer that inward Christian Sacrifice of the Person's Conversion of the heart, altho' he does his Part completely. The same may be said with Regard to all the other sacerdotal Functions. He can perform the outward Offices of preaching, praying, and administring the Sacraments, and that is all. *Paul* can plant, and *Apollos* can water, but God giveth the Encrease. God concurs with the outward Act of the Priest in bestowing the Blessings upon the true Believer. It is therefore a great Mistake to say, as Dr. *Waterland* does, that the sacerdotal Oblation consists in offering the inward spiritual Sacrifices of the People's contrite Hearts, their Faith, Hope, Self-humiliation, the *redempta civitas*, or the elect Members of the invisible Church, their Sacrifice of Prayer from a

10. pure Heart, the Sacrifice of true Converts or sincere Penitents: All the Priest can do, is to present the vocal Prayers, Praises, Commemorations and Professions of Obedience, which the People are to take care by their own Integrity and Holiness shall be profitable to them.

Now these vocal Sacrifices are acceptable in themselves, by whomsoever offered, and may be called spiritual, in Opposition to the gross, carnal and typical Rites of the Jews, which were abolished by Christianity, for these Reasons: Because in themselves they signify those inward spiritual Sacrifices which every Christian ought to offer; and because through the Intercession of Christ they bring down spiritual Blessings upon those who offer them worthily. Now the Jewish Sacrifices related primarily to the purifying of the Flesh and to temporal Blessings and Punishments. For which Cause they were no longer to be continued, but on course being but mere Shadows of Christ's grand Sacrifice did vanish and expire. But tho' these vocal ones are, I grant, true and proper Christian Sacrifices, and in a large Sense may be called spiritual, yet they are much to blame who oppose these to all Sacrifice of the material Kind, under Pretence that every material Sacrifice must necessarily be Jewish. It may, I think, as well be argued that all external or bodily Worship is Jewish, as that a material Sacrifice as such is so. The Words of Prayer are as much Signs of the Matter they express, and bowing the

Body or kneeling and the like significative (or ought to be so) of the inward Dispositions of the Soul, as material or visible Sacrifice is a sacred Sign of the Thing it represents. Now if this outward and bodily Service may be dignified with the Name of spiritual, as being sacred Actions whereby we reverence and honour God, and holy Duties which God hath required of us to 11. his Glory and our own Salvation, if we perform them as we ought; I can't see why a material Sacrifice should not be equally a Thing of a spiritual Nature, since by it we pay direct Homage to God, and keep up our League of Amity with him; and through Christ's all-sufficient expiatory Oblation (of which it is the instituted Memorial and Representation) have all the good Things promised in the Gospel bestowed upon us. All the Reason I can find why it cannot be a spiritual Sacrifice, is because it is typical, and if typical, therefore Jewish. But this methinks is a very weak Consequence, unless it is typical in the same Sense the Jewish Sacrifices were; that is not only Types of Christ to come, but also such weak and beggarly Elements as they were, such feint Resemblances as had scarce any Force or Virtue in them, and not *prima facie* or directly designed for that great End and supreme Good, by which we may truly attain everlasting Salvation. A Material therefore as well as the Vocal may be a Christian Sacrifice, and consequently a spiritual one, being ordained by Christ for spiritual Ends and Purposes, and as exactly agreeing to St. *Austin's* Definition, as any other external Sacrifice whatsoever. I am sure St. *Austin* himself thought so, nay he plainly prefers the material and visible Sacrifice of Christians before the vocal ones, as any one may perceive by the following Words: "Those who think[f], says he, these visible Sacrifices are 12. "proper for other Gods, but invisible ones to the true God as "invisible, and the greater and better to him who is greater and

---

[f] Qui autem putant hæc visibilia sacrificia diis aliis congruere, illi vero tanquam invisibili invisibilia, & majori majora, meliorique meliora, qualia sunt puræ mentis & bonæ voluntatis officia; profecto nesciunt, hæc ita esse signa illorum, sicut verba sonantia signa sunt rerum. Quo circa sicut orantes atque laudantes ad eum dirigimus significantes voces, cui res ipsas *in corde* quas significamus offerimus: ita sacrificantes non alteri visibile sacrificium offerendum esse noverimus, quam illi cujus *in cordibus nostris invisibile sacrificium* nos ipsi sumus. De civ. Dei, lib. x. c. 19.

"better, such as the Duties of a pure Mind and a good Disposi-
"tion; they do not perceive that the one are the Signs of the
"other, as Words are the Signs of Things. Wherefore as in our
"Prayers and Praises we direct our significant Words to him,
"whom we offer the Things themselves to, which are in our
"Hearts, and which we signify by them. So when we sacrifice we
"know that the visible Sacrifice is to be offered to no other, than
"to him whose invisible Sacrifice we ourselves ought to be in our
"Hearts." And what this visible or material Sacrifice is, he
informs us in the very next[g] Chapter: "The Sacrament of which
"Thing, says he, (meaning Christ's personal Sacrifice) he would
"have the daily Sacrifice of the Church to be; which, since she is
"the Body of Christ her Head, learns to offer herself by it." If
then St. *Austin* spake the Sense of the Churches before him, as
13. Dr. *Waterland* asserts, then it is plainly the Sense of all Antiquity,
that the blessed Sacrament, the material and visible Elements, is
the daily Sacrifice of the Church: It is also pretty plain too, that
according to him, praying and praising are Things somewhat
distinct from sacrificing; and are therefore to be only reckoned
Sacrifices in a large Sense, and are not to be strictly speaking
accounted as such. But I will not insist upon that; for both
Kinds of Offering may be comprehended, I presume, under St.
Austin's general Definition, but whether properly or improperly I
will not dispute; for that would be only wrangling about Words.
I proceed to discourse

2. Of the other sort of external Sacrifices of Christians, and
they are the Material. Now a material Sacrifice may agreeably
to St. *Austin*'s general Definition of Sacrifice be thus defined:

[g] Unde verus ille Mediator, in quantum formam servi accipiens Mediator effectus est Dei & hominum homo Christus Jesus, cum in forma Dei sacrificium cum patre sumat, cum quo & unus Deus est, tamen in forma servi sacrificium maluit esse quam sumere, ne vel hac occasione quisquam existimaret cuilibet sacrificandum esse creaturæ. Per hoc & sacerdos est, ipse offerens, ipse & oblatio. Cujus rei sacramentum quotidianum esse voluit ecclesiæ sacrificium: quæ cum ipsius capitis corpus sit, seipsam per ipsum discit offerre. Hujus veri sacrificii (meaning Christ's own Sacrifice, and not the Church's offering herself, as Dr. *Waterland* mistakes it in his Review, p. 529.) multiplicia variaque signa erant sacrificia prisca sanctorum, cum hoc unum per multa figuraretur, tanquam verbis multis res una diceretur, ut sine fastidio cuncta sacrificia falsa cesserunt.

"Any [h]Work, for the complete Performance of which a material Thing is offered, in order to keep up our Covenant and Communion with God, to the End that we may be everlastingly happy":

MATERIAL Sacrifice then may be divided into two sorts, private and publick. Private are such as every Christian makes, when he gives an Alms to the Poor, or feeds the Hungry, or clothes the Naked for God's Sake. In which Case the Money, the Meat, the Clothes are Oblations to God, and tho' given to Man, are as it were offered a Sacrifice to his Honour and Service. But these private Sacrifices being wide of our present Question, I shall say no more of them.

THE publick material Sacrifices are such, as are instituted by Christ to be performed by his Ministers or Priests in the publick Worship of God. And here I shall not dispute whether Baptism may not in a large Sense, conformably to St. *Austin's* Definition, be called a Sacrifice. Yet since it is not commonly called so, and the Eucharist is indeed so in the most eminent and emphatical Manner, we will set aside the Consideration of Baptism, and proceed directly to treat of the other Sacrament, as it is a part of the publick external Worship of God.

To keep close therefore to St. *Austin's* Definition: The Eucharistick Sacrifice is a Work done by a Priest, for the Performance of which Bread and Wine is used or offered in the Manner Christ has appointed, in order to keep up our Covenant and Communion with God, to the End that we may be everlastingly happy: Or in other Words: It is a sacerdotal Oblation of Bread and Wine made to God in the Manner Christ has appointed, &c. Now this is a Definition of the Eucharistick Sacrifice, the Word Sacrifice being taken, as it frequently is, for the sacrificial Ministration. And here let me take Notice, that St. *Austin*[i] says there are four Things to be considered in every Sacrifice; viz. to whom it is offered, by whom it is offered, what is offered, and for whom it is offered. And in [k]another Place, speaking of

---

[h] This falls in with Dr. *Hickes's* first Definition of a material Sacrifice, as it means the Celebration of it. See Christian Priesthood, Vol. I. p. 159.

[i] —Quatuor considerantur in omni sacrificio cui offeratur, a quo offeratur, quid offeratur, pro quibus offeratur.—De Trin. lib. IV. § 19.

[k] Recte quippe offertur sacrificium, cum offertur Deo vero, cui uni tantummodo sacrificandum est. Non autem recte dividitur, dum non discernuntur

Cain's Sacrifice, he affirms, that "a Sacrifice is rightly offered, "when it is offered to the true God, to whom alone we ought to
15. "sacrifice: But it is not rightly divided, if either the Places or the "Times of offering, or the Things themselves which are offered, or "he who offers, and to whom it is offered, or those to whom that "which is offered is distributed to be eaten are not rightly "distinguished." He seems to have forgot to mention, the essential Rites with which it is offered. But it is remarkable, that one of the Things to be considered in a material Sacrifice, (for of that he is talking) is what is offered, or the holy Gift which is presented by the Priest unto God. For in a material Sacrifice there is strict Regard had to the Gift all along through the whole Action, and without the Gift the Action or work cannot possibly proceed. In such a Work every Thing the Priest says or does apparently relates to it. The sacrificial Ministrations of the Jewish Priests, and all the particular Rites belonging to them had Respect to the Thing sacrificed, whether animate or inanimate. And if such Ministrations were Sacrifices, it must follow, that Ministrations or Works of the same Nature must be so too. In the Jewish Sacrifices the material Things were offered to maintain their League and Covenant with God. If then the Bread and Wine in the Eucharistick Sacrifice are offered, dedicated and consecrated to God, and also eaten and drunk as such, to maintain Fellowship and Communion with Christ and with God, it is as much a Sacrifice as the Jewish; and as its farther End is to bring us to everlasting Life, it is a far more valuable Sacrifice. Let it be granted then that the Eucharistick Sacrifice is a Work or Service: But then take this along with you, that this Work cannot be done, nor this Service cannot be performed without the material Thing. The Priest by our Saviour's Command, is to take something into his Hands, and give Thanks over it, and bless it, and break it, and declaring it
16. to be Christ's Body distribute it to be eaten; the like is to be said of the Cup. Now pray what is this something? 'Tis Bread and Wine, which is thus both by manual and vocal Rites dedi-

recte vel loca, vel tempora, vel res ipsæ quæ offeruntur, vel qui offert & cui offertur, vel hi quibus ad vescendum distribuitur quod oblatum est. Ib. lib. XV. c. 7, § 1.

cated and consecrated to God, and consumed in a sacrificial Feast both by Priest and People. Here is a sacrificial Work done, in which the Bread and Wine have a principal Part, since it cannot possibly be done without them: Certainly then it would be exceeding strange, if this Work should be a Sacrifice, and yet the material Part should not be a chief Ingredient. I presume it will not be denied, that the Sacrifice of the Cross was a material Sacrifice: And yet this was a Work or a Service too as well as the Sacrifice of the Eucharist. Therefore being a Work or a Service does not make a Sacrifice spiritual. For if it did, there could be no such Thing as a material Sacrifice; then the Patriarchal and Jewish Sacrifices were not material, for they were Works and Services too; neither was our blessed Saviour's Sacrifice of himself. A Work, Service, or Sacrifice therefore must be denominated spiritual or material from the Subject-matter: If the Subject-matter be spiritual, as acts of the Mind, &c. then the Work or Sacrifice is spiritual; but if it be a material Thing, then it is material. Consequently the Matter of the Eucharist being Bread and Wine, it is a material Sacrifice, or is Bread and Wine materially considered.

HAVING thus, I imagine, sufficiently shown, that the being a Work or Service does by no Means exclude the material Thing, the Bread and Wine, from being an essential Part of the Eucharistick Sacrifice; I shall consider the Thing in another View, as the Word Sacrifice means the Gift or material Thing itself offered to God by a Priest with certain Rites to pay him Honour and Service, and closely to knit and unite us to God by covenanting with him. Now the Eucharistick Elements dedicated and consecrated to God's Service may very properly be called a Sacrifice in this Sense. For we offer and present them upon God's Altar with those Rites our Lord has appointed, that we may worship him in the most solemn and beneficial Manner with them; and that through Christ commemorated, represented and applied by these consecrated Gifts, we may derive down upon us all the Benefits of our Lord's Passion. The Gifts therefore being thus offered may very justly and properly be called a Sacrifice. And indeed this Notion of a Sacrifice, as it is a material Gift offered, is a plain Consequence of the former Notion, as a Sacrifice means the actual Oblation of a material Gift. For if the sacerdotal

Oblation to God, the Work done, be a Sacrifice or Celebration of a Sacrifice, then the Thing offered is the Victim or Gift sacrificed. For Instance, the performing of all the appointed Rites over the Things presented to God by the Jewish High-Priest, was the sacrificing Action, consequently the Things presented were the Things sacrificed: Our blessed Saviour's voluntary Oblation of himself was his sacrificial Ministration; and therefore himself or his human Nature hypostatically united to the divine was the Victim. The like may be said of the sacrificial Celebration of the Eucharist, and of the material Thing offered thereby. It were needless to prove from Scripture, that the material Thing offered is frequently called a Sacrifice, because there are many known Places, where the Word might be taken in this Sense. And as to St. *Austin* I have shewn above, that he calls the Things offered visible Sacrifices, and in particular, that he calls the Eucharistick Elements the daily Sacrifice of the Church. And in this very Chapter, where he gives us the abovementioned Definition of a

18. Sacrifice, after speaking of the internal Sacrifice of Christians which they invisibly offer, he has the following [1]Words: "Which "Sacrifice, (meaning the inward one just now specified) the "Church solemnizes in the Sacrament of the Altar, for that she "herself is offered in that Thing which she offers." Now the Thing she offers or sacrifices is the Bread and Wine, which both represent Christ and his Church. The Priest then by offering the Elements, offers the Church symbolically and externally, and Christ our invisible High-Priest offers it really and visibly [? invisibly].

AND as a further Proof, that the Word Sacrifice will bear this Acceptation, in the Chapter before his famous Definition St. *Austin* tells us what a visible Sacrifice is: "A visible Sacrifice, "[m]says he, is a Sacrament, that is a sacred Sign of an invisible "Sacrifice." This is manifestly a Definition or Description of the material Gift. Now it would be very unaccountable, that he should so immediately contradict himself, if the Word Sacrifice,

---

[1] Hoc est sacrificium Christianorum: *multi unum corpus in Christo.* Quod etiam in sacramento altaris fidelibus noto frequentat Ecclesia, ut ei demonstratur, quod in ea re quam offert ipsa offeratur.

[m] Sacrificium visibile invisibilis sacrificii sacramentum, id est, sacrum signum est.

consider'd as a material one, will not admit of both these Senses, and may not be understood, not only of the obligatory Service, but also of what is offered thereby, Mr. ⁿ*Mede* observes, that St. *Austin* defines a Sacrifice in this Manner, "That which we "devote, dedicate, and render unto God, for this End, that we may "have a holy Society and Fellowship with him." According therefore to St. *Austin*, who is acknowledged to speak the Sense of the Churches before him, it is not at all inconsistent to comprehend both the Work and the Gift under the Name of Sacrifice. Let me here just intimate, that if this is a good Definition of a visible or material Sacrifice, that it is a Sacrament or sacred Sign of an invisible Sacrifice, dedicated or devoted to God for the End aforesaid, then *vice versa*, by the Rule, that Definitions and the Things defined ought to be reciprocal, such a Sacrament or sacred Sign is a visible Sacrifice. Now it cannot be denied that the Eucharist or the Thing which is offered is such a sacred Sign; therefore according to St. *Austin* it must be a visible Sacrifice. In both Views then the Eucharist is a material Sacrifice, and if St. *Austin* may still have leave to be Judge, I am much mistaken, [if] it is not proved to a Demonstration. In Confirmation of the Definition of a visible Sacrifice above set down, I beg leave to subjoin, what St. *Isidore* of *Sevil*, (an antient Writer contemporary with *Gregory* the Great) who studied St. *Austin* throughly speaks of the Eucharist as being a Sacrifice: "It is called a Sacrifice, "ᵒsays he, that is, a Thing made holy, because it is consecrated "by mystical Prayer for a Memorial of our Lord's Passion for us." From which Passage it is sufficiently manifest, that the holy

19.

ⁿ Quod Deo nuncupamus, reddimus & dedicamus, hoc fine, ut sancta societate ipsi adhæreamus. *Mede's* Works, p. 370.

ᵒ Sacrificium dictum, quasi sacrum factum, quia prece mystica consecratur in memoriam pro nobis dominicæ passionis. Isidor. Hispal. lib. VI. Orig. c. 18. (al. 19). The latter Part of this Sentence is borrowed from St. *Austin*, lib. III. de Trin. c. 4. St. *Isidore likewise gives us another Definition of a Sacrifice:* " Sacrificium est victima, & *quæcunque* crementur " in ara, vel *ponuntur* : A Sacrifice is a Victim and *whatsoever* is burnt upon an "Altar or *placed* upon it." Whatsoever then is *placed* upon an Altar for divine Worship is a Sacrifice. These abovementioned Definitions of a material Sacrifice, considered as a material Gift, agree with Dr. *Hickes's* second Definition, and with that of Mr. *Johnson* and others.

Elements offered and consecrated by Prayer are the *Sacrifice* of the *Eucharist*.

20. I HAVE already said enough to shew it is St. *Austin's* opinion, that the Eucharist is a visible or material Sacrifice; but to put the matter beyond all Question, I will produce some more Testimonies from the Works of that great Doctor of the Church. In his Book *de Civ. Dei* he endeavours to shew, that we are not to offer any sort of Sacrifice, whether visible or invisible, to any but God. He plainly distinguishes in the 3ᵈ Chapter of the 10ᵗʰ Book ᵖbetween the Service we pay to God in the outward Celebration of the Sacraments, and that we pay to him within ourselves; and both these are contained in the Worship due only to God. In the one Service something material is used, in the other the Oblation is purely spiritual. In the 4ᵗʰ Chapter he declares that external and material Sacrifice is due to God alone, and shews the Antiquity of it from the Sacrifices of *Cain* and *Abel*, of whom the Elder's Sacrifice God rejected, the Younger's he accepted. In the next Chapter he informs us of the Nature of the visible Sacrifice: That it was only the Sign of the invisible, that it was changeable at the Will and Pleasure of God, that God did not require this Kind of Sacrifices for their own Sake, but for the Sake of those Things which they signify; lastly, that the spiritual or invisible Sacrifices are more perfect and valuable, and therefore are to be preferred to them. They both indeed are true Sacrifices in their Kind, but that the one is only the Sign of the other; and both are comprised under St. *Austin's* general Definition, which introduces the 6ᵗʰ Chapter. In the 7ᵗʰ Chapter he lets us knowᵠ, that the holy Angels would not have us offer Sacri-
21. fice to them, but to him whose Sacrifice both they and we are. And in the 16ᵗʰ Chapter he asserts ʳwe are to give Credit to those Angels, who command we should sacrifice to God alone, and not to those who require we should sacrifice to themselves or to false

---

ᵖ Huic nos servitutem, quæ λατρεία Græcè dicitur, sive in quibusque sacramentis, sive in nobis ipsis debemus.

ᵠ —Nolunt nos sibi sacrificare, sed ei, cujus & ipsi nobiscum sacrificium se esse noverunt.

ʳ Quibus igitur Angelis—credendum esse censemus? Utrum eis qui *religionis ritibus* coli volunt, sibi sacra & sacrificia flagitantes a mortalibus exhiberi; an eis qui *hunc omnem cultum* uni Deo deberi dicunt?

Gods, even tho' they should work Miracles to persuade us to it. And that he means by sacrificing, offering visible or material Sacrifices, is clear both from his comparing them with the religious Rites and the Sacrifices offer'd to bad Angels and false Gods, which were confessedly material, and by his saying that this very Kind of Worship was owing to the Creator of all Things, and also by his declaring in the 19th Chapter, that visible Sacrifice is to be offered to the true God, as appears from the Passage I have cited above. To which let me add another from [s]Chapter 26. "That we need not fear the good Angels will be offended at our "not sacrificing to them. For what they know is only due to the "true God, by adhering to whom they are happy, they would not "have us pay to them either by any significant Figure, or by the "Thing itself signified by the Sacraments." Where by the significant Type or Figure is meant the Sacrament or material Sacrifice, and by the Thing signified the spiritual and invisible. From whence it follows, that God requires the visible as well as the spiritual Sacrifice as due to him. And who is ignorant, that the *Eucharist* is in the most eminent Manner the *visible Sacrifice* of Christians?

WHICH, as it was not allowed to be offered to Angels, so neither was permitted to be offered to the Martyrs. To which Purpose St. Austin is like-wise very express: "We don't, [t]says

---

[s] Non itaque debemus metuere, ne immortales & beatos uni Deo subditos non eis sacrificando offendamus. Quod enim non nisi uni vero Deo deberi sciunt, cui & ipsi adhærendo beati sunt, proculdubio neque per ullam significantem figuram, neque per ipsam rem quæ sacramentis significatur, sibi exhiberi volunt.

[t] Nec tamen nos eisdem Martyribus templa, sacerdotia, sacra & sacrificia constituimus: quoniam non ipsi, sed Deus eorum nobis est Deus. Honoramus sane Memorias eorum tanquam sanctorum hominum Dei, qui usque ad mortem corporum suorum pro veritate certarunt—Quis autem audivit aliquando fidelium stantem sacerdotem ad altare etiam super sanctum corpus Martyris ad Dei honorem cultumque constructum, dicere in precibus, Offero tibi sacrificium, Petre, vel Paule, vel Cypriane; cum apud eorum Memorias offeratur Deo, qui eos & homines & Martyres fecit?—Quæcunque igitur adhibentur religiosorum obsequia in Martyrum locis, ornamenta sunt Memoriarum, non sacra vel sacrificia mortuorum tanquam Deorum. Quicunque etiam epulas suas eo deferunt, quod quidem a Christianis melioribus non fit, & in plerisque terrarum nulla talis est consuetudo; tamen quicunque id faciunt, (quas cum apposuerint, orant, & auferunt, ut vescantur, vel ex

"he, constitute Temples, Priesthoods, holy Rites and Sacrifices to
"the Martyrs; because not they, but their God is also our God.
"We indeed honour their Memorials as of Holy Men of God, who
"even unto Death contended for the Truth.—But who of the
"Faithful ever heard a Priest standing at the Altar, built for the
"Honour and Worship of God over the holy body of a Martyr,
"say in his Prayers, I offer Sacrifices to thee, O *Peter*, or *Paul*,
"or *Cyprian*; since at their Memorials Sacrifice is offered to
"God, who made them both Men and Martyrs?—Therefore
"whatsoever Respects religious Men pay in the Places of the
23. "Martyrs, they are Ornaments of the Memorials, and not sacred
"Rites or Sacrifices to dead Men as if they were Gods. Who-
"ever also bring hither their Banquets, which yet is not done by
"the sounder Christians, and in most places there is no such
"Custom: Nevertheless, whoever does so, (which Entertainments
"when they have brought thither, they pray, and take them
"away again, that they may eat them, or bestow Part of them
"among the Poor) they only mean that their Food should be
"sanctified to them by the Merits of the Martyrs in the Name of
"the Lord of the Martyrs. But that such Banquets are not
"Sacrifices to the Martyrs he knows, who knows the one Sacrifice
"of Christians which is there offer'd." No Body can doubt but
the Sacrifice here mentioned is something material. He here
shews that the Feasts at the Tombs of the Martyrs, which were
material Things, could not be Sacrifices of Christians; for this
Reason, because the Faithful knew they had but one Sacrifice,
which as the Feasts were, was visible and material. This Reason
therefore would lose all its Force, if the one Christian Sacrifice
were purely spiritual; it therefore must be the Sacrifice of Bread
and Wine, which St. ᵛ*Austin* says all the Church offers. There
is a like Passage in his 20ᵗʰ Book against *Faustus* c. 21 where
24. heʷ informs us, they did not build Altars to the Martyrs but to

eis etiam indigentibus largiantur) sanctificari sibi eas volunt per merita
Martyrum in nomine Domini Martyrum. Non autem esse ista sacrificia
Martyrum novit, qui novit unum, quod etiam illic offertur sacrificium
Christianorum. De Civ. Dei, lib. VIII. c. 27.

ᵛ Aquarii ex illo appellati sunt, quod aquam offerunt in poculo sacramenti,
non illud quod omnis ecclesia. Lib. de Hæres. LXIV.

ʷ —Ut nulli Martyrum, sed ipsi Deo Martyrum quamvis in memoriis

God; and that the Sacrifice which was offered, was offered only to God. Now that this Sacrifice was as to its Substance material is manifest from hence, because a material Sacrifice is the only proper one for a material Altar. And this is farther clear'd from what soon after follows : "We worship the Martyr, says he, with "the Worship of Love and Society—But with that Worship called "λατρεία,—being a Service proper to God, we neither worship, "nor teach any one to worship any other but God alone. And "whereas the offering of Sacrifice appertains to this Kind of "Worship, whence it is called Idolatry in those that give it to "Idols. We neither offer nor teach any to offer any such Thing "either to any Martyr, or any holy Soul, or any Angel." Which is all manifestly to be understood of offering the external Sacrifice of the Eucharistick Elements. For soon after he assures us, that they frequently sacrificed to God in the Memories or Churches of the Martyrs, by that only Rite, whereby he ordered in the Gospel that Sacrifice should be offered to him : Which belongs to that Worship which is called *Latria*, and is due to God only. What Sacrifice is here meant is visible enough ; and what the Drift of all this is, appears sufficiently plain, to wit, that they did not celebrate the Sacrifice of Bread and Wine according to the Rite or Method prescribed by Christ to the Martyrs, but to God. And this St. *Austin* fully confirms elsewhere. For ˣsays he "We do not build to our Martyrs Temples

Martyrum constituamus altaria. Quis enim antistitum in locis sanctorum corporum assistens altari, aliquando dixit, Offerimus tibi Petre—; sed quod offertur, offertur Deo—Colimus ergo Martyres eo cultu dilectionis & societatis—At illo cultu, quæ Græcè λατρεία dicitur—, cum sit quædam propriè divinitati debita servitus, nec colimus, nec colendum docemus, nisi unum Deum. Cum autem ad hunc cultum pertineat oblatio sacrificii, unde idololatria dicitur eorum, qui hoc etiam idolis exhibent; nullo modo tale aliquid offerimus aut offerendum præcipimus, vel cuiquam Martyri, vel cuiquam sanctæ animæ vel cuiquam Angelo—Sacrificare martyribus dixi: non dixi sacrificare Deo in memoriis martyrum; quod frequentissimè facimus, illo duntaxat ritu, quo sibi sacrificari novi testamenti manifestatione præcepit: quod pertinet ad illum cultum quæ latria dicitur & uni Deo debetur.

ˣ Nos autem Martyribus nostris non templa, sicut Diis, sed memorias sicut hominibus mortuis, quorum apud Deum vivunt spiritus, fabricamus; nec ibi erigimus altaria, in quibus sacrificemus Martyribus, sed uni Deo &

"as to Gods, but Memories or Churches in Memory of them as
"to dead men, whose Spirits live with God; neither do we erect
"Altars, upon which we sacrifice to the Martyrs, but to the one
"God both theirs and ours: At which Sacrifice, as Men of God,
"who have overcome the World in confessing him, they are
"named in their Place and Order; but are not invoked by the
"Priest who sacrifices. For he sacrifices to God, and not to
"them, altho' he sacrifices in their Memorial; because he is
"God's Priest and not theirs. But the Sacrifice itself is the
"Body of Christ, which is not offered to them, for they them-
"selves also are it." That is they are the mystical Body of
Christ, as the external Sacrifice of Bread and Wine is the Body
of Christ symbolically and virtually. Here it is to be noted the
Word *Sacrificium* has a twofold Acceptation in this Passage.
The Words, *at which Sacrifice*, are to be understood, of the
Work or Celebration of the material Sacrifice at the material
Altar: And the Words, *the Sacrifice itself*, mean the material
Thing offered. So that according to St. *Austin*, not only the
Oblation of a Sacrifice may be called a Sacrifice, but the Thing
offer'd also, which confirms what I have discoursed above. This
26. may be illustrated by what St. *Austin* ʸ says about the *mensa
Cypriani*, or the Altar or Communion Table which was erected
in the place where St. *Cyprian* suffered. He tells us, "That in
"the same Place a Table was built to God; and yet it is called
"the Table of *Cyprian*, not because he himself was sacrificed
"upon it, and because by his own being sacrificed he prepared
"this Table, not upon which he eats or is fed, but upon which
"the Sacrifice is offered to God, to whom he also himself was
"offered." The Table shews what sort of Sacrifice that is, such
a one as St. *Optatus* who flourished a little before St. *Austin*,

Martyrum & nostro: ad quod sacrificium, sicut homines Dei, qui mundum
in ejus confessione vicerunt, suo loco & ordine nominantur. Deo quippe,
non ipsis, sacrificat, quamvis in memoria sacrificet eorum: quia Dei
sacerdos est non illorum. Ipsum vero sacrificium corpus est Christi, quod
non offertur ipsis, quia hoc sunt & ipsi. De Civ. Dei, lib. XXII. c. 10.

ʸ Sicut nostis, quicunque Cartaginem nostis, in eodem loco Mensa Deo
constructa est : & tamen mensa dicitur Cypriani, non quia ibi est immolatus,
& quia ipsa immolatione sua paravit hanc mensam, non in qua pascat sive
pascatur, sed in qua sacrificium Deo, cui & ipse oblatus est, offeratur.
Serm. 310, § 2.

speaks of: "Wine, ᶻsays he, is trodden and pressed out by "Workmen who are Sinners, and so of it a Sacrifice is offered to "God."

ANOTHER Argument to prove, that St. *Austin* held the Eucharist to be a material Sacrifice, may be drawn from his affirming, that *Melchisedech's* Sacrifice was a Type of it, and that the Matter was the same in both. There are several Passages in his Book *De Civ. Dei*, which I will set down in the same order as they are to be found. "*Abraham*, ᵃsays he, was blessed by "*Melchisedech*, who was Priest of the most high God—There 27. "first appeared the Sacrifice, which now through the whole "world is offered by Christians to God, and that is fulfilled which "was long after said by the Prophet to Christ, who was yet to "come in the Flesh, *Thou art a Priest for ever, after the order "of Melchisedech*." Again, upon citing the Words of God to *Eli* 1 *Sam*. ii. 36, he ᵇcomments thus: "By adding, *to eat Bread*, "he elegantly expressed the very Kind of Sacrifice, of which the "Priest himself says, *The Bread which I will give is my Flesh "for the Life of the World*. It is the very Sacrifice, not "according to the Order of *Aaron*, but according to the Order "of *Melchisedech;* he that reads, let him understand.—He "therefore said, *to eat Bread*, which is the Sacrifice of Christians "in the New Testament." A little ᶜabove he says, "There is no "Priest according to the Order of *Aaron;* and whosoever is of

---

ᶻ Nam & vinum a peccatoribus operariis & calcatur & premitur; & sic inde Deo sacrificium offertur. Lib. III.

ᵃ Sed plane tunc benedictus est a Melchisedech, qui erat sacerdos Dei excelsi.—Ibi quippe primum apparuit sacrificium, quod nunc a Christianis offertur Deo toto orbe terrarum, & impletur illud quod longe post hoc factum per prophetam dicitur ad Christum, qui fuerat adhuc venturus in carne, Tu es sacerdos in æternum secundem ordinem Melchisedech. Lib. XVI. c. 22.

ᵇ Quod ergo addidit, *manducare panem*, etiam ipsum sacrificii genus eleganter expressit, de quo dicit sacerdos ipse, *Panis quem ego dedero, caro mea est pro seculi vita*. Ipsum est sacrificium, non secundum Aaron, sed secundum ordinem Melchisedech : qui legit, intelligat.—Ideo hic dixit *manducare panem*, quod est in novo Testamento sacrificium Christianorum. Lib. XVII. c. 5, § 5.

Nullus sacerdos est secundum ordinem Aaron, & quicunque ex ejus genere est homo, cum videt sacrificium Christianorum toto orbe pollere, sibi autem honorem illum magnum esse subtractum, deficiunt oculi ejus, & defluit anima ejus tabe mœroris. Ib. § 2.

"his Race, when he sees the Sacrifice of Christians prevail all
"over the World, and himself spoiled of that great Honour, his
"Eyes fail him, and his Soul sinks down with Sorrow." The
Sacrifice of Christians then is to be seen, it must then have
something material in it. In another Place commenting on,
28. *Thou art a Priest for ever &c.* he[d] subjoins: "Since the
"Priesthood and Sacrifice according to the Order of *Aaron* is no
"where, and that is every where offered under Christ the Priest,
"which Melchisedech brought forth, who is permitted to doubt of
"whom those Things are said?" Again, expounding *Prov.* ix. 1
&c. *Wisdom has built her a House, &c.,* he thus[e] discourses:
"Here we acknowledge the Wisdom of God, that is, the Word
"coeternal with the Father,—did prepare a Table in Wine and
"Bread, where appears also the Priesthood after the Order of
"*Melchisedech.*—To be made Partaker of that Table is to begin
"to have Life. For in *Ecclesiastes* viii. 15, where it is said,
"*It is not good, but to eat and to drink,* what can more credibly
"be understood, than what relates to the partaking of this Table,
"which the Priest himself, the Mediator of the New Testament,
"furnishes after the Order of *Melchisedech* with his Body and
29. "Blood? For that Sacrifice succeeded to all the Sacrifices of the
"Old Testament, which were immolated by way of Shadow of
"that to come: On the Account of which we approve of that
"saying of the same Mediator speaking prophetically in the

[d] Ex eo quod jam nusquam est sacerdotium & sacrificium secundum ordinem Aaron, & ubique offertur sub sacerdote Christo, quod protulit Melchisedech, quando benedixit Abraham, quis ambigere permittitur, de quo ista dicantur. *Ib.*

[e] Hic certe agnoscimus Dei sapientiam, hoc est, Verbum Patri coeternum —mensam in vino & panibus præparasse, ubi apparet etiam sacerdotium secundum ordinem Melchisedech—participem autem fieri mensæ illius, ipsum est incipere habere vitam. Nam & in alio libro, qui vocatur Ecclesiastes, ubi ait, *Non est bonum homini, nisi quod manducabit & bibet,* quid credibilius dicere intelligitur, quam quod ad participationem mensæ hujus pertinet, quam sacerdos ipse Mediator testamenti novi exhibet secundum ordinem Melchisedec de corpore & sanguine suo? Id enim sacrificium successit omnibus illis sacrificiis veteris testamenti, quæ immolabantur in umbra futuri: propter quod etiam vocem in Psalmo 39, ejusdem Mediatoris per prophetiam loquentis agnoscimus: *sacrificium & oblationes noluisti, corpus autem perfecisti mihi.* Quia pro illis omnibus sacrificiis & oblationibus corpus ejus offertur, & participantibus ministratur. *Ib.* c. 20, § 2.

"xxxix[th] *Psalm: Sacrifice and offering thou wouldst not, but a*
"*Body hast thou prepared me.* For instead of all these Sacri-
"fices and Oblations his Body is offered, and is administred to the
"Communicants." From whence it is evident, that the Christian
Sacrifice is in Substance Bread and Wine, as *Melchisedech's* was,
and in Significancy and Power Christ's Body and Blood; and
that it is not completely offered till it is fully consecrated by
Prayer, and thereby made what our Saviour appointed it to be at
the Institution. He in an allegorical way accommodates the
Passage in the Psalm to the Eucharistick, which is primarily
understood of Christ's personal Sacrifice, to shew the great
Dignity and Value of it, and to declare that the Sacrifice we
partake of at the Lord's Table is not *ˡmean Cates and ignoble
Drink* but constructionally or in Virtue and Efficacy, *the Flesh
and Blood* of our Great Shepherd. From hence also we may
learn, that the Christian Sacrifice, tho' symbolical or typical, or
rather antitypical, is not such a mere cold shadow as the Jewish
Sacrifices were; neither is it *Jewish*, but Evangelical, since it
was ordained by the Mediator himself to succeed in the Room of
all the *Jewish* Sacrifices. I shall only add one more Passage out
of many that might be produced relating to this Point. It is in
his ᵍBook *de diversis* 8. 3. *quæstionibus:* "He himself is our 30.
"Priest for ever, after the Order of *Melchisedech*, who offered
"himself an entire Sacrifice for our Sins, and recommended a
"Similitude of that Sacrifice to be celebrated for a Memorial of
"his Passion, that what *Melchisedech* offered to God, we may
"behold offered through the whole World in the Church of
"Christ." What this is I need not say, because every Body's
Eyes cannot but give them full Information.

It is not here my Business to dispute, whether the Generality

---

ᶠ Invitata est postea universarum gentium multitudo, ipsa implevit
ecclesiam, ipsa accepit de mensa dominica non viles epulas aut ignobiles
potus, sed ipsius Pastoris, ipsius occisi Christi carnem prælibavit et
sanguinem. Serm. 372, § 2.

ᵍ Ipse est etiam sacerdos noster in æternum secundum ordinem Melchisedec, qui seipsum obtulit holocaustum pro peccatis nostris, & ejus
sacrificii similitudinem celebrandam in suæ passionis memoriam commen-
davit, ut illud quod Melchisedec obtulit Deo, jam per totum orbem terrarum
in Christi ecclesia videamus offerri. Quæst. LXI.

of the Fathers, and St. *Austin* in particular, were in the Right to affirm, that *Melchisedech* offered a Sacrifice of Bread and Wine as a Type of the Eucharist; and that our blessed Saviour was a Priest after his Order upon Account of his offering the same Things, when he instituted the holy Sacrament, as well as in other Respects; and that the Christian Clergy are Priests likewise after his Order for the same Reason; tho' I humbly apprehend, he must be a bold man, who will pertinaciously contradict such venerable Authority. The whole Point lies here, whether St. *Austin* did in Fact believe, that the Sacrifice of *Melchisedech*, and that of the Christian Church consist of the same Materials, and consequently are both of them to be look'd upon as material Sacrifices. Dr. Waterland[h] contends, the ancient Fathers meant, "That *Melchisedech* by a divine Instinct fore-"seeing the Sacrifice of the Cross, offered to God by Way of "Thanksgiving, a mental, vocal, manual Representation or
31. "Figuration of it, by the Symbols of Bread and Wine; and by "the same Symbols, instrumentally, conveyed to *Abraham* the "spiritual Blessings of it." Now I desire to know, whether this is not tantamount to saying, That *Melchisedech* in order to represent or prefigure the Sacrifice of the Cross, did take Bread and Wine into his Hands, and mentally and vocally give Thanks over them and blessed them, that they might become Symbols of that Sacrifice, and by performing these mental, vocal, and manual Rites over them did by Way of Address to God present them to him as such Symbols; and then gave the same Symbols so presented and consecrated by these Rites to *Abraham*, that by them the spiritual Blessings of Christ's Sacrifice might instrumentally be conveyed to him. If this is not the very same in Sense with what Dr. *Waterland* asserts, I am mightily mistaken; and I must confess, I am so shortsighted as not to be able to discern the least Disagreement. Certainly he must have a very nice Head, that can possibly distinguish between offering to God by Way of Thanksgiving a Representation or Figuration of a certain Thing by material Symbols, and offering to God by Way of Thanksgiving material Symbols to represent or figure that certain Thing. This, as it appears to me, is a Distinction

[h] Append. p. 30.

without a Difference. I must therefore take leave to say, that according to Dr. *Waterland's* own Account of the Matter, St. *Austin* and the ancient Fathers maintained, that *Melchisedech's* was a material Sacrifice of Thanksgiving, whereby the Sacrifice of the Cross was prefigured, and applied to *Abraham;* and therefore sure there can be no Harm in concluding, that the Christian is also a *material Sacrifice* of Thanksgiving, whereby the Sacrifice of the Cross is commemorated and represented, and applied to those who worthily partake of it. I beg therefore, that St. 32. *Austin* may still be permitted to say with Propriety, that the external Sacrifice of the Christian Church is an Oblation of Bread and Wine performed with such manual and vocal Rites as our Lord ordained: But whether he will be permitted or no, 'tis undoubtedly true, that he does say it, beyond all Possibility of reasonable Contradiction. For tho' it could even be made out, that this holy and learned Father is mistaken in believing *Melchisedech* offered a material Sacrifice of Bread and Wine, yet his Testimony is too strong to be resisted, that the Eucharist is a material Sacrifice, such a one as he imagined at least *Melchisedech's* to be. Which being enough for my present Purpose, I shall proceed no farther upon this Argument.

My next observation shall be, St. *Austin's* teaching that the *Jewish* material Sacrifices were changed, and that the *material Sacrifice* of the *Eucharist* succeeded in their Room. This is in Part shewn already by a Passage just now cited. And indeed it is no Wonder the *Jewish* Sacrifices ceas'd and were chang'd, for they only foretold Christ to come in an obscure Manner; but our Sacrifice openly proclaims he is come. St. Austin[1] acquaints us: "Our Saviour did not abolish those old Signs [or Sacrifices] by "blaming them, but changed them by fulfilling them, that those "which declare Christ was already come might be other than "those which were predictive of his coming." Now I hope both 33.

[1] Proinde illa vetera signa rerum non evacuavit arguendo, sed implendo mutavit: ut alia essent, quæ nuntiarent venisse jam Christum, quam fuerant illa, quæ prænuntiabant esse venturum. Tract. adv. Judæos, § 4 & contra Faust. lib. XIX. c. 13. Prima sacramenta—prænuntiativa erant Christi venturi: quæ cum suo adventu Christus implevisset, ablata sunt— & alia sunt instituta virtute majora, utilitate meliora, actu faciliora, numero pauciora.—

sorts of Signs, both new and old, are material, and you know who says, that a visible Sacrifice is a holy Sign of the invisible. "¹Again : Those Sacrifices of the Old Testament were Figures to "us, and they all signified the one Sacrifice, the Memorial of which "we now celebrate." ᵐAdd hereunto, "The *Hebrews* in Sacrifices "of Cattle, which they offered to God, celebrated a Prophecy of "the future Sacrifice, which Christ offered. Whence Christians "now celebrate the Memory of the same Sacrifice already past by "a sacred Oblation and Participation of the Body and Blood of "Christ," or which is all one, of the blessed Sacrament thereof : For you know St. *Austin* calls the *daily Sacrifice of the Church the Sacrament of this Thing*. ⁿAgain : "The Flesh and Blood of "this Sacrifice was promised before the coming of Christ by "Victims of Resemblance ; was in Verity offered in the Passion "of Christ, and is celebrated by a Sacrament of Memory after the "Ascension of Christ." Now what this Sacrament of Memory or Commemoration is let St. *Fulgentius*, who closely adhered to St. *Austin's* Doctrine, inform us : "Firmly believe, ᵒsays he, and

¹ —ipsa figura nostræ fuerunt, & omnia talia multis & variis modis unum sacrificium, cujus nunc memoriam celebramus, significaverunt. Ib. lib. IV. c. 5.

ᵐ Hebræi autem in victimis pecorum quas offerebant Deo—prophetiam celebrabant futuræ victimæ, quam Christus obtulit. Unde jam Christiani peracti ejusdem sacrificii memoriam celebrant sacrosancta oblatione & participatione corporis & sanguinis Christi. Ib. lib. XX. c. 18.

ⁿ Hujus sacrificii caro & sanguis ante adventum Christi per victimas similitudinum promittebatur; in passione Christi per ipsam veritatem reddebatur; post adscensum Christi per sacramentum memoriæ celebratur. Ib. c. 21.

ᵒ Firmissimè tene & nullatenus dubites, ipsum unigenitum Deum Verbum carnem factum, se pro nobis obtulisse sacrificium & hostiam Deo in odorem suavitatis : cui cum Patre & Spiritu sancto a Patriarchis & Prophetis & Sacerdotibus tempore veteris Testamenti animalia sacrificabantur, & cui nunc, id est, tempore novi Testamenti, cum Patre & Spiritu sancto, cum quibus illi est una divinitas, sacrificium panis & vini in fide & caritate S. Catholica Ecclesia per universum orbem terræ offerre non cessat. In illis enim carnalibus victimis significatio fuit carnis Christi, quam pro peccatis nostris ipse sine peccato fuerat oblaturus, & sanguinis quem erat effusurus in remissionem peccatorum nostrorum : in isto autem sacrificio gratiarum actio atque commemoratio est carnis Christi quam pro nobis obtulit, & sanguinis quem pro nobis idem Deus effudit.—In illis sacrificiis quid nobis esset donandum figuratè significabatur : in hoc autem sacrificio quid nobis jam

"doubt not in any wise, that the very only begotten Son, God 34.
"the WORD, being made Flesh offered himself for us a Sacrifice
"and Oblation of a sweet-smelling Savour to God: To whom with
"the Father and Holy Ghost, by Patriarchs, and Prophets, and
"Priests Animals were sacrificed in the Time of the Old Testa-
"ment; and to whom now, that is under the New, together with
"the Father and Holy Ghost, with whom he has one and the
"same Divinity, the Catholic Church throughout the World
"ceaseth not to offer a Sacrifice of Bread and Wine in Faith and
"Charity. In those carnal Sacrifices there was a Signification of
"the Flesh of Christ, which he without Sin should offer for our
"Sins, and of that Blood which he was to shed on the Cross for
"the Remission of our Sins: But in this Sacrifice there is a
"Thanksgiving and Commemoration of that Flesh of Christ, which
"he offered for us, and of that Blood which he our God has shed
"for us.—In those Sacrifices, what was to be given for us, was
"represented in a Figure; but in this Sacrifice, what is already
"given is evidently shewn." Upon which⁰ *Ratramnus* thus 35.
briefly comments: "By saying, that in those Sacrifices was
"signified what should be given for us; but that in this Sacrifice
"what is already given is commemorated; he plainly intimates,
"that as those Sacrifices were a Figure of Things to come, so this
"Sacrifice is the Figure of Things already past." It appears
from hence, that St. *Austin*'s Sacrament of Memory, is the same
with St. *Fulgentius*'s Sacrifice of Bread and Wine, whereby the
grand Sacrifice is commemorated, and with the Sacrifice of Bread
and Wine or of the Body and Blood, which St. *Austin* frequently
speaks of. From whence we may observe, that the ancient
Fathers were not so nice as we are now a-days in distinguishing
between the Sacrifice and the Sacrament. ᵖSt. *Austin* speaks of

donatum fit evidenter ostenditur. De Fide ad Petrum § 62, in the Appendix
to the 6ᵗʰ Tome of St. *Austin*'s Works. Ed. Ben.

⁰ Dicens quod in illis sacrificiis quid nobis esset donandum significabatur,
in isto verò sacrificio quid sit donatum commemoretur, patenter innuit, quod
sicut illa figuram habuerint futurorum, sic & sacrificium figura sit præteritorum. De corp. et sang. Dom. § XVI.

ᵖ And in his Epistle to *Honoratus* he calls the Sacrifice of Christ's Body
the Sacrament of the Faithful : Vota sua sacrificium vult intelligi corporis sui,
quod est fidelium sacramentum, which shews they were only different Names
for the same Thing.

eating as well as offering the Sacrifice of Christians, and of the holy Oblation and Participation of the Body of Christ, and ⁿ*Isidore Hispalensis* mentions *offering the Sacrament of Christ's Body and Blood, that is, the Oblation of Bread and Wine:* And *Tertullian* both names the *Orationes Sacrificiorum*, the Prayers by which the Sacrifice was offered, and also the *Participation of the Sacrifice.*

36. For this Remark I must acknowledge myself obliged to Archbishop *Usher,* who without Disparagement to any Body was so well acquainted both with the Language and Doctrine of the Ancients as any one either before or since his Time. It being, I think, much to my present Purpose, I will give it you in his own excellent Words out of his ʳ Book concerning the Religion of the ancient *Irish,* which by the By was wrote many Years before Mr. *Mede's* upon the Subject, and therefore Dr. *Waterland* is mistaken in supposing that he was the first Broacher of the Doctrine of a *Material Sacrifice.* " In the Relation of the Passages, says that " great and learned Prelate, that concern the Obsequies of *Colum-*" *banus* performed by *Gallus* and *Magnoaldus,* we find that " *missam celebrare* and *missas agere* is made to be the same with " *Divina celebrare mysteria* and *salutis hostiam* or *salutare* " *sacrificium immolare* : The saying of Mass the same with the " Celebration of the Divine Mysteries and Oblation of the health-" ful Sacrifice : For by that Term was the Administration of the " Sacrament of the Lord's Supper at that Time usually designed. " For as in our Beneficence and communicating unto the Neces-" sities of the Poor, (which are Sacrifices wherewith God is well-" pleased) we are taught to give both ourselves and our Alms, " first unto the Lord, and after unto our Brethren by the Will of " God, so is it in this Ministry of the blessed Sacrament. The " Service is first presented unto God (from which, as from a most " principal Part of the Duty, the Sacrament itself is called the " Eucharist ; because therein we offer a special Sacrifice of Praise " and Thanksgiving always unto God) and then communicated to

37. " the Use of God's People. In the Performance of which Part of

---

ⁿ —Corporis & sanguinis sacramentum, i.e. oblatio panis & vini, in toto orbe terrarum offertur. In Allegor. vet. Test.

ʳ Chap. IV.

"the Service, both the Minister was said *to give* and the Com-
"municant *to receive the Sacrifice:* As well as in Respect of the
"former Part they were said *to offer* the same unto the Lord.
"For they did not distinguish the *Sacrifice* from the *Sacrament*,
"as the *Romanists* do now a-days; but used the Name of *Sacrifice*
"indifferently, both of that which was offered unto God, and of
"that which was given to and received by the Communicant.
"Therefore we read of *offering the Sacrifice* to God: As in that
"Speech of *Gallus* to his Scholar *Magnoaldus, My Master* Colum-
"banus *is accustomed to offer unto the Lord the Sacrifice of Salva-
"tion in brazen Vessels.* Of *giving the Sacrifice* to Man: As when
"it is said in one of the ancient Synods of *Ireland*, that a Bishop
"by his Testament may bequeath a certain Proportion of his
"Goods for a Legacy to the Priest that *giveth him the Sacrifice*,
"and of *receiving the Sacrifice* from the Hands of the Minister:
"As in that Sentence of the Synod attributed to St. *Patrick; He
"who deserveth not to receive the Sacrifice in his Life, how can it
"help him after his Death?* And in that Gloss of *Sedulius* upon
"1 *Cor.* xi. 33, *Tarry one for another*, that is, saith he, *until you
"do receive the Sacrifice.* And in the *British* Antiquities, where
"we read of *Amon* a Nobleman in *Wales*, Father to *Samson* the
"Saint of *Dole* in little *Britain*, that being taken with a grievous
"Sickness, he was admonished by his Neighbours, that according to
"the usual Manner he should *receive the Sacrifice of the Com-
"munion.* Whereby it doth appear, that the *Sacrifice* of the
"elder Times was not like unto the new Mass of the *Romanists*,
"wherein the Priest alone doth all; but unto our *Communion*,
"where others also have free Liberty given unto them to *eat of
"the Altar*, Heb. xiii. 10, as well as they that serve the Altar." 38.
I hope this will not be look'd upon as an useless and foreign
Digression; but to return:

ST. *Austin* proves from the Prophet ᵃ *Malachi*, that the *Jewish*
Sacrifices were laid aside, and the Christian Oblation took place
every where: "*Malachi*, 'says he, prophesying of the Church

ᵃ Mal. i. 10.
ᵗ Malachias prophetans Ecclesiam, Judæis apertissimè dicit ex persona
Dei: non est mihi voluntas in vobis & munus non suscipiam de manu vestra.
Ab ortu enim solis—& in omni loco sacrificabitur & offeretur nomini meo
oblatio munda.—Hoc sacrificium per sacerdotium Christi secundum ordinem

"speaks openly to the Jews in the Person of God: *I have no* "*pleasure in You, and I will not receive a Gift at your Hands.* "*From the rising of the Sun &c. in every Place Incense shall* "*be offered unto my Name and a pure Offering.* This Sacrifice "by the Priesthood of Christ, according to the Order of *Melchi-* "*sedech,* we see offered in every Place, and they cannot deny "that the Sacrifice of the *Jews* is ceas'd, why do they yet "expect another Christ—?" And[v] again: "We ourselves, that "is, his City, are his best and most excellent Sacrifice, the "Mystery of which Thing we celebrate by our Oblations, which "are known to the Faithful.—For the *Hebrew* Prophets foretold,

39. "that the Sacrifices which the *Jews* offered for a Shadow of what "was to come should cease, and that from the rising to the set-"ting of the Sun the *Gentiles* as we now see done, should offer "the one Sacrifice." The one Sacrifice then, which the Faithful know and saw was visible and consequently material. And tho' the spiritual Oblation of ourselves is the most excellent Sacrifice, yet this, if St. *Austin* says true, is to be performed by offering the Material according to our Lord's own Ordinance; and we cannot be sure that we offer the one aright without the celebration of the other. What God has joined let not Man separate. He has pointed out the most acceptable Way of offering our spiritual Sacrifices, and that is by offering him, as frequently as we can, the instituted Symbols of them.

But now to argue a little from the preceding Passages: Nothing can be plainer from St. *Austin,* than that the Evangelical Sacrifice is *visible* and *material,* as well as the Jewish. It is granted indeed they both are Types, the one promissive, the other commemorating and representing. But surely the latter are much more noble and efficacious than the former, not such

---

Melchisedec, cum in omni loco a solis ortu ad occasum jam videamus offerri, sacrificium autem Judæorum—cessasse negare non possunt, quid adhuc expectant alium Christum—? De Civ. Dei, Lib. XVIII. c. 35.

[v] Hujus autem præclarissimum atque optimum sacrificium nos ipsi sumus, hoc est civitas ejus, cujus rei mysterium celebramus oblationibus nostris, quæ fidelibus notæ sunt—Cessaturas enim victimas, quas in umbra futuri offerebant Judæi, & unum sacrificium gentes a solis ortu usque ad occasum, sicut jam fieri cernimus, oblaturas, per prophetas Hebræos oracula increpuere divina. Ib. Lib. XIX. c. 23.

mere *Shadows*, not such obscure Similitudes. And this holy Father affirming that this material Evangelical Sacrifice was to be everywhere and always offered, that it is properly a Part of divine Christian Worship, that it is the one Christian Sacrifice offered according to the Rite prescribed in the New Testament, the Sacrifice by which we both commemorate the grand one of the Cross, and make the most excellent Oblation of our selves; it is utterly impossible he should teach that this was not Evangelical, but *Jewish*; and was *among* the symbolical, typical, umbratil Sacrifices which were to cease as unnecessary upon the Manifestation of the Gospel, and that God had rejected it upon that 40. Account. To assert this, as [u]Dr. *Waterland* seems to do, is to make him, who in his Time was famed for having a clear Head, and being an exact Reasoner, the most absurd and inconsistent Writer possible. 'Tis agreed the typical Sacrifices of the Jews were rejected, yet not barely because they were typical, but for that they were only Shadows of what was to come, and in their own Nature ceas'd of Course. It therefore does not follow, that because the symbolical Worship of the Jews was laid aside, for that Reason there could be no symbolical Worship under the Gospel, whereby we might continue a perpetual Memory of the Sacrifice of Christ's Death until his coming again. St. *Austin* never asserted any Thing like this, but the quite contrary in innumerable Places. He never oppos'd this Kind of symbolical or typical Sacrifice to real and true, but believed it real, true and substantial, because Christian and Evangelical Worship. He never could have so low and degrading a Thought as to maintain this was only the *Shadow*, not the Substance, who undoubtedly believed it the most acceptable *external* Sacrifice we can possibly make to God, and the most useful and efficacious Man can partake of. 'Tis confessed he distinguishes between external and internal Sacrifices, both which he affirms over and over to be Parts of true Christian Worship, and he justly prefers the latter before the former. He likewise says the latter are true ones, by which he does not mean to exclude visible Sacrifice from the Idea of true Sacrifice, but to affirm that one as well as the other is true, altho' the internal, which are the more valuable, are not

[u] Charge, p. 11.

commonly called by that Name, and the external are only the
41. Signs of the other, and are not required by God upon their own, but upon the others Account. And this is St. *Austin's* Method of solving the Difficulty of God's choosing internal Sacrifice rather than the outward, and not that which Dr. *Waterland* speaks of, viz. that the one is Legal, the other Evangelical, to which Pretence St. *Austin* does not give the least *Countenance*. As to the Charge of *Judaism*, which is objected to a material Sacrifice in the Eucharist, it is enough to reply almost in Dr. *Waterland's* own Words: *He forgets that it is offer'd in Christ's Name.*

My next Remark shall be, that according to St. *Austin*, St. *Paul* 1 Cor. x. 16, intended to intimate, that the Cup which we bless, and the Bread which we break, is a Sacrifice offer'd to and accepted by God, before it is eaten and drank by the Communicants, in like Manner as the *Jewish* and *Heathen* Sacrifices were offered, the first to the true God, the other to Dæmons before they were feasted on by the People. "He shews, [x] says the holy "Father, to which Sacrifice they ought to belong, saying,—*The* "*Cup of Blessing which we bless* &c. And upon this Account he
42. "subjoined: *Behold Israel after the Flesh, are not they who eat* "*of the Sacrifices Partakers of the Altar?* That they might "understand they are now so Partakers of the Body of Christ, as "those are Partakers of the Altar.—The Church offers to God "the Sacrifice of Praise in the Body of Christ, ever since God "spake and called the Earth from the rising of the Sun unto the

---

[x] —ostendit, ad quod sacrificium jam debeant pertinere, dicens,—*Calix benedictionis* &c.—Et propter hoc subjunxit, *Videte Israel secundum carnem: nonne qui de sacrificiis manducant, socii sunt altaris?* Ut intelligerent ita so jam socios esse corporis Christi, quemadmodum illi socii sunt altaris.—immolat Deo in corpore Christi sacrificium laudis, ex quo Deus deorum locutus vocavit terram a solis ortu usque ad occasum. Hæc quippe Ecclesia est Israel secundum carnem, qui serviebat in umbris sacrificiorum, quibus significabatur singulare sacrificium quod nunc offert Israel secundum Spiritum—De hujus enim domo non accipit vitulos, neque de gregibus ejus hircos. Iste immolat Deo sacrificium laudis, non secundum ordinem Aaron, sed secundum ordinem Melchisedec.—Noverunt qui legunt quid protulerit Melchisedec, quando benedixit Abraham: & si jam sunt participes ejus, vident tale sacrificium nunc offerri Deo toto orbe terrarum. Contra Advers. Leg. & Proph. lib. i. § 38, 39.

"going down thereof. For this Church is *Israel* after the Spirit;
"from which is distinguished that *Israel* after the Flesh, which
"served in the Shadows of the Sacrifices, by which was signified
"the singular Sacrifice, which *Israel* according to the Spirit now
"offers.—For out of his House he takes not Calves nor Goats out
"of his Flocks. He sacrifices to God the Sacrifice of Praise not
"after the Order of *Aaron*, but after the Order of *Melchisedech*.—
"They know who read what *Melchisedech* brought forth, when
"he blessed *Abraham;* and if they now are Partakers of it, they
"see such a Sacrifice is now offer'd to God throughout the
"World." Hence it is mighty clear it was St. *Austin's* Opinion,
that St. *Paul* designed the Eucharistick Elements should be
look'd upon as a Sacrifice, by his comparing them to those Things
which really were so: And that therefore there is not only a bare
vocal Sacrifice of Praise in the Eucharist, but also a visible
Sacrifice of Praise in the Body of Christ, or which is the same
Thing, in the material Symbols of it. This cannot be better
expressed than in the most excellent and remarkable ʸWords of
his present Grace of *Canterbury:* "the Elements were not his
"real Body and Blood, nor understood to be so by the Apostles
"or any primitive Father, but they were the Symbols of his Body
"and Blood; the partaking whereof is all one to the Receivers, 43.
"as if they should eat the Body and Blood of Christ offered upon
"the Cross. To this Purpose is the following Discourse of St.
"*Paul, The Cup of Blessing,* &c. 1 *Cor.* x. 16, 21. Where it
"may be observed, 1. That eating the Lord's Supper is the *same*
"Rite in the Christian Church with eating the Things offered in
"Sacrifice among the Jews and Gentiles. 2. That it is an Act of
"Communion and Fellowship with God, at whose Table we are
"said to be entertained, and therefore it is declared to be incon-
"sistent with eating the Gentile-Sacrifices, which is an Act of
"Communion with Devils, to whom those Sacrifices are offered.
"3. That it is an Act of Communion among Christians, who eat
"at the same Table, and by that Means are owned to be Members
"of the same evangelical Covenant under Christ. Whence the
"Apostle declares in another Place, that the *Jews*, who are not
"within the Christian Covenant, and consequently not in Com-

ʸ *Discourse of Church Government,* cap. v.

"munion with Christ and his Church, have no Right to partake of
"the Christian Altar: *We have an Altar*, says he, *whereof they
"have no Right to partake, who serve the Tabernacle*. Hence it
"is manifest, that to partake of the Lord's Supper is to partake
"of the Sacrifice of Christ, which is there commemorated and
"represented. For which Reason the most primitive Fathers
"speak of eating at the Christian Altar. *He that is not within
"the Altar*, says *Ignatius, is deprived of the Bread of God.*
"Where by the Bread of God he means the Sacrament, which
"God imparts to Christians from his own Table, which this
"Father calls the Altar. And the Lord's Supper is called an
"*Oblation*, a *Sacrifice*, and a *Gift*. Thus in *Clemens* of *Rome*: *It
"is no small Crime, if we depose them from their Episcopal office,
44. "who have unblameably and holily offered the Gifts*. Where he
"manifestly takes this Phrase of offering Gifts in the Sense
"wherein the *Jews* and our Lord used it: "*If thou bring thy
"Gift to the Altar*, &c. where Gift is put for Sacrifice. *Justin
"Martyr* in several Places of his Dialogue with *Trypho* the *Jew*
"calls the Eucharist a Sacrifice: Having cited the Passage of
"*Malachi*, where God tells the Jews: *I have no Pleasure in you
"—in every Place Incense shall be offered up in my Name and a
"pure Offering*, &c. He makes this Comment upon it: *He*, that
"is *God, then foretold the Sacrifices, which are offered to him by
"us Gentiles, namely, the Eucharist of Bread and Wine, whereby
"he saith we glorify his Name, but ye Jews profane it*. After-
"wards he hath these Words; *We* Christians *are the true Nation
"of God's Priests, as God himself witnesseth, when he saith, that
"in every Place among the Gentiles they shall offer unto him pure
"and acceptable Sacrifices: For God accepts Sacrifices from no
"Man, but his own Priests. And therefore he foretells, that all
"those shall be acceptable to him who shall offer in this* (Jesus's)
"*Name the Sacrifices, which Jesus Christ directed to be made,
"namely those which are made by the Christians in the Eucharist
"of Bread and Wine*. *Irenæus* calls the Eucharist the Oblation
"of the Church, which our Lord directed us to offer through the
"World, which he says is accounted by God a pure Sacrifice, and
"is acceptable to him. In another Place, where he speaks of
"our Lord's instituting the Eucharist he hath these Words: He
"taught the new Oblation of the New Testament which the

"Church hath received from the Apostles, and offers through the
"whole World. And in the Fathers of the next Age, to con-
"secrate the Lord's Supper is so constantly called προσφερειν in
"Greek and *offerre* in Latin, that it is needless to cite any Testi-
"monies from them. So that it is plain both from the Design
"and Nature of the Lord's Supper, and from the concurrent
"Testimony of the most primitive Fathers, who conversed with
"the Apostles or their Disciples, that it was reckoned through
"the whole World to be a commemorative Sacrifice, or the
"Memorial of our Lord offered upon the Cross; which being first
"dedicated to God by Prayer and Thanksgiving, and afterwards
"eaten by the Faithful, was to all Intents the same to them, as if
"they had really eaten the natural Body and Blood of Christ
"which are thereby represented." The great Prelate has said
somewhat more upon the Subject; but his whole Doctrine may be
resolved into these Propositions. 1. That the Eucharist is the
Sacrifice or Oblation of the Christian Church, which our Lord
directed to be offered through the whole World; and that this
Sacrifice was always believed to succeed in the Place of all other
Sacrifices. 2. That it is plain from the Nature and Design of
the Lord's Supper, and from the concurrent Testimony of the most
primitive Fathers, who conversed with the Apostles or their
Disciples, that the Lord's Supper was reckon'd through the
whole World to be a commemorative Sacrifice. 3. That Bread
and Wine, the Materials of this commemorative Sacrifice, are the
Representatives of Christ's Body and Blood, and that partaking
of them is all one to the Receivers, as if they had received the
Body and Blood of Christ which are thereby represented. 4.
That these Representatives of the Body and Blood of Christ are
first dedicated to God by Prayer and Thanksgiving, and afterwards eaten by the Faithful. 5. That therefore this Sacrifice
cannot be the one proper Sacrifice, which our Lord offered upon
the Cross, because we cannot partake of it in a literal and strict
sense without allowing Transubstantiation. 6. That Bishops
and Priests who consecrate this Sacrament or offer this commemorative Sacrifice, are Priests in the Christian Sense of that
Name, and the true and pious Sense of the Fathers, tho' not in the
unchristian, false and impious Sense of the Papists, which makes
them transubstantiating Priests, who offer the same Sacrifice in

the literal and strict Sense, that Christ offered upon the Cross. And thus you see these two great Men, the ancient Bishop of *Hippo*, and the present Archbishop of *Canterbury* concurring in their Judgments, that the Bread which we break, and the Wine which we bless is a Sacrifice first offered and dedicated to God, and then distributed to be eaten by the People.

According to their Interpretation of this Text St. *Paul's* Meaning is plainly[z] this: "The Bread and Wine which we, who "are Christ's Ministers or Priests, *offer*, *bless*, and *consecrate* by "Thanksgiving and Prayer; and which we break and put separate "in a Cup, so making a Representation of Christ's Body broken "and Blood shed upon the Cross; and lastly which we distribute; "are to those who jointly and in a Body communicate and par-
47. "take of them in Construction and Virtue the Body and Blood of "Christ, according as he ordained they should be at the Institu- "tion of this blessed Sacrament. 'Tis the Sacrifice of Bread and "Wine, in its natural Substance; 'tis the Sacrifice of the Body ' and Blood, not corporally, but spiritually, and by Christ's "divine Appointment and Power. And thus the Communion or "joint Participation of the Sacrifice of Bread and Wine, which is "[a] seen, is also the Communication of the Sacrifice of the Body and "Blood, which is understood and believed. Thus also by par- "taking of this one Bread, or by eating it in common or in Society, "we are *Socii* or Communicants of the Body of our Lord: In the "same Manner as the *Jews* by eating of the Things offered to "God, for Instance a *Lamb*, or a *Goat* considered in a *physical* "View, are joint Partakers of the Altar-Sacrifices considered in a "sacramental Respect, as they convey the Blessings of their "Religion: In the same Manner likewise as the Gentiles, by "feasting upon what seem'd not at all different from ordinary "Food, did at the same Time really feast upon diabolical "Sacrifices, it being offered to Idols and Devils; by eating

---

[z] Una eademque res secundum aliud species panis & vini consistit, secundum aliud autem corpus est & sanguis Christi. Secundum, namque quod utrumque corporaliter contingitur, species sunt creaturæ corporeæ; secundum potentiam vero, quod spiritualiter factæ sunt, mysteria sunt corporis & sanguinis Christi. Ratramnus de Corp. & Sang. Dom. § xvi.

[a] Ideo dicuntur sacramenta, quia in eis *aliud videtur, aliud intelligitur*. Serm. ad infantes apud Bedam in 1 Cor. 10.

"of which abominable and sacriligious Victims they were the "Devil's Socii or Communicants; or did join in doing Service to "them, as Christians and *Jews* by receiving their respective "Sacrifices were the Communicants of Christ and of the true "God." Thus do the three Sorts of Sacrifice illustrate each other. I have no Occasion to interpret the Context any farther, the rest is easily made out.

HAVING now sufficiently clear'd this Point from St. *Austin*, that the Eucharist, as to its Substance, is a material Sacrifice of Bread and Wine; and also that, as to its spiritual Signification and Use, it is the Sacrifice or Sacrament (for it is indifferent by which Name it is call'd) of Christ's Body and Blood; and farther, 48. that this Sacrifice is offered by the Rite, which Christ ordained in the Gospel : Let us then consider the Particulars of that Rite ; that we may have a distinct View in what Manner the Sacrifice is offered, and by what Degrees it comes to be made so sublime a Mystery. The first Step thereto which our Lord made, was to take Bread into his Hands, and separate them to be made use of in the Worship of God, or in other Words, to present them to God for that Purpose. Just so did St. *Austin* and the whole Church in his Time, which is so notorious that I need bring no [b]Proof for it here : And indeed the Passages already produced are a Demonstration of it. Those Priests therefore, that do not perform this Part of the Rite instituted by our blessed Saviour, but suffer the Clerk or the Sexton to place the Elements upon the holy Table, altho' that is also contrary to the Rubrick of our Church, cannot be said to pay any great Regard to our Lord's Command in this Particular : But I hope none of you, my Brethren, are guilty of such a slovenly Practice, but do agree in Judgment with, and practice after the Example of your worthy Archdeacon, who I do not question, being so great an Admirer and Patron of Antiquity, solemnly offers up the Bread and Wine to God, according to the Pattern of the primitive Priests.

THE second Thing set down in the Gospel Rite is *Thanksgiving;*

---

[b] In Sacramentis corporis & sanguinis Domini nihil amplius offeratur, quam ipse Dominus tradidit, hoc est panis & vinum aqua mixtum. Conc. Carth. III. can. 24.

which being said over the Elements, explains in some Degree the Nature and End of the Oblation or Sacrifice, and denotes that it is the Memorial or Sacrifice commemorative of Christ's Passion.

49. For in that Thanksgiving a peculiar Mention and Commemoration is made of the full, perfect and sufficient Sacrifice of the Death of Christ, and of the Redemption wrought by it. And this is clear from all the ancient Fathers and Liturgies, and from St. *Austin* among the rest, as several Passages above cited, which speak of celebrating the Memorial of Christ's Passion, sufficiently shew. To these let me ᵇannex what follows: "What Sacrifice of Praise "is there more sacred, than in the Eucharist or Celebration of the "Eucharist? And for what should we give greater Thanks to "God, than for his Grace by our Lord Jesus Christ? Which "the Faithful are well acquainted with in the Sacrifice of the "Church, whose Shadows all the former Sacrifices were." The Sacrifice of Praise in the Eucharist is more sacred than at any other Time, because it is the most solemn Act of Worship in the Christian Church, and is not only a bare vocal Sacrifice of Thanksgiving, which may be made without the Eucharist, but is also a visible one or sacred Sign of our Thankfulness to God ordained by Christ for that very purpose. It is best therefore when these two Sacrifices are united, and when the material Sacrifice is offered and dedicated by the other, as it is in Part: But

3. It is according to St. *Austin* completely made the representative and efficacious Sacrifice or sacred Sign of the Body and Blood of Christ once offer'd, by Prayer and the Word of God. And this is the Way by which our blessed Saviour himself completed the Eucharistick Sacrifice at the first Institu-
50. tion. He blessed the Elements and declar'd them in a most solemn Manner his Body to be given for us and his Blood to be shed upon the Cross for the Remission of our Sins. So also St. *Austin* and the Church in his Time did apply the Words of the Institution to the Bread and Wine, and did also sanctify them

---

ᵇ Quod est autem sacratius laudis sacrificium, quam in *actione gratiarum*? & unde majores agendæ sunt Deo gratiæ, quam pro ipsius gratia, per Jesum Christum Dominum nostrum? Quod totum fideles in ecclesiæ sacrificio sciunt, cujus umbræ fuerunt omnia priorum genera sacrificiorum. Cont. Adv. Legis & Proph. § 37.

by a Prayer, wherein they did desire God's Acceptance of the Gifts by beseeching him to bless and consecrate them, and in the highest Sense make them the visible Sacrifice, or the holy and effectual Signs of the Body and Blood of Christ: That so 1. putting on this high and noble Relation to our blessed Saviour, and lying in open View upon God's Altar, they might be tendered to divine Consideration, and in a most sensible and distinct Manner represent and inculcate our Lord's blessed Passion to his Father, to the End that he might for Christ's sake, according to the Tenor of his Covenant, in him be favourable and propitious to us miserable Sinners; and that 2. the Sacrifice might be useful also and beneficial to the Partakers thereof for the Pardon of their Sins, Increase of Grace, and the giving them upon their Repentance a firm and undoubted Assurance of everlasting Life.

AND thus St. *Austin* was not a mere *Vocalist,* but a *Materialist* as well as we, as I shall now particularly show. And 1. that he applied the Words of the Institution to the Elements, in order to the Consecration or most perfect Oblation of them, is plain enough from that trite [c]Saying of his, *The Word is applied to the Element and it is made a Sacrament.* And [d]in a Sermon of his: "That Bread which you see on the Altar, being sanctified by the "Word of God, is the Body of Christ; that Cup, or what the Cup 51. "contains, being sanctified by the Word of God, is the Blood of "Christ." [e]Again: "Our (Eucharistick) Bread and Cup is made "mystical to us by a certain Consecration, and is not naturally "so." This indeed may relate to Consecration by Prayer as well as by the Words of Christ. For

2. ST. *Austin* affirms they were also sanctified by Prayer. For in his Epistle to *Paulinus* explaining the Words of the Apostle, 1 *Tim.* ii. he [f]thus delivers his Mind: "By *Prayers* we

[c] Accedit verbum ad elementum & fit Sacramentum.

[d] Panis ille, quem videtis in Altari, sanctificatus per verbum Dei, corpus est Christi. Calix ille, imo quod habet calix, sanctificatum per verbum Dei, sanguis est Christi. Serm. 227.

[e] Noster panis & calix, non quodlibet,—sed certa consecratione mysticus fit nobis, non nascitur. Cont. Faust. XX. 13.

[f] Orationes, cum [quod est in mensa Domini] benedicitur & sanctificatur—

"understand that Part of the Service, wherein that which is "upon the Table of the Lord is blessed and sanctified." But what he ᵍsays, *Lib.* III. § 10 *de Trinitate*, will yet give farther Light in this Affair: "We call that only the Body and Blood of "Christ, which, being taken out of the Fruits of the Earth "and consecrated by mystical Prayer, we duly receive to our "Salvation in Memory of our Lord's Passion for us." Again in his Confutation of the *Donatist* Opinion, that the sacramental Consecrations and Administrations of Sinners were invalid, he ʰsays, "How then does God hear the Prayers of the Murderer, "'which he makes over the baptismal Water, over the Oil, or over "the Eucharist?" Where he plainly speaks of the Consecration
52. of the sacramental Signs. And against *Parmenianus*, who affirmed that the Sacrifices of wicked Men will do those harm who receive the Sacrifice from them, he ⁱdeclares, that "One "and the same Sacrifice, because of the Name of the Lord which "is invoked, is always holy, and becomes to every one according "to the Heart with which he comes to receive it." Where it is plainly implied, that the Sacrifice is made holy by a Prayer of Invocation.

AND thus it is demonstrated, that the material Oblation of Praise, and the Sacrifice commemorative and representative of our Lord's one all-sufficient Sacrifice, is offered to God by presenting the Bread and Cup upon the holy Table or Altar, and by giving Thanks over them and consecrating them into the divine Memorial, whereby God is as it were put in Mind of us, and rendered gracious to us through the Atonement made for us by the Sacrifice of the Cross. And this is farther confirmed by St. *Austin*'s declaring, that God is pleased to confer his favours upon us by our offering it to him, and tendering it to the divine

---

ᵍ Corpus Christi & sanguinem dicimus illud tantum, quod ex fructibus terræ acceptum & prece mystica consecratum rite sumimus ad salutem spiritualem in memoriam pro nobis Dominicæ passionis.

ʰ Quomodo exaudit homicidam deprecantem, vel super aquam baptismi, vel super oleum, vel super eucharistiam? De bapt. Lib. V. § 28.

ⁱ Unum atque idem sacrificium, propter nomen Domini quod invocatur, & semper sanctum est, & tale cuique fit, quali corde ad accipiendum accesserit. Cont. Ep. Parmen. Lib. II. § 11.

Consideration. For he [k]informs us, that when evil Spirits had afflicted the Cattle and Servants of one *Hesperius*, a Man of Quality, one of St. *Austin's* Priests went and offered the Sacrifice of the Body of Christ, praying that the Calamity might cease, and through the Mercy of God it accordingly did so. And it was the common Practice of the Church at that Time, as it is now of ours, to join Prayers for all Men to the Sacrifice; which shews that they believed their Prayers were likely to be most effectual, 53. when they were presented along with it; the verbal Offering being then most prevailing, when annexed to the visible One. For by Facts as well as Words, by Rites as well as Prayers, the Affections and Desires of our Hearts may be signified. For this Reason they offered their Petitions, not only for the Living, but for the Dead, that God would be pleased to hasten his Kingdom, and finally acquitting them at the last Day, grant them their perfect Consummation and Bliss both in Body and Soul in his everlasting Glory. "For, [l]says he, it is not to be denied, that "the Souls of the Dead are helped by the Piety of the Living, "when the Sacrifice of the Mediator is offered, or Alms are given "in the Church for them." In short, it was looked upon by St. *Austin* as a sensible Rite of Prayer; and the laying the Monuments or Symbols of Christ's Propitiation in View before the Divine Majesty, was considered as a most powerful Means of bringing down God's Blessings both upon the Offerers and Partakers of it, and upon those for whom it was offered: The Priest offering it both for the present Communicants, and also for all the absent Members of the Church.

HAVING thus endeavoured to explain St. *Austin's* Doctrine concerning the external Oblation of the Sacrifice according to the Rite set down in the Gospel; I come now to consider the internal and invisible Sanctification of the Sacrament. For the Priest's external Actions over the Symbols would be of little Significancy, if God did not concur with the outward Celebration. All the Priest can do is to execute Christ's Commission, and to perform

---

[k] Perrexit unus, obtulit ibi sacrificium corporis Christi, orans quantum potuit, ut cessaret illa vexatio; Deo protinus miserante cessavit.

Neque negandum est defunctorum animas pietate suorum viventium relevari, cum pro illis sacrificium Mediatoris offertur, vel eleemosynæ in Ecclesia fiunt. Enchirid. de fide, spe & caritate, § 29.

54. the Rite according to his Command. But then, since we have our Saviour's Promise, that he will be with his Ministers by his divine Presence and by his holy Spirit to the End of the World, to confirm and make authentick all they act by Virtue of his Commission, we may be sure he is as good as his Word. Whenever then the Minister, being authorized by our blessed Saviour, offers the Sacrifice to the divine Acceptance, by doing the several Acts by him prescribed, and desires God to bless it and consecrate it, that it may be the Body and Blood of Christ; we need not doubt, but God by his holy Spirit does actually make it so, and by so doing graciously accepts the Sacrifice. For as God accepted of the Patriarchal and Jewish Sacrifices by their being consum'd, either in whole or in part, by a celestial or sacred Fire, which was an Emblem of the Holy Ghost; so he now accepts the Christian Sacrifice without any such significant Ceremony immediately by sending the Holy Ghost to sanctify it. This is now the holy Flame which descends from Heaven. For as [m]St. *Chrysostome* strongly expresses it, *Not by Smoke and sweet Savour, not by Blood, but by the Grace of the Spirit the Sacrifice is offered.* [n]St. *Cyprian* likewise has something to this Purpose: "The Holy Ghost frequently appeared in Fire—In the Sacrifices "which God accepted, Fire descended from Heaven to consume "the Sacrifices." Where it is plainly intimated, that the Christian Oblation is accepted and perfected by the Holy Ghost:

55. Especially if this Place be compared with another, where he directly affirms the [o]*Oblation is sanctified by the Holy Ghost.*

AND to this St *Austin* fully agrees. For in many Places he

---

[m] Non per fumum & nidorem, non per sanguinem—sed per Spiritus gratiam offertur. Hom. adv. Jud. V. Tom. I. p. 647. Ed. Ben.

[n] Spiritum sanctum in igne frequenter apparuisse—In sacrificiis quæcunque accepta habebat Deus, descendebat ignis de cœlo, qui sacrificata consumeret. Testim. Lib. III. § 101.

[o] Quando nec oblatio sanctificari illic possit, ubi Spiritus sanctus non fit. Ep. 65. It was St. *Cyprian*'s opinion that the Holy Ghost was not present with laps'd, heretical or schismatical Bishops to sanctify their Sacraments, which proves clearly he believed, and it was the universal Opinion in his Time, that he sanctified the Catholick *Oblation.* Dr. *Waterland* has given a wrong Turn to this Passage in his Review, p. 39, by translating it, *where the Holy Ghost is not given;* It is not, *detur*, but, *fit*, which are quite different Things.

pleads, that there is a certain Sanctity or divine Virtue, which rests upon the Sacraments themselves. I shall only mention a few of them out of a Number almost infinite. I have cited one already where he says, the Sacrifice is always holy, whatsoever the Receivers be. And speaking of the Baptism and Ordination of Schismaticks, he [p]affirms: "Both Sacraments are given to Man "by a certain Consecration; and as the Baptism remains intire "in Schismaticks, so does their Ordination: For the Fault lyes in "their Schism, which is corrected by Unity, not in the Sacra-"ments, which, wherever they are, are the same." The like must by Parity of Reason be said of the Eucharist which is offered by Schismaticks. A little [q]after: "Injury is to be done "to neither Sacrament—the Perverseness of Man is to be cor-"rected, but the Sanctity of the Sacraments is to be violated in no "perverse Person. It remains in wicked Men, whether within or "without the Church, unpolluted and inviolable; but in wicked "Men the Sacraments remain to their Condemnation." There is no [r]Difference then in the Sacraments or Sacrifices themselves administered whether by the Schismaticks or Catholicks, but only in the Effects: To the one they are the Means of their Salvation, to the other of their eternal Destruction. He frequently talks of the holy Force of Baptism, and assures us, that its [s]*Sanctity cannot be polluted* by whomsoever administered, and *that a divine Virtue adheres to the Sacrament, whether to the Salvation of those who use it well, or to the Damnation of those*

---

[p] Utrumque enim sacramentum est, & quadam consecratione utrumque homini detur—sicut baptismus in eis, ita ordinatio mansit integra: quia in præcisione fuerat vitium, quod unitatis pace correctum est, non in sacramentis quæ ubicunque sunt ipsa sunt. Contra Ep. Parm. Lib. II. § 28.

[q] Neutri sacramento injuria facienda est—intelligitur perversitatem hominum esse corrigendam, sanctitatem autem sacramentorum in nullo perverso esse violandam. Constat enim eam in perversis & sceleratis hominibus, sive in eis qui intus sunt, sive in eis qui foris sunt, impollutam atque inviolabilem permanere—in malis permanent ad judicium. Ib. § 30.

[r] Sacramenta si eadem sunt, ubique integra sunt, etiamsi pravè intelliguntur & discordiosè tractantur. De Bapt. Lib. III. § 20.

[s] Ipsa ejus sanctitas pollui non potest, & sacramento suo divina virtus adsistit, sive ad salutem bene utentium, sive ad perniciem male utentium. Ib. Lib. 3, § 15.

who use it ill: ¹And "That God is present with his Sacraments "and Words, by whomsoever administered, and the Sacraments "of God are every where right." ᵛAnd, *God sanctifies his own Sacrament.* ʷAnd, *The Holy Ghost avoided the Deceit of the Man, not the Truth of the Sacrament.* The Holy Ghost therefore sanctifies the Sacrament, and for that Reason ˣ*the Sacraments*
57. *are true and holy in themselves upon Account of the holy and true God whose Sacraments they are.* As to the Eucharist in particular, St. *Austin* ᵃ allows, that schismatick Bishops can offer or consecrate the Eucharist; ᵇthey presented the Gifts to God, and others received 'em from them in their Hands; which Gifts when consecrated ᶜwere the Body and Blood of Christ notwithstanding their sacrilegious Schism. Now all this makes it evident, that the Holy Ghost imparts a divine Virtue and Energy to the Elements themselves to make them fit Instruments of conferring his Graces, and all the Fruits of Christ's Death upon the Souls of Men. For if according to St. *Austin's* Doctrine in almost every Page of his Books against the *Donatists* the Sacraments are not beneficial, but hurtful to Schismaticks, then the Sanctity or divine Virtue imparted by the Holy Ghost, when they celebrate the Eucharist, cannot be communicated to the Receivers, but must necessarily rest upon the Elements; upon which Account they are in God's Intention the Body and Blood of Christ in Power and Effect, or the Sacraments thereof in themselves holy and full of Force and Virtue, and they are so both to the Worthy

---

ᵗ Si autem Deus adest sacramentis & verbis suis, per qualescunque administrentur & sacramenta Dei ubique recta sunt. Ib. Lib. V. § 27.

ᵛ Deus ipse sanctificat sacramentum suum. Ib. Lib. VI. § 47.

ʷ Spiritus sanctus hominis fallaciam, non veritatem sacramenti fugiebat. Cont. lit. Petil. Lib. II. § 61.

ˣ Illa namque per se ipsa vera & sancta sunt propter Deum verum & sanctum cujus sunt. Cont. Crescon. Lib. IV. § 24.

ᵃ Compare Lib. VI. § 11, 12, de bapt.

ᵇ Cui ergo accedebat dona offerre Deo, ab eo cæteri conjunctis manibus accipiebant. Cont. Ep. Parm. Lib. II. § 13.

ᶜ —indigne quisque sumens Dominicum sacramentum non efficit, ut quia ipse malus est, malum sit, aut quia non ad salutem accipit, nihil acceperit. Corpus enim Domini & sanguis Domini nihilo minus erat etiam illis, quibus dicebat Apostolus, Qui manducat indigne, judicium sibi manducat & bibit. Non ergo quærant in Catholica hæretici quod habent—De bapt. Lib. V. § 9.

and Unworthy, for the Salvation of the one, and the Condemnation of the other. This is the Doctrine St. *Austin* gathers from St. *Paul*, and it is a certain and indisputable Truth. It is therefore a great Mistake to say with Dr. *Waterland*, that the primitive Church, by praying for the Descent of the Holy Ghost 58. upon the Elements, did not intend the Words should be understood in a proper Sense, but her Meaning was only to express the Operation of the holy Spirit in the Persons receiving the Sacrament, and not in the Sacrament itself. For the Elements are in themselves and absolutely the blessed Sacrament of the Body and Blood of Christ, and are so both to the Holy and Unholy; and this they could not be but by the invisible Operation of the divine Spirit, as St. *Austin* sufficiently instructs us in the following Words, where speaking of the Eucharistical Bread he [d]says, "When by the Hands of Men it is wrought into that visible "Shape, it is not sanctified into so great a Sacrament, but by "the invisible Operation of the holy Spirit." And whereas it is pretended by some, that the Holy Ghost could not operate upon inanimate or irrational Things, which was supposed to be, tho' it was not indeed, *Origen's* Opinion; St. *Austin* not only in the preceding Passages, but most especially in one other particular Place, does expressly contradict this Notion. For the Author of an *Arian* Sermon having [e]affirmed, that "it is the Work and "Care of the holy Spirit to sanctify and keep the Saints, and not "only to sanctify rational Things, as some think, but several "irrational." St. *Austin* acknowledges this Truth: "The holy 59. "Spirit does indeed do these Things, but not without the Son,— "We confess those Things are done by the Holy Ghost, which "they have mentioned to be done by him." This is home to the Point and cannot admit either of Answer or Evasion. And here

---

[d] Quod cum per manus hominum ad illam visibilem speciem perducatur, non sanctificatur ut sit tam magnum sacramentum, nisi operante invisibiliter Spiritu Dei. De Trin. Lib. III. § 10.

[e] Spiritûs sancti opus & diligentia est sanctificare & sanctos custodire, & non solum rationabilia, ut quidam putant, sed irrationabilia plura sanctificare—Facit haec quidem Spiritus sanctus, sed absit ut sine Filio faciat—Cum itaque fateamur fieri ab Spiritu sancto, quae ab illo fieri commemoraverunt—Contra Serm. Arian. § 30, 31. He no doubt has a Respect here to the baptismal Water, the Chrism, and the Eucharist.

it is said, that *some think* that only rational Creatures can be sanctified: I suppose some of the *Arian* Communion, or some few other condemn'd Hereticks: But St. *Austin* and the Catholick Church in his Time were of a contrary Judgment.

This holy Father's Doctrine will receive considerable Light from the Explanation of it by *Ratramnus*, an ancient Writer in the Ninth Century of great Authority, to whom our worthy Reformers shew'd such high Regard, that we may very justly esteem his Doctrine to be the same with that of our excellent Church. Now *Ratramnus* professes to follow the Steps of St. *Austin* and other holy Fathers; I will therefore take the Pains to transcribe some Passages out of him, for the most Part making use of the learned Dr. *William Hopkins's* accurate Translation. 'As for that Bread, "which by the Ministry of the Priest is "made Christ's Body, it sheweth one Thing outwardly to the "Senses, and inwardly proclaims quite another Thing to the "Minds of the Faithful. That which outwardly appears is "Bread, as it was before in Form, Colour, and Taste; but "inwardly there is quite another Thing presented to us, and that "much more precious and excellent, because it is heavenly and "divine, that is, Christ's Body is declared, which is beheld, "received and eaten not by our carnal Senses, but by the Sight

60. "of the believing Mind. Likewise the Wine, which by the "Priest's Consecration is made the Sacrament of Christ's Blood, "appears one Thing outwardly, and inwardly contains another. "What doth outwardly appear but the Substance of Wine—But "if you consider it inwardly, then not the Liquor of Wine, but "the Liquor of Christ's Blood is by the Minds of the Faithful "both relish'd while it is tasted, and acknowledged while it is "seen, and approved while it is smelt. Since these Things are "undeniable, 'tis evident that the Bread and Wine are figura- "tively the Body and Blood of Christ—How can that be styled "Christ's Body and Blood, in which there is not any Change to "be made—In this Sacrament if the Thing be considered in "Simplicity and Verity, and nothing else believ'd but what is "seen, we know of no Change at all made. For there is no "Change from not being to Being, as in the Production of

ᶠ §IX. &c.

"Things. Since such did not exist before, but pass'd from a
"State of Nonentity to Being. Whereas here Bread and Wine
"were real Beings before they became the Sacrament of Christ's
"Body and Blood. Nor is here a Passage from Being to not
"being, as in Things decayed or corrupted:—Now it is certain
"there is no Change of this Kind made; for it is well known, that
"the Nature of the Creatures remains in Truth the very same
"they were before. And as for that sort of Change, whereby
"one Thing is rendered another, which is seen in Things liable
"to vary in their Qualities—it is plain this Change is not made
"here. For we can perceive no Alteration either as to Touch,
"Colour or Taste. Therefore if nothing be changed the
"Elements are nothing but what they were before. And yet
"they are another Thing; for the Bread is made the Body, and
"the Wine is made the Blood of Christ.—*If they now are other
"than what they were before, they have admitted some Change.
"This being undeniable, let them now tell in what Respect they
"are changed? For we see nothing corporally changed in them.
"Therefore they must needs acknowledge either that they are
"changed in some other Respect than that of their Bodies, and
"in this Respect they are what we see they are not in Truth, but
"somewhat else which we discern them not to be in their proper
"Essence; or if they will not acknowledge this, they will be
"compelled to deny they are Christ's Body and Blood; which is
"abominable not only to speak, but even to think. But since
"they do confess them to be the Body and Blood of Christ,
"which they could not have been but by a Change for the better,
"nor is this Change wrought *corporally*, but *spiritually*; it must
"necessarily be said to be wrought *figuratively*. Because under
"the Vail of material Bread and material Wine, the Spiritual
"Body and Spiritual Blood do exist: Not that there are together
"existing two Natures so different, as a Body and a Spirit; But
"one and the same Thing in one Respect has the Nature of
"Bread and Wine, and in another Respect is the Body and
"Blood of Christ. For both as they are corporally handled are
"in their Nature corporeal Creatures; but according to their
"Virtue, and what they are spiritually made, they are Mysteries

"of the Body and Blood of Christ.—[h] If in the Font you consider
"nothing but what the bodily Sense beholdeth, you see a fluid
"Element of a corruptible Nature, and capable of washing the
62. "Body only. But the Power of the Holy Ghost came upon it by
"the Priest's Consecration, and it obtained thereby an Efficacy to
"wash not the Bodies only, but also the Souls of Men; and by a
"spiritual Virtue to take away their spiritual Filth.—[i] If you
"require what washes the Outside, it is the Element; but if you
"consider what purgeth internally, it is a quickening Power, a
"sanctifying Power, a Power conferring Immortality.—[k] Thus
"also the Body and Blood of Christ considered as to the Outside
"only, is a Creature subject to Change and Corruption. But if
"you ponder the Virtue of the Mystery, it is Life conferring
"Immortality on such as partake thereof.—[l] He now in the
"Church doth by his Almighty Power spiritually change Bread
"and Wine into the Flesh of his own Body and the Liquor of
"his own Blood.—[m] The Bread which is offered, tho' made of the
"Fruits of the Earth, while it is consecrated is changed into
"Christ's Body; as also the Wine, which flowed from the Vine, is
"by sacramental Consecration made the Blood of Christ, not
"visibly indeed, but by the invisible Operation of the Spirit of
"God.—[n] By all that hath been hitherto said it appears, that the
"Body and Blood of Christ, which are received by the Mouths of
"the Faithful in the Church, are Figures in Respect of their visible
"Nature; but in Respect of the invisible Substance, that is, the
"Power of the Word of God, they are truly Christ's Body and
"Blood. Wherefore as they are visible Creatures they feed the
"Body, but as they have a Virtue of a more powerful Substance,
"they both feed and sanctify the Souls of the Faithful.—[o] In this
63. "Mystery of the Body and Blood of Christ there is a Change
"made, and wonderfully, because it is Divine, ineffable and
"incomprehensible; I desire to know of them, who will not
"admit of an inward secret Virtue, but will judge of the whole
"Matter, as it appears to outward Sense, in what Respect this
"Change is made? As for the Substance of the Creatures, what
"they were before Consecration, the same they remain after it.—So

[h] § XVII. [i] § VIII. [k] § XIX. [l] § XXV.
[m] § XLII. [n] § XLIX. [o] LIV.

EPISTOLARY DISSERTATION. 247

"that it is changed internally by the mighty Power of the Holy
"Ghost.—[p]It is the Body of Christ indeed, yet not corporal, but
"spiritual.—[q]He plainly shews, in what Respect it is accounted
"Christ's Body, to wit, in as much as the Spirit of Christ is
"therein, that is to say, the Power of the divine Word, which
"doth not only feed, but also purifies the Soul.—[r]That, whatever
"it is, which gives the Substance of Life, is the Efficacy of a
"spiritual Power, of an invisible and divine Virtue."

Thus this ancient Writer expounds the Sentiments of St.
Austin and of the other primitive Fathers, concerning the
Change that is made by Consecration, and most accurately and
clearly shews, there is no physical Conversion, neither Generation, nor Corruption, nor Alteration in the Substance of the
Creatures: And he affirms, that it is not a corporal, but a
spiritual Conversion, the Elements being raised to a Dignity
above their Nature, and being made in an ineffable Manner,
mystically and *spiritually*, not substantially, the Body and Blood
of Christ by the divine Power of the Word of God and of the
Holy Ghost; by whose Almighty Influence they are indued with
a spiritual and internal Efficacy and Virtue. This is the Change
the primitive Fathers unanimously taught; and to deny that the
Elements are thus made the blessed Body and Blood, *Ratramnus* 64.
and in him all the primitive Saints declare to be an abominable
Impiety. Let us not then be afraid to believe and confess, that
the Bread by Consecration is sacramentally and in Power and
Virtue Christ's Body; but rather let us abhor to reduce it to a
bare empty Memorial, to an unsanctified Figure, and an insignificant Shadow; which is a Rock we shall be in great Hazard of
splitting upon, if we deny they have any Virtue in them, any Efficacy
annexed to them by the invisible Operation of the Holy Ghost.
They are the Body of Christ which was given for us, and the
Blood of Christ which was shed for us; let us never forget, that
our blessed Saviour has said it, and he is able to make it good.
'Tis a Figure of it indeed, but such a one as is in Effect the Thing
itself; 'tis a most powerful and prevalent Representation of it in
the Sight of God, and 'tis a Sacrament thereof containing in it
the sanctifying Power of the divine Spirit, which doth in a sure,

[p] § LX.   [q] § LXIV.   [r] § LXXII.

tho' invisible Manner, nourish and quicken the Souls of those who worthily partake of it.

BUT it seems this Change from common Bread to consecrated, induced with a Power and Virtue to represent and apply the Merits of Christ's Death, *is Sound without Meaning, or Words without Ideas: And it is hard to say what that inward Change means, or what Idea it carries with it. Now I am of a quite contrary Opinion, and to me there seems no Difficulty at all in conceiving, that tho' the Change is not in any physical Quality, and consequently is not a physical Change, yet God can bestow upon the Element a supernatural Quality over and above the natural, and so exalt it from the Condition of mere Corporal Food into a spiritual Sacrament, having a Force annexed to it to confer Holiness upon those who with Faith and Thanksgiving feed upon it. This is the inward Change, the inhering, intrinsick Holiness; and Dr. *Waterland* will please to think again, whether this will not very well comport both with true Philosophy and sound Theology. Not that we are to reject every Thing that we cannot explain in a philosophical Way, and which our short Understandings cannot fathom. If we were, the Pains which the worthy *Archdeacon* has taken to so good Purpose in explaining the Doctrine of the *Trinity*, not according to the rules of *Philosophy*, but according to *Scripture* and *Antiquity*, are absolutely lost. It is enough, if a Christian Mystery is not contrary to Reason and true Philosophy, altho' it be incomprehensible: And I think it cannot be made appear this inward Change contradicts true Philosophy. It is very agreeable to true Philosophy, that God by his Appointment should give our Food a Power of nourishing our Bodies, and our Medicines a Power of purging and healing them in a natural Way. I cannot see then, why Christ by his Institution and divine Concurrence may not give the Elements a Power or Quality of strengthening and refreshing the Soul in a supernatural. We know God gave the River *Jordan* a Virtue to heal *Naaman's* Leprosy, and Christ the Clay to cure Blindness, and to the Hem of his Garment to cure another Distemper, insomuch that he said, *Virtue had gone out of him:* Why then cannot Christ give to

* Append. p. 15.

the Bread and Wine a spiritual Virtue to impart Sanctification and Salvation to the Communicants? The King can make a Piece of Parchment stand for his Pardon, and yet God cannot make the Eucharist stand for his. Indeed we cannot comprehend how this is; but we know there are a great many Things in Nature as well as Religion, the Manner of which we cannot comprehend; therefore this Consideration need not trouble us. But this we can very well judge of, that it does not contradict any Principles of true Philosophy, and that I hope is abundantly sufficient. It likewise comports very well with true Theology, if the Church of *England* may be Judge, who in her 26th Article determines in this manner: "For as much as evil Ministers do "not administer the Word and Sacraments in their own Name, "but in Christ's, and do minister by his Commission and "Authority; we may use their Ministry both in hearing the "Word of God, and in receiving the Sacraments. ᵃ Neither is the "Effect of Christ's Ordinance taken away by their Wickedness; "nor the Grace of God's Gifts diminished from such as by Faith "and rightly do receive the Sacraments ministered to them, "which be effectual because of Christ's Institution and Promise, "although they be ministered by evil Men." Here it is asserted, that even evil Ministers have Christ's Commission and Authority: He with respect to the Eucharist ordered the Apostles, and in them all the Christian Clergy, to *do this*, that is, perform the sacrificial Ministration according to the Rite just before prescribed: He breathed on them, saying, *Receive ye the Holy Ghost*, by which he declared that whatever they did in the Church, was likewise the Act of the Holy Ghost; therefore what they consecrate by Prayer, the Holy Ghost really consecrates and gives it a Power or Grace to make it effectual for the Purposes intended by the Institution. With just Reason therefore doth the Church affirm likewise, that there is a divine *Grace* annexed to the Sacraments, and that they be effectual not only by Christ's Institution, but Promise. He promised to be with them

---

ᵃ It runs thus in the Latin Original: Neque per illorum malitiam, effectus institutorum Christi tollitur, aut gratia donorum Dei minuitur, quoad eos qui fide & ritè sibi oblata percipiunt, quæ propter institutionem Christi & promissionem efficacia sunt—

always by his Spirit, whom he told them he would send for that Purpose. Therefore St *Paul* calls the Offices of the Church the Gifts of the Holy Ghost. *God hath set some in the Church,* 1st *Apostles, &c.* and their Administrations, or sacramental Performances, the Administrations of the Spirit. Accordingly *by* the Virtue and Efficacy of the *one Spirit* working in and by the baptismal Water *we are all baptized into one Body,* and we are all made *to drink into one Spirit,* by drinking of the spiritual and life-giving Cup, sanctified by the Spirit of God. This then is notoriously the Doctrine of our Church, That tho' the Substance of the Creatures is not chang'd, yet the sacred Signs could not justly bear the Names of the Things themselves, except the Virtue, Power and Effect of Christ's Flesh and Blood were adjoined to them and united with them after a secret and ineffable Manner by the working of the Holy Ghost. I hope this Doctrine of our Church is very agreeable to sound Theology. I am sure it comports exactly with the Theology of St. *Austin* and all the primitive Fathers, who, if Dr. [b] *Waterland* himself say true, were at least as sound Divines, and as good Interpreters of Scripture as any Moderns whatsoever. If indeed it could be shewn, either that I have misrepresented St. *Austin's* opinion, or that he contradicts the common Doctrine of the Church in his

68. Time or before it, then I freely own myself under a Mistake in this Matter, and would frankly submit to a Recantation of it: But if this cannot be proved, as I with Great Humility, tho' with all Christian Confidence, affirm it cannot, then I must think it my Duty to exhort all Persons to reject all novel Constructions of Scripture, and stand firmly by those of the primitive Fathers: For it is an undoubted Truth, to use Dr. [c] *Waterland's* excellent Expressions, "That the Sense of the Ancients once Known, is a "useful check upon any new Interpretations of Scripture affecting "the main Doctrines. It has a negative Voice, if I may so call "it, in such a Case. And it is Reason sufficient for throwing off "any such novel Expositions, that they cross upon the undoubted

---

[b] See his Importance of the Doctrine of the holy Trinity, Chap. vii, where he shews with great Strength of Reason, and Clearness of Expression, the Use and Value of Ecclesiastical Antiquity with Respect to Controversies of Faith.

[c] Ib. p. 385.

"Faith of all the ancient Churches, or contain some Doctrine, as "of moment to be received, which the Ancients universally "rejected or never admitted." 'Tis true Dr. *Waterland* has endeavoured to obscure this Truth in his Review, but whoever reads with Attention even those very Passages from Fathers and Liturgies which he has cited, will be easily convinced, that they believed a sanctifying Virtue rested in the Elements, as well as that a sanctifying Grace was by their Means conferred upon the Receivers. There is none but *Origen* can be suspected of the contrary Opinion, and that without any good Grounds: For we are not to take his Sentiments from his Enemies, who endeavoured to make him as odious as they could, but from his own Writings, where he clearly delivers his Mind in a catholick Manner, in a Manner that I have shewed St. *Austin* did, who only spoke the Sense of all the Churches before him. But to return.

OUTWARD Relations, adventitious Uses, or Offices it seems are easily understood, and relative Holiness carries some Sense in it. Very well. But let me ask, Can Man appoint any Thing to be so much of an outward Figure of the Body and Blood of our Redeemer, or appropriate it to spiritual and salutary Uses and Offices, to be a Means and Instrument of conveying heavenly Blessings? Can Man imprint such a relative Holiness upon it, and make it bear such a near Relation to the Body and Blood of Christ, as that it should be a Means of our receiving it, and a Pledge to assure us thereof? No certainly, nothing of this can be done but by Christ's sanctifying his own Ordinance, and making it effectual to the procuring of those inestimable Benefits, for which he was pleased to ordain it. Man may pray for the Consecration of the Elements, but that would effect nothing, unless God answered his Prayer and actually made them, what the Saviour assures us he will make them, if the Rite he instituted be duly executed. If then God himself blesses the Elements and makes them, not *corporally*, but *spiritually* the Body and Blood of Christ; then certainly God's Blessing rests upon the Elements, and unless it can be truly said, that God's Blessing operates nothing at all, it must necessarily be confessed that thereby some extraordinary Efficacy and gracious Virtue is infused into them; otherwise let us give them what outward Relations we please, and set them aside to what adventitious

Uses and Offices we may invent for them or appoint them to, and suppose them vested with all the relative Holiness we can imagine, it is all to no Purpose; this will never make them Means of Grace, they will be unprofitable and lifeless Things without the divine Blessing to invigorate them. The Doctor himself is sensible of this in his [d]Review, and owns, that
70. whatever Consecration, or Benediction, or Sanctification is imparted to Things as well as Persons it is all God's doing; which makes me admire, why he should quite exclude from the sacred Signs, which are to be considered also as Means of sanctifying the Receivers, any inherent Virtue for that Purpose, and only allow them a bare relative Holiness, as Things to which we owe a Respect as bearing a certain Relation to God. They have certainly more than a bare relative Holiness belonging to them: For relative Holiness does not imply in the Idea of it, that those Things which are vested with it are in any Sense Means of Grace. Means of Grace bear indeed a very high Relation to God, and therefore are relatively holy; but that is not all, they are by God's Blessing indued with a more substantial Sanctity than that, even with an holy and divine Power of answering the Ends of their Institution; and this Things, that are only relatively holy, have not. We may illustrate this by a familiar Example of the relative Sacredness accruing to Things by the Relation they bear to earthly Majesty. The Crowns and Scepters of Princes are relatively sacred in this lower Sense, and so is their Money too: But the latter has in it more than a bare Relation to the King, it has likewise an intrinsick Value. But we will put the Case of Paper-Money, which is a Thing of no Value, but what it derives from publick Authority: This has Relation to the King too, but if it had not likewise an inherent Power or Privilege of being exchanged for Money, the Relation to the King would signify little. Shut up the Bank or the Exchequer, and then a Man will be little better for having in his Pocket a Piece of Paper that bears a Relation to the King. Just so it is with Regard to the Eucharistick Elements: They are Things of very small Value in themselves,
71. but by the Institution of Christ's and God's Blessing, being raised

[d] *Review*, p. 120.

to the Dignity of Sacraments, and to the Usefulness of Means of Grace, an holy or sacred Relation is conveyed to them: But if this were all, they would be of little or no Service to us, they might deserve our Reverence on Account of their Relation to the Deity, but they would not come up to the Intent of conferring Benefits upon us. Therefore there must necessarily something more inhere in them by the divine Sanctification, they must by God be dignified with a Power of conferring Blessings, or else undoubtedly they will confer nothing. They may possibly rise as high as Figures or Memorials, but they never can be Means of Grace, never can by any Construction in the World be accounted Christ's blessed Body and Blood for the Salvation of the worthy Receiver. From whence it may fairly be concluded, that the divine Sanctification by the Prayer of the Priest is derived upon the Elements as well as upon the Persons tho' in a different Sense; that there is an inherent Virtue residing in them, whereby they become powerful Means and effectual Instruments in God's Hand to convey sanctifying Graces to the Communicants: Not that Remission of Sins, or sanctifying Graces, or any other Benefits of Christ's Passion reside in them, but a Virtue and Power to confer Remission of Sins and so forth, and apply them to the Souls of Men. And I hope this is very intelligible, and will at length be thought very well to comport with sound Theology. I am sure it is absolutely impossible to understand how mere outward Relations and relative Holiness can be of any Value or Significancy to work any Spiritual Effect.

HAVING thus proved, that a divine Virtue is imparted to the Elements by the Holy Ghost, I come now to shew, how it makes the Eucharist a valuable Sacrifice. And this is very easy to do, if it be considered, that the Holy Ghost's imparting this Power to it makes it completely the Representative of Christ's Body and Blood, and is the Act of God's accepting the Sacrifice, while the Priest is offering it by performing the Evangelical Rite. We know that in the *Patriarchal* and *Jewish* Sacrifices, when the Priest had finished the Sacrificial Rites and done his Part in the Oblation; either a Fire from Heaven, or one that was kindled by it, did either in whole or in Part consume what was sacrificed, and this was a Token of God's accepting thereof, and made the Oblation fit to convey the Blessings they hoped to obtain by the Means of it. In like Manner God by a more sacred and celestial Flame, by the Sanctification of the Holy Ghost himself does actually accept the Christian Sacrifice, and make it completely what Christ designed it should be by his Institution. Now Christ designed it should be his Body and Blood in Power and Virtue : The Priest performs the sacrificial Rite, and desires of God that he will make it so and accept it ; and this we are assured God invisibly does, while the Priest is visibly executing the Rite. By the Power therefore of the Holy Ghost the Oblation offered and consecrated by the Prayer of the Priest is made the Body and Blood of Christ in Virtue, 1. With Regard to God, who by blessing it accepts it as such ; and in this View it represents to God in the most perfect Manner, and pleads in our Behalf the Sacrifice of Christ's Death, and God respects it upon this Account. 2. With Regard to the Communicants, that they partaking of the Sacrifice may be fulfilled with God's Grace and heavenly Benediction. The short of the Matter is this : We offer, God blesses and accepts, and then by the Hand of his Minister he communicates the Sacrifice so accepted to the Receivers, and with and by it all the Benefits of this represented grand Sacrifice, if they are worthy of them, an heavenly and divine Force being adjoined to it for that salutary Effect.

THIS then shews the Value of the Sacrifice, which we present to God, and which God gives to us. Dr. *Waterland* °acknowledges, that this divine Influence may make it a valuable Sacrament, and may shew the Value of what God gives to us, but not the Value of what we give to him. But the Ancients made no Distinction, as I have proved above, between the Sacrifice and Sacrament; this is only a modern Notion invented by the Papists to perplex the Doctrine of the Eucharist. The Sacrament according to St. *Austin* is a sacred Sign of an invisible Sacrifice, and therefore is a visible Sacrifice, first presented to God by Way of Worship and then participated by us. If then the Sacrament enriched with a divine Power is received by us as a valuable Sacrifice before offered to God, it must also be a valuable Sacrifice for the same Reason when offered to God, because in a most authentick Manner it represents to God the meritorious

° Append. p. 13.

Sacrifice of Christ, and is accepted by him as such. For the divine Power united with the Elements has a two-fold Effect: It both makes them an efficacious, commemorative and representative Sacrifice, whereby thro' Christ we address God to give us all the Benefits of Christ's Passion, and it also makes them an applicative Sacrifice, whereby all those Benefits are made over to us.

BUT it is [f]objected that the Notion of the Spirit's coming upon the Elements to make them *absolutely* the Body is a gross Notion, arising only from a popular Form of Speech. If by *absolutely*, is meant, *corporally*, I allow it is a gross Notion; but if by, *absolutely*, is meant, *spiritually*, mystically, or virtually and efficaciously the Body; then I say, this is not a gross, but a very clear and intelligible Notion. And in this Sense they are absolutely and in themselves the Body, or the sacred and efficacious Signs and Sacraments of it, replenished with the divine Power of the Word and his holy Spirit. And I cannot believe, that this should arise from a popular Form of Speech. For this Form of Speech is in all the ancient Liturgies as well as in the Writings of the primitive Fathers; and methinks it is very odd, that the Bishops and Priests of the primitive Church should suffer the People to be poison'd with gross Notions, nay, that they should not purge these gross Notions out of their Forms of publick Worship, and should mean quite another Thing than what they prayed for. I cannot make such a gross Reflection upon such excellent Men. This therefore must stand for a more certain and just Notion, and is far from being inconsistent with the true and ancient Doctrine, that the Unworthy eat not the Body, nor drink the Blood of Christ in the Eucharist, or when they partake of the Eucharist. For they may partake of the visible Sacrifice, which is the sacramental and virtual Body of Christ, and yet not spiritually partake of the real Body, or rather of the Benefits and spiritual Fruits of it. St. *Austin*, as I have shewn above, is very clear that all partake of the Body and Blood of Christ sacramentally, to which the Holy Ghost has annexed a divine Virtue: "It is the Body and "Blood of Christ, [g]says he, even to them, who eat and drink

[f] Ibid.   [g] De Bapt. Lib. V. § 9.

"Damnation to themselves." And yet he likewise [h]says that a
75. wicked Man, tho' he eats the Body and Blood sacramentally, yet he
does not eat it really or beneficially: *For this is to remain in Christ,
that Christ also may remain in him.* This only proves, that People
may eat the blessed Sacrament of the Body and Blood instituted by
Christ, and yet not eat the Flesh spoken of in *John* vi. 'Tis best to
be sure, when both spiritual and sacramental Manducation go
together : Indeed the one is hurtful and destructive without the
other. To prove that the unworthy eat not the Body of Christ
in the Eucharist, the learned Doctor cites a Passage out of
St. *Cyprian*, the Occasion of which was, that one who had
sacrificed to Idols had without being discovered taken a Part
of the Sacrament, but he could make no use of it, for when
he opened his Hands he found it turned into Ashes: "Hence by
"this Example we may learn, says he, that the Lord departs, when
"he is denied; nor does that which is received tend to the
"Salvation of the unworthy, since the salutary Grace is changed
"into Ashes, the Sanctity or Virtue flying from it." Now this
proves the contrary to what he intended : For according to St.
Cyprian the Sacrifice is a salutary Grace and has a real
Sanctity or Virtue inherent in it, and therefore is not only
relatively holy. Indeed when the salutary Grace or the
Sacrament is changed into Ashes, and, ceasing to be what it was,
loses its Virtue, it is impossible for any Body to receive it : But
so long as it preserves its true Substance, so long its Virtue
76. continues with it. From this Passage indeed we may learn, that
the Sacrament's being turn'd into Ashes was an Emblem of
Christ's leaving the Wicked; and as in this Case the Sanctity
fled from the Sacrament, so the Lord flies from ill Men; and
that the Lord departs from the Wicked, altho' even they should
receive what has not only a relative Holiness, but a real Virtue in
itself, and therefore the unworthy Partaker is not profited by it.
For tho' he receives *Sanctum Domini*, as St. *Cyprian* calls it, the

---

[h] Ipse dicens, *Qui manducat carnem meam*, &c. ostendit quid sit non sacramento tenus, sed revera corpus Christi manducare—hoc est enim in Christo manere, ut in illo maneat & Christus. Sic enim hoc dixit, tanquam diceret, Qui non in me manet, & in quo ego non manco, non se dicat aut existimet manducare corpus meum, aut bibere sanguinem meum. De Civ. Dei, Lib. XXI. c. 25.

Holy of the Lord, or as St. *Austin*, *Panem Domini*, the Bread of the Lord; yet it is agreed on all Hands, he eats not *Panem Dominicum* the true Bread which came down from Heaven. This Passage then is not in the least to the Doctor's Purpose; but much to the contrary: Because the Wicked may eat the blessed Sacrament, which is in itself a salutary Grace, and has a spiritual Sanctity or Power in it to work a saving Effect, if their own Unworthiness did not hinder it. So then they may eat the sacramental Body vested with a spiritual Energy, and yet have no Fellowship with Christ, no Communion of the holy Spirit. This we very readily grant. For the sanctifying Power in the Sacrament operates only to the Salvation of the Worthy, but it works to the Condemnation of the Unworthy. And therefore, tho' these receive it with the Elements, it is as a Fire to consume them, and not as a comfortable Flame to cherish and refresh them. St. Austin admirably clears this Point, where speaking of the Sacrament of Baptism he has these very remarkable Words: ¹"The Baptism of Christ consecrated by the Evangelical Words, 77. "tho' administer'd by Adulterers and to Adulterers is holy, "altho' they are unchaste and unclean: For its Sanctity can't be "polluted, and a divine Virtue adheres to the Sacrament, whether "to the Salvation of those who use it well, or to the Destruction "of those that abuse it. Does the Light of the Sun or a Candle, "when diffused thro' dirty Places, contract no Filth from thence, "and can the Baptism of Christ be polluted thro' the Wickedness "of any?" The like may be said by Parity of Reason of the Eucharist, its Sanctity cannot be polluted, and its holy and divine Virtue will stick to it even in the Unworthy, and will be a sharp Sword piercing the very Soul, and a Flame which cannot be extinguished without a severe Repentance. This Virtue no more than the holy Spirit who is the Author of it can be quenched; the Wicked indeed do all that in them lyes to quench it by

---

¹ Baptismus Christi verbis Evangelicis consecratus, & per adulteros & in adulteris sanctus est, quamvis illi sint impudici et immundi: quia ipsa ejus sanctitas pollui non potest, & sacramento suo divina virtus adsistit, sive ad salutem bene utentium, sive ad perniciem male utentium. An vero solis vel etiam lucernæ lux, cum per cœnosa diffunditur, nihil inde sordium contrahit, & baptismus Christi potest cujusquam sceleribus inquinari? De Bapt. Lib. III. § 15.

hindering it from answering God's Design in bestowing it, but it cannot be violated, and its Activity will have its Course one Way or other: If it cannot save, it will punish; for God will revenge the Contempt of his Gift.

But it is [k]alleged the Spirit deserts ill Men in their sinful Acts; therefore the Unworthy do not receive the Spirit, but the Elements only. 'Tis granted the Spirit deserts ill Men in their sinful Acts, that is, he disallows their sinful Acts, is grieved and displeased at them for doing them, and will, if they do not repent, condemn them for it. But does it from hence follow,

78. that the Virtue derived from the Spirit deserts the Sacrament, when received by wicked Men? I trow not; I hope the Wickedness of Man does not pollute the Sacraments, so as to make the salutary Grace of God's Gifts desert them. And if not, it is easy to conceive how the sublime Virtue may adhere to the Sacraments, and yet how the Spirit deserts the unworthy Receivers, even for the very receiving this salutary Grace, and condemns them for it. The Sacrament therefore, being in itself a salutary Grace appointed instrumentally to convey the Evangelical Promises, is consequently that Body which our Lord instituted to be received for that Purpose. Even the Unworthy receive it as well as the Worthy, but to their Condemnation. Therefore they do not only receive bare Elements, having a relative Holiness and that is all, but they receive Elements made so great a Sacrament by the invisible Operation of the Holy Ghost, as St. *Austin* assures us. And surely this means much more than only a relative Holiness, of which we can have no other Idea than this, that thereby a Thing is holy merely by having a Relation to the Deity, which a Thing may have, and yet not at all contribute towards the Salvation of Man. By Consecration therefore the Elements are not only made relatively holy, and we not only pray that Bread and Wine may have a Relation to the Body and Blood, but that by partaking of the one outwardly or physically, we may partake of the other sacramentally and spiritually according to our Lord's Institution; or as the primitive Church used to word it, that the Bread may be made to us Christ's Body, and the Wine his Blood by the invisible

---

[k] Append. p. 14.

Power of the Holy Ghost. And this tho' they are not the Body and Blood in Substance, yet they are in spiritual Virtue and Power, and consequently are authentick Substitutes and Representatives of Christ's personal Sacrifice; not so as to be exclusively an Equivalent for it, or to supersede it: God forbid: No Body I believe ever dreamt of any such Thing: But to be offered to God through Christ to represent that Sacrifice, and to apply the Benefits of it to us. Now it is very odd any Body should suppose, that Persons of Learning and Sense, professing to believe a Sacrifice representative and applicative of another Sacrifice and of the Mercies of it, should yet intend to exclude and supersede it. We are so far from any such Impieties, as that we believe and confess, that our Saviour's personal Sacrifice is that from which all other Sacrifices derive their Value; and we think it is absolutely a Contradiction to affirm, that a Person can maintain the Eucharist is only a Sacrifice representative of the grand One, and yet at the same Time intend to exclude and supersede it. For how can we be said to exclude that, whose Merits we plead by setting the holy Tokens of that Sacrifice before God, and by addressing him in a visible Manner to bestow upon us those Benefits we there commemorate? To be brief, unless commemorating, representing and applying, can be proved to be superseding and excluding, there is no Room at all for this Objection.

IT is likewise strange this learned Divine should imagine, that by offering the Eucharistick Sacrifice we design to supply the Want of Christ's personal one. For we gratefully acknowledge that was once offered, and cannot be repeated. The Atonement was once made for the Sins of the whole World: But the Merits of it will not be conferred upon us, unless we carefully perform the Duties which are commanded in the Gospel. Now one of these conditional Duties is to commemorate with all Gratitude, and to represent with all Humility to God that Atonement by the Sacrifice of the Eucharist instituted by Christ himself for that End, and thereby also to entreat him to apply the Merits of it to us. We cannot therefore be said to want that Atonement, which was actually made for us upon the Cross, and by which Christ our High-Priest is perpetually interceding for us in Heaven: But we may be truly said to have a continual Want of God's Pardon and assisting Grace, that we may be enabled to perform our Duty, and have an Interest in the Atonement and Sacrifice made and offered by our Saviour; and the offering and receiving the Sacrifice of the Eucharist is the Method appointed to supply this Want. We therefore are far from supposing, that the Eucharist was instituted to supply the Want of Christ's Sacrifice; but, we say, it was ordained to supply its *Place*, and to supply our own spiritual Wants, and to be a potent Means of bestowing the Blessings purchased for us by the Sacrifice of the Cross, which while we are in this defective and imperfect State we stand continually in need of.

THE Sacrifice of the Eucharist then is not in itself an Equivalent for, or of equal Value with Christ's personal one. For it is not the real Body and Blood hypostatically united with the Person of the Son or of the holy Spirit. But it being blessed by the holy Spirit of Christ, and consequently by Christ himself, and indued with a divine Virtue to be the instituted Body and Blood, and accepted by God as such; tho' it is not in its own Nature and Oblation equivalent with Christ's own; yet by God's gracious Acceptance and Blessing it is in a lower Sense equivalent, and the same Thing as to Virtue and Effect, both with Respect to God and the Receiver. And to compare great Things with small, as a Ring, or Parchment, or Staff, tho' insignificant Things in themselves, are by Law vested with a Power to convey the Rights, Privileges and Profits of Honours, Offices, or Estates, and so stand in construction of Law for the Things they represent: So the Eucharistick Elements, tho' naturally common and mean Things, are by the Institution and divine Power of Christ and his Spirit clothed with an heavenly Virtue or Force, both to render God propitious and gracious to us, and to deliver over to the Receivers the great and inestimable Benefits our Lord purchased for them; and so they are likewise in Effect the Things they represent, even the Body and Blood of Christ. But Dr. [a] *Waterland* and I are perfectly agreed in this Point. For he is pleased to acknowledge, they may in a qualified Sense be understood to be Equivalents and Substitutes of Christ's Body and Blood (not exclusively of and to supersede the great Atone-

---

[a] Append. p. 18.

ment, which I do not know any Body affirms) but because in Conjunction with and in Dependance on it they make over to us the Benefits of Christ's crucified Body and Blood shed, of which it is not possible for us to partake by receiving the natural Body and Blood, as the Papists fondly maintain; that being but once offered and once shed, and not capable now of being actually offered again and participated. It is enough that they are sacred Instruments of appeasing God by commemorating the Atonement, and of conveying it, or which is all one, the Benefits thereof, and bringing them in Effect to us. And I presume at length it will be no such important Paradox, that the consecrated Elements are the Substitutes of the Body and Blood.

"Dr. *Waterland* observes, that if the Eucharist is made our Lord's Body *absolutely* by an Union with the Spirit, it would be more properly the Body of the Spirit, than our Lord's Body, from which it is supposed distinct. I answer, we do not suppose 82. it is made *absolutely*, that is *corporally*, our Lord's Body, but *sacramentally*. And in this Sense indeed, I grant it absolutely and strictly is so, that is, absolutely the Sacrament of our Lord's Body. Neither is it sacramentally so by a hypostatical Union with the Spirit, but an Union with a Grace or Virtue communicated to it by the Spirit. It is made this Body of Christ by the Operation of, not by a strict and personal Union with the Spirit of Christ. Now I hope the Sacrament can no more in strict Propriety be called the Body of the Spirit, merely because of its being consecrated by the Spirit, than our Saviour's real Body is called the Body of the Spirit, because it was conceived by him. Both Bodies are sanctified by the Holy Ghost, and yet who ever denominated them properly speaking the Bodies of the Spirit? I need not inform this learned Gentleman, that the holy Spirit is the Spirit of Christ, &c. his invisible Proxy or Representative in the Church: Therefore all his Actions and Operations are also the operations of the Son of God. Hence it is, that to say the Elements are made the Body and Blood by the Power of the Spirit, is the same Thing as to say they are made so by the Power of the *Divine Word*. So that Christ makes them his Body and Blood by the sanctifying Power of the Spirit, therefore

[b] Ib. p. 17, at the Bottom.

they are properly called his Body and Blood. Christ sanctifies every Thing in his Church by the working of the Spirit. Thus the Water wherein a Person is baptized is consecrated by the Spirit, and yet it is truly Christ's Baptism. The Clergy are also set apart by the Holy Ghost for the Work of the Ministry, and yet they are the Ministers of Christ. And the Faithful are regenerated by the Holy Ghost, and yet they are the Members of Christ. Our very Bodies are the Temples of the Holy Ghost, and yet they are a part of the mystical Body of Christ. If then all
83. these are properly Christ's by the operation of the Holy Ghost, what should hinder but that the Elements are properly and absolutely Christ's sacramental Body upon the same Account? In some Sense it may be called a spiritual Body, or the Body of the Spirit, as being consecrated by him. But since it is the Design of the Spirit to make it Christ's Body, who can rightly affirm the contrary? The Thing is so plain, there needs no Words about it. Well, but the sacramental Body is supposed distinct from our Lord's Body. And so it is no doubt. I imagine Dr. *Waterland* does not believe the Sacrament of Christ's Body and the natural Body are the same. But it is objected that in our Way the very Idea of our mystical Union with Christ's glorified Body would be obscured or lost, and we should be but as Aliens from the proper Body. But how can this be, when the sacramental Body, clothed with the spiritual Virtue in order to make us holy and pure, and cleanse our Souls from all sinful Defilements, is the best Means imaginable to unite us to Christ our Head, and closely to link and cement us to him. But it seems by this Account of the Matter, that absolutely two Bodies are given at once in the Eucharist, the sacramental, and I suppose, the natural. But pray who says the natural is given in the Eucharist? I am sure Dr. *Waterland* does not. He only informs us, we in the Eucharist partake of the Atonement made by Christ's natural Body crucified, and Blood shed, and thereby have a Right to be Fellow-Heirs with his glorified Body, and on this is founded our mystical Union with Christ's glorified Body. We say the very same. But this is not partaking of the natural Body, but only of the Atonement made by it, or of the spiritual and salutary Fruits of that Atonement. Therefore the natural Body itself is not given at all in the Eucharist, but only the

Fruits of the grand Sacrifice are conveyed to us thereby. And 84. this is done by partaking of the sacramental Body. Consequently there is but one Body, *viz.* the sacramental, strictly and properly speaking given in the Eucharist. This to me is very evident; and I cannot but be of Opinion, when this worthy Person re-considers the Matter, he will perceive there is little Difference in this Point between us.

BUT to return: The Elements being supposed and proved to be Substitutes of the Body and Blood, it is mighty easy to explain how they are a Sacrifice to God. For if they infallibly signify and have a divine Property of representing the Sacrifice of Christ, then by offering them by Way of sensible Worship to God we present to God's View the Death, Passion or Sacrifice of Christ, and plead the Merit of it in Behalf of ourselves and others. This Dr. *Waterland* must confess; for it is indeed the very same Doctrine in Sense with what he himself laid down in his Summary View at the ^c End of the Appendix. For there is no Difference but in the Mode of Expression, between offering to the View of God, under certain representing Symbols, the Death, Passion and Sacrifice of Christ; and pleading the Merit of it in Behalf of ourselves and others; and offering to the View of God or to divine Consideration, certain Symbols to commemorate and represent the Sacrifice of the Death of Christ, and to plead the Merit of it in Behalf of ourselves and others. Therefore as far as I can perceive we are in the main agreed.

BUT he endeavours to argue against the Sacrifice ^d thus: "The "Elements are not conceived Substitutes of the Body and Blood "any otherwise than by the Power and Presence of the Spirit." If he means by the Word *Presence* not local, but gracious 85. Presence, this is very true; but he goes on: "If the Elements "with the Spirit, not separate from the Spirit, are the sacrificed "Substitutes, then the Spirit is sacrificed along with the "Elements, which is absurd." This is as good an Argument as the following: "It is not easy to explain how ourselves can be "any Sacrifice at all to God. Ourselves are not conceived a "Matter fit for or valuable enough for Sacrifice any otherwise "than by the Power and Presence of the Spirit. Ourselves with

^c p. 59.   ^d Append. p. 19.

"the Spirit, not separate from the Spirit, which alone renders
"us so valuable, are supposed to be so. Is the Spirit then
"sacrificed along with ourselves? That is absurd." But how
can it be absurd, if it is very certain from holy Scripture, that
while we are actually offering ourselves, our Souls and Bodies as
a reasonable, holy and lively Sacrifice unto God, our Bodies are
the Temples of the Holy Ghost, and he is therefore inhabiting
and residing in us? If then it is not absurd to say, the Spirit is
sic sacrificed along without ourselves; neither can it be absurd to
say, the Spirit is sacrificed along with the Elements. We do not
mean, as I said before, that the Spirit is present with the
Elements in a local Manner, but that only a Gift of the Spirit, a
divine spiritual Property, Faculty or Virtue is annexed to the
Elements, whereby they are made proper Substitutes of the Body
and Blood both with Regard to God and Man, both to represent
to God and exhibit to us the meritorious Sacrifice of Christ.
Pray where then is the Absurdity of saying, that the Elements
replenish'd with this divine Virtue are a Sacrifice to God? I
hope there is no Absurdity in Sacrificing to God his own Gifts.
But it is objected, that "if Grace or Virtue accompanies the
"Elements in the presenting them to God, like as in the pre-
"senting the same Elements to Man, this is perfectly un-
"intelligible. We can understand that Pardon and Sanctifi-
"cation are presented to the Communicants along with the
"Symbols: But how Pardon and Sanctification should be pre-
"sented in the Way of Sacrifice to God, is not easy to explain."
To this I reply, that Grace and Virtue are ambiguous Words,
and require a Distinction: 1. Grace or Virtue as it is a Gift
imparted to the Elements by the Holy Ghost, means no more
than a Faculty or Power given to them to make them a fit
Instrument whereby to commemorate and represent Christ's
Passion, and to convey Pardon of Sin and Sanctification to the
Participants. And with this Power nothing can invest them,
but only the Omnipotence of God, who as he created all Things
out of nothing, so he can elevate mean Things to a Dignity and
heavenly Use far beyond the Powers of their Nature. 2. Grace
or Virtue as it is a Gift imparted to the Communicants, means
such good Things and Favours bestowed by God upon Men, as
tend to make them inwardly holy and pure, and in the End

to bring them to everlasting Life, such as Pardon, and personal Sanctification, and the like. There is then a two-fold Grace or Virtue, the one proper only to the Elements, the other only to the Communicants. Now Grace understood in the first Sense is only proper to the Elements; and certainly it is very easy to explain and conceive how the Elements accompanied or enriched with such a divine Power may be both presented to God first and Man afterwards, not only without any Absurdity, but also with great Propriety and Usefulness. If indeed any Body should affirm, tho' I do not know any one so weak, that Pardon of Sin, and a Sanctity proper only to Persons are in the Elements, and so accompany them in their being presented to God; I grant this is neither practicable, nor conceivable, it is mere Confusion. But it must be noted, we are not justly chargeable with it: And for our Parts we think we can distinguish very well between the sacramental View of the Eucharist, and the sacrificial, or rather between the Sacrifice as offered to God, and the same Sacrifice as given to Men. For as the Eucharist in the former View is a Representation and Commemoration and Pleading of Christ's Sacrifice, and the Merits of it to God; so it is in the latter View a bestowing of the Fruits, Benefits, and Privileges of it upon Man. Therefore the Elements are in Effect the Body both with Regard to God and Man.

It is further to be considered, that in the Eucharist not only the Body of Christ, but also the Body of the People believing in him, is figured; and therefore it is made of many Grains of Wheat, because the Body of faithful People is made up of many Believers. St. *Austin* often speaks of this symbolical Sacrifice of ourselves, and most especially in the following Words: " If you " have a Mind to understand the Body of Christ, hearken to the " Apostle who saith, Ye are the Body of Christ and his Members; " and if ye are the Body of Christ and his Members, then there is " a Mystical Representation of yourselves set on the Lord's Table. " You receive the Mystery of yourselves, and answer, *Amen;* and " by that Answer subscribe to what you are. Thou hearest the " Body of Christ named and answerest, *Amen;* become thou a " Member of Christ, that thy *Amen* may be true. But why in " the Bread? I shall offer nothing of my own; but let us hear " what the Apostle himself speaks of this Sacrament; who saith,

"*And we being many are one Bread, and one Body* in Christ." Thus St. *Austin* sufficiently teacheth us, that as in the Bread set upon the Altar, the Body of Christ is represented, so is likewise the Body of the People who receive it. In that Body which is celebrated in a Mystery, there is a Figuration not only of the
88. proper Body of Christ, but also of the Society of the Faithful who believe in Christ. It is a Figure representing both Bodies, to wit, that of Christ, in which he died and rose again, and that of the People which are regenerated, and raised from the Dead by Baptism into Christ. And thus as it is a visible Sacrifice of Christ's Passion, so it is also a visible Sacrifice of ourselves, our Souls and Bodies, and symbolically our reasonable and spiritual Service.

To this is to be referred what St. *Fulgentius* has said upon the Prayer for the Descent of the Holy Ghost upon the Elements, to consecrate them and make them the Body and Blood of Christ in Power and Effect. °*Monimus* asked him, if the Sacrifice of the Body and Blood of Christ be offered to the whole Trinity, why the Mission of the Holy Ghost was only prayed for to sanctify the Gift of our Oblation? His Answer is to this Effect: That this Prayer is not only to be understood in a literal, but in a moral Sense. And the Design of it is not only to pray for the Consecration of the Elements, that they may be in themselves the instituted Sacrifice of the Body and Blood of Christ: But since they are made so by the Power of the holy Spirit, not upon their own Account, but for the Benefit and Salvation of the Church, which is likewise represented in the Sacrifice as well as Christ her Head: We must therefore believe, that the Intent of the Prayer is to sanctify also the Faithful who are in the Communion of the Church, and are figuratively offered or sacrificed in the Oblation, and to confer upon them by the Reception of the Sacrament some principal Gift of the holy Spirit. Now Charity, as St. *Fulgentius* observes, being the principal Gift of the Holy Ghost, when the Holy Ghost is
89. desired to descend to sanctify the Sacrifice of the whole Church, which represents the Body mystical as well as the natural, nothing else or no other Gift sanctifying the Persons of the

° Ad Monimum, Lib. II.

Faithful, as it seems to St. *Fulgentius*, can be prayed for, but this Gift of Charity; that by the Grace of the Spirit Charity may be preserved inviolate in the Body of Christ which is the Church; and that while the external Sacrifice of themselves is offering, the Faithful may internally offer spiritual Sacrifices acceptable to God, and be as living Stones in the spiritual Building. Which Edification is never more seasonably requested, than when by the Body of Christ itself, which is the Church, the very Body and Blood of Christ is representatively offered in the Sacrament of the Bread and Cup: For so both the sacramental and mystical Body are upon the Prayer of the Priest, tho' in a different Sense, sanctified by the Grace of the Spirit. Now this being the Design of the Invocation to pray not only for the Consecration of the Elements themselves, but also for the Edification of the Church by Charity: Hence it is, that tho' Hereticks and Schismaticks may have true, valid and consecrated Sacraments, and other Gifts of the Spirit, which cannot in themselves be polluted by being possessed by wicked Men, yet these Gifts profit them nothing without Charity; and the Sacrifice, however acceptable in itself, yet so far forth as it is offered by bad Men utterly void of this most principal Grace of the Spirit, is not well-pleasing to God, and no spiritual Grace sanctifying the Receivers is conveyed by it. And this is perfectly agreeable to the Sentiments of St. *Fulgentius's* great Master St. *Austin*, who in a thousand Places affirms, that the holy Sacraments administered by Hereticks and Schismaticks, tho' in themselves sanctified by the Holy Ghost, do not profit the Receivers out of the Unity of the Church, according to a 90. noted ªMaxim of his, that the Sacrifice is such to every one, as he is when he offers it, and when he receives it. If a Schismatick offers and receives it, it is unprofitable to him; if a good Man in the Unity of the Church, he offers and receives it to his Salvation. This Doctrine of St. *Fulgentius* we very readily subscribe to. But I must beg leave to observe, Dr. *Waterland* is under some

---

* Nos dicemus tale cuique sacrificium fieri, qualis accedit qui offert, & qualis accedit ut sumat. Contra litt. Petiliani, Lib. II. § 120. Quilibet ubilibet offert sacrificium tali corde vel factis, hæc ut audire mereatur, perniciem sibi infert—Cont. Ep. Parm. Lib. II. § 10.

Mistake, when he notes, that the Church alone and not the Body and Blood of Christ is the Sacrifice offered according to *Fulgentius*, and that he interprets the Illapse of the Spirit only of Christ's sanctifying the mystical Body. It is certain, and will be evident to any Person carefully attending to St. *Fulgentius's* Meaning, that he believed the Sacrifice of the Church is the Sacrifice both of his mystical and natural Body, and that both are sanctified by the Illapse of the Spirit. And to this we fully agree, being satisfied it is the Doctrine of Scripture and Antiquity, from which by the Grace of God we will never swerve.

The Eucharist then being representative both of Christ's natural and mystical Body, it is a blessed and effectual Instrument to reach to the everlasting Sacrifice, and so set it out solemnly before the Eyes of God; it is the most powerful means the Church hath to strengthen their Supplications, to open the Gates of Heaven, and to force in a Manner God and his Christ to have Compassion on us: It is likewise an excellent Medium, whereby to offer up the inward Sacrifice of ourselves, as lively Members of his Body, and to present our Resolutions and Vows of holy Obedience both in our Actions and Sufferings too, if there be Occasion, and to

91. declare we are ready to follow and imitate our divine Head in all the holy Actions of his Life, and even to take up his Cross, when he calls us to it. This corporal or material [b]Sacrifice or Sacrament therefore is nothing else but as it were a certain visible and holy Word, by which we shew forth to God our Lord's Death and our Union with one another and with him; and it being accompanied with vocal and manual Services more fully to express the Design of it, it is thereby rendered a most effectual Mean to attain all the Ends of its Institution.

If vocal and manual then be spiritual Service, there can be no Reason in the World assigned, why the *Verba visibilia*, the visible Words, the material Sacrifice, should not at least be equally so. All three are designed by Christ to complete the memorial Service. The vocal Commemoration would be lame and defective without the symbolical; and the holy Prayers would want great Part of their Force and Prevalency without the

[b] Quid enim sunt aliud quæque corporalia sacramenta, nisi quædam quasi verba visibilia, sacrosancta quidem—Contra Faustum, Lib. XIX. c. 16.

holy Signs to make the Commemoration more sensible and more affecting. This is most evidently the Truth of the Case. Let us therefore offer the vocal and material Sacrifice together, and then we shall rightly according to Christ's holy Institution perform the one external Sacrifice of the Church. And that we may not offer it unprofitably, let us every one join the internal Sacrifices, the strictly speaking spiritual Sacrifices thereto; and then we may through the Merits of Christ's eternal Oblation expect God will pour down all his Mercies and Graces upon us. And thus the Offering of our visible Sacrifice will answer fully to St. *Austin's* Definition: It will be indeed *a Work done in order to keep up our Covenant and Communion with God, to the End that we may be everlastingly happy.* Let us not then think of offering any supposed spiritual Sacrifices, or even real ones, without taking in the material into our pure Offering. For unless we offer up our Devotions in the Way Christ has appointed, it is much to be feared they will be of little or no Value. The Way truly to offer up our Worship and Sacrifices in Christ's Name, is to stick close to his Commands and Ordinances; and so shall we be sure to adhere to God and Christ, and keep up a League of Amity and Friendship with them. To do otherwise is to set them at Variance with us, and make them abhor both us and our Sacrifices.

I THINK I have now answered every Objection of Moment against a material or symbolical Sacrifice, except what we meet with in *Charge*, p. 39. It is there observed, that there are two fundamental Flaws in Mr. *Mede's* System. 1. One in his endeavouring to fix the Notion or Definition of a Christian Sacrifice by the Rules of the *Levitical;* as if typical and true were the same Thing. To this I answer, that an Oblation typical of another Oblation, which is the Archetype, is equally as to Truth of Propriety a true Sacrifice with the Archetype, tho' not as typical, yet as a Thing offered to God. No Wonder therefore Mr. *Mede* took the *Jewish* Sacrifices, tho' Types, for true Sacrifices or Sacraments; St. *Austin*, as I have shewn above, did the same, declaring that they were visible Sacrifices or sacred Signs of the invisible Sacrifice of Christ which was to come. St. *Austin* likewise took the Eucharist for a true Sacrifice, tho' the Antitype of the Passion were already past. Well therefore might Mr.

Mede do so too, especially considering the Nature of those Things, they being all reducible to one common Genus. For both the *Jewish* and Christian Sacrifices, considered as Services,
93. may very properly be defined in general to be an Oblation of a material Thing made in order to keep up our Covenant and Communion with God; and considered as a Gift, they are a Thing offered to God for that Purpose. And this is perfectly conformable to St. *Austin's* Definition of Sacrifice, they being Works or Services performed with a material Thing offered to God for the End abovementioned. Mr. *Mede* therefore and St. *Austin* agree mighty well with each other. To this it is no [d] Answer to say, that the Circumstances are different; for that in the legal Sacrifices either the Whole or some Part of the Offering was supposed to be directly given to God, and either consumed by Fire or poured forth never returning to the Use of Man. For this only proves that the legal Sacrifices were Works and Services performed in a different Manner and with other Rites than the Christian; but they were Works and Services still, and if their being so makes them spiritual Sacrifices, then they were spiritual Sacrifices as well as the Christian. They were Works and Services performed by offering material Things with various Rules and Ceremonies both vocal and manual, one of which was to burn them either in whole or in part on the Fire, or to pour out their Blood: In like Manner the Christian Sacrifice is a Work performed by offering a material Symbol with other Rites both vocal and manual. Both the one and the other therefore agree in the *Genus* of material Sacrifice, and are only *specifically* different from each other. And both come under St. *Austin's* Definition: For the Legal were formerly such Works or Services, as he defines, as the Christian now is so. This therefore is a clear Confutation of Dr. *Waterland's* Notion, that St. *Austin* and the Ancients did not allow a material Sacrifice, and needs no very subtle Head or profound Understanding to apprehend it.
94. THE second Flaw in Mr. *Mede's* System according to Dr. *Waterland* is, in not being able to make out the Sacrifice he aimed at by the very Rules which himself had fixed for it. Yes he has made it out very well; for he has sufficiently proved, that

[d] *Review*, p. 489.

both the *Jewish* and the Christian come under the Definition of
material Sacrifice, tho' offered in a different Manner, and that is
enough. Indeed in the *Levitical* Peace-offerings God had as it
were his own Mess assigned in the Sacrifice or Feast, and was
considered not merely as Convivator, but as Conviva also: But in
the Eucharist God has no Portion, and we receive all ourselves.
Now this proves no more than that the Modus in offering and
feasting upon the Christian Sacrifice is different from that of the
Jewish Sacrifice and Feast; and that we Christians have not
that gross Notion complained of as entertained by the *Jews*, as
if the Deity had Need of such Things or took Delight in them.
Upon this Account therefore, because we have no gross Notion of
God, the Modus varies, but the generical Essence both of the
Jewish and Christian Sacrifices is the same. But it is farther
objected, that since the Manner is so different, why should a
Christian Sacrifice be made material by *Jewish* Rules, or why is
the Definition of Sacrifice measured by the same? Now if by
Jewish Rules are meant Rules about the Manner of offering, we
deny that we make a Christian Sacrifice material, or measure the
Definition of Sacrifice by them. But if by *Jewish* Rules are to
be understood *Jewish* Notions of the Essence of material Sacrifice,
I cannot see, why we may not very well have some Regard to
them without any Offence, unless it can be said, the Books of the
Old Testament are so strangely penned, that it is not possible to
find out the Nature of a material Sacrifice from them. Mr. *Mede*
has found the true Nature of it there, and given a very good
Definition of it in this Manner: "An offering unto the Divine
"Majesty of that which is given for the Food of Man; that the
"Offerer partaking thereof might, as by Way of Pledge, be
"certified of his Acceptation into Covenant and Fellowship with
"his God by eating and drinking at his Table." Which is the
very same with what we may justly believe to be St. *Austin's*
Sense of a material Sacrifice: *viz.* That it is a Thing offered to
God, for this End, that we may have an holy Fellowship and
Society with him, by partaking of it at his Table. Now this is a
Definition exactly agreeable to the *Jewish* Notion of the Essence
of a material Sacrifice; and since it likewise perfectly agrees
with the true Notion of it, we have all the Reason imaginable to
adhere to it. It is not at all a necessary Circumstance to

complete the federal Oblation and federal Feast, that God should be the Guest as well as the Entertainer. For it is a gross Notion to say God is a Guest, and the Sacrifice is neither offered nor received upon God's Account, but ours, that we may honour, worship and pray to him thereby, and that by eating his Entertainment, which becomes his by our presenting it to him and his accepting it, we may receive the Benefits we request at his Hand. It is very true, we give up to God as his Tribute, our Thanks, our Praises, our Acknowledgements, our Homage, our very selves, but we do this not only vocally, but visibly by the Eucharistick Elements, which being blessed God returns them to us by the Hands of his own Minister, and thereby delivers over to us the inestimable Mercies contained in the Covenant made between him and us through the Sacrifice and Mediation of Christ. We must not therefore say, we take all this blessed Food to ourselves, but that God by his commission'd Officer imparts it to us as his

96. Entertainment. We must not look upon it as a common and ordinary Repast, but as a holy and spiritual Feast upon a Thing sacrificed, because consecrated by God himself, and bestowed upon us to communicate the highest spiritual Benefits. It is a low and mean and unprimitive Notion of it to consider it as bare Bread and Wine, and to talk of it as if it were really nothing else : "Tis the one external Sacrifice of the Church, by which we pay to God the sublimest Honour and Worship ; for it is offered to him as the first Cause of our Being, and our last and principal End, by Way of Confession of his infinite Excellency, Dominion and Majesty, of our Dependence on him, and of our Service and Subjection to Him : It is likewise offered for a Sacrifice of Thanksgiving for all the Benefits of Nature, Grace and Glory conferred and to be conferred upon us by God as our chief Benefactor : It is offered also to render God propitious to us through the Atonement made by Christ's Sacrifice, and to beseech him to pardon us, and to give us all sorts of spiritual Blessings, and to apply to all those, for whom it is offered and who receive it, the Force and Virtue of the Sacrifice of the Cross. Lastly therefore tho' in Substance it be only a Loaf of Bread and a Cup of Wine, yet it being offered and received for the Ends just now specified, in that View, it is a spiritual Sacrifice of inestimable Value, whereby we covenant with God to pay him

Honour and Obedience, and he makes over to us what he has covenanted to grant to all the Faithful Disciples of Christ. We must remember, that God wants nothing from us, not even the best Service we can do him. He expects we should do our Duty for our own Sakes, not his. Since therefore he really receives nothing from us, upon his own Account, but we all from him, he has no Occasion to have any Portion or Mess assigned him; and he therefore assigns all the Sacrifice to be received by us, that we may receive all his Blessings along with it. It is consequently a manifest Mistake, that the Analogy between other material Sacrifices and the Eucharist fails in the main Thing belonging to all material Sacrifices: For assigning God a Portion does not enter into the Essence of them. On the contrary such material Sacrifices as want this Circumstance are more rational and more answerable to the infinitely perfect Nature of God, than those who have it. Besides, God has no Need to have a Part assigned him, because it being a Thing offered to him, and consecrated to his Honour and Service, to be spent in an Act of Religion, it is all his Sacrifice, both when we offer and when we receive it. 'Tis a spiritual Sacrifice and spiritual Food, and consequently not ours properly, but God's, being employed and consumed in his immediate Worship. And thus I humbly apprehend I have vindicated Mr. *Mede* to the full, and have evinced that there is no Flaw at all in his System: Which by the bye is not at all inconsistent with Dr. *Cudworth*'s, but rather includes it. For do but offer and feast upon the symbolical Sacrifice worthily, and then you will be sure to feed really upon the Sacrifice of the Cross, or upon the Fruits and Benefits of it.

Dr. *Waterland* has given us a kind of historical Account of the Sentiments of our Divines, to which I could make very just Exceptions, and shew that several of them were entirely on our Side of the Question. I shall instance in one, and that is Dr. BREVINT, who in the sixth Section of his excellent little Book, entitled, *The Christian Sacrament and Sacrifice*, explains the Doctrine of the Sacrifice exactly as we do; and therefore I do not wonder Dr. HICKES should recommend it. As to others, in their Disputes with the Papists, they asserted the Eucharist was a commemorative and representative Sacrifice, as we do, and they only differed from us in Sound, not in Sense, when they called this an improper, which we truly denominate a proper and true Sacrifice. They allowed only the Sacrifice of the Cross to be a proper Sacrifice, as that which was alone truly and properly in its Nature meritorious. And in this Sense we also acknowledge it to be so. But this is taking the Word *proper* in too strict and limited a Meaning. For as Dr. *Waterland* very rightly [f]observes, where there is properly a Gift to God by Way of Worship, to honour or to please him, there is the formal Reason of a Sacrifice. But while these Divines called the Eucharist only an improper Sacrifice, they did not totally exclude the Symbols from their pure Offering, as Dr. *Waterland* seems to do. So that the Difference between us and them is next to nothing. There are other Divines, as great, as learned, as well versed in Ecclesiastical Antiquity, as ever adorned the Church of *England*, or any other Church whatsoever, that speak our Sentiments entirely. Dr. *Hickes* was not the first after Mr. *Mede*, as the learned *Archdeacon* would insinuate, that maintained the Doctrine of the Sacrifice. Archbishop *Laud*, Dr. *Heylin*, Archbishop *Bramhall*, Mr. *Thorndike*, Bishop *Fell*, Dr. *Grabe*, Bishop *Beverege*, Bishop *Bull*, Bishop *Cosins* and many others have done it before him without Offence or Censure, I may rather say with Approbation. But Dr. [g]*Hickes* being a Person disliked by many upon Account of

[f] Charge, p. 37, at the bottom.

[g] Dr. *Waterland* observes, (Charge, p. 43) "that this learned Writer first took *material Thing* into the very Definition of Sacrifice: but upon the latest Correction he struck it out again, putting *Gift* instead of it, thereby leaving Room for spiritual Sacrifice, (which undoubtedly is a Gift) to be as proper a Sacrifice as any." Now I question not but Dr. *Hickes* did always believe that spiritual Sacrifice was true, and better than the material. But let me observe, that Dr. *Hickes* does not intend to define a Sacrifice in the most general Notion, containing Sacrifices of all sorts both spiritual and material: But he purposes only to define a material Sacrifice in general, for that is the Thing he is treating about. By a *Gift* therefore he can mean nothing else but a *material Thing*, and therefore the Alteration he made in his Definition was no more than verbal. It is much the same Definition with *J. Saubertus's*, who in his Book de Sacrificiis, cap. I. p. 13, thus defines a Sacrifice. "Sic "definio sacrificium, sacram & externam actionem, quâ res quæpiam externa "a certis personis, loco, ritibusque certis ad finem certum Diis aut Deorum "loco habitis consecrabatur & obscrebatur." Dr. *Hickes* himself tells us (Vol. I. p. 42, of his Christian Priesthood) what he means by the Word *Gift*. "The original Word for Gift, says he, is a sacrificial Term of a general

his State-Principles, when it came to be treated of by him, it was presently looked upon with an ill Eye, as if broached with a Design to pave the Way to Popery; which certainly was as idle an Imagination as could enter into the Heads of Men of Sense. And to shew that it was only opposed upon a Party-Account, let me observe, that the whole Pack of Adversaries fell with great Cry and Fury upon Dr. *Hickes*, but said not a Word to his Friend Dr. *Potter*, who now adorns the metropolitical Chair, who wrote the very same Doctrine at the same Time. This shews the sad Effect of Party-Prejudice. Afterwards Mr. *Johnson*, who was a beneficed Clergyman, undertook Dr. *Hickes*'s Defence against the unreasonable Clamours and feeble Arguments of his Opponents, and performed it with great Strength of Argument as well as Variety of Learning, insomuch that I daresay his Book will be looked upon by Posterity as an excellent Performance, and in the main unanswerable: I say in the main, for I must confess he has advanced some Things, which need Correction; which it seems he had not done, if he had submitted to the Advice and followed the Judgment of Dr. *Hickes*, whose System is not embarrassed with those Difficulties Dr. *Waterland* mentions. You, my Brethren, will find none of those Particularities in these Papers, little else but the Opinion of St. *Austin*, but in him the genuine Sense of all Antiquity. While we adhere to this, we need not fear but our Cause will have a good Exit, and we shall be at length able to remove the Confusion and Perplexity our Adversaries Cause is involved in: Nothing being really more obvious and intelligible than our System, nothing more dark and inconsistent than their's. For they do not distinguish sufficiently between the several sorts of Sacrifices, but make a Jumble of them all together: And while with Might and Main they oppose the material Sacrifice, yet at the Bottom they maintain it, and only express themselves in a

---

" Signification, and denotes a *material* Sacrifice or Offering of any sort." As to Dr. *Hickes*'s two *Discourses*, my Bookseller cannot furnish me with them: But I do not find by Dr. *Waterland*'s Account of them, that there is any Thing there advanced contrary to his other Writings, which will, I believe, always be read with Satisfaction by those who set a Value upon primitive Truths. For the Prejudices which stuck to his Person are now removed from his Books. And Men of Understanding will judge with less Partiality than formerly.

different Manner from what we do: Which shews their Ideas are not altogether so clear and distinct as could be wished. Whether what I have advanced will contribute to remove the Cloud, I cannot tell: However I hope I have said nothing which can give your worthy *Archdeacon*, whose uncommon Learning and Merit I highly reverence, any reasonable offence : And if this Controversy is to be continued, I hope it will be carried on in a friendly and Christian Manner. If I find this is kindly received by you, I intend, God willing, to examine into the Sense of the Fathers of the more early Ages ; which I perceive is a Subject not yet quite exhausted. I shall add no more at present, but that I am, Reverend Sirs, Your Affectionate Brother in Christ Jesus, To whom be Glory for ever and ever. *Amen.*

FINIS

EXCURSUS II.

Table of approximate Dates.

A.D.
354. Born at Thagaste.
5.
6.
7.
8.
9.
360.
1.
2.
3.
4.
5.
6.
7.
8.
9. Visit to Madura.
370. Studies at Carthage.
1. Death of Patricius.
2. Birth of Adeodatus.
3. Reads Cicero's *Hortensius*.
4. Reads Aristotle's *Categories*.
5.
6. Becomes an Auditor among the Manichæans, Teaches Grammar at Thagaste.
7. Teaches Rhetoric at Carthage.
8.
9.
380. Writes *De Pulchro et Apto*.
1.
2.
3. Journey to Rome.
4. Appointed Professor at Milan.
5. Reads translations of Plato's *Dialogues*.
6. Reads *S. Paul's Epistles*. Retreat to Cassiciacum. *Contra Academicos. De Beata Vita, De Ordine.*
7. *Soliloquiorum Libri.* BAPTISM. Death of S. Monica.
8. *De Quantitate Animæ, De Moribus Manichæorum, De Div. Quæst. LXXXIII. and De Lib. Arb.* (begun).
9. *De Musica, De Magistro.*

390. *De Vera Religione.*
 1. ORDINATION. *De Utilitate Credendi. De duabus Animabus.*
 2. Debate with Fortunatus.
 3.
 4. *Contra Faustum Manichæum, Expositio quarumdam Prop. ex Epistola ad Romanos.*
 5. *De Libero Arbitrio* (completed). CONSECRATION. *De Continentia.*
 6. *De Agone Christ.*
 7. *De Doctrina Christiana* (begun). *De Div. Quæst. ad Simplic. Contra Epist. Manich.*
 8.
 9.
400. *De Consensu Evang., Confessionum Libri, De Baptismo, De Trinitate* (begun). *De Catechiz. Rudibus.*
 1. *De Bono Conjugali. De Gen. ad Lit.* (begun).
 2.
 3.
 4. *De Actis cum Fel.*
 5.
 6.
 7.
 8.
 9.
410. FALL OF ROME.
 1.
 2. EDICT OF HONORIUS AGAINST DONATISTS. *De Peccat. Meritis, De Spiritu et Lit.*
 3. *De Civitate Dei* (begun).
 4. *Enarrationes in Psalmos* (in progress).
 5. *De Perf. Just. Hom., De Genesi ad Literam* XII (completed).
 6. *In Johan. Evang. Tractatus, De Trinitate* (completed).
 7.
 8. *De Gratia Christi.*
 9. *De Nuptiis, De Anima.*
420. *Contra Adv. Leg. et Proph.*
 1. *Enchiridion, De Cura pro Mortuis Gerenda.*
 2.
 3.
 4.
 5.
 6. *De Doctrina Christiana* (completed), *De Civitate Dei* (completed).
 7. *Retractationum Libri, De Gratia et Lib. Arb., De Correptione et Gratia.*
 8. *De Predestinatione Ss., De Dono Perseverantiæ.*
 9. *Imp. Op. contra Jul.*
430. Death.

INDEX.

*** Names of Authors referred to are printed in small capitals, and titles of works in italics.

Academics 19 f., 45, 162
Adam 56 n., 170
Adeodatus 15 n.
Alaric 111
Alexandria 111
ALFRED, KING 177
S. Ambrose 3, 5, 56, 57, 149, 167
S. ANSELM 35 n., 178, 150, *Cur Deus Homo* 9 n., 150, 152, *Monologion* 150, *Proslogion* 150, 158
Antinomianism 127
Antioch 111
Antipodes 140, 162
Aquinas, S. Thomas 153
Arians 12, 243
Aristotle 38, 153
Arminians 16, 176
Articles, The XXXIX 107, 123, 129 n., 130, 182, 249
Astronomy 140, 143
S. ATHANASIUS 51 n.
Atonement 152, 259, 262
Auditores 9 n.
S. AUSTIN, and Calvin 82 f., 90, 98 n., 104, 187, 197; asserted changes 29 n., 36 n., 90, 140, 175; as an example 8, 73; form of his writings 14, 46, 78, 120; influence of 15 142 f., 177 f.; interpretation of Scripture 57, 69, 156; habits of life 66 n.; charged with Manichæism 65; personal characteristics 10, 80, 137; philosophical doctrines 19 f., 49 f., 53 n., 72 n., 114, 171; unique position 35, 36, 150 Life, baptism 12 n., 14, 42, 45, consecration 14, 175; illness at Rome 20, ordination 45
Works, lost 12 n.; supposititions, 195,

225 n.; *Contra Academicos* 15 n., 21 nn., 26 nn., 145, 127; *Contra Adv. Leg. et Proph.* 63 n., 230 n., 237; *De Actis cum Fel. Man.* 172; *De Agone Christiano* 99 n.; *De Anima et Origine Ejus* 138; *De Baptismo* 118 n., 119 n., 121 n., 122, 123, 160 n., 205 n., 238, 241, 255, 257; *De Beata Vita* 14 n., 21 n., 25 n.; *De Bono Conjugali* 168, 169, 170, 193; *De Catechizandis Rudibus* 99 n., 120 n.; *De Civitate Dei* 21 n., 22 n., 28 n., 30 n., 33 n., 35 n., 38 n., 40 n., 50 nn., 51 n., 52 n., 53 n., 55 n., 61 n., 62 n., 66 n., 67 n., 68 nn., 69 n., 83 n., 92 n., 94 nn., 99 n., 103 nn., 112 nn., 113 nn., 114 n., 137 n., 157 n., 166 nn., 174, 193, 194, 196, 203, 207, 208, 209 n., 214, 218 n., 219, 227, 256; *Confessionum Libri XIII*. 11, 12, 15, 20 n., 33 nn., 37, 38 n., 40 n., 41 n., 52 n., 61 n., 66 n., 77, 139, 154, 155, 187 n., 196; *De Consensu Evangelistarum* 163 n.; *De Continentia* 98 n., 103 nn.; *De Correptione et Gratia* 95 n., 172; *Contra Cresconium* 242; *De Cura pro Mortuis Gerenda* 187 n., 188 n.; *De Diversis Quæstionibus ad Simplicianem* 71 n., 91 n.; *De Diversis Quæstionibus LXXXIII* 9 n., 29 n., 34 nn., 50 n., 51 n., 72 n., 98 n., 138, 221 n.; *De Doctrina Christiana* 58 n., 139, 141 nn., 156, 166 nn., 167; *De Dono Perseverantiæ* 77 n., 80 n., 91 n., 127; *De Duabus Animabus* 60 n., 85 n., 172; *Enarrationes in Psalmos* 63 n.,

69 n., 187 n., 188 n.; *Enchiridion* 25 n., 52 nn., 54 nn., 55 n., 93 n., 139 n., 173, 187 n., 188 n., 238; *Epistolæ* 15 n., 17 n., 21 n., 26 n., 31 n., 93 n., 111 n., 112 n., 137, 155, 159, 162, 164 n., 181, 225; *Contra Epistolam Manichæi* 60, 138, 163 n., 167; *Contra Epist. Parmeniani* 238, 241, 242, 268; *Contra Faustum* 199, 216, 223, 224, 238 n., 268; *Contra Fortunatum Disput.* 172; *De Genesi ad Literam* 11, 32 n., 69 n., 138, 150; *De Gratia Christi* 128 n.; *De Gratia et Libero Arbitrio* 86 n., 90 n., 104 n.; *De Hæresibus* 216; *In Joan. Evangel. Tractatus* 160 n., 190 n., 198; *De Libero Arbitrio* 9 n., 24 n., 27, 28 n., 32 n, 51 n., 63 n., 83 nn., 89 nn., 92 n., 145, 151 n., 193, 194; *Contra Lit. Petilian* 242, 268; *De Magistro* 31 n.; *De Moribus Ecclesiæ* 49, 50, 144 n.; *De Moribus Manichæorum* 52 n., 53 n., 54 n., 98 n.; *De Musica* 63 n., 72 n., 145; *De Nuptiis* 66 n. 124 n., 169, 170; *De Ordine* 15 n., 26 n., 28 n., 53 n., 99 n., 137, 143, 144, 145, 158 n.; *Operis imperfecti contra Julianum Libri VI.* 58 n., 63 nn., 90 n., 174; *De Peccat. Meritis* 124 n.; *De Peccato Originali* 124 n.; *De Perf. Just. Hom.* 95 n. 173; *De Prædestinatione Ss.* 127 n., 175; *De Quantitate Animæ* 30 n., 72 n., 137; *Quarumdam Prop. in Ep. ad Rom. Expos.* 194; *Retractationum Libri VI.* 13 n., 14, 30 n., 37 nn., 45 n., 85 n., 176; *Sermones* 58 n., 151, 187 n., 218, 221, 238; *Contra Serm. Arian.* 243; *De Spiritu et Litera* 84 n., 92 n.; *Soliloquiorum Libri II.* 15, 24 n., 31 nn., 37, 117; *Tract. adv. Judæos* 223; *De Trinitate* 8 n., 9 n., 10, 19 n., 21 n., 22 n., 23 n., 24 n., 25 n., 26 n., 30 n., 31 n., 38 n., 39, 40 n., 53 n., 55 n., 59 n., 61 n., 96 n., 97 nn., 124 n., 137, 138, 151, 155, 156, 157 n., 163 n., 173, 192, 209 n., 213 n., 238, 243; *De Urbis Excidio* 113 n.; *De Utilitate Credendi* 9 n., 19. n, 22 n., 157, 160 n., 161, 164 n., 168 n.; *De Utilitate Jejunii* 63 n.; *De Vera Religione* 9 n., 22 nn., 27 n., 34 n., 51 n., 61 n., 72 n., 84 n., 94 n., 137, 145, 157 n., 162, 163 n.

Authority 10 n., 11, 144, 157 f.

Bacon, Roger 153
BAIN, *Mental and Moral Science* 171
Baptism 118, 121 f., 129 f., 209, 241, 246
BAUR, *Das manichäische Religionssystem* 47 n., 48 n., 57 n. *Die christliche Lehre von der Dreieinigkeit* 146
BAYLE, PETER, *Commentaire philosophique* 191
BEAUSOBRE, *Histoire critique* 46 n.
Beauty 29
Bede 170
BERKELEY 14 n., 197
Bethlehem 3
Beverege 274
Bible 4, 167, 195, as actual history 55 f. See Scripture.
BINDEMANN, *Der h. Augustinus* 21 n., 46 nn. 120 n.
BRADLEY 62 n., 84 n
BRADWARDINE 153, 177, 178, *De Causa Dei* 105 n., 106, 107
Bramhall 274
BREERELY, *S. Austin's Religion* 179
Brevint 273
BRIGHT, *Anti-Pelagian Treatises* 78 n., 175
Brownists 182
BRUCKER 143
Buddhism 9 n., 47 f., esoteric 49
Bull 274
Butler 35

CAIRD, *Philos. of Religion* 151 n.
CALVIN 82 f., 90, 104, 127, 179; *Institutes* 82 n., 83 n., 85 nn., 86 n., 90 n., 98 n., 104 n., 116 n., 167, 187
Calvinists 16, 103, 107, 117 n., 176, 177, 180, 182, 198
CAMPBELL, Hon. Arch., *Doctrines of Middle State* 188 n.
Carthage 19
Celibacy 66, 170
Ceylon 48
CHAUCER 106
CHRISTLIEB, *Leben und Lehre des J. S. Erigena* 150
S. Chrysostom 240
Church, disorder in 17, judgment of 78, 121, authority of 159, 166; Faith in the 114, 167, Calvinistic view of 115; Mediæval 15, 66, 178, Gallican 16, 177, Fifth Century 17, 117. See English
Cicero 19, 80, 161

INDEX. 281

Classics 141
CLAUSEN, *A. A. Hippo* 155
COLLETTE, *Saint Augustine* 180 n.
COLLIER, *Ecclesiastical History* 106 n
Consciousness 22, moral, 60
Constantinople 111
Continence 45, 64, 168
Cornelius 130, 132
Cosins 274
Councils 160
Cranmer 177, 180
Creation 56, 165, 175
Credulity 9 n., 104 n.
CROMPTON, *Saint Austin's Religion* 179
Cudworth 273
S. CYPRIAN 121, 216, 240, 256

Dead, Prayers for 187 n.
Death 58 f., 164, its sting 60
Deism 104 n., 196.
DESCARTES 16, 25, 39 f., 105, 126, 150
Determinism 96, 172
Dialectic 26, 143, 152
Digitus Dei 196
Dionysius 146, 150
Discussions, public 12, 46, 120
Dissenters 190
Dogma 5, 6
DÖLLINGER 180 n.
Dominion 153, 193
Donatists 77, 120 f., 160, 163, 183
DORNER, *Augustinus* 14, 124 n.
DUBIEF, *Les idées politiques* 116 n., 195

Edwards, President 196
Elect 10 n., 48
Empirical knowledge 137, 161
ENDERT, C. VAN, *Gottesbeweis* 38 n., 151 n., 153 n.
English Church, revived life 3, 16, Mediæval 105, 170, 175, S. Austin and 177, and Calvinism 182 f.
ERIGENA 6 n., 10 n., 35 n., 69 n., 70, 143 f., 158, 166, *De Predestinatione* 146 n., *De Divisione Naturæ* 144 n., 146, 147, 149, 158
Essays and Reviews 4
S. Etheldreda 170
Eucharist 117 n., 154, 198 f., for the Dead 187 n., 215
Evangelicalism 117 n., 131
Evil 51, 87, 97, its nature, 51, 71, its origin 54, 82, permission of 97

Faith, and knowledge 9, 73, 101, 114, 158, 163, 175, Christian 17, 41, 157, temporal 163
Fall of man 56 f., 149, 175

C.

Fatherhood of God 125
Faustus 46
Fell 274
Filmer, Sir R. 193
FOGG, *God's infinite Grace* 182
FONTEAU 82 n.
Foreknowledge 88, 97, 126, 133
Fortunatus 46
Free Choice 95, 172, 182
Free Will 79, 91 f., 104, 171, 182, 187, 196, Pelagian 93
Friends, Society of 134
S. FULGENTIUS 224, 266 f.
FULLER, *Church History* 106 n.

GALE, T. *True idea of Jansenisme* 179
GANGAUF, *Metaphysische Psychologie* 9 n., 35 n., 36 n., 37 n., 82 n., 171; *Speculative Lehre* 93 n., 103 n., 105 n., 151 n., 176
Geometry 28, 143
Goodness, of God 99 f.
Gottschalk 146
Grace 56 n., its power 71, 72, 93 n., means of 123, 133, its conditions 126
Greek 41 n., 154
S. Gregory 149
S. GREGORY OF NYSSA 51 n.
GROSSETESTE, Robert 153
GYFFARD, George, *Plaine Declaration* 183

HAMILTON, Bp. 198
HASSE, *Anselm* 150
HAURÉAU, *Philosophie scolastique* 142 n., 143
Heathenism 47, 57, 79
Hebrews, Epistle to 72, 80 n.
HEGEL 7 n., 37 n., 115, 151 n.
Heredity 81
HERMANN, Archbishop, *Consultatio* 182
Hermetic doctrine 9 n.
HEWIT, *Studies in S. Augustine* 82 n., 180 n.
Heylin 274
HICKES, Dean 188 n., 201, 209, n., 213 n., 273, 274
Hippo 3, 45, 111, 142
History, Philosophy of 114
Homilies 182
HOPKINS 244
Hume 164

Immortality, minor 58
Incontinence 64, 168
Independents 117 n.
India 41

19

Intellect 27 f.
Irving, Edward 117 n.
Isidore of Seville 213

Jains 48
Jansenists 16, 176
S. Jerome 3, 112
Jesuits 176, 179, 192, 196
John of Salisbury 152
Johnson 213 n., 226, 275
Jonah 166
Judgment of the Learned and Pious S. Augustine 191

Kant 7, 105
Knowledge, kinds of 25, 157, elements of 26, limitations of 37, 99, 101

Lactantius 140 n.
Laud, Archbishop 177, 274
Law 158
Lechler, *De Thoma Bradwardino* 107 n.
Leibnitz 35
Locke 180, *Reasonableness of Christianity* 167, *Toleration* 191
Luther 16, 179

Magicians 138
Mahommedanism 87
Malthusians 86
Mani 45
Manichæans 12, 19, 45 f., 54, 57, 71, 77, 80, 120, 160, 167
Manichæism 53, 65, 66, 71, 81, 170
Marriage 65, 168 f. 182
Matthew, Sir J. 179 n.
Maurice, F. D. 4, 122, *The Old Testament* 11 n.
Mede 213, 226, 269 f.
Memory 137
Methodists 130, 197
Middle Ages 15, 66, 105, 142, 166
Milan 3, 12 n.
Milman 65 n., 170
Miracles 160, 163
Molina 179
Monarchy 193
S. Monica 187 n.
Mozley, 107
Müller, Julius 180 n.
Mysticism 33, 35, 150

Nature, study of 10, 141, observation of 157, philosophy of, 52 n.
Neander 65 n., 80 n., 91 n., 171, 175
Nebridius 21 n.
Neo-Platonism 37, 61
Nitzsch 163 n.

Non-conformists 190
Numbers 27, 28, 143

Obedience, civil 192 f.
Olympius 111 n.
Omnipotence 102, 133
Ontological Proof 150
Orange, Council of 78
Ordination 241
Origen 6, 51 n., 56, 69 n., 243, 251
Owen, Robert 168
Oxford 16, 179, 196, 198

Parsis 48
Pattison, Mark *Sermons* 6
S. Paul 58, 59, 71, 119, 126, 231, 234, 250
Pelagianism 105, 106, 126, 132, 178
Pelagius 77, 80, 93, 105 n., 174
Penal Laws 190 f.
Penalty of sin 59, 90
Perfectionism 81, 87 n.
Persia 41, 47
Pessimism 87
Philosophy, Christian 6, no finality in 7, Academic 21 ; Greek 6, 79, 41 n., 49, 154, 174 ; Scholastic 35, 142.
Physics 10, 138
Pilate 19
Plato 14 n., 20 n., 29 n., 33 n., 34 n., 36, 41, 51, 155, 197, Theology of 37
Pliny 58, 140 n.
Plotinus 33 n.
Poole, R. L. *Illustrations* 152
Possidius 66 n.
Potter, Achbp. 231
Prayer 127, 134, 204, for dead 187
Prayer Book 135, 169, 181 f.
Preaching 120 n., 128
Predestination 90, 126, 145, 182, 196
Prescience 90, 126 n., 145, 182
Prudentius, *De Predestinatione* 145, 146
Punishment 61 f., 84, proportion in, 67 f., deliverance from 70 ; corrective 86, foreknown 146, physical 69, 146
Purgatory 187
Puritans 182 f., 192
Pusey, E. B. 16
Pythagoras 28 n.

Quadrivium 143

Ranke, *History of England* 190 n.
Ratramnus 225, 244
Ravenna 111
Reason 10 n., 144, 157 f.

Regeneration 118
REINKENS, *Die Geschichtsphilosophie des h. A.* 115 nn.
Reminiscence, doctrine of 29 n.
Repentance 130
Responsibility 84
REUTER, *Geschichte der rel. Aufklärung* 144
Rhetoric 143
RITTER, *Geschichte der Philosophie* 36 n., 37 n., 139, 151 n.
Rome 19, 45, 47, 111, 113
ROUSSELOT, *Philosophie dans le moyen âge* 144

Sacraments 117 n., 129 f., 202, 239 f.; *see* Baptism, Eucharist, Ordination
Sacrifice 201 f.
Satisfaction 151
Schelling 14 n.
Schism 117, 118, 121
Scholastics 16, 35, 38, 142, 152
Science 10, 141
SCIPIO, *Des A. A. Metaphysik* 53 n., 72 n.
Scotists 178
Scotland 117, 192
Scripture, Authority of 11, 104 n., 159 f., interpretation of 28 n., 56, 69, 157 f., 165
SCRIVENER 196
Secularists 57
Senses, Evidence of 21, 40, 162
SHIRLEY 153
Sin 164, 175, Original 82, Penalty of 59, 90 n.
SMITH, GEORGE 198
SPELMAN, Sir H. 195
Statistical Society's Journal 87 n.
STILLINGFLEET 196
Stoics 82 n., 175

STORZ, *Philosophie des h. Augustinus* 25 n., 36 n.
Suffering 50, 70, 99 f., 112 f.
SUTCLIFFE, *Unmasking of a Masse Monger* 179

Teetotalism 66 n.
Tertullian 9 n., 188
Theosophy 9 n., 49
Thomists 153, 178
THORNDIKE, *Epilogue* 182, 274
Time 56, 70, 157
Transubstantiation 198
Trent, Council of 78, 178
Trivium, 152
Truth 7, 37, 157, love of, 10, search for, 19, and light, 29

USHER 226

Vandals 112 n.
Vegetarianism 66 n.

WALDENSIS, Thomas 153 n., 154 n.
WATERLAND 198, 206, 208, 222, 229, 248, 250, 261
WESLEY, John 131 n., 177, 196, 198
Wheatley 201
WHITFIELD, *The New Birth* 130 n.
WIGGERS, *Augustinismus und Pelagianismus* 35 n., 171
Will, defect of 55, arbitrary 103, of God 93 f., 96, 103, 165, 194, human 91, 98; *see* Free Will
WYCLIF 153, 177, 193, 195

ZELLER, *Stoics, Epicureans, and Sceptics* 21 n.
Zoroaster 47, 48
Zosimus 111 n.
Zwinglian doctrine 117 n.

CAMBRIDGE: PRINTED BY C. J. CLAY, M.A. & SONS, AT THE UNIVERSITY PRESS.

BY THE SAME AUTHOR.

THE INFLUENCE OF DESCARTES ON METAPHYSI-
CAL SPECULATION IN ENGLAND. Royal 8vo., pp. xlviii+188. [Out of Print.]

A DISSERTATION ON THE EPISTLE OF S. BARNABAS.
To this are added a Greek Text, the Latin Version, with a new English Translation and Commentary by G. H. Rendall, M.A., Fellow of Trinity College. Crown 8vo., pp. cxvii+130. 7s. 6d.

THE CHURCHES OF ASIA, A METHODICAL SKETCH
OF THE SECOND CENTURY. Crown 8vo., pp. xvi+299. 6s.

CHRISTIAN CIVILISATION WITH SPECIAL REFER-
ENCE TO INDIA. Crown 8vo., pp. vi+152. 5s.

CHRISTIAN OPINION ON USURY WITH SPECIAL
REFERENCE TO ENGLAND. Crown 8vo., pp. x+84. [Out of Print.]

Macmillan and Co.

POLITICS AND ECONOMICS, AN ESSAY ON THE
PRINCIPLES OF POLITICAL ECONOMY, TOGETHER WITH A SURVEY OF RECENT LEGISLATION. Crown 8vo., pp. xvi+275. 5s.

Kegan Paul, Trench and Co.

THE GROWTH OF ENGLISH INDUSTRY AND
COMMERCE. Crown 8vo., pp. xiv+492. 12s.

Cambridge University Press.

UNIVERSITY PRESS, CAMBRIDGE.
September, 1886.

CATALOGUE OF

WORKS

PUBLISHED FOR THE SYNDICS

OF THE

Cambridge University Press.

London: C. J. CLAY AND SONS,
CAMBRIDGE UNIVERSITY PRESS WAREHOUSE,
AVE MARIA LANE.

GLASGOW: 263, ARGYLE STREET.

Cambridge: DEIGHTON, BELL AND CO.
Leipzig: F. A. BROCKHAUS.

1000
1.9/86

PUBLICATIONS OF
The Cambridge University Press.

THE HOLY SCRIPTURES, &c.

THE CAMBRIDGE PARAGRAPH BIBLE of the Authorized English Version, with the Text Revised by a Collation of its Early and other Principal Editions, the Use of the Italic Type made uniform, the Marginal References remodelled, and a Critical Introduction prefixed, by F. H. A. SCRIVENER, M.A., LL.D., Editor of the Greek Testament, Codex Augiensis, &c., and one of the Revisers of the Authorized Version. Crown 4to. gilt. 21s.

From the Times.
"Students of the Bible should be particularly grateful (to the Cambridge University Press) for having produced, with the able assistance of Dr Scrivener, a complete critical edition of the Authorized Version of the English Bible, an edition such as, to use the words of the Editor, 'would have been executed long ago had this version been nothing more than the greatest and best known of English classics.' Falling at a time when the formal revision of this version has been undertaken by a distinguished company of scholars and divines, the publication of this edition must be considered most opportune."

From the Athenæum.
"Apart from its religious importance, the English Bible has the glory, which but few sister versions indeed can claim, of being the chief classic of the language, of having, in conjunction with Shakspeare, and in an immeasurable degree more than he, fixed the language beyond any possibility of important change. Thus the recent contributions to the literature of the subject, by such workers as Mr Francis Fry and Canon Westcott, appeal to a wide range of sympathies; and to these may now be added Dr Scrivener, well known for his labours in the cause of the Greek Testament criticism, who has brought out, for the

Syndics of the Cambridge University Press, an edition of the English Bible, according to the text of 1611, revised by a comparison with later issues on principles stated by him in his Introduction. Here he enters at length into the history of the chief editions of the version, and of such features as the marginal notes, the use of italic type, and the changes of orthography, as well as into the most interesting question as to the original texts from which our translation is produced."

From the Methodist Recorder.
"This noble quarto of over 1300 pages is in every respect worthy of editor and publishers alike. The name of the Cambridge University Press is guarantee enough for its perfection in outward form, the name of the editor is equal guarantee for the worth and accuracy of its contents. Without question, it is the best Paragraph Bible ever published, and its reduced price of a guinea brings it within reach of a large number of students."

From the London Quarterly Review.
"The work is worthy in every respect of the editor's fame, and of the Cambridge University Press. The noble English Version, to which our country and religion owe so much, was probably never presented before in so perfect a form."

THE CAMBRIDGE PARAGRAPH BIBLE. STUDENT'S EDITION, on *good writing paper*, with one column of print and wide margin to each page for MS. notes. This edition will be found of great use to those who are engaged in the task of Biblical criticism. Two Vols. Crown 4to. gilt. 31s. 6d.

THE AUTHORIZED EDITION OF THE ENGLISH BIBLE (1611), ITS SUBSEQUENT REPRINTS AND MODERN REPRESENTATIVES. Being the Introduction to the Cambridge Paragraph Bible (1873), re-edited with corrections and additions. By F. H. A. SCRIVENER, M.A., D.C.L., LL.D., Prebendary of Exeter and Vicar of Hendon. Crown 8vo. 7s. 6d.

THE LECTIONARY BIBLE, WITH APOCRYPHA, divided into Sections adapted to the Calendar and Tables of Lessons of 1871. Crown 8vo. 3s. 6d.

London: C. J. CLAY & SONS, Cambridge University Press Warehouse,
Ave Maria Lane.

BREVIARIUM AD USUM INSIGNIS ECCLESIAE

SARUM. Juxta Editionem maximam pro CLAUDIO CHEVALLON ET FRANCISCO REGNAULT A.D. MDXXXI. in Alma Parisiorum Academia impressam : labore ac studio FRANCISCI PROCTER, A.M., ET CHRISTOPHORI WORDSWORTH, A.M.

FASCICULUS I. In quo continentur KALENDARIUM, et ORDO TEMPORALIS sive PROPRIUM DE TEMPORE TOTIUS ANNI, una cum ordinali suo quod usitato vocabulo dicitur PICA SIVE DIRECTORIUM SACERDOTUM. Demy 8vo. 18s.

"The value of this reprint is considerable to liturgical students, who will now be able to consult in their own libraries a work absolutely indispensable to a right understanding of the history of the Prayer-Book, but which till now usually necessitated a visit to some public library, since the rarity of the volume made its cost prohibitory to all but a few.... Messrs Procter and Wordsworth have discharged their editorial task with much care and judgment, though the conditions under which they have been working are such as to hide that fact from all but experts."—*Literary Churchman.*

FASCICULUS II. In quo continentur PSALTERIUM, cum ordinario Officii totius hebdomadae juxta Horas Canonicas, et proprio Completorii, LITANIA, COMMUNE SANCTORUM, ORDINARIUM MISSAE CUM CANONE ET XIII MISSIS, &c. &c. Demy 8vo. 12s.

"Not only experts in liturgiology, but all persons interested in the history of the Anglican Book of Common Prayer, will be grateful to the Syndicate of the Cambridge University Press for forwarding the publication of the volume which bears the above title, and which has recently appeared under their auspices."—*Notes and Queries.*
"Cambridge has worthily taken the lead with the Breviary, which is of especial value for that part of the reform of the Prayer-Book which will fit it for the wants of our time . . .

For all persons of religious tastes the Breviary, with its mixture of Psalm and Anthem and Prayer and Hymn, all hanging one on the other, and connected into a harmonious whole, must be deeply interesting."—*Church Quarterly Review.*
"The editors have done their work excellently, and deserve all praise for their labour's in rendering what they justly call 'this most interesting Service-book' more readily accessible to historical and liturgical students."—*Saturday Review.*

FASCICULUS III. In quo continetur PROPRIUM SANCTORUM quod et sanctorale dicitur, una cum accentuario. [*Nearly ready.*]

GREEK AND ENGLISH TESTAMENT, in parallel Columns on the same page. Edited by J. SCHOLEFIELD, M.A. late Regius Professor of Greek in the University. Small Octavo. New Edition, with the Marginal References as arranged and revised by Dr SCRIVENER. Cloth, red edges. 7s. 6d.

GREEK AND ENGLISH TESTAMENT. THE STUDENT'S EDITION of the above, on *large writing paper*. 4to. 12s.

GREEK TESTAMENT, ex editione Stephani tertia, 1550. Small 8vo. 3s. 6d.

THE NEW TESTAMENT IN GREEK according to the text followed in the Authorised Version, with the Variations adopted in the Revised Version. Edited by F. H. A. SCRIVENER, M.A., D.C.L., LL.D. Crown 8vo. 6s. Morocco boards or limp. 12s.

THE PARALLEL NEW TESTAMENT GREEK AND ENGLISH, being the Authorised Version set forth in 1611 Arranged in Parallel Columns with the Revised Version of 1881, and with the original Greek, as edited by F. H. A. SCRIVENER, M.A., D.C.L., LL.D. Prebendary of Exeter and Vicar of Hendon. Crown 8vo. 12s. 6d. *The Revised Version is the Joint Property of the Universities of Cambridge and Oxford.*

London: C. J. CLAY & SONS, *Cambridge University Press Warehouse*, *Ave Maria Lane.*

THE BOOK OF ECCLESIASTES, with Notes and Introduction. By the Very Rev. E. H. PLUMPTRE, D.D., Dean of Wells. Large Paper Edition. Demy 8vo. 7s. 6d.

"No one can say that the Old Testament is a dull or worn-out subject after reading this singularly attractive and also instructive commentary. Its wealth of literary and historical illustration surpasses anything to which we can point in English exegesis of the Old Testament; indeed, even Delitzsch, whose pride it is to leave no source of illustration unexplored, is far inferior on this head to Dr Plumptre."—*Academy*, Sept. 10, 1881.

THE GOSPEL ACCORDING TO ST MATTHEW in Anglo-Saxon and Northumbrian Versions, synoptically arranged: with Collations of the best Manuscripts. By J. M. KEMBLE, M.A. and Archdeacon HARDWICK. Demy 4to. 10s.

NEW EDITION. By the Rev. Professor SKEAT. [*In the Press.*

THE GOSPEL ACCORDING TO ST MARK in Anglo-Saxon and Northumbrian Versions, synoptically arranged: with Collations exhibiting all the Readings of all the MSS. Edited by the Rev. W. W. SKEAT, Litt.D., Elrington and Bosworth Professor of Anglo-Saxon. Demy 4to. 10s.

THE GOSPEL ACCORDING TO ST LUKE, uniform with the preceding, by the same Editor. Demy 4to. 10s.

THE GOSPEL ACCORDING TO ST JOHN, uniform with the preceding, by the same Editor. Demy 4to. 10s.

"*The Gospel according to St John, in Anglo-Saxon and Northumbrian Versions:* Edited for the Syndics of the University Press, by the Rev. Walter W. Skeat, M.A., completes an undertaking designed and commenced by that distinguished scholar, J. M. Kemble, some forty years ago. Of the particular volume now before us, we can only say it is worthy of its two predecessors. We repeat that the service rendered to the study of Anglo-Saxon by this Synoptic collection cannot easily be overstated."—*Contemporary Review.*

THE POINTED PRAYER BOOK, being the Book of Common Prayer with the Psalter or Psalms of David, pointed as they are to be sung or said in Churches. Royal 24mo. 1s. 6d.

The same in square 32mo. cloth. 6d.

THE CAMBRIDGE PSALTER, for the use of Choirs and Organists. Specially adapted for Congregations in which the "Cambridge Pointed Prayer Book" is used. Demy 8vo. cloth extra, 3s. 6d. cloth limp, cut flush. 2s. 6d.

THE PARAGRAPH PSALTER, arranged for the use of Choirs by BROOKE FOSS WESTCOTT, D.D., Regius Professor of Divinity in the University of Cambridge. Fcap. 4to. 5s.

The same in royal 32mo. Cloth 1s. Leather 1s. 6d.

"The Paragraph Psalter exhibits all the care, thought, and learning that those acquainted with the works of the Regius Professor of Divinity at Cambridge would expect to find, and there is not a clergyman or organist in England who should be without this Psalter as a work of reference."—*Morning Post.*

THE MISSING FRAGMENT OF THE LATIN TRANSLATION OF THE FOURTH BOOK OF EZRA, discovered, and edited with an Introduction and Notes, and a facsimile of the MS., by ROBERT L. BENSLY, M.A., Reader in Hebrew, Gonville and Caius College, Cambridge. Demy 4to. 10s.

"It has been said of this book that it has added a new chapter to the Bible, and, startling as the statement may at first sight appear, it is no exaggeration of the actual fact, if by the Bible we understand that of the larger size which contains the Apocrypha, and if the Second Book of Esdras can be fairly called a part of the Apocrypha."—*Saturday Review.*

GOSPEL DIFFICULTIES, or the Displaced Section of S. Luke. By the Rev. J. J. HALCOMBE, Rector of Balsham and Rural Dean of North Camps, formerly Reader and Librarian at the Charterhouse. Crown 8vo. 10s. 6d.

London: C. J. CLAY & SONS, Cambridge University Press Warehouse, Ave Maria Lane.

THEOLOGY—(ANCIENT).

THE GREEK LITURGIES. Chiefly from original Authorities. By C. A. SWAINSON, D.D., Master of Christ's College, Cambridge. Crown 4to. Paper covers. 15s.

"Jeder folgende Forscher wird dankbar anerkennen, dass Swainson das Fundament zu einer historisch-kritischen Geschichte der Griechischen Liturgien sicher gelegt hat."—ADOLPH HARNACK, *Theologische Literaturzeitung*.

THE PALESTINIAN MISHNA. By W. H. LOWE, M.A., Lecturer in Hebrew at Christ's College, Cambridge. Royal 8vo. 21s.

SAYINGS OF THE JEWISH FATHERS, comprising Pirqe Aboth and Pereq R. Meir in Hebrew and English, with Critical and Illustrative Notes. By CHARLES TAYLOR, D.D. Master of St John's College, Cambridge, and Honorary Fellow of King's College, London. Demy 8vo. 10s.

"The 'Masseketh Aboth' stands at the head of Hebrew non-canonical writings. It is of ancient date, claiming to contain the dicta of teachers who flourished from B.C. 200 to the same year of our era. The precise time of its compilation in its present form is, of course, in doubt. Mr Taylor's explanatory and illustrative commentary is very full and satisfactory."—*Spectator*.

"A careful and thorough edition which does credit to English scholarship, of a short treatise from the Mishna, containing a series of sentences or maxims ascribed mostly to Jewish teachers immediately preceding, or immediately following the Christian era..."—*Contemporary Review*.

THEODORE OF MOPSUESTIA'S COMMENTARY ON THE MINOR EPISTLES OF S. PAUL. The Latin Version with the Greek Fragments, edited from the MSS. with Notes and an Introduction, by H. B. SWETE, D.D., Rector of Ashdon, Essex, and late Fellow of Gonville and Caius College, Cambridge. In Two Volumes. Vol. I., containing the Introduction, with Facsimiles of the MSS., and the Commentary upon Galatians—Colossians. Demy 8vo. 12s.

"In dem oben verzeichneten Buche liegt uns die erste Hälfte einer vollständigen, ebenso sorgfältig gearbeiteten wie schön ausgestatteten Ausgabe des Commentars mit ausführlichen Prolegomena und reichhaltigen kritischen und erläuternden Anmerkungen vor."—*Literarisches Centralblatt*.

"It is the result of thorough, careful, and patient investigation of all the points bearing on the subject, and the results are presented with admirable good sense and modesty."—*Guardian*.

"Auf Grund dieser Quellen ist der Text bei Swete mit musterhafter Akribie hergestellt. Aber auch sonst hat der Herausgeber mit unermüdlichem Fleisse und eingehendster Sachkenntniss sein Werk mit allen denjenigen Zugaben ausgerüstet, welche bei einer solchen Text-Ausgabe nur irgend erwartet werden können. ... Von den drei Haupt-

handschriften ... sind vortreffliche photographische Facsimile's beigegeben, wie überhaupt das ganze Werk von der *University Press* zu Cambridge mit bekannter Eleganz ausgestattet ist."—*Theologische Literaturzeitung*.

"It is a hopeful sign, amid forebodings which arise about the theological learning of the Universities, that we have before us the first instalment of a thoroughly scientific and painstaking work, commenced at Cambridge and completed at a country rectory."—*Church Quarterly Review* (Jan. 1881).

"Herrn Swete's Leistung ist eine so tüchtige dass wir das Werk in keinen besseren Händen wissen möchten, und mit den sichersten Erwartungen auf das Gelingen der Fortsetzung entgegen sehen."—*Göttingische gelehrte Anzeigen* (Sept. 1881).

VOLUME II., containing the Commentary on 1 Thessalonians—Philemon, Appendices and Indices. 12s.

"Eine Ausgabe ... für welche alle zugänglichen Hülfsmittel in musterhafter Weise benützt wurden ... eine reife Frucht siebenjährigen Fleisses."—*Theologische Literaturzeitung* (Sept. 23, 1882).

"Mit deiselben Sorgfalt bearbeitet wie die wir bei dem ersten Theile gerühmt haben."—*Literarisches Centralblatt* (July 29, 1882).

"M. Jacobi...commença...une édition du texte. Ce travail a été repris en Angleterre et mené à bien dans les deux volumes que je signale en ce moment...Elle est accompagnée de notes érudites, suivie de divers appendices, parmi lesquels on appréciera surtout un recueil des fragments des oeuvres dogmatiques de Théodore, et précédée d'une introduction où sont traitées à fond toutes les questions d'histoire littéraire qui se rattachent soit au commentaire lui-même, soit à sa version Latine."—*Bulletin Critique*, 1885.

London: C. J. CLAY & SONS, Cambridge University Press Warehouse,
Ave Maria Lane.

SANCTI IRENÆI EPISCOPI LUGDUNENSIS libros quinque adversus Hæreses, versione Latina cum Codicibus Claromontano ac Arundeliano denuo collata, præmissa de placitis Gnosticorum prolusione, fragmenta necnon Græce, Syriace, Armeniace, commentatione perpetua et indicibus variis edidit W. WIGAN HARVEY, S.T.B. Collegii Regalis olim Socius. 2 Vols. 8vo. 18s.

M. MINUCII FELICIS OCTAVIUS. The text newly revised from the original MS., with an English Commentary, Analysis, Introduction, and Copious Indices. Edited by H. A. HOLDEN, LL.D. Examiner in Greek to the University of London. Crown 8vo. 7s. 6d.

THEOPHILI EPISCOPI ANTIOCHENSIS LIBRI TRES AD AUTOLYCUM edidit, Prolegomenis Versione Notulis Indicibus instruxit GULIELMUS GILSON HUMPHRY, S.T.B. Collegii Sanctiss. Trin. apud Cantabrigienses quondam Socius. Post 8vo. 5s.

THEOPHYLACTI IN EVANGELIUM S. MATTHÆI COMMENTARIUS, edited by W. G. HUMPHRY, B.D. Prebendary of St Paul's, late Fellow of Trinity College. Demy 8vo. 7s. 6d.

TERTULLIANUS DE CORONA MILITIS, DE SPECTACULIS, DE IDOLOLATRIA, with Analysis and English Notes, by GEORGE CURREY, D.D. Preacher at the Charter House, late Fellow and Tutor of St John's College. Crown 8vo. 5s.

FRAGMENTS OF PHILO AND JOSEPHUS. Newly edited by J. RENDEL HARRIS, M.A., Fellow of Clare College, Cambridge. With two Facsimiles. Demy 4to. 12s. 6d.

THEOLOGY—(ENGLISH).

WORKS OF ISAAC BARROW, compared with the Original MSS., enlarged with Materials hitherto unpublished. A new Edition, by A. NAPIER, M.A. of Trinity College, Vicar of Holkham, Norfolk. 9 Vols. Demy 8vo. £3. 3s.

TREATISE OF THE POPE'S SUPREMACY, and a Discourse concerning the Unity of the Church, by ISAAC BARROW. Demy 8vo. 7s. 6d.

PEARSON'S EXPOSITION OF THE CREED, edited by TEMPLE CHEVALLIER, B.D. late Fellow and Tutor of St Catharine's College, Cambridge. New Edition. Revised by R. Sinker, B.D., Librarian of Trinity College. Demy 8vo. 12s.

"A new edition of Bishop Pearson's famous work *On the Creed* has just been issued by the Cambridge University Press. It is the well-known edition of Temple Chevallier, thoroughly overhauled by the Rev. R. Sinker, of Trinity College. The whole text and notes have been most carefully examined and corrected, and special pains have been taken to verify the almost innumerable references. These have been more clearly and accurately given in very many places, and the citations themselves have been adapted to the best and newest texts of the several authors—texts which have undergone vast improvements within the last two centuries. The Indices have also been revised and enlarged......Altogether this appears to be the most complete and convenient edition as yet published of a work which has long been recognised in all quarters as a standard one."—*Guardian.*

AN ANALYSIS OF THE EXPOSITION OF THE CREED written by the Right Rev. JOHN PEARSON, D.D. late Lord Bishop of Chester, by W. H. MILL, D.D. late Regius Professor of Hebrew in the University of Cambridge. Demy 8vo. 5s.

WHEATLY ON THE COMMON PRAYER, edited by G. E. CORRIE, D.D. late Master of Jesus College. Demy 8vo. 7s. 6d.

London: C. J. CLAY & SONS, Cambridge University Press Warehouse, Ave Maria Lane.

TWO FORMS OF PRAYER OF THE TIME OF QUEEN ELIZABETH. Now First Reprinted. Demy 8vo. 6*d*.

"From 'Collections and Notes' 1867—1876, by W. Carew Hazlitt (p. 340), we learn that—'A very remarkable volume, in the original vellum cover, and containing 25 Forms of Prayer of the reign of Elizabeth, each with the autograph of Humphrey Dyson, has lately fallen into the hands of my friend Mr H. Pyne. It is mentioned specially in the Preface to the Parker Society's volume of Occasional Forms of Prayer, but it had been lost sight of for 200 years.' By the kindness of the present possessor of this valuable volume, containing in all 25 distinct publications, I am enabled to reprint in the following pages the two Forms of Prayer supposed to have been lost."—*Extract from the* PREFACE.

CÆSAR MORGAN'S INVESTIGATION OF THE TRINITY OF PLATO, and of Philo Judæus, and of the effects which an attachment to their writings had upon the principles and reasonings of the Fathers of the Christian Church. Revised by H. A. HOLDEN, LL.D., formerly Fellow of Trinity College, Cambridge. Crown 8vo. 4*s*.

SELECT DISCOURSES, by JOHN SMITH, late Fellow of Queens' College, Cambridge. Edited by H. G. WILLIAMS, B.D. late Professor of Arabic. Royal 8vo. 7*s*. 6*d*.

"The 'Select Discourses' of John Smith, collected and published from his papers after his death, are, in my opinion, much the most considerable work left to us by this Cambridge School [the Cambridge Platonists]. They have a right to a place in English literary history."—Mr MATTHEW ARNOLD, in the *Contemporary Review*.
"Of all the products of the Cambridge School, the 'Select Discourses' are perhaps the highest, as they are the most accessible and the most widely appreciated...and indeed no spiritually thoughtful mind can read them unmoved. They carry us so directly into an atmosphere of divine philosophy, luminous with the richest lights of meditative genius... He was one of those rare thinkers in whom largeness of view, and depth, and wealth of poetic and speculative insight, only served to evoke more fully the religious spirit, and while he drew the mould of his thought from Plotinus, he vivified the substance of it from St Paul."—Principal TULLOCH, *Rational Theology in England in the 17th Century*.
"We may instance Mr Henry Griffin Williams's revised edition of Mr John Smith's 'Select Discourses,' which have won Mr Matthew Arnold's admiration, as an example of worthy work for an University Press to undertake."—*Times*.

THE HOMILIES, with Various Readings, and the Quotations from the Fathers given at length in the Original Languages. Edited by G. E. CORRIE, D.D. late Master of Jesus College. Demy 8vo. 7*s*. 6*d*.

DE OBLIGATIONE CONSCIENTIÆ PRÆLECTIONES decem Oxonii in Schola Theologica habitæ a ROBERTO SANDERSON, SS. Theologiæ ibidem Professore Regio. With English Notes, including an abridged Translation, by W. WHEWELL, D.D. late Master of Trinity College. Demy 8vo. 7*s*. 6*d*.

ARCHBISHOP USHER'S ANSWER TO A JESUIT, with other Tracts on Popery. Edited by J. SCHOLEFIELD, M.A. late Regius Professor of Greek in the University. Demy 8vo. 7*s*. 6*d*.

WILSON'S ILLUSTRATION OF THE METHOD OF explaining the New Testament, by the early opinions of Jews and Christians concerning Christ. Edited by T. TURTON, D.D. late Lord Bishop of Ely. Demy 8vo. 5*s*.

LECTURES ON DIVINITY delivered in the University of Cambridge, by JOHN HEY, D.D. Third Edition, revised by T. TURTON, D.D. late Lord Bishop of Ely. 2 vols. Demy 8vo. 15*s*.

S. AUSTIN AND HIS PLACE IN THE HISTORY OF CHRISTIAN THOUGHT. Being the Hulsean Lectures for 1885. By W. Cunningham, B.D., Chaplain and Birkbeck Lecturer, Trinity College, Cambridge. Demy 8vo.

London: C. J. CLAY & SONS, Cambridge University Press Warehouse,
Ave Maria Lane.

ARABIC, SANSKRIT, SYRIAC, &c.

THE DIVYÂVADÂNA, a Collection of Early Buddhist Legends, now first edited from the Nepalese Sanskrit MSS. in Cambridge and Paris. By E. B. COWELL, M.A., Professor of Sanskrit in the University of Cambridge, and R. A. NEIL, M.A., Fellow and Lecturer of Pembroke College. Demy 8vo. 18s.

POEMS OF BEHA ED DIN ZOHEIR OF EGYPT. With a Metrical Translation, Notes and Introduction, by E. H. PALMER, M.A., Barrister-at-Law of the Middle Temple, late Lord Almoner's Professor of Arabic, formerly Fellow of St John's College, Cambridge. 2 vols. Crown 4to.
Vol. I. The ARABIC TEXT. 10s. 6d.; cloth extra. 15s.
Vol. II. ENGLISH TRANSLATION. 10s. 6d.; cloth extra. 15s.

"We have no hesitation in saying that in both Prof. Palmer has made an addition to Oriental literature for which scholars should be grateful; and that, while his knowledge of Arabic is a sufficient guarantee for his mastery of the original, his English compositions are distinguished by versatility, command of language, rhythmical cadence, and, as we have remarked, by not unskilful imitations of the styles of several of our own favourite poets, living and dead."—*Saturday Review.*

"This sumptuous edition of the poems of Behá-ed-dín Zoheir is a very welcome addition to the small series of Eastern poets accessible to readers who are not Orientalists."—*Academy.*

THE CHRONICLE OF JOSHUA THE STYLITE, composed in Syriac A.D. 507 with an English translation and notes, by W. WRIGHT, LL.D., Professor of Arabic. Demy 8vo. 10s. 6d.

"Die lehrreiche kleine Chronik Josuas hat nach Assemani und Martin in Wright einen dritten Bearbeiter gefunden, der sich um die Emendation des Textes wie um die Erklärung der Realien wesentlich verdient gemacht hat ... W's. Josua-Ausgabe ist eine sehr dankenswerte Gabe und besonders empfehlenswert als ein Lehrmittel für den syrischen Unterricht; es erscheint auch gerade zur rechten Zeit, da die zweite Ausgabe von Roedigers syrischer Chrestomathie im Buchhandel vollständig vergriffen und diejenige von Kirsch-Bernstein nur noch in wenigen Exemplaren vorhanden ist."—*Deutsche Litteraturzeitung.*

KALĪLAH AND DIMNAH, OR, THE FABLES OF BIDPAI; being an account of their literary history, together with an English Translation of the same, with Notes, by I. G. N. KEITH-FALCONER, M.A., Trinity College. Demy 8vo. 7s. 6d.

NALOPÁKHYÁNAM, OR, THE TALE OF NALA; containing the Sanskrit Text in Roman Characters, followed by a Vocabulary and a sketch of Sanskrit Grammar. By the late Rev. THOMAS JARRETT, M.A. Trinity College, Regius Professor of Hebrew. Demy 8vo. 10s.

NOTES ON THE TALE OF NALA, for the use of Classical Students, by J. PEILE, Litt.D., Fellow and Tutor of Christ's College. Demy 8vo. 12s.

CATALOGUE OF THE BUDDHIST SANSKRIT MANUSCRIPTS in the University Library, Cambridge. Edited by C. BENDALL, M.A., Fellow of Gonville and Caius College. Demy 8vo. 12s.

"It is unnecessary to state how the compilation of the present catalogue came to be placed in Mr Bendall's hands; from the character of his work it is evident the selection was judicious, and we may fairly congratulate those concerned in it on the result... Mr Bendall has entitled himself to the thanks of all Oriental scholars, and we hope he may have before him a long course of successful labour in the field he has chosen."—*Athenæum.*

London: C. J. CLAY & SONS, Cambridge University Press Warehouse,
Ave Maria Lane.

GREEK AND LATIN CLASSICS, &c.

SOPHOCLES: The Plays and Fragments, with Critical Notes, Commentary, and Translation in English Prose, by R. C. JEBB, Litt.D., LL.D., Professor of Greek in the University of Glasgow.
Part I. Oedipus Tyrannus. Demy 8vo. 15s.
Part II. Oedipus Coloneus. Demy 8vo. 12s. 6d.
Part III. The Antigone. [*In the Press.*

"Of his explanatory and critical notes we can only speak with admiration. Thorough scholarship combines with taste, erudition, and boundless industry to make this first volume a pattern of editing. The work is made complete by a prose translation, upon pages alternating with the text, of which we may say shortly that it displays sound judgment and taste, without sacrificing precision to poetry of expression."—*The Times.*

"This larger edition he has deferred these many years for reasons which he has given in his preface, and which we accept with entire satisfaction, as we have now the first portion of a work composed in the fulness of his powers and with all the resources of fine erudition and laboriously earned experience...We will confidently aver, then, that the edition is neither tedious nor long; for we get in one compact volume such a cyclopædia of instruction, such a variety of helps to the full comprehension of the poet, as not so many years ago would have needed a small library, and all this instruction and assistance given, not in a dull and pedantic way, but in a style of singular clearness and vivacity. In fact, one might take this edition with him on a journey, and, without any other help whatever, acquire with comfort and delight a thorough acquaintance with the noblest production of, perhaps, the most difficult of all Greek poets—the most difficult, yet possessed at the same time of an immortal charm for one who has mastered him, as Mr Jebb has, and can feel so subtly perfection of form and language...We await with lively expectation the continuation, and completion of Mr Jebb's great task, and it is a fortunate thing that his power of work seems to be as great as the style is happy in which the work is done."—*The Athenæum.*

"An edition which marks a definite advance, which is whole in itself, and brings a mass of solid and well-wrought material such as future constructors will desire to adapt, is definitive in the only applicable sense of the term, and such is the edition of Professor Jebb. No man is better fitted to express in relation to Sophocles the mind of the present generation."—*The Saturday Review.*

AESCHYLI FABULAE.—ΙΚΕΤΙΔΕΣ ΧΟΗΦΟΡΟΙ IN LIBRO MEDICEO MENDOSE SCRIPTAE EX VV. DD. CONIECTURIS EMENDATIUS EDITAE cum Scholiis Graecis et brevi adnotatione critica, curante F. A. PALEY, M.A., LL.D. Demy 8vo. 7s. 6d.

THE AGAMEMNON OF AESCHYLUS. With a Translation in English Rhythm, and Notes Critical and Explanatory. **New Edition Revised.** By BENJAMIN HALL KENNEDY, D.D., Regius Professor of Greek. Crown 8vo. 6s.
"One of the best editions of the masterpiece of Greek tragedy."—*Athenæum.*

THE THEÆTETUS OF PLATO with a Translation and Notes by the same Editor. Crown 8vo. 7s. 6d.

ARISTOTLE.—ΠΕΡΙ ΨΥΧΗΣ. ARISTOTLE'S PSYCHOLOGY, in Greek and English, with Introduction and Notes, by EDWIN WALLACE, M.A., late Fellow and Tutor of Worcester College, Oxford. Demy 8vo. 18s.

"The notes are exactly what such notes ought to be,—helps to the student, not mere displays of learning. By far the more valuable parts of the notes are neither critical nor literary, but philosophical and expository of the thought, and of the connection of thought, in the treatise itself. In this relation the notes are invaluable. Of the translation, it may be said that an English reader may fairly master by means of it this great treatise of Aristotle."—*Spectator.*

"Wallace's Bearbeitung der Aristotelischen Psychologie ist das Werk eines denkenden und in allen Schriften des Aristoteles und grösstenteils auch in der neueren Litteratur zu Hause belesenen Mannes... Der schwächste Teil der Arbeit ist der kritische... Aber in allen diesen Dingen liegt auch nach der Absicht des Verfassers nicht der Schwerpunkt seiner Arbeit, sondern."—Prof. Susemihl in *Philologische Wochenschrift.*

ARISTOTLE.—ΠΕΡΙ ΔΙΚΑΙΟΣΤΝΗΣ. THE FIFTH BOOK OF THE NICOMACHEAN ETHICS OF ARISTOTLE. Edited by HENRY JACKSON, Litt.D., Fellow of Trinity College, Cambridge. Demy 8vo. 6s.

"It is not too much to say that some of the points he discusses have never had so much light thrown upon them before.... Scholars will hope that this is not the only portion of the Aristotelian writings which he is likely to edit."—*Athenæum.*

London: C. J. CLAY & SONS, Cambridge University Press Warehouse, Ave Maria Lane.

ARISTOTLE. THE RHETORIC. With a Commentary by the late E. M. COPE, Fellow of Trinity College, Cambridge, revised and edited by J. E. SANDYS, Litt.D. With a biographical Memoir by the late H. A. J. MUNRO, Litt.D. 3 Vols., Demy 8vo. **Now reduced to 21s.** (*originally published at 31s. 6d.*)

"This work is in many ways creditable to the University of Cambridge. If an English student wishes to have a full conception of what is contained in the *Rhetoric* of Aristotle, to Mr Cope's edition he must go."—*Academy.*

"Mr Sandys has performed his arduous duties with marked ability and admirable tact. ...... In every part of his work—revising, supplementing, and completing—he has done exceedingly well."—*Examiner.*

PINDAR. OLYMPIAN AND PYTHIAN ODES. With Notes Explanatory and Critical, Introductions and Introductory Essays. Edited by C. A. M. FENNELL, Litt. D., late Fellow of Jesus College. Crown 8vo. 9s.

"Mr Fennell deserves the thanks of all classical students for his careful and scholarly edition of the Olympian and Pythian odes. He brings to his task the necessary enthusiasm for his author, great industry, a sound judgment, and, in particular, copious and minute learning

in comparative philology."—*Athenæum.*
"Considered simply as a contribution to the study and criticism of Pindar, Mr Fennell's edition is a work of great merit."—*Saturday Review.*

—— **THE ISTHMIAN AND NEMEAN ODES.** By the same Editor. Crown 8vo. 9s.

"... As a handy and instructive edition of a difficult classic no work of recent years surpasses Mr Fennell's 'Pindar.'"—*Athenæum.*
"This work is in no way inferior to the previous volume. The commentary affords

valuable help to the study of the most difficult of Greek authors, and is enriched with notes on points of scholarship and etymology which could only have been written by a scholar of very high attainments."—*Saturday Review.*

PRIVATE ORATIONS OF DEMOSTHENES, with Introductions and English Notes, by F. A. PALEY, M.A. Editor of Aeschylus, etc. and J. E. SANDYS, Litt.D. Fellow and Tutor of St John's College, and Public Orator in the University of Cambridge.

PART I. Contra Phormionem, Lacritum, Pantaenetum, Boeotum de Nomine, Boeotum de Dote, Dionysodorum. Crown 8vo. 6s.
[*New Edition. Nearly ready.*

"Mr Paley's scholarship is sound and accurate, his experience of editing wide, and if he is content to devote his learning and abilities to the production of such manuals as these, they will be received with gratitude throughout the higher schools of the country. Mr Sandys is deeply read in the German

literature which bears upon his author, and the elucidation of matters of daily life, in the delineation of which Demosthenes is so rich, obtains full justice at his hands. ... We hope this edition may lead the way to a more general study of these speeches in schools than has hitherto been possible."—*Academy.*

PART II. Pro Phormione, Contra Stephanum I. II.; Nicostratum, Cononem, Calliclem. Crown 8vo. 7s. 6d.
[*New Edition. In the Press.*

"It is long since we have come upon a work evincing more pains, scholarship, and varied research and illustration than Mr Sandys's contribution to the 'Private Orations of De-

mosthenes'."—*Saturday Review.*
"...... the edition reflects credit on Cambridge scholarship, and ought to be extensively used."—*Athenæum.*

DEMOSTHENES AGAINST ANDROTION AND AGAINST TIMOCRATES, with Introductions and English Commentary, by WILLIAM WAYTE, M.A., late Professor of Greek, University College, London. Crown 8vo. 7s. 6d.

"These speeches are highly interesting, as illustrating Attic Law, as that law was influenced by the exigences of politics ... As vigorous examples of the great orator's style, they are worthy of all admiration; and they have the advantage—not inconsiderable when the actual attainments of the average schoolboy are considered—of having an easily com-

prehended subject matter .... Besides a most lucid and interesting introduction, Mr Wayte has given the student effective help in his running commentary. We may note, as being so well managed as to form a very valuable part of the exegesis, the summaries given with every two or three sections throughout the speech."—*Spectator.*

PLATO'S PHÆDO, literally translated, by the late E. M. COPE, Fellow of Trinity College, Cambridge, revised by HENRY JACKSON, Litt.D., Fellow of Trinity College. Demy 8vo. 5s.

London: C. J. CLAY & SONS, Cambridge University Press Warehouse, Ave Maria Lane.

THE BACCHAE OF EURIPIDES. With Introduction, Critical Notes, and Archæological Illustrations, by J. E. SANDYS, Litt.D., Fellow and Tutor of St John's College, Cambridge, and Public Orator. New and Enlarged Edition. Crown 8vo. 12s. 6d.

"Of the present edition of the *Bacchæ* by Mr Sandys we may safely say that never before has a Greek play, in England at least, had fuller justice done to its criticism, interpretation, and archæological illustration, whether for the young student or the more advanced scholar. The Cambridge Public Orator may be said to have taken the lead in issuing a complete edition of a Greek play, which is destined perhaps to gain redoubled favour now that the study of ancient monuments has been applied to its illustration."—*Saturday Review.*
"The volume is interspersed with well-executed woodcuts, and its general attractiveness of form reflects great credit on the University Press. In the notes Mr Sandys has more than sustained his well-earned reputation as a careful and learned editor, and shows consider-

able advance in freedom and lightness of style. ... Under such circumstances it is superfluous to say that for the purposes of teachers and advanced students this handsome edition far surpasses all its predecessors."—*Athenæum.*
"It has not, like so many such books, been hastily produced to meet the momentary need of some particular examination; but it has employed for some years the labour and thought of a highly finished scholar, whose aim seems to have been that his book should go forth *totus teres atque rotundus*, armed at all points with all that may throw light upon its subject. The result is a work which will not only assist the schoolboy or undergraduate in his tasks, but will adorn the library of the scholar."—*The Guardian.*

THE TYPES OF GREEK COINS. By PERCY GARDNER, Litt. D., F.S.A., Disney Professor of Archæology. With 16 Autotype plates, containing photographs of Coins of all parts of the Greek World. Impl. 4to. Cloth extra, £1. 11s. 6d.; Roxburgh (Morocco back), £2. 2s.

"Professor Gardner's book is written with such lucidity and in a manner so straightforward that it may well win converts, and it may be distinctly recommended to that omnivorous class of readers—'men in the schools'."—*Saturday Review.*
"'The Types of Greek Coins' is a work which

is less purely and dryly scientific. Nevertheless, it takes high rank as proceeding upon a truly scientific basis at the same time that it treats the subject of numismatics in an attractive style and is elegant enough to justify its appearance in the drawing-room."—*Athenæum.*

A SELECTION OF GREEK INSCRIPTIONS, with Introductions and Annotations by E. S. ROBERTS, M.A., Fellow and Tutor of Gonville and Caius College. [*Nearly ready.*

ESSAYS ON THE ART OF PHEIDIAS. By C. WALD-STEIN, M.A., Phil. D., Reader in Classical Archæology in the University of Cambridge. Royal 8vo. With numerous Illustrations. 16 Plates. Buckram, 30s.

"I acknowledge expressly the warm enthusiasm for ideal art which pervades the whole volume, and the sharp eye Dr Waldstein has proved himself to possess in his special line of study, namely, stylistic analysis, which has led him to several happy and important discoveries. His book will be universally welcomed as a

very valuable contribution towards a more thorough knowledge of the style of Pheidias."—*The Academy.*
"'Essays on the Art of Pheidias' form an extremely valuable and important piece of work. ... Taking it for the illustrations alone, it is an exceedingly fascinating book."—*Times.*

M. TULLI CICERONIS AD. M. BRUTUM ORATOR. A revised text edited with Introductory Essays and with critical and explanatory notes, by J. E. SANDYS, Litt.D., Fellow and Tutor of St John's College, and Public Orator. Demy 8vo. 16s.

M. TULLI CICERONIS DE FINIBUS BONORUM ET MALORUM LIBRI QUINQUE. The text revised and explained; With a Translation by JAMES S. REID, Litt. D., Fellow and Tutor of Gonville and Caius College. 3 Vols. [*In the Press.*
VOL. III. Containing the Translation. Demy 8vo. 8s.

M. T. CICERONIS DE OFFICIIS LIBRI TRES, with Marginal Analysis, an English Commentary, and copious Indices, by H. A. HOLDEN, LL.D., Examiner in Greek to the University of London. **Sixth Edition**, Revised and Enlarged. Crown 8vo. 9s.

"Dr Holden has issued an edition of what is perhaps the easiest and most popular of Cicero's philosophical works, the *de Officiis*, which, especially in the form which it has now

assumed after two most thorough revisions, leaves little or nothing to be desired in the fullness and accuracy of its treatment alike of the matter and the language."—*Academy.*

London: C. J. CLAY & SONS, Cambridge University Press Warehouse, Ave Maria Lane.

M. TVLLI CICERONIS PRO C RABIRIO [PERDVE-LIONIS REO] ORATIO AD QVIRITES With Notes Introduction and Appendices by W. E. HEITLAND, M.A., Fellow and Tutor of St John's College, Cambridge. Demy 8vo. 7s. 6d.

M. TULLII CICERONIS DE NATURA DEORVM Libri Tres, with Introduction and Commentary by JOSEP. MAYOR, M.A., late Professor of Moral Philosophy at King's College, London, together with a new collation of several of the En. sh MSS. by J. H. SWAINSON, M.A.

Vol. I. Demy 8vo. 10s. 6d. Vol. II. 12s. 6d. Vol. III. 10

"Such editions as that of which Prof. Mayor has given us the first instalment wi'l doubtless do much to remedy this undeserved neglect. It is one on which great pains and much learning have evidently been expended, and is in every way admirably suited to meet the needs of the student... The notes of the editor are all that could be expected from his well-known learning and scholarship." *Academy*.

"Der vorliegende zweite Band enthält N. D. II. und zeigt eben o wie der erste e n erheblichen F rtschritt g gen d l- her v r- handenen commentirten Au gaben M in dorf

jetzt, nach lem der grösste Theil ersehen, ist, sagen, dass niemand, welcher sich s- oder kritisch mit der Schrift De Nat. beschäftigt, die neue Ausgabe wird ign durfen."- P Schwencke in *JB. f. c.* vol. 3s. p. 93 foll.

"Nell' edizione sua è più compiuto, qualun que altra edizione anteriore, e in nuove, n n men l' apparato critico d che l' esim e l il c m ento del conten lit r. "- R l istait in *Nuo s Antolog* 1 1, 1 P 7l" 7 lt

P. VERGILI MARONIS OPERA cum Prolegomen et Commentario Critico edidit B. H. KENNEDY, S.T.P., Gra. Linguae Prof. Regius. Extra Fcap. 8vo. 5s.

See also Pitt Press Series, pp. 24—27.

MATHEMATICS, PHYSICAL SCIENCE, &c.

MATHEMATICAL AND PHYSICAL PAPERS. Sir W. THOMSON, LL.D., D C.L, F.R.S., Professor of Natural 1 losophy in the University of Glasgow. Collected from differ. Scientific Periodicals from May 1841, to the present time. V. Demy 8vo. 18s. Vol. II. 15s. [Volume III. *In the P*

"Wherever exa t scien c h. s f id a f l- lower Sir William Th ms n's name is k wn as a leader and a master. I :r a s;ace of 4 years each of his successive c ntributi ns to kn w- ledge in the domain of experime tal and mathematical physics has been recognized as m rking a stage in the progress of the subject. But, unhappily for the mere learner, he is no writer of text-books. His eager fertility overfl ws into the nearest available journal ... The paper in this volume deal largely with the subject of the dynamics of heat. They begin with two or three articles which were in part written at the

a. e f 17, l- f re tle author had com- re - lence . s an undergraduate in Camb r — *The Tim*

"We are c nvinced that nothing has re greater effect on the progress of the theori electricity an l magnetism during the la t years than the publicati n of Sir W Thom reprint of papers on electrostatics and ma i m, and we believe that the present volu d tine l in no le s degree to farther the v t cement of physical science."—*Glas Herald*.

MATHEMATICAL AND PHYSICAL PAPERS, by GEORGE GABRIEL STOKES, M.A., D.C.L., LL.D., F.R.S., Fellow Pembroke College, and Lucasian Professor of Mathematics in U University of Cambridge. Reprinted from the Original Journals a Transactions, with Additional Notes by the Author. Vol. I. De v 8vo. 15s. Vol. II. 15s. [Volume III. *In the Pr*.

"...The same spirit pervades the papers on pure mathematics which are included in the volume. They have a severe accuracy of style

which well befits the subtle nature of the ject , and inspire the c mpletest confiden their author."—*The Times*.

A HISTORY OF THE THEORY OF ELASTICIT AND OF THE STRENGTH OF MATERIALS, from Galilei the present time. VOL. I. Galilei to Saint-Venant, 1639-18: By the late I. TODHUNTER, D. Sc., F.R.S., edited and comple by KARL PEARSON, M.A. Demy 8vo. 25s.

London : C. J. CLAY & SONS, Cambridge University Press Warehou. Ave Maria Lane

M. TVLLI CICERONIS PRO C RABIRIO [PERDVEL-LIONIS REO] ORATIO AD QVIRITES With Notes Introduction and Appendices by W. E. HEITLAND, M.A., Fellow and Tutor of St John's College, Cambridge. Demy 8vo. 7s. 6d.

M. TULLII CICERONIS DE NATURA DEORUM Libri Tres, with Introduction and Commentary by JOSEPH B. MAYOR, M.A., late Professor of Moral Philosophy at King's College, London, together with a new collation of several of the English MSS. by J. H. SWAINSON, M.A.
Vol. I. Demy 8vo. 10s. 6d. Vol. II. 12s. 6d. Vol. III. 10s.

"Such editions as that of which Prof. Mayor has given us the first instalment will doubtless do much to remedy this undeserved neglect. It is one on which great pains and much learning have evidently been expended, and is in every way admirably suited to meet the needs of the student... The notes of the editor are all that could be expected from his well-known learning and scholarship."—*Academy*.

"Der vorliegende zweite Band enthält N. D. II. und zeigt ebenso wie der erste einen erheblichen Fortschritt gegen die bisher vorhandenen commentirten Ausgaben. Man darf jetzt, nachdem der grösste Theil erschienen ist, sagen, dass niemand, welcher sich sachlich oder kritisch mit der Schrift De Nat. Deor. beschäftigt, die neue Ausgabe wird ignoriren dürfen."—P. SCHWENCKE in *JB. f. cl. Alt.* vol. 35, p. 90 foll.

"Nell' edizione sua è più compiuto, che in qualunque altra edizione anteriore, e in parte nuove, non meno l' apparato critico dal testo che l' esame ed il commento del contenuto del libro."—R. BONGHI in *Nuova Antologia*, Oct. 1881, pp. 717—731.

P. VERGILI MARONIS OPERA cum Prolegomenis et Commentario Critico edidit B. H. KENNEDY, S.T.P., Graecae Linguae Prof. Regius. Extra Fcap. 8vo. 5s.

See also Pitt Press Series, pp. 24—27.

MATHEMATICS, PHYSICAL SCIENCE, &c.

MATHEMATICAL AND PHYSICAL PAPERS. By Sir W. THOMSON, LL.D., D.C.L., F.R.S., Professor of Natural Philosophy in the University of Glasgow. Collected from different Scientific Periodicals from May 1841, to the present time. Vol. I. Demy 8vo. 18s. Vol. II. 15s. [Volume III. *In the Press.*

"Wherever exact science has found a follower Sir William Thomson's name is known as a leader and a master. For a space of 40 years each of his successive contributions to knowledge in the domain of experimental and mathematical physics has been recognized as marking a stage in the progress of the subject. But, unhappily for the mere learner, he is no writer of text-books. His eager fertility overflows into the nearest available journal... The papers in this volume deal largely with the subject of the dynamics of heat. They begin with two or three articles which were in part written at the age of 17, before the author had commenced residence as an undergraduate in Cambridge."—*The Times*.

"We are convinced that nothing has had a greater effect on the progress of the theories of electricity and magnetism during the last ten years than the publication of Sir W. Thomson's reprint of papers on electrostatics and magnetism, and we believe that the present volume is destined in no less degree to further the advancement of physical science."—*Glasgow Herald*.

MATHEMATICAL AND PHYSICAL PAPERS, by GEORGE GABRIEL STOKES, M.A., D.C.L., LL.D., F.R.S., Fellow of Pembroke College, and Lucasian Professor of Mathematics in the University of Cambridge. Reprinted from the Original Journals and Transactions, with Additional Notes by the Author. Vol. I. Demy 8vo. 15s. Vol. II. 15s. [Volume III. *In the Press.*

"...The same spirit pervades the papers on pure mathematics which are included in the volume. They have a severe accuracy of style which well befits the subtle nature of the subjects, and inspires the completest confidence in their author."—*The Times*.

A HISTORY OF THE THEORY OF ELASTICITY AND OF THE STRENGTH OF MATERIALS, from Galilei to the present time. VOL. I. Galilei to Saint-Venant, 1639-1850. By the late I. TODHUNTER, D. Sc., F.R.S., edited and completed by KARL PEARSON, M.A. Demy 8vo. 25s.

---

*London : C. J. CLAY & SONS, Cambridge University Press Warehouse,
Ave Maria Lane.*

THE SCIENTIFIC PAPERS OF THE LATE PROF.
J. CLERK MAXWELL. Edited by W. D. NIVEN, M.A. In 2 vols. Royal 4to. [*In the Press.*

A TREATISE ON NATURAL PHILOSOPHY. By Sir W. THOMSON, LL.D., D.C.L., F.R.S., Professor of Natural Philosophy in the University of Glasgow, and P. G. TAIT, M.A., Professor of Natural Philosophy in the University of Edinburgh. Part I. Demy 8vo. 16s. Part II. Demy 8vo. 18s.

ELEMENTS OF NATURAL PHILOSOPHY. By Professors Sir W. THOMSON and P. G. TAIT. Demy 8vo. *Second Edition.* 9s.

AN ATTEMPT TO TEST THE THEORIES OF CAPILLARY ACTION by FRANCIS BASHFORTH, B.D., and J. C. ADAMS, M.A., F.R.S. Demy 4to. £1. 1s.

A TREATISE ON THE THEORY OF DETERMInants and their applications in Analysis and Geometry, by R. F. SCOTT, M.A., Fellow of St John's College. Demy 8vo. 12s.

HYDRODYNAMICS, a Treatise on the Mathematical Theory of the Motion of Fluids, by HORACE LAMB, M.A., formerly Fellow of Trinity College, Cambridge. Demy 8vo. 12s.

THE ANALYTICAL THEORY OF HEAT, by JOSEPH FOURIER. Translated, with Notes, by A. FREEMAN, M.A., Fellow of St John's College, Cambridge. Demy 8vo. 16s.

THE ELECTRICAL RESEARCHES OF THE Hon. H. CAVENDISH, F.R.S. Written between 1771 and 1781. Edited from the original MSS. in the possession of the Duke of Devonshire, K. G., by the late J. CLERK MAXWELL, F.R.S. Demy 8vo. 18s.

"Every department of editorial duty appears to have been most conscientiously performed; and it must have been no small satisfaction to Prof. Maxwell to see this goodly volume completed before his life's work was done."—*Athenæum.*

AN ELEMENTARY TREATISE ON QUATERNIONS. By P. G. TAIT, M.A., Professor of Natural Philosophy in the University of Edinburgh. *Second Edition.* Demy 8vo. 14s.

THE MATHEMATICAL WORKS OF ISAAC BARROW, D.D. Edited by W. WHEWELL, D.D. Demy 8vo. 7s. 6d.

COUNTERPOINT. A Practical Course of Study, by Professor Sir G. A. MACFARREN, M.A., Mus. Doc. New Edition, revised. Crown 4to. 7s. 6d.

A TREATISE ON THE GENERAL PRINCIPLES OF CHEMISTRY, by M. M. PATTISON MUIR, M.A., Fellow and Prælector in Chemistry of Gonville and Caius College. Demy 8vo. 15s.

"The value of the book as a digest of the historical developments of chemical thought is immense."—*Academy.*
"Theoretical Chemistry has moved so rapidly of late years that most of our ordinary text books have been left far behind. German students, to be sure, possess an excellent guide to the present state of the science in 'Die Modernen Theorien der Chemie' of Prof. Lothar Meyer; but in this country the student has had to content himself with such works as Dr Tilden's 'Introduction to Chemical Philosophy', an admirable book in its way, but rather slender. Mr Pattison Muir having aimed at a more comprehensive scheme, has produced a systematic treatise on the principles of chemical philosophy which stands far in advance of any kindred work in our language. It is a treatise that requires for its due comprehension a fair acquaintance with physical science, and it can hardly be placed with advantage in the hands of any one who does not possess an extended knowledge of descriptive chemistry. But the advanced student whose mind is well equipped with an array of chemical and physical facts can turn to Mr Muir's masterly volume for unfailing help in acquiring a knowledge of the principles of modern chemistry."—*Athenæum.*

NOTES ON QUALITATIVE ANALYSIS. Concise and Explanatory. By H. J. H. FENTON, M.A., F.I.C., Demonstrator of Chemistry in the University of Cambridge. Cr. 4to. *New Edition.* 6s.

London: C. J. CLAY & SONS, Cambridge University Press Warehouse. Ave Maria Lane.

PUBLICATIONS OF

LECTURES ON THE PHYSIOLOGY OF PLANTS, by S. H. VINES, M.A., D.Sc., Fellow of Christ's College. Demy 8vo. With Illustratious. 21s.

A SHORT HISTORY OF GREEK MATHEMATICS. By J. Gow, Litt.D., Fellow of Trinity College. Demy 8vo. 10s. 6d.

DIOPHANTOS OF ALEXANDRIA; a Study in the History of Greek Algebra. By T. L. HEATH, B.A., Fellow of Trinity College, Cambridge. Demy 8vo. 7s. 6d.

"This study in the history of Greek Algebra is an exceedingly valuable contribution to the history of mathematics."—*Academy*.
"Der Verfasser des uns vorliegenden Werkes hat die vorhandenen Schriften Diophants einem genauen Studium unterworfen. Er hat die sämtlichen erhaltenen Aufgaben nicht ihrem Wortlaut nach übersetzt, sondern in die algebraische Zeichensprache unserer Zeit übertragen, und diese moderne Darstellung hat er auf 86 S. anhangsweise zum Abdrucke gebracht, während eine fast doppelt so starke Abhandlung vorausgeht.... Wir haben zu zeigen gesucht, dass es in dem uns vorliegenden Buche nicht an neuen Gedanken fehlt. Wir hoffen in der nicht vollständigen Uebereinstimmung, in welcher wir uns mit dem Verf. befinden, das Lob nicht ersticht zu haben, welches in jener Anerkennung liegt."—M. Cantor, *Berl. Phil. Wochenschrift*.
"The most thorough account extant of Diophantus's place, work, and critics.... [The classification of Diophantus's methods of solution taken in conjunction with the invaluable abstract, presents the English reader with a capital picture of what Greek algebraists had really accomplished.]"—*Athenæum*.

THE FOSSILS AND PALÆONTOLOGICAL AFFINITIES OF THE NEOCOMIAN DEPOSITS OF UPWARE AND BRICKHILL with Plates, being the Sedgwick Prize Essay for the Year 1879. By W. KEEPING, M.A., F.G.S. Demy 8vo. 10s. 6d.

A CATALOGUE OF BOOKS AND PAPERS ON PROTOZOA, CŒLENTERATES, WORMS, and certain smaller groups of animals, published during the years 1861—1883, by D'ARCY W. THOMPSON, B.A., Professor of Biology in University College, Dundee. Demy 8vo. 12s. 6d.

ASTRONOMICAL OBSERVATIONS made at the Observatory of Cambridge by the late Rev. JAMES CHALLIS, M.A., F.R.S., F.R.A.S. For various Years, from 1846 to 1860.

ASTRONOMICAL OBSERVATIONS from 1861 to 1865. Vol. XXI. Royal 4to. 15s. From 1866 to 1869. Vol. XXII. Royal 4to. [*Nearly ready.*

A CATALOGUE OF THE COLLECTION OF BIRDS formed by the late H. E. STRICKLAND, now in the possession of the University of Cambridge. By O. SALVIN, M.A. Demy 8vo. £1. 1s.

A CATALOGUE OF AUSTRALIAN FOSSILS (including Tasmania and the Island of Timor), Stratigraphically and Zoologically arranged, by R. ETHERIDGE, Jun., F.G.S., Acting Palæontologist, H.M. Geol. Survey of Scotland. Demy 8vo. 10s. 6d.

ILLUSTRATIONS OF COMPARATIVE ANATOMY, VERTEBRATE AND INVERTEBRATE, for the Use of Students in the Museum of Zoology and Comparative Anatomy. Second Edition. Demy 8vo. 2s. 6d.

A SYNOPSIS OF THE CLASSIFICATION OF THE BRITISH PALÆOZOIC ROCKS, by the Rev. ADAM SEDGWICK, M.A., F.R.S., and FREDERICK M^cCOY, F.G.S. One vol., Royal 4to. Plates, £1. 1s.

A CATALOGUE OF THE COLLECTION OF CAMBRIAN AND SILURIAN FOSSILS contained in the Geological Museum of the University of Cambridge, by J. W. SALTER, F.G.S. With a Portrait of PROFESSOR SEDGWICK. Royal 4to. 7s. 6d.

CATALOGUE OF OSTEOLOGICAL SPECIMENS contained in the Anatomical Museum of the University of Cambridge. Demy 8vo. 2s. 6d.

London: C. J. CLAY & SONS, Cambridge University Press Warehouse, Ave Maria Lane.

LAW.

A SELECTION OF CASES ON THE ENGLISH LAW OF CONTRACT. By GERARD BROWN FINCH, M.A., of Lincoln's Inn, Barrister at Law; Law Lecturer and late Fellow of Queens' College, Cambridge. Royal 8vo. 28s.

"An invaluable guide towards the best method of legal study."—*Law Quarterly Review.*

THE INFLUENCE OF THE ROMAN LAW ON THE LAW OF ENGLAND. Being the Yorke Prize Essay for 1884. By T. E. SCRUTTON, M.A. Demy 8vo. 10s. 6d.

"Legal work of just the kind that a learned University should promote by its prizes."—*Law Quarterly Review.*

LAND IN FETTERS. Being the Yorke Prize Essay for 1885. By T. E. SCRUTTON, M.A. Demy 8vo.

AN ANALYSIS OF CRIMINAL LIABILITY. By E. C. CLARK, LL.D., Regius Professor of Civil Law in the University of Cambridge, also of Lincoln's Inn, Barrister-at-Law. Crown 8vo. 7s. 6d.

"Prof. Clark's little book is the substance of lectures delivered by him upon those portions of Austin's work on jurisprudence which deal with the "operation of sanctions"... Students of jurisprudence will find much to interest and instruct them in the work of Prof. Clark."—*Athenæum.*

PRACTICAL JURISPRUDENCE, a Comment on AUSTIN. By E. C. CLARK, LL.D. Regius Professor of Civil Law. Crown 8vo. 9s.

"Damit schliesst dieses inhaltreiche und nach allen Seiten anregende Buch über Practical Jurisprudence."—König. *Centralblatt für Rechtswissenschaft.*

A SELECTION OF THE STATE TRIALS. By J. W. WILLIS-BUND, M.A., LL.B., Barrister-at-Law, Professor of Constitutional Law and History, University College, London. Crown 8vo. Vols. I. and II. In 3 parts. **Now reduced to 30s.** (*originally published at 46s.*)

"This work is a very useful contribution to that important branch of the constitutional history of England which is concerned with the growth and development of the law of treason, as it may be gathered from trials before the ordinary courts. The author has very wisely distinguished these cases from those of impeachment for treason before Parliament, which he proposes to treat in a future volume under the general head 'Proceedings in Parliament.'"—*The Academy.*

"This is a work of such obvious utility that the only wonder is that no one should have undertaken it before... In many respects therefore, although the trials are more or less abridged, this is for the ordinary student's purpose not only a more handy, but a more useful work than Howell's."—*Saturday Review.*

"But, although the book is most interesting to the historian of constitutional law, it is also not without considerable value to those who seek information with regard to procedure and the growth of the law of evidence. We should add that Mr Willis-Bund has given short prefaces and appendices to the trials, so as to form a connected narrative of the events in history to which they relate. We can thoroughly recommend the book."—*Law Times.*

"To a large class of readers Mr Willis-Bund's compilation will thus be of great assistance, for he presents in a convenient form a judicious selection of the principal statutes and the leading cases bearing on the crime of treason ... For all classes of readers these volumes possess an indirect interest, arising from the nature of the cases themselves, from the men who were actors in them, and from the numerous points of social life which are incidentally illustrated in the course of the trials."—*Athenæum.*

THE FRAGMENTS OF THE PERPETUAL EDICT OF SALVIUS JULIANUS, collected, arranged, and annotated by BRYAN WALKER, M.A., LL.D., Law Lecturer of St John's College, and late Fellow of Corpus Christi College, Cambridge. Crown 8vo. 6s.

"In the present book we have the fruits of the same kind of thorough and well-ordered study which was brought to bear upon the notes to the Commentaries and the Institutes... Hitherto the Edict has been almost inaccessible to the ordinary English student, and such a student will be interested as well as perhaps surprised to find how abundantly the extant fragments illustrate and clear up points which have attracted his attention in the Commentaries, or the Institutes, or the Digest."—*Law Times.*

London: C. J. CLAY & SONS, Cambridge University Press Warehouse,
Ave Maria Lane.

**AN INTRODUCTION TO THE STUDY OF JUS-
TINIAN'S DIGEST.** Containing an account of its composition
and of the Jurists used or referred to therein. By HENRY JOHN
ROBY, M.A., formerly Prof. of Jurisprudence, University College,
London. Demy 8vo. 9s.

JUSTINIAN'S DIGEST. Lib. VII., Tit. I. De Usufructu
with a Legal and Philological Commentary. By H. J. ROBY. Demy
8vo. 9s.

Or the Two Parts complete in One Volume. Demy 8vo. 18s.

"Not an obscurity, philological, historical, or legal, has been left unsifted. More informing aid still has been supplied to the student of the Digest at large by a preliminary account, covering nearly 300 pages, of the mode of composition of the Digest, and of the jurists whose decisions and arguments constitute its substance. Nowhere else can a clearer view be obtained of the personal succession by which the tradition of Roman legal science was sustained and developed. Roman law, almost more than Roman legions, was the backbone of the Roman commonwealth. Mr Roby, by his careful sketch of the sages of Roman law, from Sextus Papirius, under Tarquin the Proud, to the Byzantine Bar, has contributed to render the tenacity and durability of the most enduring polity the world has ever experienced somewhat more intelligible."—*The Times.*

**THE COMMENTARIES OF GAIUS AND RULES OF
ULPIAN.** With a Translation and Notes, by J. T. ABDY, LL.D.,
Judge of County Courts, late Regius Professor of Laws in the
University of Cambridge, and BRYAN WALKER, M.A., LL.D., Law
Lecturer of St John's College, Cambridge, formerly Law Student of
Trinity Hall and Chancellor's Medallist for Legal Studies. New
Edition by BRYAN WALKER. Crown 8vo. 16s.

"As scholars and as editors Messrs Abdy and Walker have done their work well... For one thing the editors deserve special commendation. They have presented Gaius to the reader with few notes and those merely by way of reference or necessary explanation. Thus the Roman jurist is allowed to speak for himself, and the reader feels that he is really studying Roman law in the original, and not a fanciful representation of it."—*Athenæum.*

THE INSTITUTES OF JUSTINIAN, translated with
Notes by J. T. ABDY, LL.D., and BRYAN WALKER, M.A., LL.D.
Crown 8vo. 16s.

"We welcome here a valuable contribution to the study of jurisprudence. The text of the *Institutes* is occasionally perplexing, even to practised scholars, whose knowledge of classical models does not always avail them in dealing with the technicalities of legal phraseology. Nor can the ordinary dictionaries be expected to furnish all the help that is wanted. This translation will then be of great use. To the ordinary student, whose attention is distracted from the subject-matter by the difficulty of struggling through the language in which it is contained, it will be almost indispensable."—*Spectator.*
"The notes are learned and carefully compiled, and this edition will be found useful to students."—*Law Times.*

SELECTED TITLES FROM THE DIGEST, annotated
by B. WALKER, M.A., LL.D. Part I. Mandati vel Contra. Digest
XVII. 1. Crown 8vo. 5s.

"This small volume is published as an experiment. The author proposes to publish an annotated edition and translation of several books of the Digest if this one is received with favour. We are pleased to be able to say that Mr Walker deserves credit for the way in which he has performed the task undertaken. The translation, as might be expected, is scholarly."—*Law Times.*

—— Part II. De Adquirendo rerum dominio and De Adquirenda vel
amittenda possessione. Digest XLI. 1 and 11. Crown 8vo. 6s.

—— Part III. De Condictionibus. Digest XII. 1 and 4—7 and Digest
XIII. 1—3. Crown 8vo. 6s.

GROTIUS DE JURE BELLI ET PACIS, with the Notes
of Barbeyrac and others; accompanied by an abridged Translation
of the Text, by W. WHEWELL, D.D. late Master of Trinity College.
3 Vols. Demy 8vo. 12s. The translation separate, 6s.

---

*London: C. J. CLAY & SONS, Cambridge University Press Warehouse,
Ave Maria Lane.*

HISTORY.

LIFE AND TIMES OF STEIN, OR GERMANY AND PRUSSIA IN THE NAPOLEONIC AGE, by J. R. SEELEY, M.A., Regius Professor of Modern History in the University of Cambridge, with Portraits and Maps. 3 Vols. Demy 8vo. 30s.

"DR BUSCH's volume has made people think and talk even more than usual of Prince Bismarck, and Professor Seeley's very learned work on Stein will turn attention to an earlier and an almost equally eminent German statesman. It has been the good fortune of Prince Bismarck to help to raise Prussia to a position which she had never before attained, and to complete the work of German unification. The frustrated labours of Stein in the same field were also very great, and well worthy to be taken into account. He was one, perhaps the chief, of the illustrious group of strangers who came to the rescue of Prussia in her darkest hour, about the time of the inglorious Peace of Tilsit, and who laboured to put life and order into her dispirited army, her impoverished finances, and her inefficient Civil Service. Stein strove, too, —no man more,—for the cause of unification when it seemed almost folly to hope for success. Englishmen will feel very pardonable pride at seeing one of their countrymen undertake to write the history of a period from the investigation of which even laborious Germans are apt to shrink."—*Times*.

"In a notice of this kind scant justice can be done to a work like the one before us; no short *résumé* can give even the most meagre notion of the contents of these volumes, which contain no page that is superfluous, and none that is uninteresting.... To understand the Germany of to-day one must study the Germany of many yesterdays, and now that study has been made easy by this work, to which no one can hesitate to assign a very high place among those recent histories which have aimed at original research."—*Athenæum*.

"We congratulate Cambridge and her Professor of History on the appearance of such a noteworthy production. And we may add that it is something upon which we may congratulate England that on the especial field of the Germans, history, on the history of their own country, by the use of their own literary weapons, an Englishman has produced a history of Germany in the Napoleonic age far superior to any that exists in German."—*Examiner*.

THE DESPATCHES OF EARL GOWER, English Ambassador at the court of Versailles from June 1790 to August 1792, to which are added the Despatches of Mr Lindsay and Mr Munro, and the Diary of Lord Palmerston in France during July and August 1791. Edited by OSCAR BROWNING, M.A., Fellow of King's College, Cambridge. Demy 8vo. 15s.

THE GROWTH OF ENGLISH INDUSTRY AND COMMERCE. By W. CUNNINGHAM, B.D., late Deputy to the Knightbridge Professor in the University of Cambridge. With Maps and Charts. Crown 8vo. 12s.

"Mr Cunningham is not likely to disappoint any readers except such as begin by mistaking the character of his book. He does not promise, and does not give, an account of the dimensions to which English industry and commerce have grown. It is with the process of growth that he is concerned; and this process he traces with the philosophical insight which distinguishes between what is important and what is trivial."—*Guardian*.

CHRONOLOGICAL TABLES OF GREEK HISTORY. Accompanied by a short narrative of events, with references to the sources of information and extracts from the ancient authorities, by CARL PETER. Translated from the German by G. CHAWNER, M.A., Fellow of King's College, Cambridge. Demy 4to. 10s.

CHRONOLOGICAL TABLES OF ROMAN HISTORY. By the same. [*Preparing*.

KINSHIP AND MARRIAGE IN EARLY ARABIA, by W. ROBERTSON SMITH, M.A., LL.D., Lord Almoner's Professor of Arabic in the University of Cambridge. Crown 8vo. 7s. 6d.

"It would be superfluous to praise a book so learned and masterly as Professor Robertson Smith's; it is enough to say that no student of early history can afford to be without *Kinship in Early Arabia*."—*Nature*.

"It is clearly and vividly written, full of curious and picturesque material, and incidentally throws light, not merely on the social history of Arabia, but on the earlier passages of Old Testament history.... We must be grateful to him for so valuable a contribution to the early history of social organisation."—*Scotsman*.

London: C. J. CLAY & SONS, Cambridge University Press Warehouse, Ave Maria Lane.

TRAVELS IN NORTHERN ARABIA IN 1876 AND 1877. By CHARLES M. DOUGHTY, of Gonville and Caius College. With Illustrations. Demy 8vo. [*In the Press.*

HISTORY OF NEPĀL, translated by MUNSHĪ SHEW SHUNKER SINGH and PANDIT SHRĪ GUNĀNAND; edited with an Introductory Sketch of the Country and People by Dr D. WRIGHT, late Residency Surgeon at Kāthmāndū, and with facsimiles of native drawings, and portraits of Sir JUNG BAHĀDUR, the KING OF NEPĀL, &c. Super-royal 8vo. 10s. 6d.

"The Cambridge University Press have done well in publishing this work. Such translations are valuable not only to the historian but also to the ethnologist;... Dr Wright's

Introduction is based on personal inquiry and observation, is written intelligently and candidly, and adds much to the value of the volume"—*Nature.*

A JOURNEY OF LITERARY AND **ARCHÆOLOGICAL RESEARCH IN NEPAL AND NORTHERN INDIA**, during the Winter of 1884-5. By CECIL BENDALL, M.A., Fellow of Gonville and Caius College, Cambridge; Professor of Sanskrit in University College, London. Demy 8vo. 10s.

THE UNIVERSITY OF CAMBRIDGE FROM THE EARLIEST TIMES TO THE ROYAL INJUNCTIONS OF 1535, by J. B. MULLINGER, M.A., Lecturer on History and Librarian to St John's College. Part I. Demy 8vo. (734 pp.), 12s.

Part II. From the Royal Injunctions of 1535 to the Accession of Charles the First. Demy 8vo. 18s.

"That Mr Mullinger's work should admit of being regarded as a continuous narrative, in which character it has no predecessors worth mentioning, is one of the many advantages it possesses over annalistic compilations, even so valuable as Cooper's, as well as over *Athenae.*"—Prof. A. W. Ward in the *Academy.*

"Mr Mullinger's narrative omits nothing which is required by the fullest interpretation of his subject. He shews in the statutes of the Colleges, the internal organization of the University, its connection with national problems, its studies, its social life, and the activity of its leading members. All this he combines in a form which is eminently readable."—PROF. CREIGHTON in *Cont. Review.*

"Mr Mullinger has succeeded perfectly in presenting the earnest and thoughtful student with a thorough and trustworthy history."—*Guardian.*

"The entire work is a model of accurate and industrious scholarship. The same qualities that distinguished the earlier volume are again visible, and the whole is still conspicuous for minuteness and fidelity of workmanship and breadth and toleration of view."—*Notes and Queries.*

"Mr Mullinger displays an admirable thoroughness in his work. Nothing could be more exhaustive and conscientious than his method: and his style...is picturesque and elevated."—*Times.*

HISTORY OF THE COLLEGE OF ST JOHN THE EVANGELIST, by THOMAS BAKER, B.D., Ejected Fellow. Edited by JOHN E. B. MAYOR, M.A. Two Vols. Demy 8vo. 24s.

"To antiquaries the book will be a source of almost inexhaustible amusement, by historians it will be found a work of considerable service on questions respecting our social progress in past times; and the care and thoroughness with which Mr Mayor has discharged his editorial functions are creditable to his learning and industry."—*Athenæum.*

"The work displays very wide reading, and it will be of great use to members of the college and of the university, and, perhaps, of still greater use to students of English history, ecclesiastical, political, social, literary and academical, who have hitherto had to be content with 'Dyer.'"—*Academy.*

SCHOLAE ACADEMICAE: some Account of the Studies at the English Universities in the Eighteenth Century. By CHRISTOPHER WORDSWORTH, M.A., Fellow of Peterhouse. Demy 8vo. 10s. 6d.

"Mr Wordsworth has collected a great quantity of minute and curious information about the working of Cambridge institutions in the last century, with an occasional comparison of the corresponding state of things at Oxford. ... To a great extent it is purely a book of reference, and as such it will be of permanent value for the historical knowledge of English

education and learning."—*Saturday Review.*

"Of the whole volume it may be said that it is a genuine service rendered to the study of University history, and that the habits of thought of any writer educated at either seat of learning in the last century will, in many cases, be far better understood after a consideration of the materials here collected."—*Academy.*

London: C. J. CLAY & SONS, Cambridge University Press Warehouse, Ave Maria Lane.

THE ARCHITECTURAL HISTORY OF THE UNI-
VERSITY OF CAMBRIDGE AND OF THE COLLEGES OF
CAMBRIDGE AND ETON, by the late ROBERT WILLIS, M.A.
F.R.S., Jacksonian Professor in the University of Cambridge. Edited
with large Additions and a Continuation to the present time by
JOHN WILLIS CLARK, M.A., formerly Fellow of Trinity College,
Cambridge. Four Vols. Super Royal 8vo. £6. 6s.

Also a limited Edition of the same, consisting of 120 numbered
Copies only, large paper Quarto; the woodcuts and steel engravings
mounted on India paper; of which 100 copies are now offered for
sale, at Twenty-five Guineas net each set.

MISCELLANEOUS.

A CATALOGUE OF ANCIENT MARBLES IN GREAT
BRITAIN, by Prof. ADOLF MICHAELIS. Translated by C. A. M.
FENNELL, Litt. D., late Fellow of Jesus College. Royal 8vo. Rox-
burgh (Morocco back), £2. 2s.

"The object of the present work of Michaelis is to describe and make known the vast
treasures of ancient sculpture now accumulated
in the galleries of Great Britain, the extent and
value of which are scarcely appreciated, and
chiefly so because there has hitherto been little
accessible information about them. To the
loving labours of a learned German the owners
of art treasures in England are for the second
time indebted for a full description of their rich
possessions. Waagen gave to the private collections of pictures the advantage of his in-
spection and cultivated acquaintance with art,
and now Michaelis performs the same office
for the still less known private hoards of an-
tique sculptures for which our country is so

remarkable. The book is beautifully executed,
and with its few handsome plates, and excellent indexes, does much credit to the Cambridge Press. It has not been printed in
German, but appears for the first time in the
English translation. All lovers of true art and
of good work should be grateful to the Syndics
of the University Press for the liberal facilities
afforded by them towards the production of
this important volume by Professor Michaelis."
—*Saturday Review.*

"Professor Michaelis has achieved so high
a fame as an authority in classical archæology
that it seems unnecessary to say how good
a book this is."—*The Antiquary.*

RHODES IN ANCIENT TIMES. By CECIL TORR, M.A.
With six plates. Demy 8vo. 10s. 6d.

THE WOODCUTTERS OF THE NETHERLANDS
during the last quarter of the Fifteenth Century. In three parts.
I. History of the Woodcutters. II. Catalogue of their Woodcuts.
III. List of the Books containing Woodcuts. By WILLIAM MARTIN
CONWAY. Demy 8vo. 10s. 6d.

A GRAMMAR OF THE IRISH LANGUAGE. By Prof.
WINDISCH. Translated by Dr NORMAN MOORE. Crown 8vo. 7s. 6d.

LECTURES ON TEACHING, delivered in the University
of Cambridge in the Lent Term, 1880. By J. G. FITCH, M.A., LL.D.
Her Majesty's Inspector of Training Colleges. Cr. 8vo. New Edit. 5s.

"As principal of a training college and as a
Government inspector of schools, Mr Fitch has
got at his fingers' ends the working of primary
education, while as assistant commissioner to
the late Endowed Schools Commission he has
seen something of the machinery of our higher
schools... Mr Fitch's book covers so wide a
field and touches on so many burning questions
that we must be content to recommend it as
the best existing *vade mecum* for the teacher."
—*Pall Mall Gazette.*

"Therefore, without reviewing the book for
the second time, we are glad to avail ourselves
of the opportunity of calling attention to the
re-issue of the volume in the five-shilling form,
bringing it within the reach of the rank and
file of the profession. We cannot let the occasion pass without making special reference to
the excellent section on 'punishments' in the
lecture on 'Discipline.'"—*School Board Chronicle.*

For other books on Education, see Pitt Press Series, pp. 30, 31.

*London: C. J. CLAY & SONS, Cambridge University Press Warehouse,
Ave Maria Lane.*

FROM SHAKESPEARE TO POPE: an Inquiry into the causes and phenomena of the rise of Classical Poetry in England. By EDMUND GOSSE, M.A., Clark Lecturer in English Literature at Trinity College, Cambridge. Crown 8vo. 6s.

THE LITERATURE OF THE FRENCH RENAISSANCE. An Introductory Essay. By A. A. TILLEY, M.A., Fellow and Tutor of King's College, Cambridge. Crown 8vo. 6s.

STUDIES IN THE LITERARY RELATIONS OF ENGLAND WITH GERMANY IN THE SIXTEENTH CENTURY. By C. H. HERFORD, M.A. Crown 8vo. 9s.

CATALOGUE OF THE HEBREW MANUSCRIPTS preserved in the University Library, Cambridge. By Dr S. M. SCHILLER-SZINESSY. Volume I. containing Section 1. *The Holy Scriptures;* Section II. *Commentaries on the Bible.* Demy 8vo. 9s. Volume II. *In the Press.*

A CATALOGUE OF THE MANUSCRIPTS preserved in the Library of the University of Cambridge. Demy 8vo. 5 Vols. 10s. each. INDEX TO THE CATALOGUE. Demy 8vo. 10s.

A CATALOGUE OF ADVERSARIA and printed books containing MS. notes, preserved in the Library of the University of Cambridge. 3s. 6d.

THE ILLUMINATED MANUSCRIPTS IN THE LIBRARY OF THE FITZWILLIAM MUSEUM, Catalogued with Descriptions, and an Introduction, by W. G. SEARLE, M.A., late Fellow of Queens' College, Cambridge Demy 8vo. 7s. 6d

A CHRONOLOGICAL LIST OF THE GRACES, Documents, and other Papers in the University Registry which concern the University Library. Demy 8vo. 2s. 6d.

CATALOGUS BIBLIOTHECÆ BURCKHARDTIANÆ. Demy 4to. 5s.

GRADUATI CANTABRIGIENSES: SIVE CATALOGUS exhibens nomina eorum quos ab Anno Academico Admissionum MDCCC usque ad octavum diem Octobris MDCCCLXXXIV gradu quocunque ornavit Academia Cantabrigiensis, e libris subscriptionum desumptus. Cura HENRICI RICHARDS LUARD S. T. P. Coll. SS. Trin. Socii atque Academiæ Registrarii. Demy 8vo. 12s. 6d.

STATUTES OF THE UNIVERSITY OF CAMBRIDGE and for the Colleges therein, made published and approved (1878—1882) under the Universities of Oxford and Cambridge Act, 1877. With an Appendix. Demy 8vo. 16s.

STATUTES OF THE UNIVERSITY OF CAMBRIDGE. With some Acts of Parliament relating to the University. Demy 8vo. 3s. 6d.

ORDINANCES OF THE UNIVERSITY OF CAMBRIDGE. Demy 8vo., cloth. 7s. 6d.

TRUSTS, STATUTES AND DIRECTIONS affecting (1) The Professorships of the University. (2) The Scholarships and Prizes. (3) Other Gifts and Endowments. Demy 8vo. 5s.

COMPENDIUM OF UNIVERSITY REGULATIONS, for the use of persons in Statu Pupillari. Demy 8vo. 6d.

London: C. J. CLAY & SONS, Cambridge University Press Warehouse, Ave Maria Lane.

The Cambridge Bible for Schools and Colleges.

GENERAL EDITOR: THE VERY REVEREND J. J. S. PEROWNE, D.D., DEAN OF PETERBOROUGH.

"It is difficult to commend too highly this excellent series, the volumes of which are now becoming numerous."—*Guardian.*

"The modesty of the general title of this series has, we believe, led many to misunderstand its character and underrate its value. The books are well suited for study in the upper forms of our best schools, but not the less are they adapted to the wants of all Bible students who are not specialists. We doubt, indeed, whether any of the numerous popular commentaries recently issued in this country will be found more serviceable for general use."—*Academy.*

"Of great value. The whole series of comments for schools is highly esteemed by students capable of forming a judgment. The books are scholarly without being pretentious: information is so given as to be easily understood."—*Sword and Trowel.*

The Very Reverend J. J. S. PEROWNE, D.D., Dean of Peterborough, has undertaken the general editorial supervision of the work, assisted by a staff of eminent coadjutors. Some of the books have been already edited or undertaken by the following gentlemen:

Rev. A. CARR, M.A., *late Assistant Master at Wellington College.*
Rev. T. K. CHEYNE, M.A., D.D., *late Fellow of Balliol College, Oxford.*
Rev. S. COX, *Nottingham.*
Rev. A. B. DAVIDSON, D.D., *Professor of Hebrew, Edinburgh.*
The Ven. F. W. FARRAR, D.D., *Archdeacon of Westminster.*
Rev. C. D. GINSBURG, LL.D.
Rev. A. E. HUMPHREYS, M.A., *late Fellow of Trinity College, Cambridge.*
Rev. A. F. KIRKPATRICK, M.A., *Fellow of Trinity College, Regius Professor of Hebrew.*
Rev. J. J. LIAS, M.A., *late Professor at St David's College, Lampeter.*
Rev. J. R. LUMBY, D.D., *Norrisian Professor of Divinity.*
Rev. G. F. MACLEAR, D.D., *Warden of St Augustine's College, Canterbury.*
Rev. H. C. G. MOULE, M.A., *late Fellow of Trinity College, Principal of Ridley Hall, Cambridge.*
Rev. W. F. MOULTON, D.D., *Head Master of the Leys School, Cambridge.*
Rev. E. H. PEROWNE, D.D., *Master of Corpus Christi College, Cambridge.*
The Ven. T. T. PEROWNE, M.A., *Archdeacon of Norwich.*
Rev. A. PLUMMER, M.A., D.D., *Master of University College, Durham.*
The Very Rev. E. H. PLUMPTRE, D.D., *Dean of Wells.*
Rev. W. SIMCOX, M.A., *Rector of Weyhill, Hants.*
W. ROBERTSON SMITH, M.A., *Lord Almoner's Professor of Arabic.*
Rev. H. D. M. SPENCE, M.A., *Hon. Canon of Gloucester Cathedral.*
Rev. A. W. STREANE, M.A., *Fellow of Corpus Christi College, Cambridge.*

London: C. J. CLAY & SONS, Cambridge University Press Warehouse, Ave Maria Lane.

THE CAMBRIDGE BIBLE FOR SCHOOLS & COLLEGES.
Continued.
Now Ready. Cloth, Extra Fcap. 8vo.

THE BOOK OF JOSHUA. By the Rev. G. F. MACLEAR, D.D. With 2 Maps. 2s. 6d.

THE BOOK OF JUDGES. By the Rev. J. J. LIAS, M.A. With Map. 3s. 6d.

THE FIRST BOOK OF SAMUEL. By the Rev. Professor KIRKPATRICK, M.A. With Map. 3s. 6d.

THE SECOND BOOK OF SAMUEL. By the Rev. Professor KIRKPATRICK, M.A. With 2 Maps. 3s. 6d.

THE BOOK OF JOB. By the Rev. A. B. DAVIDSON, D.D. 5s.

THE BOOK OF ECCLESIASTES. By the Very Rev. E. H. PLUMPTRE, D.D., Dean of Wells. 5s.

THE BOOK OF JEREMIAH. By the Rev. A. W. STREANE, M.A. With Map. 4s. 6d.

THE BOOK OF HOSEA. By Rev. T. K. CHEYNE, M.A., D.D. 3s.

THE BOOKS OF OBADIAH AND JONAH. By Archdeacon PEROWNE. 2s. 6d.

THE BOOK OF MICAH. By Rev. T. K. CHEYNE, M.A., D.D. 1s. 6d.

THE BOOKS OF HAGGAI AND ZECHARIAH. By Archdeacon PEROWNE. 3s.

THE GOSPEL ACCORDING TO ST MATTHEW. By the Rev. A. CARR, M.A. With 2 Maps. 2s. 6d.

THE GOSPEL ACCORDING TO ST MARK. By the Rev. G. F. MACLEAR, D.D. With 4 Maps. 2s. 6d.

THE GOSPEL ACCORDING TO ST LUKE. By Archdeacon F. W. FARRAR. With 4 Maps. 4s. 6d.

THE GOSPEL ACCORDING TO ST JOHN. By the Rev. A. PLUMMER, M.A., D.D. With 4 Maps. 4s. 6d.

THE ACTS OF THE APOSTLES. By the Rev. Professor LUMBY, D.D. With 4 Maps. 4s. 6d.

THE EPISTLE TO THE ROMANS. By the Rev. H. C. G. MOULE, M.A. 3s. 6d.

THE FIRST EPISTLE TO THE CORINTHIANS. By the Rev. J. J. LIAS, M.A. With a Map and Plan. 2s.

THE SECOND EPISTLE TO THE CORINTHIANS. By the Rev. J. J. LIAS, M.A. 2s.

THE EPISTLE TO THE EPHESIANS. By the Rev. H. C. G. MOULE, M.A. 2s. 6d.

THE EPISTLE TO THE HEBREWS. By Arch. FARRAR. 3s. 6d.

THE GENERAL EPISTLE OF ST JAMES. By the Very Rev. E. H. PLUMPTRE, D.D., Dean of Wells. 1s. 6d.

THE EPISTLES OF ST PETER AND ST JUDE. By the same Editor. 2s. 6d.

THE EPISTLES OF ST JOHN. By the Rev. A. PLUMMER, M.A., D.D. 3s. 6d.

London: C. J. CLAY & SONS, Cambridge University Press Warehouse, Ave Maria Lane.

THE CAMBRIDGE BIBLE FOR SCHOOLS & COLLEGES.
Continued.

Preparing.

THE BOOK OF GENESIS. By the Very Rev. the DEAN OF PETERBOROUGH.
THE BOOKS OF EXODUS, NUMBERS AND DEUTERONOMY. By the Rev. C. D. GINSBURG, LL.D.
THE FIRST AND SECOND BOOKS OF KINGS. By the Rev. Prof. LUMBY, D.D.
THE BOOK OF PSALMS. By the Rev. Prof. KIRKPATRICK, M.A.
THE BOOK OF ISAIAH. By Prof. W. ROBERTSON SMITH, M.A.
THE BOOK OF EZEKIEL. By the Rev. A. B. DAVIDSON, D.D.
THE EPISTLE TO THE GALATIANS. By the Rev. E. H. PEROWNE, D.D.
THE EPISTLES TO THE PHILIPPIANS, COLOSSIANS AND PHILEMON. By the Rev. H. C. G. MOULE, M.A.
THE BOOK OF REVELATION. By the Rev. W. SIMCOX, M.A.

THE CAMBRIDGE GREEK TESTAMENT
FOR SCHOOLS AND COLLEGES,
with a Revised Text, based on the most recent critical authorities, and English Notes, prepared under the direction of the General Editor,
THE VERY REVEREND J. J. S. PEROWNE, D.D.

Now Ready.

THE GOSPEL ACCORDING TO ST MATTHEW. By the Rev. A. CARR, M.A. With 4 Maps. 4s. 6d.
"Copious illustrations, gathered from a great variety of sources, make his notes a very valuable aid to the student. They are indeed remarkably interesting, while all explanations on meanings, applications, and the like are distinguished by their lucidity and good sense."—*Pall Mall Gazette.*

THE GOSPEL ACCORDING TO ST MARK. By the Rev. G. F. MACLEAR, D.D. With 3 Maps. 4s. 6d.
"The Cambridge Greek Testament, of which Dr Maclear's edition of the Gospel according to St Mark is a volume, certainly supplies a want. Without pretending to compete with the leading commentaries, or to embody very much original research, it forms a most satisfactory introduction to the study of the New Testament in the original... Dr Maclear's introduction contains all that is known of St Mark's life, with references to passages in the New Testament in which he is mentioned; an account of the circumstances in which the Gospel was composed, with an estimate of the influence of St Peter's teaching upon St Mark; an excellent sketch of the special characteristics of this Gospel; an analysis, and a chapter on the text of the New Testament generally... The work is completed by three good maps."—*Saturday Review.*

THE GOSPEL ACCORDING TO ST LUKE. By Archdeacon FARRAR. With 4 Maps. 6s.

THE GOSPEL ACCORDING TO ST JOHN. By the Rev. A. PLUMMER, M.A., D.D. With 4 Maps. 6s.
"A valuable addition has also been made to 'The Cambridge Greek Testament for Schools, Dr Plummer's notes on 'the Gospel according to St John' are scholarly, concise, and instructive, and embody the results of much thought and wide reading."—*Expositor.*

THE ACTS OF THE APOSTLES. By the Rev. Prof. LUMBY, D.D., with 4 Maps. 6s.

THE FIRST EPISTLE TO THE CORINTHIANS. By the Rev. J. J. LIAS, M.A. 3s.

THE EPISTLE TO THE HEBREWS. By Archdeacon FARRAR.
[*In the Press.*

THE EPISTLES OF ST JOHN. By the Rev. A. PLUMMER, M.A., D.D. 4s.

London: C. J. CLAY & SONS, Cambridge University Press Warehouse, Ave Maria Lane.

THE PITT PRESS SERIES.

I. GREEK.

SOPHOCLES.—OEDIPUS TYRANNUS. School Edition, with Introduction and Commentary, by R. C. JEBB, Litt. D., LL.D., Professor of Greek in the University of Glasgow. 4s. 6d.

XENOPHON.—ANABASIS, BOOKS I. III. IV. and V. With a Map and English Notes by ALFRED PRETOR, M.A., Fellow of St Catharine's College, Cambridge. 2s. each.

"In Mr Pretor's edition of the Anabasis the text of Kühner has been followed in the main, while the exhaustive and admirable notes of the great German editor have been largely utilised. These notes deal with the minutest as well as the most important difficulties in construction, and all questions of history, antiquity, and geography are briefly but very effectually elucidated."—*The Examiner.*

"We welcome this addition to the other books of the *Anabasis* so ably edited by Mr Pretor. Although originally intended for the use of candidates at the university local examinations, yet this edition will be found adapted not only to meet the wants of the junior student, but even advanced scholars will find much in this work that will repay its perusal."—*The Schoolmaster.*

"Mr Pretor's 'Anabasis of Xenophon, Book IV.' displays a union of accurate Cambridge scholarship, with experience of what is required by learners gained in examining middle-class schools. The text is large and clearly printed, and the notes explain all difficulties. . . . Mr Pretor's notes seem to be all that could be wished as regards grammar, geography, and other matters."—*The Academy.*

BOOKS II. VI. and VII. By the same Editor. 2s. 6d. each.

"Another Greek text, designed it would seem for students preparing for the local examinations, is 'Xenophon's Anabasis,' Book II., with English Notes, by Alfred Pretor, M.A. The editor has exercised his usual discrimination in utilising the text and notes of Kuhner, with the occasional assistance of the best hints of Schneider, Vollbrecht and Macmichael on critical matters, and of Mr R. W. Taylor on points of history and geography. . . . When Mr Pretor commits himself to Commentator's work, he is eminently helpful. . . Had we to introduce a young Greek scholar to Xenophon, we should esteem ourselves fortunate in having Pretor's text-book as our chart and guide."—*Contemporary Review.*

XENOPHON.—ANABASIS. By A. PRETOR, M.A., Text and Notes, complete in two Volumes. 7s. 6d.

XENOPHON.—AGESILAUS. The Text revised with Critical and Explanatory Notes, Introduction, Analysis, and Indices. By H. HAILSTONE, M.A., late Scholar of Peterhouse. 2s. 6d.

XENOPHON.—CYROPAEDIA. With Introduction and Notes. By Rev. HUBERT A. HOLDEN, M.A., LL.D. [*Nearly ready.*

ARISTOPHANES—RANAE. With English Notes and Introduction by W. C. GREEN, M.A., late Assistant Master at Rugby School. 3s. 6d.

ARISTOPHANES—AVES. By the same Editor. *New Edition.* 3s. 6d.

"The notes to both plays are excellent. Much has been done in these two volumes to render the study of Aristophanes a real treat to a boy instead of a drudgery, by helping him to understand the fun and to express it in his mother tongue. —*The Examiner.*

ARISTOPHANES—PLUTUS. By the same Editor. 3s. 6d.

London: C. J. CLAY & SONS, Cambridge University Press Warehouse,
Ave Maria Lane.

EURIPIDES. HERCULES FURENS. With Introductions, Notes and Analysis. By A. GRAY, M.A., Fellow of Jesus College, and J. T. HUTCHINSON, M.A., Christ's College. New Edition, with additions. 2s.

"Messrs Hutchinson and Gray have produced a careful and useful edition."—*Saturday Review.*

EURIPIDES. HERACLEIDÆ. With Introduction and Critical Notes by E. A. BECK, M.A., Fellow of Trinity Hall. 3s. 6d.

LUCIANI SOMNIUM CHARON PISCATOR ET DE LUCTU, with English Notes by W. E. HEITLAND, M.A., Fellow of St John's College, Cambridge. New Edition, with Appendix. 3s. 6d.

PLUTARCH'S LIVES OF THE GRACCHI. With Introduction, Notes and Lexicon by Rev. HUBERT A. HOLDEN, M.A., LL.D., Examiner in Greek to the University of London. 6s.

PLUTARCH'S LIFE OF SULLA. With Introduction, Notes, and Lexicon. By the Rev. HUBERT A. HOLDEN, M.A., LL.D. 6s.

OUTLINES OF THE PHILOSOPHY OF ARISTOTLE. Edited by E. WALLACE, M.A. (See p. 31.)

II. LATIN.

M. T. CICERONIS DE AMICITIA. Edited by J. S. REID, Litt. D., Fellow and Tutor of Gonville and Caius College. New Edition, with Additions. 3s. 6d.

"Mr Reid has decidedly attained his aim, namely, 'a thorough examination of the Latinity of the dialogue.' ..... The revision of the text is most valuable, and comprehends sundry acute corrections.... This volume, like Mr Reid's other editions, is a solid gain to the scholarship of the country."—*Athenæum.*

"A more distinct gain to scholarship is Mr Reid's able and thorough edition of the *De Amicitia* of Cicero, a work of which, whether we regard the exhaustive introduction or the instructive and most suggestive commentary, it would be difficult to speak too highly.... When we come to the commentary, we are only amazed by its fulness in proportion to its bulk. Nothing is overlooked which can tend to enlarge the learner's general knowledge of Ciceronian Latin or to elucidate the text."—*Saturday Review.*

M. T. CICERONIS CATO MAJOR DE SENECTUTE. Edited by J. S. REID, Litt. D. 3s. 6d.

"The notes are excellent and scholarlike, adapted for the upper forms of public schools, and likely to be useful even to more advanced students."—*Guardian.*

M. T. CICERONIS ORATIO PRO ARCHIA POETA. Edited by J. S. REID, Litt. D. Revised Edition. 2s.

"It is an admirable specimen of careful editing. An Introduction tells us everything we could wish to know about Archias, about Cicero's connexion with him, about the merits of the trial, and the genuineness of the speech. The text is well and carefully printed. The notes are clear and scholar-like.... No boy can master this little volume without feeling that he has advanced a long step in scholarship."—*The Academy.*

M. T. CICERONIS PRO L. CORNELIO BALBO ORATIO. Edited by J. S. REID, Litt. D. 1s. 6d.

"We are bound to recognize the pains devoted in the annotation of these two orations to the minute and thorough study of their Latinity, both in the ordinary notes and in the textual appendices."—*Saturday Review.*

M. T. CICERONIS PRO P. CORNELIO SULLA ORATIO. Edited by J. S. REID, Litt. D. 3s. 6d.

"Mr Reid is so well known to scholars as a commentator on Cicero that a new work from him scarcely needs any commendation of ours. His edition of the speech *Pro Sulla* is fully equal in merit to the volumes which he has already published ... It would be difficult to speak too highly of the notes. There could be no better way of gaining an insight into the characteristics of Cicero's style and the Latinity of his period than by making a careful study of this speech with the aid of Mr Reid's commentary ... Mr Reid's intimate knowledge of the minutest details of scholarship enables him to detect and explain the slightest points of distinction between the usages of different authors and different periods ... The notes are followed by a valuable appendix on the text, and another on points of orthography; an excellent index brings the work to a close."—*Saturday Review.*

London: C. J. CLAY & SONS, Cambridge University Press Warehouse, Ave Maria Lane.

M. T. CICERONIS PRO CN. PLANCIO ORATIO.
Edited by H. A. HOLDEN, LL.D., Examiner in Greek to the University of London. 4s. 6d.

"As a book for students this edition can have few rivals. It is enriched by an excellent introduction and a chronological table of the principal events of the life of Cicero; while in its appendix, and in the notes on the text which are added, there is much of the greatest value. The volume is neatly got up, and is in every way commendable."—*The Scotsman.*

M. T. CICERONIS IN Q. CAECILIUM DIVINATIO
ET IN C. VERREM ACTIO PRIMA. With Introduction and Notes by W. E. HEITLAND, M.A., and HERBERT COWIE, M.A., Fellows of St John's College, Cambridge. 3s.

M. T. CICERONIS ORATIO PRO L. MURENA, with
English Introduction and Notes. By W. E. HEITLAND, M.A., Fellow and Classical Lecturer of St John's College, Cambridge. **Second Edition, carefully revised.** 3s.

"Those students are to be deemed fortunate who have to read Cicero's lively and brilliant oration for L. Murena with Mr Heitland's handy edition, which may be pronounced 'four-square' in point of equipment, and which has, not without good reason, attained the honours of a second edition."—*Saturday Review.*

M. T. CICERONIS IN GAIUM VERREM ACTIO
PRIMA. With Introduction and Notes. By H. COWIE, M.A., Fellow of St John's College, Cambridge. 1s. 6d.

M. T. CICERONIS ORATIO PRO T. A. MILONE,
with a Translation of Asconius' Introduction, Marginal Analysis and English Notes. Edited by the Rev. JOHN SMYTH PURTON, B.D., late President and Tutor of St Catharine's College. 2s. 6d.

"The editorial work is excellently done."—*The Academy.*

M. T. CICERONIS SOMNIUM SCIPIONIS. With Introduction and Notes. By W. D. PEARMAN, M.A., Head Master of Potsdam School, Jamaica. 2s.

P. OVIDII NASONIS FASTORUM LIBER VI. With
a Plan of Rome and Notes by A. SIDGWICK, M.A., Tutor of Corpus Christi College, Oxford. 1s. 6d.

"Mr Sidgwick's editing of the Sixth Book of Ovid's *Fasti* furnishes a careful and serviceable volume for average students. It eschews 'construes' which supersede the use of the dictionary, but gives full explanation of grammatical usages and historical and mythical allusions, besides illustrating peculiarities of style, true and false derivations, and the more remarkable variations of the text."—*Saturday Review.*

"It is eminently good and useful.... The Introduction is singularly clear on the astronomy of Ovid, which is properly shown to be ignorant and confused; there is an excellent little map of Rome, giving just the places mentioned in the text and no more; the notes are evidently written by a practical schoolmaster."—*The Academy.*

M. ANNAEI LUCANI PHARSALIAE LIBER
PRIMUS, edited with English Introduction and Notes by W. E. HEITLAND, M.A. and C. E. HASKINS, M.A., Fellows and Lecturers of St John's College, Cambridge. 1s. 6d.

"A careful and scholarlike production."—*Times.*

"In nice parallels of Lucan from Latin poets and from Shakspeare, Mr Haskins and Mr Heitland deserve praise."—*Saturday Review.*

London: C. J. CLAY & SONS, Cambridge University Press Warehouse,
Ave Maria Lane.

GAI IULI CAESARIS DE BELLO GALLICO COM-
MENT. I. II. III. With Maps and English Notes by A. G. PESKETT, M.A., Fellow of Magdalene College, Cambridge. 3s.

"In an unusually succinct introduction he gives all the preliminary and collateral information that is likely to be useful to a young student; and, wherever we have examined his notes, we have found them eminently practical and satisfying... The book may well be recommended for careful study in school or college."—*Saturday Review*.

"The notes are scholarly, short, and a real help to the most elementary beginners in Latin prose."—*The Examiner*.

—— COMMENT. IV. AND V. AND COMMENT. VII. by the same Editor. 2s. each.

—— COMMENT. VI. AND COMMENT. VIII. by the same Editor. 1s. 6d. each.

P. VERGILI MARONIS AENEIDOS LIBRI I., II., III., IV., V., VI., VII., VIII., IX., X., XI., XII. Edited with Notes by A. SIDGWICK, M.A., Tutor of Corpus Christi College, Oxford. 1s. 6d. each.

"Much more attention is given to the literary aspect of the poem than is usually paid to it in editions intended for the use of beginners. The introduction points out the distinction between primitive and literary epics, explains the purpose of the poem, and gives an outline of the story." —*Saturday Review*.

"Mr Arthur Sidgwick's 'Vergil, Aeneid, Book XII.' is worthy of his reputation, and is distinguished by the same acuteness and accuracy of knowledge, appreciation of a boy's difficulties and ingenuity and resource in meeting them, which we have on other occasions had reason to praise in these pages."—*The Academy*.

"As masterly in its clearly divided preface and appendices as in the sound and independent character of its annotations.... There is a great deal more in the notes than mere compilation and suggestion.... No difficulty is left unnoticed or unhandled."—*Saturday Review*.

BOOKS IX. X. in one volume. 3s.

BOOKS X., XI., XII. in one volume. 3s. 6d.

P. VERGILI MARONIS GEORGICON LIBRI I. II.
By the same Editor. 2s.

QUINTUS CURTIUS. A Portion of the History.
(ALEXANDER IN INDIA.) By W. E. HEITLAND, M.A., Fellow and Lecturer of St John's College, Cambridge, and T. E. RAVEN, B.A., Assistant Master in Sherborne School. 3s. 6d.

"Equally commendable as a genuine addition to the existing stock of school-books is *Alexander in India*, a compilation from the eighth and ninth books of Q. Curtius, edited for the Pitt Press by Messrs Heitland and Raven.... The work of Curtius has merits of its own, which, in former generations, made it a favourite with English scholars, and which still make it a popular text-book in Continental schools...... The reputation of Mr Heitland is a sufficient guarantee for the scholarship of the notes, which are ample without being excessive, and the book is well furnished with all that is needful in the nature of maps, indices, and appendices."—*Academy*.

BEDA'S ECCLESIASTICAL HISTORY, BOOKS
III., IV., the Text from the very ancient MS. in the Cambridge University Library, collated with six other MSS. Edited, with a life from the German of EBERT, and with Notes, &c. by J. E. B. MAYOR, M.A., Professor of Latin, and J. R. LUMBY, D.D., Norrisian Professor of Divinity. Revised edition. 7s. 6d.

"To young students of English History the illustrative notes will be of great service, while the study of the texts will be a good introduction to Mediæval Latin."—*The Nonconformist*.

"In Bede's works Englishmen can go back to *origines* of their history, unequalled for form and matter by any modern European nation. Prof. Mayor has done good service in rendering a part of Bede's greatest work accessible to those who can read Latin with ease. He has adorned this edition of the third and fourth books of the 'Ecclesiastical History' with that amazing erudition for which he is unrivalled among Englishmen and rarely equalled by Germans. And however interesting and valuable the text may be, we can certainly apply to his notes the expression, *La sauce vaut mieux que le poisson*. They are literally crammed with interesting information about early English life. For though ecclesiastical in name, Bede's history treats of all parts of the national life, since the Church had points of contact with all."—*Examiner*.

BOOKS I. and II. *In the Press.*

London: C. J. CLAY & SONS, Cambridge University Press Warehouse, Ave Maria Lane.

III. FRENCH.

JEANNE D'ARC by A. DE LAMARTINE. With a Map and Notes Historical and Philological and a Vocabulary by Rev. A. C. CLAPIN, M.A., St John's College, Cambridge, and Bachelier-ès-Lettres of the University of France. 2s.

LE BOURGEOIS GENTILHOMME, Comédie-Ballet en Cinq Actes. Par J.-B. POQUELIN DE MOLIÈRE (1670). With a life of Molière and Grammatical and Philological Notes. By the same Editor. 1s.6d.

LA PICCIOLA. By X. B. SAINTINE. The Text, with Introduction, Notes and Map, by the same Editor. 2s.

LA GUERRE. By MM. ERCKMANN-CHATRIAN. With Map, Introduction and Commentary by the same Editor. 3s.

LAZARE HOCHE—PAR ÉMILE DE BONNECHOSE. With Three Maps, Introduction and Commentary, by C. COLBECK, M.A., late Fellow of Trinity College, Cambridge. 2s.

LE VERRE D'EAU. A Comedy, by SCRIBE. With a Biographical Memoir, and Grammatical, Literary and Historical Notes. By the same Editor. 2s.

"It may be national prejudice, but we consider this edition far superior to any of the series which hitherto have been edited exclusively by foreigners. Mr Colbeck seems better to understand the wants and difficulties of an English boy. The etymological notes especially are admirable.... The historical notes and introduction are a piece of thorough honest work."—*Journal of Education.*

HISTOIRE DU SIÈCLE DE LOUIS XIV PAR VOLTAIRE. Part I. Chaps. I.—XIII. Edited with Notes Philological and Historical, Biographical and Geographical Indices, etc. by GUSTAVE MASSON, B.A. Univ. Gallic., Officier d'Académie, Assistant Master of Harrow School, and G. W. PROTHERO, M.A., Fellow and Tutor of King's College, Cambridge. 2s. 6d.

"Messrs Masson and Prothero have, to judge from the first part of their work, performed with much discretion and care the task of editing Voltaire's *Siècle de Louis XIV* for the 'Pitt Press Series.' Besides the usual kind of notes, the editors have in this case, influenced by Voltaire's 'summary way of treating much of the history,' given a good deal of historical information, in which they have, we think, done well. At the beginning of the book will be found excellent and succinct accounts of the constitution of the French army and Parliament at the period treated of."—*Saturday Review.*

—— Part II. Chaps. XIV.—XXIV. With Three Maps of the Period. By the same Editors. 2s. 6d.

—— Part III. Chap. XXV. to the end. By the same Editors. 2s. 6d.

M. DARU, par M. C. A. SAINTE-BEUVE, (Causeries du Lundi, Vol. IX.). With Biographical Sketch of the Author, and Notes Philological and Historical. By GUSTAVE MASSON. 2s.

LA SUITE DU MENTEUR. A Comedy in Five Acts, by P. CORNEILLE. Edited with Fontenelle's Memoir of the Author, Voltaire's Critical Remarks, and Notes Philological and Historical. By GUSTAVE MASSON. 2s.

LA JEUNE SIBÉRIENNE. LE LÉPREUX DE LA CITÉ D'AOSTE. Tales by COUNT XAVIER DE MAISTRE. With Biographical Notice, Critical Appreciations, and Notes. By G. MASSON. 2s.

London: C. J. CLAY & SONS, Cambridge University Press Warehouse, Ave Maria Lane.

LE DIRECTOIRE. (Considérations sur la Révolution Française. Troisième et quatrième parties.) Par MADAME LA BARONNE DE STAËL-HOLSTEIN. With a Critical Notice of the Author, a Chronological Table, and Notes Historical and Philological, by G. MASSON, B.A., and G. W. PROTHERO, M.A. Revised and enlarged Edition. 2s.

"Prussia under Frederick the Great, and France under the Directory, bring us face to face respectively with periods of history which it is right should be known thoroughly, and which are well treated in the Pitt Press volumes. The latter in particular, an extract from the world-known work of Madame de Staël on the French Revolution, is beyond all praise for the excellence both of its style and of its matter."—*Times*.

DIX ANNÉES D'ÉXIL. LIVRE II. CHAPITRES 1—8. Par MADAME LA BARONNE DE STAËL-HOLSTEIN. With a Biographical Sketch of the Author, a Selection of Poetical Fragments by Madame de Staël's Contemporaries, and Notes Historical and Philological. By GUSTAVE MASSON and G. W. PROTHERO, M.A. Revised and enlarged edition. 2s.

FRÉDÉGONDE ET BRUNEHAUT. A Tragedy in Five Acts, by N. LEMERCIER. Edited with Notes, Genealogical and Chronological Tables, a Critical Introduction and a Biographical Notice. By GUSTAVE MASSON. 2s.

LE VIEUX CÉLIBATAIRE. A Comedy, by COLLIN D'HARLEVILLE. With a Biographical Memoir, and Grammatical, Literary and Historical Notes. By the same Editor. 2s.

"M. Masson is doing good work in introducing learners to some of the less-known French play-writers. The arguments are admirably clear, and the notes are not too abundant."— *Academy*.

LA MÉTROMANIE, A Comedy, by PIRON, with a Biographical Memoir, and Grammatical, Literary and Historical Notes. By the same Editor. 2s.

LASCARIS, OU LES GRECS DU XVE. SIÈCLE, Nouvelle Historique, par A. F. VILLEMAIN, with a Biographical Sketch of the Author, a Selection of Poems on Greece, and Notes Historical and Philological. By the same Editor. 2s.

LETTRES SUR L'HISTOIRE DE FRANCE (XIII— XXIV.). Par AUGUSTIN THIERRY. By GUSTAVE MASSON, B.A. and G. W. PROTHERO, M.A. With Map. 2s. 6d.

IV. GERMAN.

DIE KARAVANE von WILHELM HAUFF. Edited with Notes by A. SCHLOTTMANN, Ph. D. 3s. 6d.

CULTURGESCHICHTLICHE NOVELLEN, von W. H. RIEHL, with Grammatical, Philological, and Historical Notes, and a Complete Index, by H. J. WOLSTENHOLME, B.A. (Lond.). 4s. 6d.

ERNST, HERZOG VON SCHWABEN. UHLAND. With Introduction and Notes. By H. J. WOLSTENHOLME, B.A. (Lond.), Lecturer in German at Newnham College, Cambridge. 3s. 6d.

ZOPF UND SCHWERT. Lustspiel in fünf Aufzügen von KARL GUTZKOW. With a Biographical and Historical Introduction, English Notes, and an Index. By the same Editor. 3s. 6d.

"We are glad to be able to notice a careful edition of K. Gutzkow's amusing comedy 'Zopf and Schwert' by Mr H. J. Wolstenholme.... These notes are abundant and contain references to standard grammatical works."—*Academy*.

Goethe's Knabenjahre. (1749—1759.) GOETHE'S BOYHOOD: being the First Three Books of his Autobiography. Arranged and Annotated by WILHELM WAGNER, Ph. D., late Professor at the Johanneum, Hamburg. 2s.

London: C. J. CLAY & SONS, Cambridge University Press Warehouse,
Ave Maria Lane.

HAUFF. DAS WIRTHSHAUS IM SPESSART. Edited by A. SCHLOTTMANN, Ph.D., late Assistant Master at Uppingham School. 3s. 6d.

DER OBERHOF. A Tale of Westphalian Life, by KARL IMMERMANN. With a Life of Immermann and English Notes, by WILHELM WAGNER, Ph.D., late Professor at the Johanneum, Hamburg. 3s.

A BOOK OF GERMAN DACTYLIC POETRY. Arranged and Annotated by the same Editor. 3s.

Der erste Kreuzzug (THE FIRST CRUSADE), by FRIEDRICH VON RAUMER. Condensed from the Author's 'History of the Hohenstaufen', with a life of RAUMER, two Plans and English Notes. By the same Editor. 2s.

"Certainly no more interesting book could be made the subject of examinations. The story of the First Crusade has an undying interest. The notes are, on the whole, good."—*Educational Times.*

A BOOK OF BALLADS ON GERMAN HISTORY Arranged and Annotated by the same Editor. 2s.

"It carries the reader rapidly through some of the most important incidents connected with the German race and name, from the invasion of Italy by the Visigoths under their King Alaric, down to the Franco-German War and the installation of the present Emperor. The notes supply very well the connecting links between the successive periods, and exhibit in its various phases of growth and progress, or the reverse, the vast unwieldy mass which constitutes modern Germany." —*Times.*

DER STAAT FRIEDRICHS DES GROSSEN. By G. FREYTAG. With Notes. By the same Editor. 2s.

"Prussia under Frederick the Great, and France under the Directory, bring us face to face respectively with periods of history which it is right should be known thoroughly, and which are well treated in the Pitt Press volumes."—*Times.*

GOETHE'S HERMANN AND DOROTHEA. With an Introduction and Notes. By the same Editor. Revised edition by J. W. CARTMELL, M.A. 3s. 6d.

"The notes are among the best that we know, with the reservation that they are often too abundant."—*Academy.*

Das Jahr 1813 (THE YEAR 1813), by F. KOHLRAUSCH. With English Notes. By W. WAGNER. 2s.

V. ENGLISH.

COWLEY'S ESSAYS. With Introduction and Notes. By the Rev. J. RAWSON LUMBY, D.D., Norrisian Professor of Divinity; late Fellow of St Catharine's College. [*Nearly ready.*

SIR THOMAS MORE'S UTOPIA. With Notes by the Rev. J. RAWSON LUMBY, D.D. 3s. 6d.

"To Dr Lumby we must give praise unqualified and unstinted. He has done his work admirably..... Every student of history, every politician, every social reformer, every one interested in literary curiosities, every lover of English should buy and carefully read Dr Lumby's edition of the 'Utopia.' We are afraid to say more lest we should be thought extravagant, and our recommendation accordingly lose part of its force."—*The Teacher.*

"It was originally written in Latin and does not find a place on ordinary bookshelves. A very great boon has therefore been conferred on the general English reader by the managers of the *Pitt Press Series*, in the issue of a convenient little volume of *More's Utopia* not in the original Latin, but in the quaint *English Translation thereof made by Raphe Robynson*, which adds a linguistic interest to the intrinsic merit of the work. . . . All this has been edited in a most complete and scholarly fashion by Dr J. R. Lumby, the Norrisian Professor of Divinity, whose name alone is a sufficient warrant for its accuracy. It is a real addition to the modern stock of classical English literature."—*Guardian.*

BACON'S HISTORY OF THE REIGN OF KING HENRY VII. With Notes by the Rev. J. RAWSON LUMBY, D.D. 3s.

London: C. J. CLAY & SONS, Cambridge University Press Warehouse, Ave Maria Lane.

THE CAMBRIDGE UNIVERSITY PRESS. 31

MORE'S HISTORY OF KING RICHARD III. Edited with Notes, Glossary and Index of Names. By J. RAWSON LUMBY, D.D. Norrisian Professor of Divinity, Cambridge; to which is added the conclusion of the History of King Richard III. as given in the continuation of Hardyng's Chronicle, London, 1543. 3s. 6d.

THE TWO NOBLE KINSMEN, edited with Introduction and Notes by the Rev. Professor SKEAT, Litt.D., formerly Fellow of Christ's College, Cambridge. 3s. 6d.

"This edition of a play that is well worth study, for more reasons than one, by so carefu a scholar as Mr Skeat, deserves a hearty welcome."—*Athenæum*.
"Mr Skeat is a conscientious editor, and has left no difficulty unexplained."—*Times*.

LOCKE ON EDUCATION. With Introduction and Notes by the Rev. R. H. QUICK, M.A. 3s. 6d.

"The work before us leaves nothing to be desired. It is of convenient form and reasonable price, accurately printed, and accompanied by notes which are admirable. There is no teacher too young to find this book interesting; there is no teacher too old to find it profitable."—*The School Bulletin, New York*.

MILTON'S TRACTATE ON EDUCATION. A facsimile reprint from the Edition of 1673. Edited, with Introduction and Notes, by OSCAR BROWNING, M.A., Senior Fellow of King's College, Cambridge, and University Lecturer. 2s.

"A separate reprint of Milton's famous letter to Master Samuel Hartlib was a desideratum, and we are grateful to Mr Browning for his elegant and scholarly edition, to which is prefixed the careful *résumé* of the work given in his 'History of Educational Theories.'"—*Journal of Education*.

THEORY AND PRACTICE OF TEACHING. By the Rev. EDWARD THRING, M.A., Head Master of Uppingham School, late Fellow of King's College, Cambridge. New Edition. 4s. 6d.

"Any attempt to summarize the contents of the volume would fail to give our readers a taste of the pleasure that its perusal has given us."—*Journal of Education*.

GENERAL AIMS OF THE TEACHER, AND FORM MANAGEMENT. Two Lectures delivered in the University of Cambridge in the Lent Term, 1883, by F. W. FARRAR, D.D. Archdeacon of Westminster, and R. B. POOLE, B.D. Head Master of Bedford Modern School. 1s. 6d.

THREE LECTURES ON THE PRACTICE OF EDUCATION. Delivered in the University of Cambridge in the Easter Term, 1882, under the direction of the Teachers' Training Syndicate. 2s.

JOHN AMOS COMENIUS, Bishop of the Moravians. His Life and Educational Works, by S. S. LAURIE, A.M., F.R.S.E., Professor of the Institutes and History of Education in the University of Edinburgh. Second Edition, revised. 3s. 6d.

OUTLINES OF THE PHILOSOPHY OF ARISTOTLE. Compiled by EDWIN WALLACE, M.A., LL.D. (St Andrews), late Fellow of Worcester College, Oxford. Third Edition Enlarged. 4s. 6d.

"A judicious selection of characteristic passages, arranged in paragraphs, each of which is preceded by a masterly and perspicuous English analysis."—*Scotsman*.
"Gives in a comparatively small compass a very good sketch of Aristotle's teaching."—*Sat. Review*.

A SKETCH OF ANCIENT PHILOSOPHY FROM THALES TO CICERO, by JOSEPH B. MAYOR, M.A., late Professor of Moral Philosophy at King's College, London. 3s. 6d.

"Professor Mayor contributes to the Pitt Press Series *A Sketch of Ancient Philosophy* in which he has endeavoured to give a general view of the philosophical systems illustrated by the genius of the masters of metaphysical and ethical science from Thales to Cicero. In the course of his sketch he takes occasion to give concise analyses of Plato's Republic, and of the Ethics and Politics of Aristotle; and these abstracts will be to some readers not the least useful portions of the book."—*The Guardian*.

[*Other Volumes are in preparation.*]

London: C. J. CLAY & SONS, Cambridge University Press Warehouse, Ave Maria Lane.

University of Cambridge.

LOCAL EXAMINATIONS.
Examination Papers, for various years, with the *Regulations for the Examination*. Demy 8vo. 2s. each, or by Post, 2s. 2d.
Class Lists, for various years, Boys 1s., Girls 6d.
Annual Reports of the Syndicate, with Supplementary Tables showing the success and failure of the Candidates. 2s. each, by Post 2s. 3d.

HIGHER LOCAL EXAMINATIONS.
Examination Papers for various years, *to which are added the Regulations for the Examination*. Demy 8vo. 2s. each, by Post 2s. 2d.
Class Lists, for various years. 1s. By post, 1s. 2d.
Reports of the Syndicate. Demy 8vo. 1s., by Post 1s. 2d.

LOCAL LECTURES SYNDICATE.
Calendar for the years 1875—80. Fcap. 8vo. *cloth*. 2s.; for 1880—81. 1s.

TEACHERS' TRAINING SYNDICATE.
Examination Papers for various years, *to which are added the Regulations for the Examination*. Demy 8vo. 6d., by Post 7d.

CAMBRIDGE UNIVERSITY REPORTER.
Published by Authority.
Containing all the Official Notices of the University, Reports of Discussions in the Schools, and Proceedings of the Cambridge Philosophical, Antiquarian, and Philological Societies. 3d. weekly.

CAMBRIDGE UNIVERSITY EXAMINATION PAPERS.
These Papers are published in occasional numbers every Term, and in volumes for the Academical year.
VOL. XIII. Parts 177 to 195. PAPERS for the Year 1883—84, 15s. *cloth*.
VOL. XIV. „ 1 to 20. „ „ 1884—85, 15s. *cloth*.
VOL. XV. „ 21 to 43. „ „ 1885—86, 15s. *cloth*.

Oxford and Cambridge Schools Examinations.
Papers set in the Examination for Certificates, July, 1885. 2s. 6d.
List of Candidates who obtained Certificates at the Examinations held in 1885 and 1886; and Supplementary Tables. 6d.
Regulations of the Board for 1887. 9d.
Report of the Board for the year ending Oct. 31, 1885. 1s.

Studies from the Morphological Laboratory in the University of Cambridge. Edited by ADAM SEDGWICK, M.A., Fellow and Lecturer of Trinity College, Cambridge. Vol. II. Part I. Royal 8vo. 10s.

London: C. J. CLAY AND SONS,
CAMBRIDGE UNIVERSITY PRESS WAREHOUSE,
AVE MARIA LANE.

GLASGOW: 263, ARGYLE STREET.

www.ingramcontent.com/pod-product-compliance
Lightning Source LLC
Chambersburg PA
CBHW021208230426
43667CB00006B/609